The New York Times

BOOK OF

CRIME

MORE THAN 166 YEARS OF COVERING THE BEAT

Edited by KEVIN FLYNN

Foreword by RICHARD PRICE

STERLING
New York

STERLING
New York

An Imprint of Sterling Publishing Co.
1166 Avenue of the Americas
New York, NY 10036

ISBN 978-1-4027-9323-3

Distributed in Canada by Sterling Publishing Co., Inc.
c/o Canadian Manda Group, 664 Annette Street
Toronto, Ontario, Canada M6S 2C8
Distributed in the United Kingdom by GMC Distribution Services
Castle Place, 166 High Street, Lewes, East Sussex, England BN7 1XU
Distributed in Australia by NewSouth Books
45 Beach Street, Coogee, NSW 2034, Australia

For information about custom editions, special sales, and premium and corporate
purchases, please contact Sterling Special Sales at 800-805-5489 or
specialsales@sterlingpublishing.com.

Manufactured in the United States of America

2 4 6 8 10 9 7 5 3

www.sterlingpublishing.com

Design by Ashley Prine, Tandem Books

Photo Credits–see page 400

CONTENTS

Foreword viii

Introduction xii

CHAPTER 1

ASSASSINATIONS

Awful Event: President Lincoln Shot by an Assassin 2

Heir to Austria's Throne Is Slain with His Wife by a Bosnian
  Youth to Avenge Seizure of His Country 6

Gandhi Is Killed by a Hindu; India Shaken, World Mourns;
  15 Die in Rioting in Bombay *Robert Trumbull* 8

Kennedy Is Killed by Sniper as He Rides in Car in Dallas; Johnson
  Sworn in on Plane *Tom Wicker* 12

Malcolm X Shot to Death at Rally Here *Peter Kihss* 21

Martin Luther King Is Slain in Memphis; A White Is Suspected;
  Johnson Urges Calm *Earl Caldwell* 27

Kennedy Is Dead, Victim of Assassin; Suspect, Arab Immigrant,
  Arraigned; Johnson Appoints Panel on Violence *Gladwin Hill* 32

Sadat Assassinated at Army Parade as Men Amid Ranks Fire into
  Stands; Vice President Affirms "All Treaties" *William E. Farrell* 36

Bhutto Is Killed at Rally, and Pakistan Faces
  Outrage and New Turmoil *Salman Masood and Carlotta Gall* 40

CHAPTER 2

HEISTS

Masked Men Rob a Train: The Bold Exploit of a Gang of Missouri Outlaws 46

Dillinger Defied Capture for Year. 50

Bandits Rob Mail Train Outside London; Record Loss
  May Exceed $5,000,000 *James Feron* 55

Star of India and 8 Other Stolen Gems Returned to City From
  Miami Locker *Jack Roth* 60

The Big Lufthansa Robbery and Its Trail of Murder *Leslie Maitland* 65

Boston Thieves Loot a Museum of Masterpieces *Fox Butterfield* 70

Willie Sutton, Urbane Scoundrel *Peter Duffy* 73
FBI Brings a Fresh Set of Eyes to a '71 Plane
    Hijacking Mystery *Susan Saulny* 76
Graying Thieves and a Record Heist Undone in London *Dan Bilefsky* 78

CHAPTER 3
KIDNAPPINGS

Franks Slayers Get Life Imprisonment; Youth Averts Noose 84
Lindbergh Baby Kidnapped from Home of Parents on Farm
    Near Princeton; Taken from His Crib; Wide Search On 89
Bronfman's Son Rescued in City After a Payment of
    $2.3 Million; Money Recovered, 2 Suspects Held *Peter Kihss* 92
Miss Hearst Is Convicted on Bank Robbery Charges *Wallace Turner* 96
Agony Lingers, 20 Years After the Moro Killing *Alessandra Stanley* 103
Captive's Own Account of 18 Years as a Hostage *Jesse McKinley* 105

CHAPTER 4
MASS MURDER

School Dynamiter First Slew Wife 110
Suspect Seized in Chicago in Slaying of Eight Nurses *Austin C. Wehrwein* 114
Terror in Littleton: The Overview; 2 Students in Colorado School Said to
    Gun Down as Many as 23 and Kill Themselves in a Siege *James Brooke* 117
Massacre in Virginia; Drumbeat of Shots,
    Broken by Pauses to Reload *Shaila Dewan* 121
Gunman Kills 12 at Colorado Theater; Scores Are Wounded,
    Reviving Debate *Dan Frosch and Kirk Johnson* 124
Norwegian Mass Killer Gets Maximum Sentence: 21 Years
    Mark Lewis and Sarah Lyall 128
Sandy Hook Pupils Were All Shot Multiple Times with a Semiautomatic,
    Officials Say *James Barron* 131
A Hectic Day at Church, and Then a Hellish Visitor
    Richard Fausset, John Eligon, Jason Horowitz and Frances Robles 134
Praising Isis, Gunman Attacks Gay Nightclub,
    Leaving 50 Dead in Worst Shooting on U.S. Soil
    Lizette Alavarez and Richard Pérez-Peña 140

CHAPTER 5

THE MOB

7 Chicago Gangsters Slain by Firing Squad of Rivals,
   Some in Police Uniforms 146
The Crime Hearings: Television Provides Both a Lively Show
   and a Notable Public Service *Jack Gould* 153
65 Hoodlums Seized in a Raid and Run Out of Upstate Village 156
Valachi Names 5 as Crime Chiefs in New York Area *Emanuel Perlmutter* 159
Galante and 2 Shot to Death in a Brooklyn Restaurant *Robert D. McFadden* 164
The Mafia of the 1980s: Divided and Under Siege *Robert D. McFadden* 168
John Gotti Dies in Prison at 61; Mafia Boss Relished
   the Spotlight *Selwyn Raab* 175
A Mafia Boss Breaks a Code in Telling All *William K. Rashbaum* 182
Long Elusive, Irish Mob Legend Ended Up
   a California Recluse *Adam Nagourney and Abby Goodnough* 185

CHAPTER 6

MURDER

Thaw Murders Stanford White; Shoots Him on the
   Madison Square Garden Roof 192
Trial Under Way in Youth's Killing *John N. Popham* 198
Manson, 3 Women Guilty; Prosecution to Ask Death *Earl Caldwell* 201
John Lennon of Beatles Is Killed; Suspect Held in
   Shooting at Dakota *Les Ledbetter* 208
Mrs. Harris Found Guilty of Murder and She Is
   Quickly Removed to Jail *James Feron* 211
Not Guilty: The Overview; Jury Clears Simpson in Double Murder;
   Spellbound Nation Divides on Verdict *David Margolick* 217
Colorado Murder Mystery Lingers as Police Press On *James Brooke* 222
Kitty, 40 Years Later *Jim Rasenberger* 225
Freed by DNA, Now Charged in New Crime *Monica Davey* 231
Grisly Murder Case Intrigues Italian University City *Ian Fisher* 235
A Trial Ends, but for South Africans, the Debate May
   Be Just Beginning *Sarah Lyall and Alan Cowell* 237
Straight From TV to Jail: Durst Is Charged
   in Killing *Charles V. Bagli and Vivian Yee* 240

CHAPTER 7

PRISON

Showering and Yoking 246

9 Hostages and 28 Prisoners Die as 1,000 Storm
 Prison in Attica—"Like a War Zone" *Fred Ferretti* 250

No Way Out: Dashed Hopes—Serving Life,
 with No Chance of Redemption *Adam Liptak* 257

Tale of 3 Inmates Who Vanished from Alcatraz Maintains
 Intrigue 50 Years Later *Robert D. McFadden*. 262

How El Chapo Was Finally Captured, Again *Azam Ahmed*. 266

Prison Rate Was Rising Years Before 1994 Law *Erik Eckholm* 273

CHAPTER 8

SERIAL KILLERS

Dismay in Whitechapel: Two More Murdered Women Found 278

Holmes Cool to the End 281

DeSalvo, Confessed "Boston Strangler," Found Stabbed
 to Death in Prison Cell *John Kifner*. 289

.44 Killer Wounds 12th and 13th Victims *Robert D. McFadden* 291

The Suspect Is Quoted on Killings:
 "It Was a Command . . . I Had a Sign" *Howard Blum* 296

Suspect in Mass Deaths Is Puzzle to All *Douglas E. Kneeland* 300

Bundy Is Put to Death in Florida After
 Admitting Trail of Killings *Jon Nordheimer*. 306

Jeffrey Dahmer, Multiple Killer,
 Is Bludgeoned to Death in Prison *Don Terry* 310

Retracing a Trail: The Sniper Suspects; Serial Killing's
 Squarest Pegs: Not Solo, White, Psychosexual or Picky
 N. R. Kleinfield and Erica Goode 313

CHAPTER 9

SEX CRIMES

Polanski Guilty Plea Accepted in Sex Case *Grace Lichtenstein* 320

Crimmins Found Guilty of Murder as the Jury
 Accepts His Confession *E. R. Shipp* 322

Darkness Beneath the Glitter:

    Life of Suspect in Park Slaying *Samuel G. Freedman* 325

Lorena Bobbitt Acquitted in Mutilation

    of Husband *David Margolick* 330

A Crime Revisited: The Decision; 13 Years Later, Official

    Reversal in Jogger Attack *Robert D. McFadden and Susan Saulny* 334

Boston Church Papers Released; A Pattern of

    Negligence Is Cited *Pam Belluck* 339

Sandusky Guilty of Sexual Abuse of 10 Young Boys *Joe Drape* 344

CHAPTER 10

VICE

Marijuana Smoking Is Reported Safe 350

Speakeasy Census Shows Brisk Trade *C. G. Poore* 354

Kingpin of Crime Syndicate *Robert D. McFadden* 358

Head of Medellín Cocaine Cartel Is Killed by

    Troops in Colombia *Robert D. McFadden* 362

Spitzer, Linked to a Sex Ring as a Client,

    Gives an Apology *Danny Hakim and William K. Rashbaum* 366

CHAPTER 11

WHITE COLLAR

Exchange "Wizard" Is Paying Claims 372

Van Doren Pleads Guilty; Is Freed *Alfred E. Clark* 376

Milken Gets 10 Years for Wall St. Crimes *Kurt Eichenwald* 378

2 Enron Chiefs Are Convicted in Fraud and Conspiracy Trial *Alexei Barrionuevo* 382

Madoff Goes to Jail After Guilty Pleas *Diana B. Henriques and Jack Healy* 386

Acknowledgments 389

Contributors 390

Index 396

Picture Credits 400

FOREWORD

By RICHARD PRICE

THE PLEASURES TO BE HAD in reading this book are legion.

There's the consistent quality of the reportage, the rich yet precise presentations of backstory and the overall handsomeness of the prose. There's the revisiting of historical events unfolding in real time, the ramifications of a singular act often unknown (except to the reader, who feels like a reverse-oracle predicting the past) for weeks, months and even years to come. The early days' speculations on looming verdicts, the progress of manhunts, the (sometimes empty) vows of law enforcement to bring the perps to heel, the prosecutorial and defense team strategies that will succeed or fail. The unfolding of criminal deeds—the Enron and Madoff trials; the assassinations of Lincoln, of JFK, of Malcolm X; the massacres at Columbine, at Sandy Hook and in Charleston—that still sear the national psyche. The scramble to make immediate sense of fresh events, ("Heir to Austria's Throne Is Slain . . . by Bosnian Youth") that will end up reshaping the world map.

I've always assumed that the best crime reporting—sports reporting, too—was to be found in the tabloids, but after inhaling the contents of this anthology, which cover more than a century and a half of criminal mayhem as filed with *The New York Times*, the shingles have fallen from my eyes. Lurid writing can overwhelm lurid deeds. Excitable adjectives, judgmental prose and the egging on of public outrage can often obscure rather than illuminate the facts at the core.

In most of the articles contained herein, the thoroughness of the research combined with the implacableness of the tone, especially when flying in the face of a popular taboo or sentiment of the times, often reads like a fortress of probity.

A 1926 article debunks the era's hysteria over marijuana by carefully extrapolating the results of an investigation into the physiological and psychological impact of smoking marijuana on a number of subjects, "soberly" concluding: "The influence of the drug when used for smoking is uncertain and appears to be have been greatly exaggerated. . . . There is no evidence that [marijuana] is a habit-forming drug in the sense of the term as applied to alcohol, opium, cocaine . . . or that it has any appreciable deleterious effect on the individuals using it." I repeat: 1926.

An even earlier investigative piece written in 1852 regards the systematic use of capital punishment as meted out by the guards at Sing Sing prison. The report gathers physicians and physiologists to refute the prison staff's claims that the punishments (including an hours'-long form of water torture) were carefully monitored, when in fact, due to either unchecked sadism or sheer ignorance regarding the limits of human endurance, they often ended in either death or madness.

Occasionally, the stoniness of the prose can feel chillingly blunt given the subject at hand. The unnamed writer covering the aftermath of Lincoln's assassination in 1865, reports: "The pistol ball entered the back of the president's head and penetrated nearly through the head. The wound is mortal. The president has been insensible ever since it was inflicted, and is now dying."

At other times, the measured tone and objective formalism of the writing, when set against the grain of an outrage, can powerfully serve to isolate and heighten the darkness of the deed. At first glance, John N. Popham's atmospheric description of the Sumner, Mississippi, courtroom during jury selection for the trial of Emmett Till's murderers in 1955 reads like a rough draft of *To Kill a Mockingbird*; the judge in shirtsleeves, the defendants and rubberneckers free to smoke up a storm, bailiffs passing out cups of ice water to their friends in the sweltering pews, the jarring intimacy between the state-appointed prosecutor and the prospective jurors during voir dire: "He seemed to be familiar with everyone's personal habits and family background, even to the nicknames they had for friends who might be interested in the outcome of the trial." And last, but not least, the defendants' children "played around the knees of their fathers and occasionally ran up and down the corridors" of the courtroom.

This effortless sketch of southern comfort has become a trope of countless Hollywood legal dramas, from *Inherit the Wind* to *My Cousin Vinny*, yet in this soon-to-be-infamous courtroom, the barely mentioned true crime that has brought this assembly together—the torturing and murder of a 14-year-old African American boy for allegedly whistling at a white woman—infuses every folksy detail with an aftertaste of revulsion. On the other hand, Popham's description of the courthouse hangers-on as "several hundred white persons who strongly support a strict pattern of racial segregation" seems, pardon the oxymoron, a feat of excessive understatement.

At the other end of tone spectrum, and maybe the biggest revelation of all, is the discovery that certain crimes—especially those found in the heists and capers chapter—demand a punchier, almost sporty, narrative. Who didn't root for Willie Sutton? How could you not like a jewel thief named Murph the Surf? The articles can read like a cross between a tense noir thriller and a riff on Jimmy Breslin's *The Gang That Couldn't Shoot Straight*.

In the report on the 1965 recovery (from a bus terminal locker in Miami) of the Star of India diamond (563.35 carats) and eight other eye-popping jewels stolen by the afore-mentioned Murph and two other part-time beach bums, the Florida paparazzi chasing three NYPD detectives, Assistant District Attorney Maurice Nadjari and a handcuffed perp, Allan Kuhn, seem more villainous than the bad guys, some of them "hiding in bushes . . . carrying walkie-talkies and . . . pulling ignition wires on cars the authorities had rented so they would not start."

At one point in this Marxian (Groucho, not Karl) game of hide-and-seek, Nadjari, the cops and the arrestee, after having already switched hotels and motels ten or twelve times, "jumped 20 feet from a motel window to shake off" the press—a caper within a caper—after which the collared Kuhn said to his captors, "I'm glad you fellows aren't burglars. You'd put me out of business."

In a similar vein, Dan Bilefsky's 2015 piece, "Graying Thieves and a Record Heist Undone in London," which could have just as easily been entitled "One Last Score," offers up a blow-by-blow recreation of another doomed heist, this one led by a 76-year-old lifetime criminal. As much a character study as a detailed accounting of star-crossed events, it begs to be rewritten as a vehicle for an ensemble of aging hard-guy actors.

But sometimes the melodrama can run as thick as in any news rag, including the account of the 1929 Saint Valentine's Day Massacre that consolidated Al Capone's gang rule in Chicago: after two of the killers entered the murder garage dressed as policemen, "their stars gleaming against the blue of the cloth." The seven victims were lined up against a wall. The likely order to "give it to them" was followed by "the roar of the shotguns mingled with the rat-a-tat of the machine gun, a clatter like that of a gigantic type-writer." (Love the hyphenated "type-writer.")

However, the same reporter redeems himself when he describes one of the victims in a sleek three-sentence word burst worthy of James M. Cain: "The body of Mays, the overall-clad mechanic, had only a few dollars in the pockets. He was the father of seven children. A machine gun bullet had penetrated two medals of St. Christopher."

In another gem of succinctness written 78 years later, Shaila Dewan describes the sound of another deadly barrage, this one slow and steady, resulting in the deaths of 33 Virginia Tech students (including the shooter, who killed himself) and the wounding of

17 more: "[the gunshots] went on and on, for what seemed like 10 or 15 or 20 minutes, an eternity with punctuation."

Jumping back from 2007 to the Jean Harris murder trial in 1981, that same tight prose is on display in James Feron's deft description of the defense table's reaction to the guilty verdict: "Two lawyers at the . . . table burst into tears, but Mrs. Harris showed no emotion, watching as each juror was polled. 'I can't sit in jail,' she said to one of her attorneys. She then walked forcefully from the courtroom, shrugging off a police matron." Afterward, "She sat in the back of a sheriff's car, appearing stunned and staring straight ahead. Photographers' flashbulbs glinted on her headband."

But my favorite example of how novelistically hardcore the writing in *The Times* can be is in one the most recent filings to be included, Azam Ahmed's 2016 account of El Chapo's escape and recapture in Mexico. Here's the lede 'graph: "Stripped to his under-shirt and covered in filth, the world's most notorious drug lord dragged himself out of the sewers and into the middle of traffic. Disoriented from his long trudge underground, with gun-toting marines on his heels, he found himself standing across the street from a Walmart. Joaquín Guzmán Loera, the kingpin known . . . as El Chapo, would have to improvise. His cavalry was not coming."

Over three centuries, the Gray Lady of journalism has time and again earned her moniker, but as often on display in this volume, when it comes to her crime reporting, she can just as easily come off as a bottle blonde.

Enjoy.

INTRODUCTION

By KEVIN FLYNN

WHAT CONSTITUTES A CRIME has often been a matter of time and place, as the histories of marijuana and gambling make clear. In 1901, *The New York Times* reported with alarm on the "long, deathlike sleep" that marijuana was thought to induce. In 1926, though, the newspaper suggested the still-illicit drug might actually be "safe," a perspective now held by many voters in the seven states that recently legalized its recreational use. The article from 1926 is reprinted in this book, one of the many included here that demonstrate how *The Times* has worked since 1851 to track the shifting discussion about crime, to study the people who commit it and to analyze the ground from which those criminals grew.

This book is organized into chapters that focus on particular types of crime, and within each chapter the articles unroll chronologically. Some stretch back to depict criminals who went on to eternal fame, such as Jesse James, whose penchant for relieving trains of their valuables in the era after the Civil War made his a household name. Others recount little remembered "crimes of the century," a phrase now weary from overuse. One such report comes from 1906, when the world was transfixed by the strange story of Henry Kendall Thaw, a rich man who murdered Stanford White, a leading American architect, by shooting White to death in public to avenge the honor of his wife, Evelyn Nesbit, America's first supermodel.

For 166 years, *The Times* has been a rich resource for novelists, nonfiction writers and filmmakers. Erik Larson, in his brilliant best seller *The Devil in the White City*, credits many sources, including *The Times*, for helping him unveil the mysteries of Henry Howard Holmes, a serial killer from a time before the term had even been coined. Holmes, despite a medical degree from the University of Michigan, demonstrated little interest in the healing arts. He chose instead to open the World's Fair Hotel in Chicago near the fairgrounds of the 1893 World's Columbian Exposition, advertise for guests and then murder some in rooms he had specially constructed to conceal their screams.

A *Times* article about him, published on July 26, 1895, began almost jocularly: "It is regarded as a rather uneventful day in police circles when the name of H. H. Holmes is not connected with the mysterious disappearance of one or more persons who were last seen in his company." Holmes, who was born Herman Mudgett and whose death is recounted in these pages, ultimately confessed to more than two dozen murders. In several cases, he had made an extra buck by selling the skeletons of his victims to medical schools.

A *Times* report from 2005 spurred the filmmakers Laura Ricciardi and Moira Demos to explore the story of Steven Avery, who would become the subject of their Netflix documentary, *Making a Murderer*. The precipitating article by Monica Davey, reprinted in this book, recounts how Avery, a Wisconsin man just freed from prison after serving 18 years for a rape he did not commit—a person who had become the poster child for wrongful prosecution—became implicated in the murder of another young woman. Avery would end up being convicted, but the documentary challenged the investigation, the prosecution and the verdict of his case. More than 500,000 people have signed a petition seeking a presidential pardon for Avery, though that is impossible since Avery was tried in a state, not a federal, court. He still remains in prison, though efforts to free him continue.

The Times has long shown admirable restraint in depicting the most squalid of criminal settings, but crime reporting has always appealed to the voyeur in all of us. Readers are stirred by their visceral response to the possibility that, but for fate, they too might have suffered. For all our genuine repulsion at violence, crime, it seems, makes rubberneckers of us all.

And reading about it is, unquestionably, a guilty pleasure.

"Simply put, we are compelled to understand why serial killers do such horrible things to (generally) complete strangers," Scott Bonn, a professor of criminology at Drew University, wrote in a 2011 article on the blog *Criminology on the Streets*. Such understanding does not come easy, though. Spend some time in chapter 8 reading about John Wayne Gacy and see if you think you could have detected that this seemingly community-spirited man who served as a Democratic precinct captain, shook hands with a president's wife and entertained children as Pogo the Clown was capable of murdering nearly three dozen young men and boys.

It's not enough for crime reporters to just examine individual atrocities and predators. The best of them have always tried to take a deeper look for underlying explanations, but the answers they arrive at are not always uniformly embraced. What sent crime plummeting in the 1990s: effective policing, or the waning of what had been epidemic use of crack cocaine? But still, crime reporting does provide some basis upon which to shape public policy. Governments, after all, are often judged by their ability to control crime and the attending fear, social disorder and economic decline it fosters. However systemic the root causes, unabated crime is a trapdoor for any elected leader. Several of the articles included here, primarily in the chapter on prison, undertake that broader analysis, whether the review is about rising incarceration rates or the surprising attraction of capital punishment to some inmates facing a lifetime behind bars.

The constraints of space, though, prevented us from delving into perhaps the most complicated of crime topics: policing. I worked as the police bureau chief for *The Times* in New York City between 1998 and 2002, a time, if it's possible to imagine, when the debate over how law enforcement conceived and performed its mission was even more contentious than it is today. New York enjoyed record-setting declines in crime in those years, which sparked the economy and created the calm of an earlier era on the streets. Some New York Police Department enforcement strategies, most notably Compstat—the use of data to map crime and distribute resources—were widely applauded and copied. Others, such as stop-and-frisk—the practice of confronting someone based on the suspicion they were carrying a concealed weapon—were criticized as excessive. And a series of police missteps and abuses—the torture of Abner Louima, the reckless shooting of Amadou Diallo, to name but two—tarnished the department's success, sowed mistrust in minority neighborhoods and foreshadowed the sort of police-community tensions so prevalent today. In New York, the debate over these issues was muted by the events of 9/11, but it was not resolved. So today, not unlike the issue of gun control, the matter of proper policing—what works, what doesn't and at what cost—remains a matter of robust disagreement. It is simply too complicated and important a topic to be dealt with in a single chapter of this book.

Similarly excluded are the topics of terrorism and political corruption, again for the reason that each is worthy of a more extended discussion. The rest of our selections could similarly be matters of debate. Susan Beachy, the researcher for this book, and I spent many hours reading through *Times* articles to pick material that was both consequential and well written, but one could fill five more books with the articles we passed on: Bernie Goetz, the subway vigilante. The kidnapping of Elizabeth Smart. The mob assassination of Paul Castellano outside a popular New York City steakhouse. The murders that inspired Truman Capote to author *In Cold Blood*. Even the articles we did pick sometimes had to be condensed for space.

In our reading we encountered articles by many of the great reporters who have covered crime for *The Times* like Gay Talese and David Halberstam, both of whom did time at New York City police headquarters in the press room known as the Shack. Tossed from headquarters in 1875, the cop reporters for several newspapers ended up occupying a tenement across the street, thus the nickname. The journalists were let back into headquarters years later, though the press room in the building continued to be called the Shack, a fitting name for the congested rabbit's warren of offices I once occupied. (I'm told the offices have since moved across the floor without gaining any space or losing any of their grimy charm.)

Crime reporting at *The Times* has, in more recent days, been graced by the participation of fine successors to the Taleses and the Halberstams, such as Robert McFadden, Selwyn Raab, Al Baker, William Rashbaum and Michael Wilson, some of whose work you'll find within these pages. The focus of these journalists was largely pointed toward crime that affected New York and its surroundings, but the breadth of *Times* resources is particularly evident in dispatches you will see filed from far afield:. From the city in Italy where a young student, Amanda Knox, was charged with murder. From a parade route in Egypt where Anwar Sadat was gunned down. From the killing fields in Norway where a mass murderer made clear that xenophobia was an international concern. Their work in these and other settings can never heal the injured or mitigate the grief. But it does help to address the questions that any society must confront if it wants to thrive: How can we stop the people who do bad things? And how can we be sure, when we punish them, that we have gotten it right?

CHAPTER 1

ASSASSINATIONS

"From Dallas, Texas, the flash, apparently official, President Kennedy died at 1 p.m. central standard time, 2 o'clock eastern standard time, some 38 minutes ago."

—CBS News anchor Walter Cronkite reporting the death of John F. Kennedy on November 22, 1963

THEY OFTEN STOP TIME, or seem to. Where were you when . . . ? Many people can remember where they were when they learned that John F. Kennedy or Martin Luther King Jr. had been shot. The killing of a leader is never just a murder, and the aftermath is never just about finding the assassin. It's about the death of an idea or the damage to a movement or, in some cases, the stirrings of war. *The Times* measured all of that as it reported on some of the most stunning acts of violence that the world has seen.

OPPOSITE: The funeral of President John F. Kennedy at Arlington National Cemetery, November 25, 1963. First Lady Jacqueline Kennedy and U.S. Attorney General Robert F. Kennedy are in the center foreground; President Lyndon B. Johnson is in the back row, left.

AWFUL EVENT:
PRESIDENT LINCOLN SHOT BY AN ASSASSIN

This evening at about 9:30 p.m. at Ford's Theatre, the president, while sitting in his private box with Mrs. Lincoln, Mr. Harris, and Major Rathburn, was shot by an assassin, who suddenly entered the box and appeared behind the president.

The assassin then leaped upon the stage, brandishing a large dagger or knife, and made his escape in the rear of the theatre.

The pistol ball entered the back of the president's head and penetrated nearly through the head. The wound is mortal. The president has been insensible ever since it was inflicted, and is now dying.

About the same hour an assassin, whether the same or not, entered [Secretary of State] Mr. Seward's apartments, and under the pretense of having a prescription, was shown to the secretary's sick chamber. The assassin rushed to the bed, and inflicted stabs on the throat and the face. It is hoped the wounds may not be mortal.

The nurse alarmed Mr. Frederick Seward, who was in an adjoining room, and hastened to the door of his father's room, when he met the assassin, who inflicted upon him one or more dangerous wounds. The recovery of Frederick Seward is doubtful.

It is not probable that the president will live throughout the night.

At a cabinet meeting at which Gen. Grant was present, the prospect of a speedy peace was discussed. The president was cheerful and hopeful, and spoke kindly of Gen. Lee and others of the Confederacy.

All the members of the cabinet except Mr. Seward are now in attendance upon the president.

I have seen Mr. Seward, but he and Frederick were both unconscious.

—Edwin M. Stanton,
Secretary of War

Detail of the Occurrence

Washington, Friday, April 14, 12:30 a.m.—The president was shot in a theatre tonight, and is perhaps mortally wounded. Secretary of State Seward was also assassinated.

President Lincoln and wife, with other friends, this evening visited Ford's Theatre for the purpose of witnessing the performance of the *American Cousin*.

The theatre was densely crowded, and everybody seemed delighted with the scene before them. During the third act, a sharp report of a pistol was heard, which suggested nothing serious until a man rushed to the front of the president's box, waving a long dagger, and exclaiming "Sic semper tyrannis," and leaped from the box, which was in the second tier, to the opposite side, making his escape from the rear of the theatre, and mounting a horse, fled.

The screams of Mrs. Lincoln first disclosed to the audience that the president had been shot, when all present rose to their feet, rushing toward the stage, many exclaiming, "Hang him! Hang him!"

The excitement was of the wildest possible description, and of course there was an abrupt termination of the theatrical performance.

President Lincoln's box at Ford's Theatre, April 1865.

There was a rush toward the president's box, when cries were heard: "Stand back and give him air." "Has any one stimulants?" On a hasty examination, it was found that the president had been shot through the head, above and back of the temporal bone, and that some of the brain was oozing out. He was removed to a private house opposite the theatre, and the surgeon-general of the army and other surgeons were sent for.

On an examination of the private box blood was discovered on the back of the rocking chair on which the president had been sitting, also on the partition and on the floor. A single-barreled pocket pistol was found on the carpet.

A military guard was placed in front of the private residence to which the president had been conveyed. An immense crowd was in front, all deeply anxious to learn the condition of the president. It had been previously announced that the wound was mortal but all hoped otherwise.

The president was totally insensible, and breathing slowly. Blood oozed from the wound at the back of his head. The surgeons exhausted every effort, but all hope was gone. The parting of his family with the dying president is too sad for description.

At midnight, the cabinet, with Messrs. Sumner, Colfax and Farnsworth, Judge Curtis, Gov. Oglesby, Gen. Meigs, Col. Hay, and a few personal friends, with Surgeon-General Barnes and his immediate assistants, were around his bedside.

The president and Mrs. Lincoln had not started for the theatre until 15 minutes after 8 o'clock. Speaker Colfax was at the White House at the time, and the president stated to him that he was going, although Mrs. Lincoln had not been well, because the papers had announced that Gen. Grant and they were to be present, and, as Gen. Grant had gone north, he did not wish the audience to be disappointed.

> ## A single-barreled pocket pistol was found on the carpet.

He went with apparent reluctance and urged Mr. Colfax to go with him; but that gentleman had made other engagements, and with Mr. Ashman, of Massachusetts, bid him good-bye.

When the excitement at the theater was at its wildest height, reports circulated that Secretary Seward had also been assassinated.

On reaching this gentleman's residence a crowd and a military guard were found at the door, and on entering it was ascertained that the reports were true.

Everybody there was so excited that scarcely an intelligible word could be gathered, but the facts are substantially as follows:

About 10 o'clock a man rang the bell, and the call having been answered by a colored servant, he said he had come from Dr. Verdi, Secretary Seward's family physician, with a prescription, at the same time holding in his hand a small piece of paper, and saying in answer to a refusal that he must see the secretary. The man struck the servant on the head with a "billy," severely injuring the skull and felling him almost senseless. The assassin then rushed into the chamber and attacked Major Seward, paymaster of the United States army, and Mr. Hansell, a messenger of the State Department and two male nurses. Disabling them all, he then rushed upon the secretary, who was lying in bed in the same room, and inflicted three stabs in the neck, but severing, it is hoped, no arteries, though he bled profusely.

The assassin then rushed downstairs, mounted his horse, and rode off before an alarm could be sounded, and in the same manner as the assassin of the president.

It is believed that the injuries of the secretary are not fatal, nor those of either of the others, although the secretary and the assistant secretary are seriously injured.

Secretaries Stanton and Welles, and other officers of the government, called at Secretary Seward's home and there heard of the assassination of the president.

They then proceeded to the house where he was lying, exhibiting of course intense anxiety and solicitude. An immense crowd was gathered in front of the president's house, and a guard was also stationed there, many persons evidently supposing he would be brought to his home.

The entire city tonight presents a scene of wild excitement, accompanied by violent expressions of indignation, and the profoundest sorrow; many shed tears. The military authorities have dispatched mounted patrols in every direction, to arrest the assassins. The whole metropolitan police are vigilant for the same purpose.

The attacks both at the theatre and at Secretary Seward's house, took place at about the same hour—10 o'clock—showing a preconcerted plan to assassinate those gentlemen. Some evidences of the guilt of the party who attacked the president are in the possession of the police.

—*April 15, 1865*

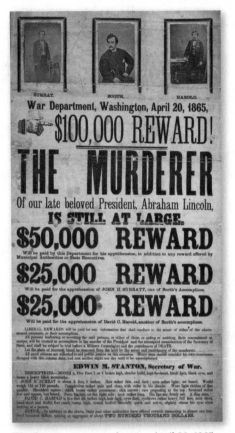

War Department reward poster, April 20, 1865.

NOTE: *The assassin, John Wilkes Booth, an actor and Confederate sympathizer, fled to Maryland where he was found 12 days later hiding in a barn. He was shot and killed by Boston Corbett, a Union soldier. Eight other suspected accomplices to the assassination were rounded up and put on trial before a military tribunal. All were convicted and four were hanged, including Mary Surratt, the first woman to be executed by the U.S. government.*

HEIR TO AUSTRIA'S THRONE IS SLAIN
WITH HIS WIFE BY A BOSNIAN YOUTH TO
AVENGE SEIZURE OF HIS COUNTRY

Archduke Francis Ferdinand, heir to the throne of Austria-Hungary, and his wife, the Duchess of Hohenberg, were shot and killed by a Bosnian student here in Sarajevo. The fatal shooting was the second attempt upon the lives of the couple during the day, and is believed to have been the result of a political conspiracy.

This morning, as Archduke Francis Ferdinand and the duchess were driving to a reception at the town hall, a bomb was thrown at their motorcar. The archduke pushed it off with his arm.

The bomb did not explode until after the archduke's car had passed on, and the occupants of the next car, Count von Boos-Waldeck and Col. Morizzi, the archduke's aide de camp, were slightly injured. Among the spectators, six persons were hurt.

The author of the attempt at assassination was a compositor named Gabrinovics, who comes from Trebinje.

After the attempt upon his life the archduke ordered his car to halt, and after he found out what had happened he drove to the town hall, where the town councilors, with the mayor at their head, awaited him. The mayor was about to begin his address of welcome when the archduke interrupted him angrily, saying:

> *The fatal shooting was the second attempt upon the lives of the couple during the day.*

"Herr burgermeister, it is perfectly outrageous! We have come to Sarajevo on a visit and have had a bomb thrown at us."

The archduke paused and then said: "Now you may go on."

Thereupon the mayor delivered his address and the archduke made a suitable reply.

The public by this time had heard of the bomb attempt, and burst into the hall with loud cries of "Zivio!" the Slav word for "hurrah."

After going around the town hall, the archduke started for the garrison hospital to visit Col. Morizzi, who had been taken there after the outrage.

As the archduke reached the corner of Rudolf Street two pistol shots were fired by an individual who called himself Gavrilo Princip. The first shot struck the duchess in the

HEIR TO AUSTRIA'S THRONE IS SLAIN WITH HIS WIFE BY A BOSNIAN YOUTH TO AVENGE SEIZURE OF HIS COUNTRY

Francis Ferdinand Shot During State Visit to Sarajevo.

TWO ATTACKS IN A DAY

Archduke Saves His Life First Time by Knocking Aside a Bomb Hurled at Auto.

SLAIN IN SECOND ATTEMPT

Lad Dashes at Car as the Royal Couple Return from Town Hall and Kills Both of Them.

New York Times front page, June 29, 1914.

abdomen, while the second hit the archduke in the neck and pierced the jugular vein. The duchess became unconscious immediately and fell across the knees of her husband. The archduke also lost consciousness.

The motorcar in which they were seated drove straight to the Konak, where an army surgeon rendered first aid, but in vain. Neither the archduke nor the duchess gave any sign of life, and the head of the hospital could only certify they were dead.

The authors of both attacks upon the archduke are Bosnians. Gabrinovics is a compositor, and worked briefly in the government printing works at Belgrade. He returned to Sarajevo a Servian chauvinist, and made no concealment of his sympathies with the king of Servia. Both he and the actual murderer of the archduke and the duchess expressed themselves to the police in the most cynical fashion about their crimes.

—June 29, 1914

NOTE: *The assassination helped trigger World War I. The assassin, 19-year-old Gavrilo Princip, a Yugoslav nationalist who opposed Austro-Hungarian rule, died in prison in 1918.*

GANDHI IS KILLED BY A HINDU; INDIA SHAKEN, WORLD MOURNS; 15 DIE IN RIOTING IN BOMBAY

By ROBERT TRUMBULL

Mohandas K. Gandhi was killed by an assassin's bullet today. The assassin was a Hindu who fired three shots from a pistol at a range of three feet.

The 78-year-old Gandhi, the one person who held discordant elements together and kept some sort of unity in this turbulent land, was shot down at 5:15 p.m. as he was proceeding through the Biria House gardens to the pergola from which he was to deliver his daily prayer meeting message.

The assassin was immediately seized. He later identified himself as Nathuram Vinayak Godse, 36, a Hindu of the Mahratta tribes in Poona. This has been a center of resistance to Gandhi's ideology.

Mr. Gandhi died 25 minutes later. His death left all India stunned and bewildered as to the direction that this newly independent nation would take without its "Mahatma" (Great Teacher).

The loss of Mr. Gandhi brings this country of 300,000,000 abruptly to a crossroads. Mingled with the sadness in New Delhi tonight was an undercurrent of fear and uncertainty, for now the strongest influence for peace in India that this generation has known is gone.

Riots quickly swept Bombay when news of Mr. Gandhi's death was received. The Associated Press reported that 15 persons were killed and more than 50 injured.

Appeal Made by Nehru

Prime Minister Pandit Jawaharlal Nehru, in a voice choked with emotion, appealed in a radio address tonight for a sane approach to the future. He asked that India's path be turned away from violence in memory of the great peacemaker who had departed.

Mr. Gandhi's body will be cremated in the orthodox Hindu fashion, according to his expressed wishes. His body will be carried from his New Delhi residence on a simple wooden cot covered with a sheet at 11:30 tomorrow morning. The funeral procession will wind through every principal street of the two cities of New and Old Delhi and reach the burning ghats on the bank of the sacred Jumna River at 4 p.m. There the remains of the greatest Indian since Gautama Buddha will be wrapped in a sheet, laid on a pyre of wood and burned. His ashes will be scattered on the Jumna's waters, eventually to mingle with the Ganges where the two holy rivers meet at the temple city of Allahabad.

These simple ceremonies were announced tonight by Pandit Nehru in respect to Mr. Gandhi's wishes. India will see the last of Mr. Gandhi as it saw him when he lived—as a humble and unassuming Hindu.

News Spreads Quickly

News of the assassination of Mr. Gandhi—only a few days after he had finished a five-day fast to bring about communal friendship—spread quickly through New Delhi. Immediately there was spontaneous movement of thousands to Biria House, home of G. D. Biria, the millionaire industrialist, where Mr. Gandhi and his six secretaries had been guests since he came to New Delhi in the midst of the disturbances in India's capital.

While walking through the gardens to this evening's prayer meeting Mr. Gandhi had just reached the top of a short flight of brick steps, his slender brown arms around the shoulders of his granddaughters, Manu, 17, and Ava, 20.

Someone spoke to him and he turned and gave the appealing Hindu salute—palms together and the points of the fingers brought to the chin as in a Christian attitude of prayer.

At once a youngish Indian stepped from the crowd, which had opened to form a pathway for Mr. Gandhi's walk to the pergola, and fired the fatal shots from a pistol. One bullet struck Mr. Gandhi in the chest and two in the abdomen. He seemed to lean forward and then crumpled to the ground. His two granddaughters fell beside him in tears.

Crowd Is Stunned

A crowd of about 500, according to witnesses, was stunned. There was no outcry or excitement for a second or two. Then the onlookers began to push the assassin more as if in bewilderment than in anger.

The assassin was seized by Tom Reiner of Lancaster, Mass., a vice consul attached to the American embassy and a recent arrival in India.

Mr. Reiner grasped the assailant by the shoulders and shoved him toward several police guards. Only then did the crowd begin to grasp what had happened, and a forest of fists belabored the assassin as he was dragged toward the pergola where Mr. Gandhi was to have prayed, leaving a trail of blood.

Mr. Gandhi was picked up by attendants and carried back to the unpretentious bedroom where he had passed most of his working and sleeping hours. Hindu onlookers who could see him began to wail and beat their breasts.

Less than half an hour later a member of Mr. Gandhi's entourage came out of the room and said to those about the door:

"Bapu [father] is finished."

But not until Mr. Gandhi's death was announced by All India Radio, at 6 p.m. did the words spread widely.

Assassin Taken Away

Meanwhile the assassin was taken to a police station. He identified himself as coming from Poona.

It was remarked that the first of three attempts on Mr. Gandhi's life was made in Poona on June 25, 1934, when a bomb was thrown at a car believed to be Mr. Gandhi's. Poona is a center of the extremist anti-Gandhi orthodox Hindu Mahasabha (Great Society).

The second possible attempt to assassinate Mr. Gandhi was by means of a crude bomb planted on his garden wall on Jan. 20 of this year.

The only statement known to have been made by the assassin was his remark to a foreign correspondent: "I am not at all sorry."

He is large for a Hindu and was dressed in gray slacks, blue pullover and khaki bush jacket. His pistol, which was snatched from him immediately after the shooting by Royal Indian Air Force Flight Sergeant D. R. Singh, contained four undischarged cartridges.

Lying on a wooden cot in his bedroom, Mr. Gandhi said no word before his death except to ask for water. Most of the time he was unconscious. When he was pronounced dead by his physician, weeping members of his staff covered the lower half of his face with a sheet in the Hindu fashion and the women present sat on the floor and chanted verses from the sacred scriptures of the Hindus.

Pandit Nehru arrived at 6 o'clock. Silently he inspected the spot where Mr. Gandhi was shot and then entered the house. Later he stood at the front gate of Biria House and related the tentative funeral arrangements to several thousand persons gathered in the street. His voice shook with grief, and hundreds in the crowd were weeping uncontrollably.

Several thousand mourners formed queues at all doors leading into Biria House and for a time they were permitted to file past the body. Later, when it became evident that only a small fraction of the gathering would be able to view Mr. Gandhi's remains tonight, the body was taken to a second-floor balcony and placed on a cot fitted under a flood lamp so all in the grounds would see their departed leader.

His head was illuminated by a lamp with five wicks representing the five elements—air, light, water, earth, and fire—and also to light his soul to eternity according to Hindu belief.

Pandit Nehru delivered Mr. Gandhi's valedictory in his radio address late this evening. In a quivering voice, he said:

"Gandhi has gone out of our lives and there is darkness everywhere. The father of our nation is no more—no longer will we run to him for advice and solace. This is a terrible blow to millions and millions in this country.

"I can only call him a madman."

"Our light has gone out, but the light that shone in this country was no ordinary light. For a thousand years that light will be seen in this country and the world will see it. . . . Oh, that this has happened to us! There was so much more to do."

Referring to the assassin, Pandit Nehru said: "I can only call him a madman."

He pleaded for a renewed spirit of peace, which had been Mr. Gandhi's last project, saying:

"His spirit looks upon us—nothing would displease him more than to see us indulge in violence. All our petty conflicts and difficulties must be ended in the face of this great disaster. . . . In his death he has reminded us of the big things in life."

—January 31, 1948

NOTE: *The assassin, Nathuram Godse, a Hindu nationalist, said at his trial that he was angry because he believed Gandhi, a Hindu, had "pandered" to Muslims. Godse was sentenced to death and hanged on November 15, 1949.*

KENNEDY IS KILLED BY SNIPER AS HE RIDES IN CAR IN DALLAS; JOHNSON SWORN IN ON PLANE

By TOM WICKER

President John Fitzgerald Kennedy was shot and killed by an assassin today.

He died of a wound in the brain caused by a rifle bullet that was fired at him as he was riding through downtown Dallas in a motorcade.

Vice President Lyndon Baines Johnson, who was riding in the third car behind Mr. Kennedy's, was sworn in as the 36th president of the United States 99 minutes after Mr. Kennedy's death.

Mr. Johnson is 55 years old; Mr. Kennedy was 46.

Shortly after the assassination, Lee H. Oswald, who once defected to the Soviet Union and has been active in the Fair Play for Cuba Committee, was arrested by the Dallas police. Tonight he was accused of the killing.

Suspect Captured after Scuffle

Oswald, 24, was also accused of slaying a policeman who had approached him in the street. Oswald was subdued after a scuffle with a second policeman in a nearby theater.

President Kennedy was shot at 12:30 p.m., central standard time. He was pronounced dead at 1 p.m. and Mr. Johnson was sworn in at 2:39 p.m.

Mr. Johnson, who was uninjured in the shooting, took his oath in the presidential jet plane as it stood on the runway at Love Field. The body of Mr. Kennedy was aboard. Immediately after the oath-taking, the plane took off for Washington.

Standing beside the new president as Mr. Johnson took the oath of office was Mrs. John F. Kennedy. Her stockings were spattered with her husband's blood.

Gov. John B. Connally Jr. of Texas, who was riding in the same car with Mr. Kennedy, was severely wounded in the chest, ribs and arm.

The killer fired the rifle from a building just off the motorcade route. Mr. Kennedy, Governor Connally and Mr. Johnson had just received an enthusiastic welcome from a large crowd in downtown Dallas.

Mr. Kennedy apparently was hit by the first of what witnesses believed were three shots. He was driven at high speed to Dallas's Parkland Hospital. There, in an emergency operating room, he died without regaining consciousness.

Mrs. Kennedy, Mrs. Connally and a Secret Service agent were in the car with Mrs. Kennedy and Governor Connally. Two Secret Service agents flanked the car. Other than Mr. Connally, none of this group was injured in the shooting. Mrs. Kennedy cried, "Oh, no!" immediately after her husband was struck.

Mrs. Kennedy was in the hospital near her husband when he died, but not in the operating room. When the body was taken from the hospital in a bronze coffin about 2 p.m., Mrs. Kennedy walked beside it.

Her face was sorrowful. She looked steadily at the floor. She still wore the raspberry-colored suit in which she had greeted welcoming crowds in Fort Worth and Dallas. But she had taken off the matching pillbox hat she wore earlier in the day, and her dark hair was windblown and tangled. Her hand rested lightly on her husband's coffin as it was taken to a waiting hearse.

Mrs. Kennedy climbed in beside the coffin. Then the ambulance drove to Love Field, and Mr. Kennedy's body was placed aboard the presidential jet. Mrs. Kennedy then attended the swearing-in ceremony for Mr. Johnson.

Priests Administer Last Rites

Two priests administered last rites to Mr. Kennedy, a Roman Catholic. They were the Very Rev. Oscar Huber, the pastor of Holy Trinity Church in Dallas, and the Rev. James Thompson.

Mr. Johnson was sworn in as president by Federal Judge Sarah T. Hughes of the Northern District of Texas. The ceremony, delayed about five minutes for Mrs. Kennedy's arrival, took place in the private presidential cabin in the rear of the plane.

About 25 to 30 persons—members of the late president's staff, members of Congress who had been accompanying the president on a two-day tour of Texas cities and a few reporters—crowded into the little room.

Mrs. Kennedy stood at the left of Mr. Johnson, her eyes and face showing the signs of weeping that had apparently shaken her since she left the hospital not long before. Mrs. Johnson stood at her husband's right. As Judge Hughes read the brief oath of office, her eyes, too, were red from weeping. Mr. Johnson's hands rested on a black, leather-bound Bible as Judge Hughes read and he repeated: "I do solemnly swear that I will perform the duties of the president of the United States to the best of my ability and defend, protect and preserve the Constitution of the United States."

Those 34 words made Lyndon Baines Johnson, one-time farm boy and school-teacher of Johnson City, Texas, the president.

President Kennedy, Jacqueline Kennedy, and Gov. and Mrs. John Connally of Texas riding in a motorcade, approximately one minute before the president was shot in Dallas on November 22, 1963.

Johnson Embraces Mrs. Kennedy

Mr. Johnson made no statement. He embraced Mrs. Kennedy and she held his hand for a long moment. He also embraced Mrs. Johnson and Mrs. Evelyn Lincoln, Mr. Kennedy's private secretary.

"O.K.," Mr. Johnson said. "Let's get this plane back to Washington."

At 2:46 p.m., 7 minutes after he had become president and 106 minutes after Mr. Kennedy had become the fourth American president to succumb to an assassin's wounds, the jet took off for Washington.

Mr. Kennedy's staff members appeared stunned and bewildered. Lawrence F. O'Brien, the Congressional liaison officer, and Kenneth P. O'Donnell, the appointment secretary, both long associates of Mr. Kennedy, showed evidence of weeping. None had anything to say.

14

Other staff members believed to be in the cabin for the swearing-in included David F. Powers, the White House receptionist; Miss Pamela Turnure, Mrs. Kennedy's press secretary, and Malcolm Kilduff, the assistant White House press secretary.

Mr. Kilduff announced the president's death, with choked voice and red-rimmed eyes, at about 1:36 p.m.

"President John F. Kennedy died at approximately 1 o'clock central standard time today here in Dallas," Mr. Kilduff said at the hospital. "He died of a gunshot wound in the brain. I have no other details regarding the assassination of the president."

Mr. Kilduff also announced that Governor Connally had been hit by a bullet or bullets and that Mr. Johnson, who had not yet been sworn in, was in the protective custody of the Secret Service at an unannounced place.

Mr. Kilduff indicated that the president had been shot once. Later medical reports raised the possibility that there had been two wounds. But the death was apparently caused by a massive wound in the brain.

Later in the afternoon, Dr. Malcolm Perry, an attending surgeon, and Dr. Kemp Clark, chief of neurosurgery at Parkland Hospital, gave more details. Mr. Kennedy was hit by a bullet in the throat, just below the Adam's apple, they said. This wound had the appearance of a bullet's entry.

Mr. Kennedy also had a massive wound in the back and one on the right side of the head. However, the doctors said it was impossible to determine immediately whether the wounds had been caused by one bullet or two.

Resuscitation Attempted

Dr. Perry, the first physician to treat the president, said a number of resuscitative measures had been attempted, including oxygen, anesthesia, an indotracheal tube, a tracheotomy, blood and fluids. An electrocardiogram monitor was attached to measure Mr. Kennedy's heartbeats.

Dr. Clark was summoned and arrived in a minute or two. By then, Dr. Perry said, Mr. Kennedy was near death.

Dr. Clark said that on his first sight of the president, he had concluded immediately that Mr. Kennedy could not live.

"It was apparent that the president had sustained a lethal wound," he said. "A missile had gone in and out of the back of his head causing external lacerations and loss of brain tissue."

Shortly after he arrived, Dr. Clark said, "the president lost his heart action by the electrocardiogram."

In Operating Room 40 Minutes

The president was on the emergency table at the hospital for about 40 minutes, the doctors said. At the end, perhaps 8 physicians were in Operating Room No. 1, where Mr. Kennedy remained until his death. The doctors said officially that it occurred at 1 p.m.

Later, there were unofficial reports that Mr. Kennedy had been killed instantly. The source of these reports, Dr. Tom Shires, chief surgeon at the hospital and professor of surgery at the University of Texas Southwest Medical School, issued this statement tonight:

"Medically, it was apparent the president was not alive when he was brought in," he said, adding, "It was obvious he had a lethal head wound.

"Technically, however, by using vigorous resuscitation, intravenous tubes and all the usual supportive measures, we were able to raise a semblance of a heartbeat."

Dr. Shires said he was "positive it was impossible" that President Kennedy could have spoken after being shot. "I am absolutely sure he never knew what hit him," Dr. Shires said.

Dr. Shires was not present when Mr. Kennedy was being treated at Parkland Hospital. He issued his statement after conferences with the doctors who had attended the president.

The details of what happened when shots first rang out, as the president's car moved along at about 25 miles an hour, were sketchy.

Kennedys Hailed at Breakfast

Mr. Kennedy had opened his day in Fort Worth, with a speech in a parking lot and then at a chamber of commerce breakfast. The breakfast appearance was a particular triumph for Mrs. Kennedy, who was given an ovation.

Then the presidential party, including Governor and Mrs. Connally, flew on to Dallas, an eight-minute flight. Mr. Johnson, as is customary, flew in a separate plane. The president and the vice president do not travel together, out of fear of a double tragedy.

At Love Field, Mr. and Mrs. Kennedy shook hands with an enthusiastic group lining the fence.

Mr. Kennedy then entered his open Lincoln convertible at the head of the motorcade. He sat in the rear seat on the right-hand side. Mrs. Kennedy, who appeared to be enjoying one of the first political outings she had ever made with her husband, sat at his left.

In the jump seat, directly ahead of Mr. Kennedy, sat Governor Connally, with Mrs. Connally at his left in another jump seat. A Secret Service agent was driving and the two others ran alongside.

Behind the president's limousine was an open sedan carrying Secret Service agents. Behind them, in an open convertible, rode Mr. and Mrs. Johnson and Texas's senior senator, Ralph W. Yarborough, a Democrat.

The motorcade proceeded along a 10-mile route through downtown Dallas, aiming for the Merchandise Mart. Mr. Kennedy was to address a group of the city's leading citizens at a luncheon.

In downtown Dallas, crowds were enthusiastic and cheering. The turnout was unusual for this center of conservatism, where only a month ago Adlai E. Stevenson was attacked by a rightist crowd. As the motorcade neared its end and the president's car moved out of the thick crowds onto Stemmons Freeway near the Merchandise Mart, Mrs. Connally recalled later, "we were all very pleased with the reception in downtown Dallas."

Approaching 3-Street Underpass

Behind the three leading cars were a string of others carrying Texas and Dallas dignitaries, two buses of reporters, several open cars carrying photographers and other reporters, and a bus for White House staff members.

As Mrs. Connally recalled later, the president's car was almost ready to go underneath a triple underpass beneath three streets—Elm, Commerce and Main—when the first shot was fired. That shot apparently struck Mr. Kennedy. Governor Connally turned in his seat and appeared immediately to be hit in the chest.

Mrs. Mary Norman of Dallas was standing at the curb and aiming her camera at the president. She saw him slump forward, then slide down in the seat.

"My God!" Mrs. Norman screamed, as she recalled later. "He's shot!"

Mrs. Connally said that Mrs. Kennedy had reached and "grabbed" her husband. Mrs. Connally put her arms around the governor. She said that she and Mrs. Kennedy then ducked in the car as it sped off.

Most reporters in the press buses were too far back to see the shootings, but they observed scurrying by motor policemen accompanying the motorcade. It was noted that the president's car had picked up speed and raced away, but reporters were only aware that anything serious had occurred when they reached the Merchandise Mart a few minutes later.

Rumors Spread at Trade Mart

Rumors of the shooting already were spreading through the luncheon crowd of hundreds. No White House officials or Secret Service agents were present, but the reporters were taken quickly to Parkland Hospital on the strength of the rumors.

There they encountered Senator Yarborough, white, shaken and horrified.

The shots, he said, seemed to have come from the right and the rear of the car in which he was riding, the third in the motorcade. Another eyewitness, Mel Crouch, a Dallas television reporter, reported that as the shots rang out he saw a rifle extended and then withdrawn from a window on the "fifth or sixth floor" of the Texas Public School Book Depository, a state building on Elm Street, to the right of the motorcade route.

Senator Yarborough said there had been a slight pause between the first two shots and a longer pause between the second and third. A Secret Service man riding in the senator's car ordered Mr. and Mrs. Johnson to get down below the level of the doors. The leading cars of the motorcade then pulled away at high speed toward nearby Parkland Hospital by the fast highway.

"We knew by the speed that something was terribly wrong," Senator Yarborough reported. When he put his head up, he said, he saw a Secret Serve man in the car ahead beating his fists against the trunk deck of the car in which he was riding, apparently in frustration and anguish.

Mrs. Kennedy's Reaction

Only White House staff members spoke with Mrs. Kennedy. A Dallas medical student, David Edwards, saw her in Parkland Hospital while she was waiting for news of her husband. He gave this description:

"The look in her eyes was like an animal that had been trapped, like a little rabbit—brave, but fear was in the eyes."

Dr. Clark was reported to have informed Mrs. Kennedy of her husband's death.

Mr. Kennedy's limousine pulled up at the emergency entrance of Parkland Hospital. By the time reporters arrived at the hospital, the police were guarding the presidential car closely. They would allow no one to approach it. A bucket of water stood by the car, suggesting that the back seat had been scrubbed out.

Robert Clark of the American Broadcasting Company, who had been riding near the front of the motorcade, said Mr. Kennedy was motionless when he was carried inside. There was a great amount of blood on Mr. Kennedy's suit and shirtfront and the front of his body, Mr. Clark said.

Mrs. Kennedy was leaning over her husband when the car stopped, Mr. Clark said, and he walked beside the wheeled stretcher into the hospital. Mr. Connally was also moved into the hospital in a stretcher.

Eyewitness Describes Shooting

An unidentified Dallas man, interviewed on television here, said he had been waving at the president when the shots were fired. His belief was that Mr. Kennedy had been struck twice—once, as Mrs. Norman recalled, when he slumped in his seat, and again when he slid down in it.

"It seemed to just knock him down," the man said.

Governor Connally's condition was reported as "satisfactory" tonight after four hours in surgery at Parkland Hospital.

Dr. Robert R. Shaw, a thoracic surgeon, operated on the governor to repair damage to his left chest. Later, Dr. Shaw said Governor Connally had been hit in the back just below the shoulder blade, and that the bullet had gone through the governor's chest. After leaving the body, he said, the bullet struck the governor's right wrist and then lodged in the left thigh.

Tour by Mrs. Kennedy Unusual

Mrs. Kennedy's presence near her husband's bedside at his death resulted from somewhat unusual circumstances. She had rarely accompanied him on his trips about the country and almost never made political trips with him.

The tour on which Mr. Kennedy was engaged was only quasi-political; the only open political activity was to have been a speech tonight to a fund-raising dinner at the state capitol in Austin.

In visiting Texas, Mr. Kennedy was seeking to improve his political fortunes in a pivotal state that he barely won in 1960. He was also hoping to patch an internal dispute among Texas's Democrats.

At 8:45 a.m., when Mr. Kennedy left the Texas Hotel in Fort Worth, where he spent his last night, to address the parking lot crowd across the street, Mrs. Kennedy was not with him. There appeared to be some disappointment.

"Mrs. Kennedy is organizing herself," the president said good-naturedly. "It takes longer, but, of course, she looks better than we do when she does it."

Later, Mrs. Kennedy appeared late at the chamber of commerce breakfast in Fort Worth.

Again, Mr. Kennedy took note of her presence. "Two years ago," he said, "I introduced myself in Paris by saying that I was the man who had accompanied Mrs. Kennedy to Paris. I am getting somewhat that same sensation as I travel around Texas. Nobody wonders what Lyndon and I wear."

The speech Mr. Kennedy never delivered at the Merchandise Mart luncheon contained a passage commenting on a recent preoccupation of his, and a subject of much interest in this city, where right-wing conservatism is the rule rather than the exception.

Voices are being heard in the land, he said, "voices preaching doctrines wholly unrelated to reality, wholly unsuited to the sixties, doctrines which apparently assume that words will suffice without weapons, that vituperation is as good as victory and that peace is a sign of weakness."

The speech went on: "At a time when the national debt is steadily being reduced in terms of its burden on our economy, they see that debt as the greatest threat to our security. At a time when we are steadily reducing the number of federal employees serving every thousand citizens, they fear those supposed hordes of civil servants far more than the actual hordes of opposing armies.

"We cannot expect that everyone, to use the phrase of a decade ago, will 'talk sense to the American people.' But we can hope that fewer people will listen to nonsense. And the notion that this nation is headed for defeat through deficit, or that strength is but a matter of slogans, is nothing but just plain nonsense."

—November 23, 1963

NOTE: *Lee Harvey Oswald, the man who shot Kennedy, was himself shot to death two days later by Dallas nightclub owner Jack Ruby while being transported to a county jail. The question of whether Oswald acted alone has been debated by conspiracy theorists for decades.*

MALCOLM X SHOT TO DEATH AT RALLY HERE

By PETER KIHSS

Malcolm X, the 39-year-old leader of a militant black nationalist movement, was shot to death yesterday afternoon at a rally of his followers in a ballroom in Washington Heights.

Shortly before midnight, a 22-year-old Negro, Thomas Hagan, was charged with the killing. The police rescued him from the ballroom crowd after he had been shot and beaten.

Malcolm, a bearded extremist, had said only a few words of greeting when a fusillade rang out. The bullets knocked him over backward.

Pandemonium broke out among the 400 Negroes in the Audubon Ballroom at 166th Street and Broadway. As men, women and children ducked under tables and flattened themselves on the floor, more shots were fired. Some witnesses said 30 shots had been fired.

Malcolm X at a news conference in New York, March 12, 1964.

Three Weapons Fired

The police said seven bullets had struck Malcolm. Three other Negroes were shot.

About two hours later the police said the shooting was apparently a result of a feud between followers of Malcolm and members of the extremist group he broke with last year, the Black Muslims. The police declined to say whether Hagan is a Muslim.

The medical examiner's office said early this morning that a preliminary autopsy showed Malcolm had died of "multiple gunshot wounds." The office said that bullets of two different calibers as well as shotgun pellets had been removed from his body.

One police theory was that up to five conspirators might have been involved, two creating a diversionary disturbance.

Hagan was shot in the left thigh and his left leg was broken, apparently by kicks. He was under treatment in the Bellevue Hospital prison ward last night; perhaps a dozen policemen were guarding him, according to a hospital superintendent. The police said they had found a cartridge case with four unused .45-caliber shells in his pocket.

Two other Negroes, described as "apparent spectators" by Assistant Chief Inspector Harry Taylor, in command of Manhattan North uniformed police, also were shot. They were identified as William Harris, wounded seriously in the abdomen, and William Parker, shot in a foot. Both were taken to Columbia Presbyterian Medical Center, which is near the ballroom.

Capt. Paul Glaser of the police department's Community Relations Bureau said early today that Hagan, using a double-barreled shotgun with shortened barrels and stock, had killed Malcolm X.

Malcolm, a slim, reddish-haired six-footer with a gift for bitter eloquence against what he considered white exploitation of Negroes, broke in March 1964 with the Black Muslim movement called the Nation of Islam, headed by Elijah Muhammad.

A weapon described as a 12-gauge shotgun was found behind the ballroom stage wrapped in a man's gray jacket.

As Hagan fired at Malcolm, Captain Glaser said, Reuben Francis, a follower of Malcolm, drew a .45-caliber automatic pistol and shot Hagan in the leg. Francis, 33, of East 179th Street, the Bronx, was charged with felonious assault and violation of the Sullivan Law.

Records of the FBI showed that Hagan's real name is Talmadge Hayer, the police said this morning. The FBI records showed that the suspect's address was on Marshall Street in Paterson, N.J., and he was arrested Nov. 7, 1963, in Passaic for possession of stolen property.

Sanford Garelick, assistant chief inspector in charge of the police Central Office Bureau and Squads, said at 5 p.m. that "this is the result, it would seem, of a long-standing feud between the followers of Elijah Muhammad and the people who broke away from him, headed by Malcolm X."

At 7:30 p.m., Chief of Detectives Philip J. Walsh predicted "a long drawn-out investigation."

Muslim Denies Involvement

James X, New York spokesman for the Black Muslims, denied his organization had anything to do with the killing.

Just a week before the slaying, Malcolm was bombed out of the small brick home in East Elmhurst, Queens, where he had been living. James X suggested that Malcolm had set off firebombs himself "to get publicity."

Assemblyman Percy Sutton, Malcolm's lawyer, said the murdered leader had planned to disclose at yesterday's rally "the names of those who were trying to kill him."

Mr. Sutton added that Malcolm had taken to carrying a pistol "because he feared for his life" and had notified the police that he was doing so even though he did not have a permit. Assistant Chief Inspector Taylor, however, said Malcolm was unarmed when he was shot.

Chief Walsh said he believed "proper action was taken on all considerations of protection" for Malcolm, and "many of our requests in this connection were turned down."

Captain Glaser said that since Jan. 27, Malcolm had been offered police protection on seven different occasions, but had refused each time.

Remarks Criticized

One factor in Malcolm's break with the Black Muslims was his comment on the assassination of President Kennedy. He called it a case of "chickens coming home to roost" and an outgrowth of violence that whites had used against Negroes. He was suspended by Elijah Muhammad and then started his own movement.

While the Nation of Islam searches for weapons anyone attending its meetings, Malcolm's new movement emphasized self-defense even with weapons. And so there was no search of anyone at yesterday's rally, a regular Sunday affair of Malcolm's Organization of Afro-American Unity. White persons were barred.

The Audubon Ballroom is in a two-story building on West 166th Street between Broadway and St. Nicholas Avenue. The meeting had been called for 2:30 p.m. in the second-floor hall, where 400 chairs had been set up with two aisles going down the sides.

"Would Give His Life"

Witnesses said one of the speakers who preceded Malcolm had asserted: "Malcolm is a man who would give his life for you."

Gene Simpson, a WMCA newsman, said he was sitting in the front row when Malcolm was introduced. He said Malcolm gave the traditional Arabic greeting, "Salaam aleikum"—"peace be unto you."

"The crowd responded, 'Aleikum salaam,'" Mr. Simpson said, "and then there was some disturbance about eight rows back. Everybody turned, and so did I, and then I heard Malcolm saying, 'Be cool now, don't get excited.'

"And then I heard this muffled sound, and I saw Malcolm hit with his hands still raised, and then he fell back over the chairs behind him. And everybody was shouting, and I saw one man firing a gun from under his coat behind me.

"And he was firing like he was in some Western, running backward toward the door and firing at the same time."

Sharon Six X Shabazz, 19, who said she was a member of Malcolm's organization, told this story:

"I think he only said 'Brothers and Sisters' when there was a commotion in the back of the room. I thought it was some rowdy drunks."

Someone ran toward the stage, she said, there were loud noises, and she saw blood on Malcolm's face.

"Then everybody started screaming and running and he fell down," she said. "There was blood on his chest, too."

Stanley Scott, a United Press International reporter, said he had been admitted with this admonition by a Malcolm lieutenant: "As a Negro, you will be allowed to enter as a citizen if you like, but you must remove your press badge."

After Malcolm stepped to the rostrum and said a few words, Mr. Scott reported, "there was a scuffle at the back of the auditorium, possibly to distract attention from the assassins."

"Shots rang out," Mr. Scott went on. "Men, women and children ran for cover. They stretched out on the floor and ducked under tables. His wife, Betty, who was in the audience, ran about screaming hysterically, 'They're killing my husband!'"

A woman wearing a black felt hat and who would identify herself only as a registered nurse, said she had seen "two men rushing toward the stage and firing from underneath their coats."

Rushed to the Stage

"I rushed to the stage even while the firing was going on," she said. "I don't know how I got on the stage, but I threw myself down on who I thought was Malcolm, but it wasn't. I was willing to die for the man. I would have taken the bullets myself. Then I saw Malcolm, and the firing had stopped, and I tried to give him artificial respiration.

"I think he was dead then."

Witnesses differed on the number of shots fired; some said as many as 30. Assistant Chief Inspector Taylor estimated the number at nearer eight. Six shots hit Malcolm in the chest and one hit him on the chin; some of the shots struck Malcolm after piercing the plywood rostrum in front of him.

Sgt. Alvin Aronoff and Patrolman Louis Angelos, who were in a radio car, heard the shooting. Sergeant Aronoff said he and his partner got to the ballroom just in time to see several persons run out, followed by a mob of perhaps 150, many of them pummeling Hagan.

"I've been shot, help me!" he quoted Hagan as shouting. The sergeant said he fired a warning shot into the air to halt the crowd, then pushed Hagan into the police car and drove him to the Wadsworth Avenue station house. From there the wounded man was taken to Jewish Memorial Hospital and later to the Bellevue prison ward.

"In the car, I found four unused .45 cartridges in Hagan's pocket," Sergeant Aronoff said.

Malcolm was placed on a stretcher and wheeled one block up Broadway to the Vanderbilt Clinic emergency entrance at 167th Street. It was about 3:15 p.m., a Columbia Presbyterian Medical Center spokesman said, when he reached a third-floor emergency operating room.

A team of doctors cut through his chest to massage his heart. But Malcolm was "either dead or in a death-appearing state," the spokesman said. The effort was given up at 3:30 p.m.

"The person you know as Malcolm X is dead," the spokesman reported.

Malcolm's birth name was Malcolm Little. He considered it a "slave name" and abandoned it when he joined the Black Muslims. The other wounded men, in addition to Hagan, were believed to have been hit by random shots. Parker was described as being 36 years old and living in Astoria, Queens. Harris's age was given as 51, and he was living in Brooklyn.

The police declined to discuss any suspects.

Patrolman Thomas Hoy said he had been stationed outside the 166th Street entrance when "I heard the shooting, and the place exploded." He rushed in, saw Malcolm lying on the stage and "grabbed a suspect" who, he said, some people were chasing.

"As I brought him to the front of the ballroom, the crowd began beating me and the suspect," Patrolman Hoy said. He said he put this man, not otherwise identified later for newsmen, into a police car to be taken to the Wadsworth Avenue station.

At the station house later, one man said he had told investigators he believed the killers were "two short fellows, about 5 foot 6," who had been in the audience and had walked toward the stage with their hands in their pockets. This witness said he believed the men fired several shots from pistols when they were only about eight feet from Malcolm.

An alarm was issued for a 1963 blue Oldsmobile. The police said the car was registered in the name of a Muslim Mosque in East Elmhurst, Queens, which was the address of the home Malcolm had occupied until it was burned. The Nation of Islam had him evicted last week.

According to the police, Malcolm, his wife, Betty, and their four children moved last week into the Theresa Hotel, 125th Street and Seventh Avenue, and then into the New York Hilton Hotel, Avenue of the Americas and 53rd Street. They checked out at noon yesterday.

The couple was married in 1958. The children are Attilah, 6; Quiblah, 4, and Lamumbah, 5 months, all daughters, and Llyasha, a son, 2.

The widow held a brief press conference last night at George's Supper Club, on Astoria Boulevard in East Elmhurst. She said her husband had received telephone calls at the Hilton Saturday night and yesterday morning saying he had "better wake up before it's too late."

Assemblyman Sutton, the family lawyer, said: "Malcolm X died broke, without even an insurance policy. Every penny that he received from books, magazine articles and so on was assigned to the Black Muslims before he broke with them, and after that to the Muslim Mosque, Inc.," the sect Malcolm set up at the Theresa Hotel.

At 7:15 p.m. the police left the ballroom. Three cleaning women scrubbed blood off the stage. Musical instruments were placed on the stage, and a dance sponsored by the Metro Associates of Brooklyn went on as scheduled at 11 p.m.

—February 22, 1965

NOTE: *Thomas Hagan, who said he was upset because Malcolm X had split from the Nation of Islam, confessed to the killing. He was imprisoned until 2010, when he was released on parole. Two other men were convicted with him but maintained they were innocent. They were released on parole in the 1980s.*

MARTIN LUTHER KING IS SLAIN IN MEMPHIS; A WHITE IS SUSPECTED; JOHNSON URGES CALM

By EARL CALDWELL

The Rev. Dr. Martin Luther King Jr., who preached nonviolence and racial brotherhood, was fatally shot here in Memphis last night by a distant gunman who raced away and escaped.

Four thousand National Guard troops were ordered into Memphis by Gov. Buford Ellington after the 39-year-old Nobel Prize–winning civil rights leader died.

A curfew was imposed on the shocked city of 550,000 inhabitants, 40 percent of whom are Negro. But the police said the tragedy had been followed by incidents that included sporadic shooting, fires, bricks and bottles thrown at policemen, and looting that started in Negro districts and then spread over the city.

Police Director Frank Holloman said the assassin might have been a white man who was "50 to 100 yards away in a flophouse."

Chief of Detectives W. P. Huston said a late model white Mustang was believed to have been the getaway car. Its occupant was described as a white man in his 30s, wearing a black suit and black tie.

Rifle Found Nearby

A high-powered .30-06-caliber rifle was found a block from the scene of the shooting, on South Main Street.

"We think it's the gun," Chief Huston said, reporting it would be turned over to the Federal Bureau of Investigation.

Dr. King was shot while he leaned over a second-floor railing outside his room at the Lorraine Motel. He was chatting with two friends just before starting for dinner.

One of the friends was a musician, and Dr. King had just asked him to play a Negro spiritual, "Precious Lord, Take My Hand," at a rally that was to have been held two hours later in support of striking Memphis sanitation men.

Paul Hess, assistant administrator at St. Joseph's Hospital, where Dr. King died despite emergency surgery, said the minister had "received a gunshot wound on the right side of the neck, at the root of the neck, a gaping wound."

"He was pronounced dead at 7:05 p.m. central standard time by staff doctors," Mr. Hess said. "They did everything humanly possible."

There was concern by law enforcement officers here and elsewhere over potential reactions. In a television broadcast after the curfew was ordered here, Mr. Holloman said, "rioting has broken out in parts of the city" and "looting is rampant."

Dr. King had come back to Memphis Wednesday morning to organize support once again for 1,300 sanitation workers who have been striking since Lincoln's birthday. Just a week ago yesterday he led a march in the strikers' cause that ended in violence. A 16-year-old Negro was killed, and 62 persons were injured.

Yesterday Dr. King had been in his second-floor room—number 306—throughout the day. About 6 p.m. he emerged, wearing a black suit and white shirt.

Solomon Jones Jr., his driver, had been waiting to drive him to the home of the Rev. Samuel Kyles of Memphis for dinner. Mr. Jones said later he had observed, "It's cold outside, put your topcoat on," and Dr. King had replied, "O.K., I will."

Two Men in Courtyard

Dr. King, an open-faced, genial man, leaned over a green iron railing to chat with an associate, Jesse Jackson, standing just below him in a courtyard parking lot:

"Do you know Ben?" Mr. Jackson asked, introducing Ben Branch of Chicago, a musician who was to play at the night's rally.

"Yes, that's my man!" Dr. King glowed.

The two men recalled Dr. King's asking for the playing of the spiritual. "I really want you to play that tonight," Dr. King said.

The Rev. Ralph W. Abernathy, perhaps Dr. King's closest friend, was just about to come out of the motel room when the sudden loud noise burst out.

Dr. King toppled to the concrete second-floor walkway. Blood gushed from the jaw and neck area. His necktie had been ripped off by the blast.

"He had just bent over," Mr. Jackson recalled later. "If he had been standing up, he wouldn't have been hit in the face."

Policemen "All Over"

"When I turned around," Mr. Jackson went on, "I saw police coming from everywhere. They said, 'Where did it come from?' And I said, 'Behind you.' The police were coming from where the shot came."

"We didn't need to call the police," Mr. Jackson said. "They were here all over the place."

Mr. Jones, the driver, said that a squad car with four policemen in it drove down the street only moments before the gunshot. The police had been circulating throughout the motel area on precautionary patrols.

After the shot, Mr. Jones said, he saw a man "with something white on his face" creep away from a thicket across the street.

Someone rushed up with a towel to stem the flow of Dr. King's blood. Mr. Kyles said he put a blanket over Dr. King, but "I knew he was gone." He ran down the stairs and tried to telephone from the motel office for an ambulance.

Police with Helmets

Policemen were pouring into the motel area, carrying rifles and shotguns and wearing helmets. But the King aides said it seemed to be 10 or 15 minutes before a fire department ambulance arrived.

Dr. King was apparently still living when he reached the St. Joseph's Hospital operating room for emergency surgery.

It was the same emergency room to which James H. Meredith, first Negro enrolled at the University of Mississippi, was taken after he was shot in June 1965, at Hernando, Miss., south of Memphis; Mr. Meredith was not seriously hurt.

Outside the emergency room some of Dr. King's aides waited. One was Chauncey Eskridge, his legal adviser. He broke into sobs when Dr. King's death was announced.

"A man full of life, full of love, and he was shot," Mr. Eskridge said. "He had always lived with that expectation—but nobody ever expected it to happen."

But the Rev. Andrew Young, executive director of Dr. King's Southern Christian Leadership Conference, recalled there had been talk Wednesday night about possible harm to Dr. King in Memphis.

Mr. Young recalled: "He said he had reached the pinnacle of fulfillment with his nonviolent movement, and these reports did not bother him."

There were perhaps 15 persons in the motel courtyard area when Dr. King was shot, all believed to be Negroes and Dr. King's associates.

Past the courtyard is a small swimming pool. Then comes Mulberry Street, a short street only three blocks away from storied Beale Street on the fringe of downtown Memphis.

Fire Station Nearby

On the other side of the street is a six-foot brick restraining wall, with bushes and grass atop it and a hillside leading to a patch of trees. Behind the trees is a wire fence enclosing backyards of brick and frame houses. At the corner at Butler Street is a white brick fire station.

Police were reported to have chased a late-model blue or white car through Memphis and north to Millington. A civilian in another car that had a citizens band radio was also reported to have pursued the fleeing car and to have opened fire on it.

The police first cordoned off an area of five blocks around the Lorraine Motel, chosen by Dr. King for his stay here because it is Negro-owned. The two-story motel is an addition to a small two-story hotel in a largely Negro area.

Mayor Henry Loeb had ordered a curfew here after last week's disorder, and National Guard units had been on duty for five days until they were deactivated Wednesday.

Last night the mayor reinstated the curfew at 6:35 and declared: "After the tragedy which has happened in Memphis tonight, for the protection of all our citizens, we are putting the curfew back in effect. All movement is restricted except for health or emergency reasons."

Governor Ellington, calling out the National Guard and pledging all necessary action by the state to prevent disorder, announced: "For the second time in recent days, I most earnestly ask the people of Memphis and Shelby County to remain calm. I do so again tonight in the face of this most regrettable incident."

"Every possible action is being taken to apprehend the person or persons responsible for committing this act."

National Guard planes flew over the state to bring in contingents of riot-trained highway patrolmen.

Assistant Chief Bartholomew early this morning said that unidentified persons had shot from rooftops and windows at policemen 8 or 10 times. He said bullets had shattered one police car's windshield, wounding two policemen with flying glass.

Numerous minor injuries were reported in four hours of clashes between civilians and law enforcement officers. But any serious disorders were under control by 11:15 p.m., Chief Bartholomew said. Early this morning streets were virtually empty except for patrol cars.

Once Stabbed in Harlem

In his career Dr. King had suffered beatings and blows. On Sept. 20, 1958, he was stabbed in a Harlem department store in New York by a Negro woman later adjudged insane.

That time he underwent a four-hour operation to remove a steel letter opener that had been plunged into his chest. For a time he was on the critical list, but he told his wife while in the hospital, "I don't hold any bitterness toward this woman."

In Memphis, Dr. King's chief associates met in his room after he died. They included Mr. Young, Mr. Abernathy, Mr. Jackson, the Rev. James Bevel and Hosea Williams. They had to step across a drying pool of Dr. King's blood to enter.

After 15 minutes they emerged. Mr. Jackson looked at the blood. He embraced Mr. Abernathy.

"Stand tall!" somebody exhorted.

"Murder! Murder!" Mr. Bevel groaned. "Doc said that's not the way."

"Doc" was what they often called Dr. King.

Coretta Scott King, center, wife of the Rev. Martin Luther King Jr., and their daughter, Bernice, right, at the slain civil rights leader's funeral services in Atlanta, April 9, 1968.

Then the murdered leader's aides said they would go on to the hall where tonight's rally was to have been held. They wanted to urge calm upon the mourners.

At the Federal Bureau of Investigation office here, Robert Jensen, special agent in charge, said the FBI had entered the murder investigation at the request of Attorney General Ramsey Clark.

—April 5, 1968

NOTE: *James Earl Ray, whose family said he harbored a hatred for black people, initially confessed to the killing. After recanting his confession, in 1997 Ray was able to persuade members of the King family that he was innocent and that others had killed Rev. King as part of a broader conspiracy. He died in prison in 1998.*

KENNEDY IS DEAD, VICTIM OF ASSASSIN; SUSPECT, ARAB IMMIGRANT, ARRAIGNED; JOHNSON APPOINTS PANEL ON VIOLENCE

By GLADWIN HILL

Senator Robert F. Kennedy, the brother of a murdered president, died at 1:44 a.m. today of an assassin's shots.

The New York senator was wounded more than 20 hours earlier, moments after he had made his victory statement in the California primary.

At his side when he died today in Good Samaritan Hospital were his wife, Ethel; his sisters, Mrs. Stephen Smith and Mrs. Patricia Lawford; his bother-in-law, Stephen Smith, and his sister-in-law, Mrs. John F. Kennedy, whose husband was assassinated four and a half years ago in Dallas.

In Washington, President Johnson issued a statement calling the death a tragedy. He proclaimed next Sunday a national day of mourning.

The Final Report

Hopes had risen slightly when more than eight hours went by without a new medical bulletin on the stricken senator, but the grimness of the final announcement was signaled when Frank Mankiewicz, Mr. Kennedy's press secretary, walked slowly down the street in front of the hospital toward the gymnasium that served as press headquarters.

Mr. Mankiewicz bit his lip. His shoulders slumped. He stepped to a lectern in front of a chalkboard and bowed his head for a moment while the television lights snapped on. Then, at one minute before 2 a.m., he told of the death of Mr. Kennedy.

Following is the text of his statement:

"I have a short announcement to read which I will read at this time. Senator Robert Francis Kennedy died at 1:44 a.m. today, June 6, 1968. With Senator Kennedy at the time of his death was his wife, Ethel; his sisters, Mrs. Patricia Lawford and Mrs. Stephen Smith, his brother-in-law, Stephen Smith and his sister-in-law, Mrs. John F. Kennedy.

"He was 42 years old."

Senator Kennedy's body will be taken to New York this morning and then to Washington.

The man accused of shooting Mr. Kennedy early yesterday in a pantry of the Ambassador Hotel was identified as Sirhan Bishara Sirhan, 24, who was born in Palestinian Jerusalem of Arab parentage and had lived in the Los Angeles area since 1957. Sirhan had been a clerk.

$250,000 Bail

Yesterday, he was hurried through an early-morning court arraignment and held in lieu of $250,000 bail.

Sirhan was charged with six counts of assault with intent to murder, an offense involving a prison term of 1 to 14 years.

Five other persons in addition to the 42-year-old senator were wounded by the eight bullets from a .22-caliber revolver fired at almost point-blank range into a throng of Democratic rally celebrants surging between ballrooms in the hotel. The shots came moments after Senator Kennedy had made a speech celebrating his victory in yesterday's Democratic presidential primary in California.

The defendant, seized moments after the shooting, refused to give the police any information about himself.

Three hours later, Mayor Samuel W. Yorty announced that the defendant had been identified as Sirhan. He said the identity had been confirmed by Sirhan's brother and a second individual.

Senator Kennedy, accompanied by his wife, was wheeled into the Good Samaritan Hospital shortly after 1 a.m. yesterday after a brief stop at the Central Receiving Hospital. A score of the senator's campaign aides swarmed around the scene.

Grim Reminder

Less than five years back many of them had experienced the similar tragedy that ended the life of President John F. Kennedy.

At 2:22 a.m., the press secretary, Mr. Mankiewicz, came out of the hospital into a throng of hundreds of news people to announce that the senator would be taken into surgery "in 5 or 10 minutes" for an operation of "45 minutes or an hour."

One bullet had gone into the senator's brain past the mastoid bone back of the right ear, with some fragments going near the brain stem. Another bullet lodged in the back of the neck.

It was after 7 a.m. when Mr. Mankiewicz reported that more than three hours of surgery had been completed, and all but one fragment of the upper bullet had been removed. The neck bullet was not removed but "is not regarded as a major problem," Mr. Mankiewicz said.

He also reported that the senator's vital signs remained about as they had been, except that he was now breathing on his own, which he had not been doing before the surgery. Then Mr. Mankiewicz said:

"There may have been an impairment of the blood supply to the midbrain, which the doctors explained as governing certain of the vital signs—heart, eye track, level of consciousness—although not directly the thinking process."

> *Senator Kennedy was taken from surgery to an intensive-care unit.*

Senator Kennedy was taken from surgery to an intensive-care unit.

At 2:15 p.m. Mr. Mankiewicz announced that Senator Kennedy had not regained consciousness and that a series of medical tests had been "inconclusive and don't show measurable improvement in Senator Kennedy's condition."

"His condition as of 1:30 p.m. remains extremely critical," the spokesman continued. "His life forces—pulse, temperature, blood pressure and heart—remain good, and he continues to show the ability to breathe on his own, although he is being assisted by a resuscitator."

Mrs. Kennedy remained at the hospital.

Mrs. John F. Kennedy arrived at the hospital at 7:30 p.m. yesterday, after a chartered flight from New York.

A team of surgeons treating Senator Kennedy included Dr. James Poppen, head of neurosurgery at the Lahey Clinic in Boston. He was rushed to Los Angeles in an air force plane on instructions from Vice President Humphrey.

Mr. Humphrey and Senator Eugene J. McCarthy of Minnesota have been Senator Kennedy's rivals in the Democratic presidential competition.

Mayor Yorty said the defendant's identification had come through a brother, Adel Sirhan, after the police had traced the ownership of the .22-caliber revolver involved in the shooting to a third brother, Munir Bishari Salameh Sirhan, also known as Joe Sirhan.

The weapon was traced through three owners, one in suburban Alabama, the next in Marin County, adjacent to San Francisco, and back to an 18-year-old in suburban Pasadena. The youth said he had sold it to "a bushy-haired guy named Joe" whom he knew only as an employee of a Pasadena department store.

Detectives identified the bushy-haired man as Munir Sirhan. From him, the trail led to the two other brothers, who have been living in Pasadena.

The snub-nosed .22-caliber Iver Johnson Cadet model revolver seized after the shooting was described as having been picked out of a list of 2.5 million weapons registered in California in "just seconds" after the disclosure of its serial number. The defendant was arraigned at 7 a.m. before Municipal Judge Joan Dempsey Klein.

The other victims of the shooting were Paul Schrade, 43, a regional director of the United Automobile and Aerospace Workers Union, a prominent Kennedy campaigner; William Weisel, 30, a unit manager for the American Broadcasting Company; Ira Goldstein, 19, an employee of Continental News Service at nearby Sherman Oaks; Mrs. Elizabeth Evans, 43, of Saugus, in Los Angeles County, and Irwin Stroll, 17.

Sirhan was represented at the arraignment by the chief public defender, Richard S. Buckley. He asked Mr. Buckley to get in touch with the American Civil Liberties Union about getting private counsel for him.

—June 6, 1968

NOTE: *Sirhan was convicted in 1969 and is now serving a life sentence. He said in a 1989 interview that he shot Kennedy because of the senator's support for Israel.*

SADAT ASSASSINATED AT ARMY PARADE AS MEN AMID RANKS FIRE INTO STANDS; VICE PRESIDENT AFFIRMS "ALL TREATIES"

By WILLIAM E. FARRELL

President Anwar el-Sadat of Egypt was shot and killed today by a group of men in military uniforms who hurled hand grenades and fired rifles at him as he watched a military parade in Cairo commemorating the 1973 war against Israel.

Vice President Hosni Mubarak said Egypt's treaties and international commitments would be respected. He said the speaker of parliament, Sufi Abu Taleb, would serve as interim president pending an election in 60 days.

The assassins' bullets ended the life of a man who earned a reputation for making bold decisions in foreign affairs, a reputation based in large part on his decision in 1977 to journey to the camp of Egypt's foe, Israel, to make peace.

Regarded as an interim ruler when he came to power in 1970 on the death of Gamal Abdel Nasser, Mr. Sadat forged his own regime and ran Egypt single-handedly. He was bent on moving this impoverished country into the late 20th century, a drive that led him to abandon an alliance with the Soviet Union and embrace the West.

That rule ended abruptly and violently today. As jet fighters roared overhead, the killers sprayed the reviewing stand with bullets while thousands of horrified people—officials, diplomats and journalists, including this correspondent—looked on.

Killers' Identity Not Disclosed

Information gathered from a number of sources indicated that 8 persons had been killed and 27 wounded. Later reports, all unconfirmed, put the toll at 11 dead and 38 wounded. The authorities did not disclose the identity of the assassins. They were being interrogated, and there were no clear indications whether the attack was part of a coup attempt.

In Washington, American officials said an army major, a lieutenant and four enlisted men had been involved in the attack. The major and two of the soldiers were killed and the others captured, the officials said. The assassination followed a recent crackdown by Mr. Sadat against religious extremists and other political opponents.

Those standing nearby at the parade today said six to eight soldiers riding in a truck towing an artillery piece had broken away from the line of march and walked toward the

Assassins attack the presidential viewing stand during a military parade in Cairo, killing President Sadat and ten others, October 7, 1981.

reviewing stand. Onlookers thought the procession was part of the pageant. Suddenly, a hand grenade exploded and bursts of rifle fire erupted while French-made Mirage jets screeched overhead. The 62-year-old leader was rushed to Maadi Military Hospital by helicopter and died several hours later.

A medical bulletin said he had no heartbeat when he arrived at the hospital. It attributed his death, at 2:40 p.m., to "violent nervous shock and internal bleeding in the chest cavity, where the left lung and major blood vessels below it were torn."

The death of Mr. Sadat raised serious questions about the direction the nation would now take. At least for the time being, affairs of state are expected to be run largely by Vice President Mubarak, a longtime associate who promptly took over direction of the armed forces after the president died. Egypt's ruling National Democratic Party announced that Vice President Mubarak would be its candidate in the presidential election.

Mr. Mubarak, in his broadcast announcing Mr. Sadat's death seven hours after the assassination, indicated that Egypt would continue to respect the peace treaty with Israel.

"I hereby declare," he said, "in the name of the great soul passing away and in the name of the people, its constitutional institutions and its armed forces, that we are committed to all charters, treaties, and international obligations that Egypt has concluded."

Security police patrolled Cairo's streets, nearly empty because of the holiday marking the 1973 war, and government buildings were being closely guarded.

Regular television programming was canceled after the announcement of Mr. Sadat's death and was replaced by readings from the Koran and film clips of his achievements—the 1973 war against Israel, which Mr. Sadat said restored Egyptian dignity after its defeat in 1967, the peace treaty with Israel and other milestones. No film of the attack at today's parade was shown on Egyptian television.

Reviewing Stand Awash in Blood

Within seconds of the attack, the reviewing stand was awash in blood. Bemedaled officials dived for cover. Screams and panic followed as guests tried to flee. Some were crushed under foot.

This correspondent saw one assailant, a stocky, dark-haired man, standing in a half crouch, firing a rifle into the stand used by Mr. Sadat, who was wearing black leather boots and military attire crossed by a green sash. The reviewing stand was a blood-soaked horror.

Mr. Sadat was promptly carried away, but others felled by bullets remained writhing on the ground. A few did not move. One man, seriously wounded, was slumped over a railing separating Mr. Sadat and his party from the parade about 20 yards away.

Among those hit was reported to be Bishop Samuel, whom Mr. Sadat had named one of five clerics to run the Coptic Christians' affairs after he deposed their pope, Shenouda III. The bishop was later reported to have died.

Others said to have died were two presidential aides—Mohammed Rashwan, the official photographer, and Sayed Marei, a confidant. The Belgian ambassador, Claude Ruelle, was seriously wounded, and three American military officers were hurt. Egypt's Defense Minister, Gen. Abdel Halim Abu Ghazala, who had opened the parade with a speech, stood in the midst of the carnage. His face was bleeding, and his gold-braided uniform was blood-soaked. He waved away attempts to assist him and began issuing orders.

Soldiers wearing red berets and perfectly creased uniforms promptly joined hands to cordon off the scene of the attack, widening the circle as more soldiers arrived. Some of the soldiers were sobbing, a few screamed hysterically.

Overhead, the air show continued. Planes looped and dived and sent colorful sprays of vapor over the pandemonium below. The roar of engines drowned out the screams and the clatter of chairs.

Camel Corps on Parade

The parade ground, which had witnessed a joyful procession of Egypt's most advanced arms as well as the colorful camel corps, with its turbaned soldiers, and the cavalry, with its elegant Arabian horses, was littered with little Egyptian souvenir flags dropped by panicked guests. As members of military bands scattered, the brilliant sun beamed off shiny brass instruments.

The Egyptian military establishment has long been regarded as the ingredient needed by any leader to remain in power. Diplomatic and military analysts said Mr. Sadat had the support of the military and that it assured the stability of his regime and permitted him to take daring steps, such as the peace overture to Israel and, finally, the peace treaty. In the absence of information, it was hard to tell whether the assassins represented a disenchantment with Mr. Sadat within the military.

Speculation abounded. Some thought the attackers might be Muslim fundamentalists opposed to the alliance with Israel and to Mr. Sadat's recent crackdown.

About a month ago, he ordered the arrest of some 1,500 Coptic and Muslim extremists, along with some of his political opponents. He said they had fomented sectarian strife and endangered his efforts to bring democracy to Egypt.

A devout Muslim, Mr. Sadat was harsh toward fundamentalist groups, such as the Muslim Brotherhood and the Islamic Association. He banned both groups, calling them illegal. He said that he would not tolerate mixing religion and politics.

Arrest of Some Military Rumored

The published names of those arrested in the crackdown did not include those of military personnel. But there were reports that some of those detained were in the armed forces.

After Mr. Sadat's helicopter had left the scene, diplomats rushed to their limousines. Soldiers cleared the grounds and drove away the stunned spectators. Ambulances wailed, and women clutching their children raced away. The air show above continued.

Early in the parade, a rocketlike object had been launched. It rained down Egyptian flags and portraits of Mr. Sadat hanging from tiny parachutes. Most of them floated over a nearby housing development called Nasser City. As the grounds were being cleared, one portrait was seen hanging from a flagpole on which it had become impaled in landing. The portrait had been torn by the sharp tip of the Egyptian flag that was fluttering from it.

—*October 7, 1981*

NOTE: *The attack was carried out by Islamic militants angered that Egypt had entered into a peace treaty with Israel. The assailants included an Egyptian army officer, Khalid Islambouli, who was executed along with several other of the assailants in 1982.*

BHUTTO IS KILLED AT RALLY, AND PAKISTAN FACES OUTRAGE AND NEW TURMOIL

By SALMAN MASOOD AND CARLOTTA GALL

Benazir Bhutto, the Pakistani opposition leader and twice-serving prime minister, was assassinated Thursday evening as she left a political rally in Rawalpindi, a scene of fiery carnage that plunged Pakistan deeper into political turmoil and ignited widespread violence by her enraged supporters.

Ms. Bhutto, 54, was shot in the neck or head, according to differing accounts, as she stood in the open sunroof of a car and waved to crowds. Seconds later a suicide attacker detonated his bomb, damaging one of the cars in her motorcade, killing more than 20 people and wounding 50, the Interior Ministry said.

News of her death sent angry protesters swarming the emergency ward of the nearby hospital, where doctors declared Ms. Bhutto dead at 6:16 p.m. Supporters later jostled to carry her bare wooden coffin as it began its journey to her hometown, Larkana, in southern Pakistan, for burial. In Karachi and other cities, frenzied crowds vented their rage, blocking the streets, burning tires and throwing stones.

The death of Ms. Bhutto, leader of Pakistan's largest political party, threw politics into disarray less than two weeks before parliamentary elections and just weeks after a state of emergency was lifted. There was speculation that elections would be postponed and another state of emergency declared.

A deeply polarizing figure, Ms. Bhutto spent 30 years navigating the turbulent and often violent world of Pakistani politics, becoming in 1988 the first woman to lead a modern Muslim country.

She had narrowly escaped an assassination attempt upon her return to Pakistan two months ago. Her death now presents President Pervez Musharraf with one of

> *The attack bore hallmarks of the Qaeda-linked militants in Pakistan.*

the most potent crises of his turbulent eight years in power, and Bush administration officials with a new challenge in their efforts to stabilize a front-line state—home to both Al Qaeda and nuclear arms—in their fight against terrorism.

The attack bore hallmarks of the Qaeda-linked militants in Pakistan. But witnesses described a sniper firing from a nearby building, raising questions about how well the government had protected her in a usually well-guarded garrison town and fueling speculation that government sympathizers had played a part.

On Thursday, officials from the FBI and the Department of Homeland Security issued a bulletin to local law enforcement agencies informing them about posts on some Islamic Web sites saying that Al Qaeda was claiming responsibility for the attack, and that the plot was orchestrated by Ayman al-Zawahri, the group's second-ranking official.

As world leaders lined up to express outrage at the killing of arguably Pakistan's most pro-Western political figure, a grim-faced President Bush said that the best way to honor her would be "by continuing with the democratic process for which she so bravely gave her life."

Benazir Bhutto at a press conference in Islamabad, November 6, 2007.

Speaking to reporters while vacationing at his ranch in Crawford, Tex., Mr. Bush attributed Ms. Bhutto's death to "murderous extremists who are trying to undermine Pakistan's democracy."

Mr. Musharraf went on national television on Thursday evening, describing the killing as "a great national tragedy" and announcing a three-day period of national mourning. He called it a terrorist attack and vowed to continue to fight to root out the terrorists. "I appeal to the nation to remain peaceful and show restraint," he said.

Despite the president's appeal, politicians and government officials said they feared more violence from those protesting her death, but also from militants who would try to take advantage of the uncertain situation.

Before her return in October, Ms. Bhutto had spent nearly eight years in self-imposed exile to avoid corruption charges stemming from her time as prime minister in the 1990s. Her return had been promoted by Washington as part of an agreement to share power with Mr. Musharraf and give his increasingly unpopular government a more democratic face.

She was a leading contender to become prime minister after the Jan. 8 elections, campaigning as an advocate for Pakistan's return to party politics after eight years of military rule under Mr. Musharraf. She also presented herself as the individual who could best combat growing militancy in Pakistan.

Her comments condemning militancy and suicide bombing had made her a target of Qaeda-linked militants in Pakistan. Her homecoming procession in Karachi was attacked by two bomb blasts that killed 150 supporters and narrowly missed killing her.

Much of the rage over her death is nonetheless likely to be directed at Mr. Musharraf, who kept her out of power for over eight years and had shown her only a grudging welcome at first, and later outright hostility.

The country's other main opposition leader, another former prime minister, Nawaz Sharif, announced Thursday evening that he was pulling his party out of the elections. A longtime political rival of Ms. Bhutto's, he had lately become an ally in pressing for a return to democracy in Pakistan.

"This is a tragedy for her party, and a tragedy for our party and the entire nation," Mr. Sharif said.

Tauqir Zia, a retired general who recently joined Ms. Bhutto's party, the Pakistan Peoples Party, said it seemed that elections were unlikely to go ahead now. "P.P.P. is now in turmoil for the time being," he said. "It has to find a new leadership."

Other officials and politicians said they, too, thought elections would be postponed. "This is going to lead to chaos and turmoil," said the former interior minister, Aftab Ahmad Khan Sherpao, who was nearly killed last week in a suicide bombing at a mosque in his home village. "I was anticipating this, that suicide bombings would increase. . . . This was bound to happen."

There were differing accounts of the attack. Zamrud Khan, a member of her party, said Ms. Bhutto was shot in the head from gunfire that originated from behind her car in a building nearby. Seconds later a suicide bomber detonated his bomb, damaging a car in her motorcade and killing some 15 people on the ground, Mr. Khan said.

The Interior Ministry spokesman, quoted by the state news agency, the Associated Press of Pakistan, said that the suicide bomber first fired on Ms. Bhutto and then blew himself up.

After the explosion, the site was littered with pools of blood. Shoes and caps of party workers were lying on the asphalt. More than a dozen ambulances pushed through crowds of dazed and wounded people.

Witnesses described hearing gunfire a minute before the explosion. Sajid Hussain, who had a shrapnel wound on his left hand, said he had heard at least three shots fired: "Then there was a big explosion, the earth seemed to tremble, I fell down. And everything was covered in black smoke."

Mr. Zia, the retired general, said he was in a car ahead of Ms. Bhutto before the blast. "A leader has to come out and lead, and she did exactly that," he said. "But I would ask, where was the security? How did they allow people to come so close to her? It is inconceivable."

Dr. Abbas Hayat of Rawalpindi General Hospital said that doctors had tried for 35 minutes to resuscitate Ms. Bhutto, who he said had wounds to her head as well as shrapnel injuries.

Dr. Mohamed Mussadik, head of the medical college in Rawalpindi and a top surgeon who attended to Ms. Bhutto at the hospital, said she was clinically dead on arrival, according to Athar Minallah, a lawyer who had served in the Musharraf government but who has since helped lead the movement against him.

Mr. Minallah said an independent investigation into the assassination was critical. A precedent for this, he said, was the investigation into the murder of Ms. Bhutto's brother 11 years ago. "The government has to allow it," he said, "because the entire blame is on the government. Everyone I have spoken to believes it is the government that has done this."

Apparently no autopsy was done because the police did not request one, Dawn TV reported. Lawyers calling for an international neutral investigation are raising questions about the speed with which Ms. Bhutto's body was moved. The body arrived in her southern home province, Sindh, before dawn, party officials told Agence-France Presse.

The assassination is likely to deepen suspicion among Ms. Bhutto's supporters of Pakistan's security agencies. Ms. Bhutto has long accused parts of the government, namely the country's premier military intelligence agency, the Inter-Services Intelligence, or I.S.I., of working against her and her party because they oppose her liberal, secular agenda.

A former senior Pakistani intelligence official said he did not believe that the country's intelligence agency was involved. He blamed militants for the assassination, but said government-provided protection was far too lax and the area surrounding the rally should have been better secured.

"For sure, the government was complicit in the security aspects," said the official. "I think the security arrangements of the police, they were not professionally handled."

—December 28, 2007

NOTE: *The gun and bomb attack was blamed on Pakistan's Taliban, led by Baitullah Mehsud, who denied responsibility. The CIA killed Mehsud in a drone attack in 2009.*

CHAPTER 2

HEISTS

"We have to be patient. Sooner or later that $1,000,000 [reward] is going to take hold of someone, and they'll talk. That's the way it usually happens."

—An FBI agent on the Isabella Stewart Gardner Museum theft, quoted in *The New York Times*, June 2, 1992

MYSTERY IS A POWERFUL DRUG. Decades later, the world still waits eagerly for answers to some of the questions raised by the greatest robberies in history. Where are those masterpieces that once decorated the Isabella Stewart Gardner Museum in Boston? Who has them? Are they lost for all time? Victims of theft are seldom fascinated by the puzzle of it all, but newspaper readers have long been riveted by robbers and the crimes they commit.

OPPOSITE: Empty frames still hang on the walls of the Isabella Stewart Gardner Museum, where paintings were cut out of their frames in the heist of March 1990. This frame held Rembrandt's *The Storm on the Sea of Galilee* (1633).

MASKED MEN ROB A TRAIN:
THE BOLD EXPLOIT OF A GANG OF
MISSOURI OUTLAWS

At 8:40 o'clock last evening, as the passenger express train No. 48 over the Chicago and Alton Road approached a deep cut four miles east of here [Independence, Missouri] and two miles west of Glendale, where the Missouri Pacific track crosses the Chicago and Alton, engineer L. Foote was signaled to stop his train. Thinking possibly that a delayed freight train was in his way, he whistled "down brakes," and brought the train to a standstill, but not until he had discovered a pile of rocks on the track and that the man who had given the signal wore a mask and proved to be the leader of a well-armed force of men who successfully carried out one of the most daring and skillfully planned robberies that ever occurred.

As the leader appeared in sight, he shouted, as though addressing a large body of followers: "Now, men, to your work! Fire!" Instantly there came a sharp discharge of firearms, which gave the impression that the gang the trainmen had to cope with was a large one. Passengers and trainmen were panic-stricken by the fusillade, and before they could recover from their fright the robbers had complete possession of the train. All the robbers were masked, and, as the expression goes, "armed to the teeth" with revolvers and Henry rifles.

At each door of each passenger car stood one of the gang with revolvers cocked and a threat that the first one who attempted to move would be killed. The advice to remain quiet was heeded by all except Frank Burton, the brakeman upon the front platform of the sleeping car, who heard a freight train coming up behind his train. Intent upon preventing a collision, he jumped from his car, and, lantern in hand, ran down the track toward the on-coming freight. As the robbers saw him going down the track, they opened fire upon him, and though their bullets passed unpleasantly near he was not hurt.

That his life was saved was due to the fact that the engineer shouted to the captain of the band: "For God's sake, don't shoot him, he's trying to save the lives of these people!" Instantly the captain threw up his hands and shouted, "Stop shooting!" The command was obeyed, and Burton succeeded in stopping the freight train and preventing a collision.

Before this incident, the engine had been taken possession of by four of the desperadoes, and engineer Foote and fireman John Steading were compelled to leave the cab, the party threatening to kill them if they refused. They complied, as did the engineer when he was instructed to take his coal pick from the tender and go with the party to the express car. On arriving he was forced to break down the door. It was then discovered that the express messenger, Fox, of St. Louis, was missing, but he was discovered in some bushes at the side of the track, where he had hidden. He was taken from his hiding place and forced to open the safe. The contents were transferred to the pockets of the gang, but the amount secured was so small that the robbers were disgusted, and they knocked the messenger on the head with a revolver.

It is supposed that the robbers at first only intended to rob the express car, for when this job was completed they held a consultation, after which a party of six entered the passenger cars. Many of the passengers, suspecting what was in progress, had taken their valuables from their pockets and hidden them in whatever place seemed to offer security. The scene when the robbers entered the cars beggars description, for women and children wept and men begged as for their lives that they might be allowed to retain their money, which, for a number of emigrants, was all they had in the world.

One of the passengers states that one robber had a huge sack, into which was dumped all the valuables that were secured. The train hands were placed under guard, each with one of the gang holding a revolver at his head. Each person was compelled, under threat of death, to empty the contents of his or her pockets. Ladies were compelled to sit on the floor of the car while the desperadoes stripped them of their jewelry. It is estimated that the amount obtained from the passengers aggregates at least $15,000. When the robbery was completed, the gang left the train and made for the woods, where, it is supposed, they had horses ready to convey them to a place of safety.

Each person was compelled, under threat of death, to empty the contents of his or her pockets.

As soon as possible the obstructions on the track were removed, and the train proceeded to Kansas City, when a posse of men was organized to capture, the gang. The authorities at Marshall were also informed of the robbery, and from there another posse of men under the charge of a sheriff started to head off the desperadoes if they attempted to head east. From this place also a body of men, under Marshal Murphy, started in pursuit, and scarcely a settlement in the vicinity has not contributed its quota of men to assist. The country is now being thoroughly scoured in every direction.

Conductor Hazelbaker was fired at several times by the robbers, but escaped injury. Fox, the express messenger, who was so badly wounded on the head, passed through here this morning en route from Kansas City to his home in St. Louis. He denies the charges of cowardice made against him, says he was struck down while endeavoring to save the property of his employers—the United States Express Company—and refuses to state the amount of money he had in his safe, a sum reported as having been between $100 and $20,000.

It is generally supposed the robbers were a gang under the command of the famous James brothers, who have a worldwide notoriety for their desperate deeds. The number in the party is estimated at from 12 to 16. The leader is described as a tall man with a dark beard, who wore his mask only when in the light. In general he answers to the description of the man who led the gang that robbed a Rock Island train on July 17 last. He introduced himself to the

Photograph, c. 1864, of a young Jesse James posing with three revolvers, likely when he was a member of the guerilla Confederate group Quantrill's Rangers, during the Civil War.

engineer as Jesse James and his "partner," a short, heavy man, as Dick Little, and several times during the robbery the man calling himself James addressed his companion as Dick.

It was near the same spot that a train on the Chicago and Alton Road was robbed in a similar manner on Oct. 8, 1879. The express messenger was assaulted, the safe broken open, and $50,000 in cash secured.

Engineer Foote makes the following statement: "Between three and four miles east of Independence there is a deep cut, over which the Missouri Pacific track crosses the Chicago and Alton, and it was just before entering the deepest part of this cut that I saw the pile of stones, which was about five feet high, and on the top of which was a stick, to which was attached a red rag, and behind the whole stood the leader of the robbers. Of course, I stopped. I was then approached by four of the gang, and the leader, who said, 'Step down off that engine and do as I tell you or I will kill you.' He then told me to get the coal pick, which I did after some parleying, but as a revolver was pointed at my head I could not refuse to obey them.

"They then marched me and John Steading, the fireman, to the express car, and told me to break down the door, which I did. Messenger Fox had hidden himself in the weeds by the roadside, but they swore they would kill me if he didn't come out, and so I called for him, and he entered the car with two of the robbers, who forced him to open the safe and pour its contents into a sack. They were disappointed at not getting more booty and knocked Fox down twice with the butt end of a navy revolver, cutting his head in a fearful manner. They then marched us to the coaches, where, they kept us covered with revolvers while they robbed the passengers.

"After the last coach had been gone through they marched us back to the engine, when the leader said, 'Now get back there and we will remove the stones. You have been a bully boy and, here is a little present for you,' and he handed me two silver dollars. I told him I would remove the obstructions, and the entire gang skipped up over the embankment and were out of sight in a moment. In going through the passengers each one was made to hold up his hands, and what was taken from them was put into a two-bushel sack, which was nearly full of watches, money, and other valuables."

Later.—A posse of men under Sheriff Casen, of Saline County, tonight brought in three of the robbers, all of whom were captured near the scene of the robbery. They gave their names as Creed Chapman and Sam Chapman, brothers, and John Burgler. J. Wilkinson, alias Nolan, is being "shadowed," and will be arrested on the arrival of the train he boarded near here bound for Kansas City. One of the persons interested implicates him as a member of the gang. The names of the entire party are known, and their capture is considered a certainty.

—September 9, 1881

NOTE: *In January 1882, Missouri governor Thomas Crittenden promised Jesse James's associate Robert Ford a $10,000 reward and a pardon in exchange for killing the outlaw. Ford shot and killed James three months later. Robert and his brother Charles pleaded guilty to murder and were sentenced to hang, but Crittenden made good on his pledge and pardoned them.*

DILLINGER DEFIED CAPTURE FOR YEAR

John Dillinger, the Midwest outlaw who, in the space of a year, became one of the country's most notorious badmen, a killer of the old frontier tradition, had left a trail of dead and wounded across several states and of terror through the Northwest.

A small army had been on his trail, and several times he had been ambushed. But each time he was able to shoot his way out and flee. Each time, except when he achieved the daring exploit of walking out of the supposedly escape-proof Lake County jail at Crown Point, Ind., last March 4.

Then he cowed guards and other inmates with a piece of wood whittled to resemble a pistol and stained with shoe blacking.

Only last fall did his exploits begin to attract attention. He had been sentenced in 1924, a farm boy who had committed an amateur holdup in his home town, to six years in the Indiana State Prison for robbing a grocery in Groveton.

Met Band in Prison

The prison schooled him in the ways of the outlaw. There he met most of the criminals who later formed his band.

On the request of his father, the family's minister and the grocer he had held up, he was released by the parole board in May 1933. This, although he had been in trouble since the very beginning of his term, having "hid out" in the machine shop to which he was first assigned, sawed through the bars of his cell door and made his way into an adjoining cell block, fought with another inmate, and given all evidence of being incorrigible. The governor revoked the board's decision, however, and he was declared a delinquent patrolist.

Scoffing at the revocation of his parole, Dillinger, free in spite of the governor, never

John Dillinger, c. 1933.

did return. The old charges became back numbers. He resumed his career of crime. His holdups, carried out in a sensational, almost flamboyant manner, won for him and his mob the reputation of being supercriminals.

In the late summer he staged three robberies, in one holding up the girl cashier of a small-town bank, obtaining $25,000 in all. A fellow inmate of reformatory days was with him. But he wandered into Ohio, was captured and held there as a bank robber.

Engineered Prison Break

From that time on Dillinger grew to his present stature, to which fact and fable have contributed. While he was being held at Lima, Ohio, he engineered a plot by which Harry Pierpont, Russell Clark, John Hamilton and Charles Makley, who had come to know the daring with which he planned for those he dominated at Michigan City penitentiary, escaped from the prison. Six others fled with them.

Hamilton, Makley and Pierpont came to Lima. Working as if they were following well-laid plans, they raided the jail and released their chief. Sheriff Jess Sarber of Allen County resisted. They shot and killed him. That was on Oct. 12.

Dillinger gave an indication of the bravado that would later attract the attention of London, Paris and Berlin as well as the United States when he next appeared in Chicago. The police got wind of it.

A trap was set for him by the Chicago police as he visited a doctor's office on Nov. 16. Dillinger adopted a device that later was to insure his death by violence, but his escape until then. He shot his way out.

Federal Reward Offered

Events followed swiftly after that, multiplying until his name became a byword for outlawry, his career a reason for the passage of laws in Congress and the posting of a $10,000 reward by the United States government for his capture.

Only four days after he had walked from the trap he appeared at Racine, Wis., at the head of his lawless band. They raided the American Bank and Trust Company, obtained more than $10,000 and escaped.

Spectacular in the way he staged his lawless escapades, devil-may-care in his encounters with the law, he nevertheless brought every possible modern facility into play in his skirmishes. He used fast cars. He had bulletproof vests. His men used machine guns.

And when, with Hamilton and Makley, he took possession of the safe-deposit vault of the Unity Trust and Savings Bank in Chicago on Dec. 13, he reached his loot with electric torches. A haul of $8,700 and a large amount of jewelry was netted.

John Hamilton, Dillinger's lieutenant, and probably others of the gang remained in Chicago. The following day the police picked up Hamilton's trail. Police sergeant William T. Shanley set a trap for him. Hamilton, following his chief's cue, shot his way out, killing Shanley. A second victim lay dead on the Dillinger trail.

Six days later another Dillinger group fell afoul of the police at Paris, Ill. Edward Shouse, an aide of the outlaw, was captured. But in the gun battle, Eugene Teague, an Indiana State policeman, was killed, the third victim.

Dillinger was traced to a North Side apartment. The Chicago police closed in on Dec. 21. This time the casualties were on Dillinger's side. Lewis Katzewitz of Streator, Sam Ginsburg, an escaped Michigan prisoner, and Charles Tilden, who had broken out of an Illinois prison, were slain.

> *He used fast cars. He had bullet-proof vests. His men used machine guns.*

Ten days later the battle was declared a fight to the finish. The Chicago police received orders to shoot members of the gang on sight. But that very night, Dillinger declared his defiance by staging a hold-up of the Beverly Gardens, a resort, wounding two highway policemen in escaping.

On Jan. 6, 1934, the police picked up the trail of Jack Klutas, a gang leader affiliated with Dillinger, in Bellwood, a Chicago suburb. He was shot and killed, and five were dead.

Then another policeman fell, mortally wounded, before a Dillinger onslaught. He, Hamilton and another member of the mob held up the First National Bank of East Chicago. Escaping with more than $20,000, the careening Dillinger automobile passed Policeman William P. O'Malley. Before the policeman become aware of his antagonist, shots burst out and the policeman was dead.

Captured by "Hick Cops"

Dillinger was captured on Jan. 25. He, Makley, Clark and Pierpont appeared quietly in Tucson, Ariz.. They had considerable luggage and their hotel caught fire. They offered large rewards for the rescue of the luggage and obtained it.

One of the firemen read a detective story magazine and saw Dillinger's picture. He told the local police. One by one the members of the gang were captured before they could resort to arms. The luggage held a miniature arsenal. Dillinger was chagrined at his capture by what he called "hick cops."

Pierpont, Makley and Clark were sent to Ohio. Pierpont and Makley were sentenced to death for the Sarber murder, Clark to life imprisonment. Dillinger was taken to the Crown Point Jail.

The desperado announced to his fellow prisoners that he intended to break jail. They guffawed. In his cell, from a block of wood, he fashioned what looked like an automatic pistol. The morning of March 3 he held up a guard and the warden, cowed other guards, robbed 33 persons of $15 "for expenses" and helped himself to two of the jail's machine guns.

Stealing the automobile of the woman sheriff, he drove away with a murderer, Herbert Youngblood, a Negro. He carried with him a deputy sheriff and a garage attendant as hostages, throwing them out later on.

A nationwide search was started. The Indiana officials were criticized by Attorney General Cummings, the prosecutor of Lake County. Dillinger picked up where he had left off.

Ten days later he raided the Mason City, Iowa, bank. He was wounded in the shoulder. He forced a physician in St. Paul to treat him, and was able to continue. But on March 16, two more deaths marked his trail.

Youngblood turned up in Port Huron, Mich., and boasted of his successful jailbreak. The police heard of it. In the ensuing battle Youngblood and Under-Sheriff Charles Cavanaugh were killed.

Dillinger himself was trapped on March 31 in St. Paul. Government operatives had thrown a cordon about him. Confronted in an apartment with Eugene Green and a woman companion, he made his way to freedom behind a barrage of bullets. He and Green were wounded.

Green died of these and other wounds a few days later, on April 11. Dillinger, with pistol leveled, forced Dr. Clayton E. May of Minneapolis to treat him. The doctor was imprisoned because, terror-stricken, he had not informed the authorities.

Then the outlaw's exploits became unbelievable. He visited his father, John Sr., at the latter's homestead near Mooresville, Ind., and the neighbors marked the visit by petitioning the governor for a pardon for the killer.

Raided a Police Station

With posses on his trail, he and a companion raided a police station at Warsaw, Ind., stealing two bulletproof vests and two pistols, and made contact again with Hamilton by visiting the criminal's sister in Michigan.

Although the federal authorities were massing agents against him, he and his gang decided on a holiday in the Wisconsin woods. They motored to a resort near Mercer, practiced target shooting and enjoyed restful card games.

The federal agents got wind of the hideout. The resort was surrounded. But dogs barked the alarm and a battle began. Two Civilian Conservation Corps members and a local resident were fired on, and one of the CCC men was killed.

Terrific battles were fought about the resort, in which W. Carter Baum, a federal agent, was killed, but Dillinger and his men stole cars and escaped to St. Paul.

There they fought a gun battle with sheriff's deputies and escaped. But the gang was scattered. A small army was marshaled to close in on Dillinger. Congress was stirred. Ten anticrime bills were passed by the House and his name resounded in debate.

But for three months he eluded pursuers. He had been wounded in the battle around Mercer. Albert Reilly, one of his aides, was captured in Minneapolis and said his chief was dead. But Dillinger's father exhibited a letter from the son in denial.

Two detectives were shot to death in East Chicago on May 24. Dillinger was suspected. The kidnapping of Edward Bremer, St. Paul banker, was laid to a plot kindled by a fertile, twisted brain. By that time the legend began outrunning the story.

The amount of his thefts has been estimated at $5,000,000. Gunmen copied his methods, however, and fact became inseparable from fiction. The deaths he caused directly totaled about a score, including police, federal agents, bystanders and the thugs who had allied themselves with him.

—July 23, 1934

BANDITS ROB MAIL TRAIN OUTSIDE LONDON; RECORD LOSS MAY EXCEED $5,000,000

By JAMES FERON

Masked bandits robbed a mail train near London early today and escaped with at least $2,800,000, and perhaps more than $5,000,000, in cash and gems. The robbery may have been the biggest ever.

The gang of 8 to 15 men ambushed the Glasgow-to-London train before dawn in the outskirts of London.

Most of the loot consisted of more than £1 million ($2,800,000) in used pound banknotes, which are easily disposable. They were being sent to big London banks from provincial branches.

If the estimate of the loot proves accurate, the robbery was larger than the Brink's robbery in Boston on Jan. 17, 1950, in which cash and securities totaling $2,775,395 were stolen. The cash amounted to $1,218,211.

Last Aug. 15, a mail robbery on Cape Cod amounted to $1,551,277 in cash, exceeding the cash lost in the Brink's robbery.

For audacity and skillful planning, the post office and the British railways could not recall a parallel to the predawn raid.

Briefly, the gang stopped a Glasgow-to-London mail train with two faked signals, one to slow it and the other to halt it. The diesel engine rumbled to a stop near Cheddington, a village of 539 inhabitants 36 miles northwest of London.

The robbers, some carrying firearms against a completely unarmed mail crew, uncoupled the engine and the first two cars. They then forced the engineer to

> *The robbery may have been the biggest ever.*

drive ahead to a bridge over a road where they dumped about 120 registered mailbags into a waiting truck.

So expertly was the raid carried out that the 75 mail sorters in the last 10 cars of the train knew nothing about it until it was over.

Experts were impressed with the gang's intimate knowledge of railroading and their detailed planning. When they uncoupled the train, for example, they were able to operate both the hydraulic and steambrake systems without raising attention.

Detectives step across the rails to retrieve a crowbar near Bridego Railway Bridge in Buckinghamshire, England, on August 10, 1963, the day after the "Great Train Robbery."

They were so thorough that they cut roadside telephone lines into the village. When they shackled the engineer and his co-engineer together after the raid, they used the very latest type of handcuffs.

Det. Superintendent Malcolm Fewtrell of the Buckinghamshire Criminal Investigation Department said that "this was obviously a brilliantly planned operation." Reginald Bevins, the postmaster general, who rushed to London tonight from his home in Liverpool, said the robbery might have been an inside job.

Asked whether he felt any sneaking admiration for the way the raid had been carried out, Mr. Bevins said: "I don't feel any admiration for these gentlemen at all; in fact, I would not use the word gentlemen."

All of London's big banks were believed to have had packages of banknotes aboard the train.

The insurance position of the banknotes is vague. One bank, the Midland, said that it did not insure banknotes in transit but that this might not be a universal practice.

Mr. Bevins said that £20 ($56) was the maximum compensation for the loss of a registered package. This, however, is the maximum compensation for the minimum fee of 25 cents.

The postmaster general offered a reward of £10,000 leading to the criminals' arrest, but this was a third of the amount offered by two banks.

The National Provincial Bank alone estimated its loss in excess of £500.000 ($1.4 million), almost all in banknotes. The British Linen Bank of Scotland said it had lost £55,000 ($154,000).

Insurance adjusters were offering rewards equivalent to $70,000 on behalf of the two banks. Tonight railroad detectives were combing the records of past employees. Every available officer in Scotland Yard's flying squad of detectives was checking the bureau's files or seeking known "snouts," underworld contacts, for clues to the gang.

The ambush had all the drama of the Western train robberies that British television audiences have grown to recognize. Missing only were the ping of bullets against steel and a coachful of terrified passengers.

The traveling post office, rarely seen by the public and unmentioned in published timetables, was one of four such specials that streak through the dark each night. Each carries 75 postal workers and is called either an "up special," if it carries mail "up" to London, or a "down special" to the provinces or Scotland.

With staggering thoroughness, the gang had cut the telephone lines to nearby farmhouses and set a railroad signal a mile north of the ambush at amber, or "slow," to prepare the engineer for the fake stop signal. Armed with crowbars, their faces hidden, the gang waited.

The big diesel stopped for the signal. The signal's green light had been covered with an old glove and its red light had been illuminated with four batteries brought by the gang.

David Whitby, the 26-year-old co-engineer, said later: "We stopped and I got out to go to the telephone at the signal. On examining it, I found the wires had been cut. I went back to tell the driver and saw a man looking out from between the second and third coaches. I told my driver and went back to this man and said: 'What's up, mate?' He walked across the line and said, 'Come here.' He pushed me down the bank and another man grabbed me and put his hand over my mouth. He said: 'If you shout, I will kill you.' I said: 'I won't shout.'"

"They took me back to the engine and I found they had coshed [slugged] my driver," said Jack Mills, the engineer. "They put one end of a pair of handcuffs on one of my wrists and one of the men held the other end."

A second group of bandits had uncoupled the last 10 cars of the train, separating the registered mail in the second coach from the ordinary mail in the rest of the train.

"They knew what they were doing," a railroad official said later.

Mr. Whitby said: "They made my driver go forward to Sears Crossing. When we stopped, they handcuffed me to him.

Two Forced to Lie Down

"They made us get out of the engine and lie down at the side of the train while they went to unload the coach. They left one man to guard us and he made us walk down to the second coach."

Mr. Mills, suffering from a crowbar blow to the head, had recovered sufficiently to follow the gang's orders to take the shortened train to a small marking near the bridge at Sears Crossing.

A truck waited in a narrow road under the bridge. Members of the gang threw the mailbags onto the track shoulder, where others carried them to the truck.

The robbery took place on a busy, four-track line that links northwestern England and western Scotland with London. The mail train, heading south, was stopped at an overhead signal three miles north of Cheddington Station. The front section was taken another mile south to Bridego bridge, two miles north of the station.

Sears Crossing, which the railroad men referred to in their account of the robbery, is a dirt road that crosses the tracks leading to a farmhouse. It is three-fourths of a mile north of the bridge.

"When they had finished unloading," Mr. Whitby said, "they made my driver and me get in with the four G.P.O. [General Post Office] men in there."

He was referring to the mail car that had contained the valuable shipment.

"They told us to wait for half an hour and then they left," he continued.

"I believe they threatened the G.P.O. men verbally that they would use a gun on them. The G.P.O. men tried to stop them getting in, but they broke in apparently."

Meanwhile, the mail sorters in the rear cars were still busy at work, unaware of the robbery.

Rear Guard Knocked Out

The rear guard put lanterns on the tracks to warn oncoming trains and walked to the front to determine the cause of the long delay.

The guard, Thomas Miller, said:

"You can imagine my surprise when I saw the two coaches and engine gone."

"The post office were just finishing up their work and they thought the engine had broken down. I hopped it up the line after that, trying to find a phone, but all the lines had been cut. Then, about 200 yards down, I came across the coaches and engine. There was blood in the cab and the windows on the near side of the coach had been smashed in and the door busted open."

The entire incident took 15 minutes and the police were not alerted until 45 minutes after the robbery was over. It was not discovered until a signalman realized that the mail train had not passed through the signal block. He summoned a search train.

After the robbers had gone, a trainman in a rear coach, realizing that something was amiss, ran to a nearby farmhouse to summon help. He found that there was no phone in the house. It wouldn't have mattered, however, because the roadside cables had been cut.

Britain has had her share of dramatic mail-train robberies, but none approaching this one.

Other robbers have dressed up as railway men, started fires in passenger compartments and even tried to cause a diversion by releasing a swarm of bees.

The previous record mail robbery in Britain took place May 21, 1952, when seven men held up a post office truck on Oxford Street in London. They got away with £238,000 ($666,400), mostly in banknotes. Some 400 informers and suspects were questioned, but no one was ever brought to justice for that robbery.

—August 9, 1963

NOTE: *Scotland Yard caught most of the robbers within a month of the crime, and they received prison terms of up to 30 years. The most notorious member of the gang, Ronnie Biggs, escaped from Wandsworth Prison in 1965 and ended up in Brazil, where for decades he lived a sometimes lavish lifestyle under his real name. In failing health, Biggs voluntarily returned to England in 2001 to serve the remainder of his term. He was given compassionate release in 2009 and died in 2013. Most of the loot taken in the heist was never recovered.*

STAR OF INDIA AND 8 OTHER STOLEN GEMS RETURNED TO CITY FROM MIAMI LOCKER

By JACK ROTH

The fabulous Star of India, the world's largest sapphire, and 8 of the 23 other gems stolen from the American Museum of Natural History were returned to New York yesterday in the coat pocket of an assistant district attorney.

The gems were recovered in two waterlogged suede pouches from a locker in a Miami bus terminal with the help of Allan Dale Kuhn, one of three ne'er-do-wells who have been charged with the daring burglary of last Oct. 29.

The other defendants are Jack Roland Murphy, known as Murph the Surf, and Roger Frederick Clark. All three describe themselves as skin divers, surfers and beach boys. The authorities call them "notorious jewel thieves."

Still missing is the magnificent DeLong Star Ruby, which weighs 100 carats, and a diamond crystal called the Eagle Diamond, of 15.37 carats. The other stones are smaller. All were removed from the museum's J. P. Morgan gem gallery.

Agreement Cuts Charges

Under an arrangement agreed to by District Attorney Frank S. Hogan's office, the defendants will plead guilty to third-degree burglary, a crime punishable by up to 10 years in prison.

It was learned that Mr. Hogan's office, despite the DeLong ruby's not being returned, will still recommend a sentence of one year. Earlier Mr. Hogan was said to be insisting that both the Star of India and the DeLong ruby be returned in the arrangement.

It was understood that the agreement did not cover any of the other robbery charges against the defendants.

Murphy faces a charge of assault and robbery in a $250 holdup of a clerk in the Algonquin Hotel here in New York. In Miami, along with Kuhn, he is accused of the pistol-whipping of Eva Gabor, the actress, and stealing $550,000 in jewels from her. And last Saturday, Murphy and Clark were charged with the burglary of $52,000 worth of costume jewelry from a private home.

Gems Displayed on Scarf

Mr. Hogan displayed the recovered gems on a $1.98 black scarf borrowed from one of his secretaries.

In addition to the Star of India, which weighs 563.35 carats, the other pieces recovered were the Midnight Star sapphire, 116 carats; an engraved emerald, 87 carats; an engraved emerald keystone-shaped stone, 67 carats; a 32-carat emerald; a smaller emerald; an inch-long emerald carved in an egg shape; an aquamarine-faceted stone nearly square, 400 carats, and an oval aquamarine weighing 737 carats.

On Tuesday night, Kuhn, Assistant District Attorney Maurice Nadjari and three detectives, Richard Maline, Peter Meenan and John McNally, flew to Florida. The mission was to recover as many of the gems as possible in return for leniency in sentencing.

Newsmen Enter Chase

On arriving Kuhn made a series of phone calls and said he expected to have the gems by Wednesday evening. By that time, newspapers had carried stories of the supposedly secret trip and newsmen started following the group.

Evasive maneuvering began, most of it to avoid reporters and photographers, some of them hiding in bushes, some carrying walkie-talkies and some pulling ignition wires on cars the authorities had rented so they would not start.

Kuhn, the detectives and Mr. Nadjari moved from one hotel to another in their hectic effort to lose the reporters. At one point, they nimbly jumped 20 feet from a motel window to shake off their pursuers. Detectives said that caused Kuhn to comment, as he jumped with the group: "I'm glad you fellows aren't burglars. You'd put me out of business."

Finally, 10 or 12 hotels and motels later, they succeeded in shaking off the newsmen. But Kuhn was continually making and receiving phone calls. To a fence or a friend who held the gems? The answer has not been disclosed. The key call was made about 3 a.m. yesterday. Kuhn and the authorities were at the University Inn, a motel near the University of Miami.

Caller Gives Secret

A caller told a detective who picked up the phone: "The jewels are in a locker in the bus terminal at Northeast Fourth Street."

The caller then gave the location of the locker and the place where the key to it was hidden. Det. Maline left the motel and picked up the key, which belonged to a locker in

Jack "Murph the Surf" is escorted to the Miami Beach police station by detectives after he was arrested with three other men for armed robbery, January 28, 1968—three years after he was released from prison after serving time for the museum heist.

a bus terminal in downtown Miami. The detective found two wet brown suede pouches in locker 0911, located in a tier of lockers on a loading platform outside the waiting room. After removing the pouches from the locker, the detective opened the drawstrings and found the jewels, each wrapped in wet tissue paper.

Had the pouches been in the ocean? The defendants are expert swimmers and divers. Mr. Hogan declined to comment.

It was reported that the locker had been used every day since Dec. 12. An employee of the terminal said: "Someone put a quarter in the locker every day until today."

Mr. Maline, still alone, returned to the motel with the pouches, and Mr. Nadjari called Mr. Hogan at his home.

"Chief, I'm sorry to wake you up," he told Mr. Hogan. "We've completed our mission and we're leaving on an 8:15 a.m. plane." The prosecutor said he did not go into "specifics" with Mr. Nadjari, and Mr. Hogan refused to talk about anything the group had done in Miami other than to say that most of the time had been spent trying to elude newsmen.

It is known that on Wednesday afternoon Kuhn called his lawyer, Gilbert S. Rosenthal, and told him: "We ought to have the stuff in a few hours and get back to New York some time tonight."

Aboard the plane for New York, Mr. Nadjari took the gems from the pouches and transferred them, each in fresh tissue paper, into an air-sickness bag.

The Northeast Airlines jet touched down at the Kennedy International Airport with Kuhn, the detectives and Mr. Nadjari at 10:55 a.m. Six detectives boarded the plane. When everyone else was off the aircraft, Kuhn, his hands manacled in front of him, stepped off the plane with the detectives. He was tanned, his orange-colored hair neatly combed, and he was dressed in a camel hair coat with a fur collar.

The group proceeded to two unmarked detective cars. Kuhn traveled in a vehicle with Assistant Chief Inspector Joseph Coyle, who has headed the investigation into the burglary.

At 11:53 a.m. a plainclothes man carrying three suitcases pushed into the door at 155 Leonard Street, Mr. Hogan's office. Only after he had entered an elevator did newsmen realize there were airport tags on the luggage.

As he went up the elevator, he said he was carrying "Nadjari's luggage."

The car carrying Kuhn stopped at the intersection of Leonard and Centre Streets rather than pull up at the entrance to the prosecutor's office. Across the street, walking casually and unnoticed, was Mr. Nadjari carrying the gems in his black coat pocket.

The district attorney said that as soon as Mr. Nadjari had laid the gems on his desk, Dr. Bryan Mason, curator of gems at the museum, was called into his office. Mr. Hogan said that Dr. Mason, after examining the stones through a jeweler's eyepiece, had found them to be undamaged during their absence from the museum.

The expected plea of guilty by the defendants is to cover the three other counts in the indictment that value the gems at $300,000, as well as a charge of felonious possession of marijuana against Clark.

Federal Action Weighed

Federal authorities were said to be concerned as to whether to proceed against the three defendants on charges of interstate theft, a crime punishable by 10 years and a $10,000 fine. The government isn't bound by any arrangement made by Mr. Hogan, but there has always been close cooperation between Mr. Hogan and U.S. Attorney Robert M. Morgenthau.

The defendants appeared briefly before Supreme Court Justice Mitchell D. Schweitzer yesterday and Mr. Rosenthal was granted an adjournment in the case until Tuesday. Bail was continued for Kuhn, Murphy and Clark.

Kuhn was returned to his cell in Manhattan City Prison where Clark and Murphy are also held. None could raise bail.

The district attorney declined to answer questions as to whether the jewels not recovered had been cut up and disposed of and whether he had hopes of recovering any of the stones still missing, particularly the DeLong ruby. All he would say was that the investigation was not closed.

—January 9, 1965

NOTE: *Clark, Kuhn and Murphy, who carried out the theft by lowering themselves from the museum's roof to an unlocked window, pleaded guilty and were sentenced in 1965 to three years in prison. In 1965, insurance magnate John D. MacArthur paid $25,000 to recover the DeLong Star Ruby from Florida loan sharks who had been holding it.*

THE BIG LUFTHANSA ROBBERY AND ITS TRAIL OF MURDER

By LESLIE MAITLAND

Relying on old connections in the world of crime, Steve Carbone put out the word that he was looking for Joseph Manri and Paolo LiCastri. He wanted to warn them that their lives were in danger.

He believed that the people behind the $5.8 million armed robbery of Lufthansa's air cargo building a year ago had decided that the two men had served their purposes and should be eliminated. But Mr. Carbone, a supervisor in the Federal Bureau of Investigation, could not get to them in time.

"We could have saved their lives if only they had come to us," Mr. Carbone said.

"But our efforts to warn them fell on deaf ears—they were either too greedy or too scared. You hate to see people killed. But it's also a great frustration to us. They were links in the case that are cut off now."

Mr. Manri and Mr. LiCastri were two of several suspects who received death

> *In Mr. Carbone's opinion, the murderer was likely someone they knew.*

sentences gangland style, at the hands of hired killers, following the largest cash robbery in the country's history. Investigators say they are confident their luck will turn, and that one day they will solve the most dramatic case of their careers.

Eventually, Mr. Carbone thinks, they will recover some of the $5 million in cash and almost $1 million in jewelry that the robbers loaded into a stolen van and took from the German airline's cargo building at Kennedy International Airport in the predawn hours of Dec. 11, 1978. The robbers were six or seven men wearing ski masks and carrying shotguns and automatic pistols.

"It's a case that just won't die," said Mr. Carbone, who was once a high school English teacher. "Every time it has breathed its last breath, something new comes up. It's like a gigantic puzzle, and now we have a lot of the pieces."

The bodies of Mr. Manri and a companion, Robert McMahon, were found last May 16 slumped in a brown Buick LeSabre in a deserted area in the Mill Basin section of Brooklyn. They had been shot in the back of the head. In Mr. Carbone's opinion, the murderer was likely someone they knew.

As for Mr. LiCastri, his bullet-torn body was found face down last June 13 on a pile of garbage in a lot off Flatlands Avenue in Brooklyn.

An illegal alien from Sicily who had sneaked back into the country after serving time for manslaughter and then being deported, Mr. LiCastri was the sixth victim that the FBI believes was silenced because of his role in the Lufthansa robbery. There is a seventh, whose dismembered body has yet to be identified, whom the FBI thinks is also related to the case.

Two other suspects have been missing for a year. More killings are expected. The federal agents who are working on the case, a group that varies from 3 to 100, say they may be powerless to prevent them.

Long, Unproductive Interviews

In the last year they have gone on fruitless searches for cash or bodies and have delved into murders that later proved unconnected to the Lufthansa robbery. They have spent days listening to surreptitiously recorded tapes, hoping to hear something new.

There have been long nights in the FBI's Queens office, in the shadow of the neighborhoods—Howard Beach and Ozone Park—where several of the suspects live. Fifty or sixty tips have been investigated, Mr. Carbone said, but fewer than a tenth have produced anything of value.

And yet an initial tip, provided by informers within days of the robbery, gave investigators the names of four whom they believe were involved, and what is regarded as a solid notion of the powers behind the robbery.

That information also helped provide the FBI with a legal basis for conducting electronic surveillance of the suspects, allowing them to monitor conversations that took place in the suspects' cars. Other information, gathered through almost 1,000 interviews with airport employees, led last spring to the trial of Louis Werner, a Lufthansa cargo agent who was convicted of having given the robbers crucial inside assistance. He remains the only person to be charged or tried so far in the case.

After his conviction but before his sentencing to 16 years imprisonment last June, Mr. Werner was taken before a federal grand jury, granted immunity from further prosecution and asked to tell what he knew. He was held in contempt when he refused to answer questions, apparently afraid of retribution by accomplices.

Only one suspect decided to cooperate in exchange for leniency, according to Mr. Carbone, who has supervised two special agents, Thomas Sweeney and Gary Kirby, who have worked on the case full-time. They credit the assistance of Det. Jack Fitzsimmons of the New York City Police Department's Queens task force, Sgt. James Shea of the department's 12th Homicide Zone, the personnel of the 113th Precinct, the Nassau County Police and Det. Thomas Stollard of the Port Authority of New York and New Jersey.

Termed a Double Cross

According to testimony at the trial of Mr. Werner, the idea for the robbery originated with Peter Gruenawald, a Lufthansa cargo worker who was his friend but ended up testifying against him. Mr. Gruenawald, who is now under federal protection, stalled about carrying out the plan when he became disillusioned with those originally recruited for it from a bar in Queens.

Mr. Werner, 47, was depicted at trial as a gambler who ultimately double-crossed Mr. Gruenawald by arranging the robbery without him. Authorities now believe Mr. Werner never knew the identities of the men who invaded and robbed the cargo building. But they say he received $80,000 before he was arrested and gave Mr. Gruenawald $10,000 of his share to guarantee his silence.

According to testimony at Mr. Werner's trial, the cargo agent went to his bookmaker, Frank Menna, who introduced him to a big bookmaker named Martin Krugman. Authorities have concluded that Mr. Krugman, a beautician from Nassau County, brought the scheme to the men who pulled it off. Mr. Krugman disappeared a month after the crime and has not been heard from.

Although the name never came up at Mr. Werner's trial, James Burke of Howard Beach is the man investigators are convinced was approached by Mr. Krugman to carry out the plan. According to Chief Edward J. Stoll, formerly of the Queens detectives, Mr. Burke is an associate of the Paul Vario organized crime "family," a group said to be responsible for much of the cargo thefts that have plagued the Kennedy Airport.

Mr. Vario, who now lives in Florida, has often been identified as a prominent member of the Lucchese organized crime family, now said to be headed by Anthony Corallo. Authorities believe that Mr. Vario and Mr. Corallo are both receiving tribute from the proceeds of the crime.

Federal surveillance indicated that Mr. Burke went to Florida after the robbery, but it is not known whether he met there with Mr. Vario. Mr. Burke made the trip with Angelo J. Sepe, one of the four persons named by an informer as one of the Lufthansa robbers, as was Mr. Burke's son, Frank.

Mr. Sepe, who is 38 and comes from Ozone Park, has been arrested more than a dozen times since 1955 and was on probation for an armed robbery of a bank payroll at the time of his arrest last February as one of the Lufthansa robbers.

Mr. Sepe has not been indicted. But Federal authorities had parole revoked for him and Mr. Burke on the ground that they had associated with known criminals. They are now back in prison, but are eligible for release this month.

A Loan-Sharking Conviction

At the time of the robbery, Mr. Burke was in a Manhattan halfway house, following his release from the Federal penitentiary in Atlanta where he had been sentenced to 10 years on a 1972 loansharking conviction. Mr. Burke, who is 49 and whose extensive criminal record dates to 1948, had been sent to the halfway house on Oct. 18, 1978, and was released from it on Jan. 25, 1979.

Another suspect, Thomas DeSimone, arrived at the halfway house the same day as Mr. Burke, with whom the police say he had participated in at least one previous crime. Mr. DeSimone, 34, who also came from Ozone Park, had served one-third of a 10-year sentence at the penitentiary in Lewisburg, Pa., on a conviction for theft from an interstate shipment and interfering by force with interstate commerce. Mr. DeSimone was released from the halfway house on Dec. 12, 1978, one day after the Lufthansa robbery. His wife, Cookie, reported him missing a month later, and he has not been found.

Matthew Walsh, the director of the halfway house, which rented rooms in the Woodward Hotel on Broadway and 55th Street, said that Mr. DeSimone and Mr. Burke were friends while at the center. He also said that theoretically residents could sneak away at night without being noticed.

At the time of his disappearance, Mr. DeSimone—believed to have been one of the armed robbers—was wanted in Queens for questioning in a murder that took place a week after the Lufthansa robbery. That victim, Steven Edwards, said to have been an associate of Mr. DeSimone, was found shot in the back in his Ozone Park apartment. The FBI now believes that Mr. Edwards stole the 1977 black Ford van used in the robbery.

Besides Mr. DeSimone, Mr. Sepe and Mr. Burke's 21-year-old son, Frank, the FBI also received information implicating a man named Anthony Rodriguez as another gunman in the airport robbery. Mr. Sweeney, the federal agent, said that Mr. Rodriguez and Mr. Sepe were seen together a few days after the robbery. The two men had been arrested together before by the state police in a raid of a house used by Mr. Sepe in Mattituck, L.I., where drugs and guns were said to have been found.

The only court-authorized search conducted so far by the agents in their effort to recover the stolen Lufthansa cargo was at that Long Island house. The effort was not successful.

Mr. Carbone now believes that Mr. LiCastri and Mr. Manri joined the four others in entering the cargo building the morning of the robbery. Other authorities, noting that witnesses described six or seven gunmen, said that the elder Mr. Burke may have been among them. Mr. Carbone theorizes that Mr. Manri and Mr. LiCastri were murdered because they were "susceptible to deals"—Mr. LiCastri because he was in the country illegally and Mr. Manri because he was facing trial in a robbery and a truck hijacking.

Mr. Carbone was not sure whether Mr. McMahon, who was found dead in the car with Mr. Manri, had also been involved, or whether he was just unfortunate in having "gone along for the ride." The bodies were found May 16, the day Mr. Werner was convicted.

"We are now seeking information about a known truck hijacker who provided Manri and that pulled the heist," said Mr. Carbone. "We're also looking for a well-known Long Island bookmaker who was associated with both Werner and Krugman and may have knowledge of the details of the robbery."

Although the police have theorized that Mr. Krugman and Mr. DeSimone were murdered, Mr. Carbone believes that they are still alive, because their bodies have not been found. "Whoever killed the others made no effort to hide the bodies," he said.

But another murder victim that investigators link to the case—Theresa Ferrara, 27, part owner of a beauty shop in Bellmore, L.I.,—could be identified only through x-rays after her dismembered body was washed ashore near Toms River, N.J., last May 18. Miss Ferrara is said to have previously shared a house in Queens with an associate of Mr. Burke.

In the view of investigators, the huge amount of money stolen is actually a factor in their favor.

"It's such a large amount that any movement of it would single them out," Mr. Carbone said. "Already they have had to get other people involved in moving it. The circle of people who have been involved has reached 30 or 35 by now, and the more people there are, the better our chances. It took the Brink's people five years to solve that case, so we still have four to go. We're very confident."

—January 3, 1980

NOTE: *The suspected mastermind of the heist, James "Jimmy the Gent" Burke, died in 1996 while serving a life sentence for the murder of a drug dealer. More than 35 years after the crime, reputed mobster Vincent Asaro was charged for his participation in the robbery; he was acquitted in 2015. Only one person, a Lufthansa cargo agent described as an inside man, has been convicted in the heist.*

BOSTON THIEVES LOOT A MUSEUM OF MASTERPIECES

By FOX BUTTERFIELD

Dressed as police officers, thieves broke into the Isabella Stewart Gardner Museum here in Boston early this morning and made off with 12 priceless artworks, including paintings by Rembrandt, Vermeer, Degas and Manet.

The daring theft, which the museum said was not discovered until the cleaning crew arrived this morning, is believed to be one of the largest in the world, said the Federal Bureau of Investigation and a museum spokesman.

Corey Cronin, a spokesman for the Gardner Museum, said it was difficult to place an exact value on the stolen paintings because "they were acquired by Mrs. Gardner at the turn of the century" and have never been offered for sale since. But an official of the FBI in Boston said he heard estimates today that the paintings could be worth from $100 million to $200 million.

A Major Dutch Theft

The largest previous known art theft occurred in 1988 when thieves stole three van Goghs from the Kröller-Müller Museum in Otterlo, the Netherlands, with an estimated value of $72 million to $90 million. But the skyrocketing price paid for art in the past few years makes any valuation difficult, experts cautioned today.

Mr. Cronin would not say whether the Gardner Museum, a 15th-century Venetian palace transported to Boston, had insurance on the stolen paintings. It was the first theft at the elegant museum, built around a flowered courtyard, since it opened in 1903.

According to Thomas A. Hughes, the agent in charge of the FBI's Boston office, at least two thieves gained entry to the museum by posing as police officers. They were admitted by two security guards, who were then "subdued and restrained," Mr. Hughes said in a statement. A Boston police spokesman said that the guards were overpowered and then handcuffed, and that the thieves then disabled the museum's security system.

The theft, which occurred sometime after 1 a.m., was not discovered till the regular cleaning crew arrived at 8 a.m., Mr. Hughes said.

Neither Mr. Cronin nor the FBI would comment on how the thieves stripped the paintings from the museum's walls or how they transported them after leaving. But a

Boston law-enforcement official said the thieves appeared to know precisely what they were looking for.

Among the stolen works were three by Rembrandt, *The Storm on the Sea of Galilee, A Lady and a Gentleman in Black,* and a self-portrait.

Value of the Rembrandts

Mr. Cronin described the Rembrandts as "priceless" and "irreplaceable."

In addition, the thieves also took a Vermeer called *The Concert*, which Mr. Cronin said was valuable because it is among only 35 paintings by the artist known to exist.

It was acquired by Mrs. Gardner at an auction in Paris for $6,000, using one of her favorite secret devices to signal a bid: letting drop a handkerchief covering her mouth, according to Cleveland Amory in his book *The Proper Bostonians.* Mrs. Gardner was the daughter of a wealthy New York dry-goods merchant and the wife of John Lowell Gardner, a son of one of Boston's last East India merchants who traded tea and opium with China.

The thieves also stole five works by Degas, including *La Sortie du Paysage, Cortege aux Environs de Florence, Three Mounted Jockeys* and *Program for an Artistic Soiree,* as well as another painting similar to the *Program for an Artistic Soiree.* A painting by Manet, *Chez Tortoni,* was also taken, as was a Chinese bronze beaker dating from the Shang dynasty, from 1200 to 1000 B.C.

Mr. Cronin said no damage had been done to the museum's other works or to its building and galleries, a favorite with Bostonians since it was opened to the public in 1903 while Mrs. Gardner was still living in an apartment on the top floor. She died in 1924 at the age of 85.

Many of the museum's works were acquired for Mrs. Gardner by Bernard Berenson. The museum houses 290 paintings and 280 other pieces, including tapestries, ceramics, furniture and documents.

A Delight in Shocking

Mrs. Gardner, popularly known as Mrs. Jack, was a leader of Boston society, but took pleasure in shocking Puritan Boston with her own ways. Instead of drinking tea, she drank beer. Instead of going sleigh-riding, she went walking with a lion named Rex on a leash, according to the account in *The Proper Bostonians.* Told that everybody in Boston was either a Unitarian or an Episcopalian, she became a Buddhist.

In 1898, soon after her husband died, she suffered a nervous breakdown and was advised by her doctors to take up a hobby. Her hobby turned out to be the erection of a Venetian palace in Boston's Fenway section. Mrs. Gardner is said to have acquired the palace in Europe and had it shipped back to Boston piece by piece.

When she first opened the building, one guest was her good friend William James, the philosopher. He wrote her afterwards that "the aesthetic perfection of all things . . . seemed to have a peculiar effect on the company, making them quiet and docile and self-forgetful and kind."

"It was a very extraordinary and wonderful moral influence," Mr. James went on. "Quite in the line of a Gospel miracle."

—March 19, 1990

NOTE: *More than 25 years after the heist, none of the artworks have been recovered from what remains the largest art theft in American history.*

WILLIE SUTTON, URBANE SCOUNDREL

By PETER DUFFY

For years afterward, Willie Sutton would curse himself for squeezing into the BMT subway train at Union Square station just before it rumbled toward Brooklyn that early afternoon in February 1952.

Mr. Sutton, then 52, was America's most celebrated criminal, a fixture on the FBI's Most Wanted List ever since he had escaped from a Pennsylvania prison five years earlier. He was a gentleman bandit who robbed scores of banks without firing a shot, sometimes while disguised as a policeman or a telegram messenger. He was a brainy ne'er-do-well who escaped from prison three times, read Schopenhauer for fun and loved to stroll through the roses at the Brooklyn Botanic Garden. Known variously as the Babe Ruth of Bank Robbers, Willie the Actor and Slick Willie, the Brooklyn native claimed to have stolen $2 million during his 25-year career in robbery.

In the 1940s and 1950s, New York newspapers were filled with lurid photographs of crime victims splayed on the sidewalk. But crime levels were low, and flamboyant gangsters, like Frank Costello and Bugsy Siegel, fascinated rather than repulsed the citizenry.

"Crime was less prevalent but the criminals were more glamorous," said Kenneth T. Jackson, professor of history at Columbia University and president of the New-York Historical Society. In the tense, high-crime decades that followed, that image was largely lost. No one ever had a warm feeling toward David Berkowitz, also known as Son of Sam.

He was a gentleman bandit who robbed scores of banks without firing a shot.

But Mr. Sutton, with his pencil-thin mustache and well-tailored suits, enjoyed near folk-hero status in that era. Young boys idolized him. One year, a group of them chanted his name during the St. Patrick's Day parade. He was beloved by the tabloids, too. When asked why he robbed banks, he famously replied, "Because that's where the money is." It didn't matter that he said he never uttered the phrase—or that the "Field Marshal of Crime" wasn't such a master criminal, ultimately spending nearly half his life behind bars.

Fifty years ago tomorrow, Mr. Sutton's career came to an end with that 10-cent subway ride. As his train pulled into the DeKalb Avenue station in Brooklyn, a chubby-cheeked 24-year-old named Arnold Schuster boarded for the short trip to his Borough Park home.

By the time the subway reached the next stop, Pacific Street, the young man realized he was standing near the master thief.

Willie Sutton, the gentleman bandit, entering a courtroom.

Mr. Sutton, who was living in a $6-a-week room on Dean Street, exited the station, and Mr. Schuster followed. While the bank robber fiddled with a dead battery in his gray 1951 Chevrolet sedan, Mr. Schuster flagged down two patrolmen, Donald Shea and Joseph McClellan. "I know you're going to think I'm crazy," he said. "But I just saw Willie Sutton. He's right around the corner fixing a car."

The officers approached Mr. Sutton and asked to see his registration, which listed his identity as Charles Gordon. "Thank you, Mr. Gordon," one of them said, satisfied. They returned to the station house, a few blocks away on Bergen Street, thinking they had nearly made the arrest of their careers. The two described what had just transpired to Det. Louis Weiner, who suggested taking another look at Mr. Gordon.

Det. Weiner approached Mr. Sutton and asked to see his license and registration. "Would you mind coming back to the station with me so we can check on this license a little further to make sure it's genuine?" the third-grade detective asked.

"Sure," Mr. Sutton said, in the tone of someone who had nothing to hide.

At headquarters, it didn't take long before the police knew they had their man. "OK, fellas," the fugitive said. "I'm Willie Sutton." Det. Weiner, who is retired and living in Southern California, later called him the nicest crook he ever locked up.

Word of the arrest spread quickly. Reporters flocked to the Brooklyn precinct house, where Mr. Sutton and the three proud officers were paraded in front of the flashing cameras.

A joyous Police Commissioner George P. Monaghan hugged the three officers and crowed to the assembled press: "Well, we've got Willie. We've got Willie Sutton." Mr. Monaghan immediately promoted each of the men to first-grade detective.

Forgotten in the hullabaloo was one Arnold Schuster. Hearing of the arrest, he immediately called the police station, but was unable to speak to anyone about his role. He hired a lawyer, in the hopes of obtaining the $70,000 reward that had been reported in the newspapers. It later turned out there was no such prize.

Within a few days, the police conceded they had made a mistake in not crediting Mr. Schuster, although the officers were permitted to retain their promotions. Mr. Schuster, with his fresh-faced innocence, then emerged as the story's newest hero.

He gleefully told reporters how he had studied an FBI flier on Mr. Sutton that had been sent to his father's Borough Park clothing store, where he worked. He spoke of how Mr. Sutton bowed his head when he stared at him on the subway, arousing his suspicions. Mr. Schuster's tales were transmitted nationally by the new medium of television, making him an instant celebrity.

But not everyone was impressed. The Schuster family received 12 harassing letters and so many threatening phone calls that their number was changed.

Then, on March 8, while he was walking near his home in Borough Park, Mr. Schuster was murdered, shot once in each eye and twice in the groin. The viciousness of the crime shocked the city and sparked a widespread manhunt for the killer.

"This sinks me," Mr. Sutton said of the killing, which he claimed he knew nothing about.

No one was ever arrested for the crime, although several suspects, including a longtime accomplice of Mr. Sutton, were identified. Mafia legend has it that the mob boss Albert Anastasia took one look at Mr. Schuster crowing about his achievement on television and ordered the hit simply because he hated the sight of a rat.

Mr. Sutton was convicted of robbing a Queens bank and was released from Attica in 1969 after a series of appeals. He died in 1980.

He always claimed to be heartbroken over the murder. "Arnold Schuster haunts me," he wrote in his 1976 autobiography, *Where the Money Was*. "Throughout my career I had plotted and planned my jobs to make sure that I would not have to hurt anybody, and now, after it was over and I was sitting in jail, a good-looking, promising young man had been killed because of me. The laughter of the gods."

—February 17, 2002

FBI BRINGS A FRESH SET OF EYES TO A '71 PLANE HIJACKING MYSTERY

By SUSAN SAULNY

It is considered one of the great unsolved mysteries of American crime: how a seemingly quiet man in his 40s hijacked an airliner somewhere between Seattle and Reno in November 1971, then parachuted in his loafers and trench coat, making off with $200,000 in cash.

Who was he? Did he survive? After all these years, federal authorities say they still do not know, and the case lingers and vexes and fascinates as the only unsolved airplane hijacking in United States history. "It's a mystery, frankly," agency officials said in a December news release issued periodically to update old cases.

FBI artist sketches of D. B. Cooper.

But now, with the advantage of technologies unavailable decades ago and with newfound attention from an agent on the West Coast, the FBI has announced that the cold case is officially hot again—and the search is on for the parachuter who called himself Dan, and sometimes D. B. Cooper.

And, for the first time, the FBI is providing pictures and information on the Cooper case to the public on its Web site. The agency hopes that pictures like the one of Mr. Cooper's black tie, which he removed before jumping, will prompt a memory, or that someone will offer fresh insight into what happened to all that cash, some of which was scattered in the wilderness and found by a young boy in 1980.

"This case is 36 years old, it's beyond its expiration date, but I asked for the case because I was intrigued with it," said Larry Carr, a federal agent based in Seattle who was four when the hijacking occurred. "I remember as a child reading about it and wondering what had happened. It's surreal that after 36 years here I am, the only investigator left. I wanted to take a shot at solving it."

Since the case was turned over to him six months ago, Mr. Carr has come up with a new way of seeing the incident: as a bank robbery that just happened to be on an airplane. The fresh perspective led to new investigating techniques.

"The classic way we solve bank robberies is with the public," Mr. Carr said. "Everything we know—pictures, descriptions, m.o., everything. We put it all out there."

Now, with the information made public, he said, "maybe someone will say: My uncle who disappeared in 1971—he could have been Cooper."

Included in the newly released information are updated insights on Mr. Cooper that the FBI feels are accurate: he was not an expert sky diver, he had no help on the ground, he was about six feet tall and 175 pounds, with brown eyes.

The description came from separate accounts given by attendants on the hijacked flight, Northwest Airlines 305, that left Portland, Ore., bound for Seattle on Nov. 24, 1971. After takeoff, Mr. Cooper

The fresh perspective led to new investigating techniques.

handed a flight attendant a note saying he had a bomb in his suitcase. He demanded four parachutes and $200,000 in $20 bills, the FBI says. Upon the plane's landing in Seattle, Mr. Cooper exchanged all 36 passengers for the ransom, but continued to hold several crewmembers on the plane with him as, on his orders, it took off again, this time on a flight to Mexico City.

Around 8 that night, Mr. Cooper jumped out of the back of the plane as it was flying somewhere between Seattle and Reno, Nev. It later landed safely.

The FBI opened an investigation while the airplane was still in flight, but despite years of work and the consideration of hundreds of suspects, Mr. Cooper seems to have disappeared into the night.

"If he's alive today, he'd be about 85 years old," Mr. Carr said. "Maybe one day I'll be sitting at my desk and I'll get a call from an old man who says, 'You're not going to believe this story.'"

—*January 2, 2008*

GRAYING THIEVES AND A RECORD HEIST UNDONE IN LONDON

By DAN BILEFSKY

On Friday nights for three years, they met over pints at the Castle, a pub in Islington, in North London. The four men were getting on in years, but they were not there just to talk about retirement or the aches and pains of aging.

Experienced thieves with long criminal records, they had something far more pressing in mind: an audacious, career-topping heist they boasted the world would never forget.

The operation, meticulously plotted—with the help, the police would later learn, of the book *Forensics for Dummies*—was finally set in motion the Thursday before Easter this year, as Brian Reader, the ruddy-faced ringleader whom the others called "the Master," boarded the No. 96 bus near his home in Dartford, Kent.

Mr. Reader, 76, swiped his free travel pass for seniors and began the 80-minute journey to Hatton Garden, for centuries the center of London's jewelry trade. By early evening, Mr. Reader reached an inconspicuous, seven-floor building on the handsome, manicured street. A plaque outside read: Hatton Garden Safe Deposit Ltd.

The rest of his crew was there, dressed as building workers: John Collins, also known as Kenny, 75; Daniel Jones, 60; and Terrence Perkins, 67. Mr. Reader wore a yellow hard hat and a fluorescent jacket with the word "Gas" on the back. His distinctive striped socks were later captured by surveillance cameras.

In a case that prosecutors have called the largest burglary ever in England, the four men have pleaded guilty to conspiring to steal up to $30 million in gold, jewelry and gems. Prosecutors say they used high-powered, diamond-tipped drills over the long Easter weekend to bore an 18-inch hole through a concrete wall in a basement vault at the safe deposit company and then made off with the loot.

Those four are now in prison awaiting sentencing, and may face 10 years behind bars. Four other men are standing trial on suspicion of involvement, and have denied the charges.

As details of the burglary have emerged, many have been left wondering how four aging and sometimes bungling robbers managed to break into a high-security vault in the center of London—protected by reinforced concrete, iron gates and a motion-triggered alarm system—and get away with loot-filled wheeled plastic garbage bins. Had they not violated one of the first laws in the criminal handbook and boasted about the caper, they might never have been caught.

"This offense was to be the largest burglary in English legal history," the prosecutor Philip Evans told Woolwich Crown Court. "These four ringleaders and organizers of this conspiracy, although senior in years, brought with them a great deal of experience."

With his lined face, baggy eyes and cunning, Mr. Reader, the gang's elder statesman, had a notable criminal record.

In 1983, after six armed men in balaclavas stole gold, cash and jewelry from a warehouse at Heathrow Airport in another celebrated heist, prosecutors say Mr. Reader teamed up with a Kent crime boss to help launder around $40 million in gold. He was sentenced in 1986 to nine years in prison for handling stolen bullion. Until recently, he was living in a sprawling mansion in Dartford.

His distinctive striped socks were later captured by surveillance cameras.

Mr. Perkins was sentenced to 22 years in jail for his involvement in another notorious 1983 robbery in which a gang with sawed-off shotguns stole about $7.5 million in cash from the vaults at the London headquarters of Security Express, a security company.

At Hatton Garden, despite their expertise and the gang's extensive planning, not everything went according to plan.

On the evening of April 2, Mr. Reader and the rest of the gang were greeted at Hatton Garden Safe Deposit by a red-haired man known as "Basil" who, investigators say, apparently opened the fire escape door and let the others in. The man has never been identified and remains at large.

Several men got out of a white van and unloaded bags, tools and two garbage bins, taking them in on the fire escape and down the stairs, Mr. Evans told the jury. The men communicated by walkie-talkie.

Once inside the building, they disabled the elevator, left an "out of order" sign, sent the elevator to the second floor, and shimmied down the elevator shaft to the basement, busting through a metal barrier. They cut a telephone cable jutting out of an alarm box as well as electrical wires, disabling an iron gate protecting the vault.

Then they began the arduous task of drilling through the vault's wall, reinforced with concrete—a skill they had perfected by watching clips online. Shortly after 12:21 a.m. on April 3, Alok Bavishi, whose family owns the safety-deposit company, received a call that the intruder alarm had been triggered. He testified that his concerns were initially tempered by the fact that a previous alarm had been triggered by an insect.

Kelvin Stockwell, a security guard at the building, arrived nearly an hour later. After examining the front door and peering through the letterbox of the fire escape door, he told the jury he decided that the building was secure and left.

The police were also notified of the alarm, but no response was deemed necessary. Meanwhile, the thieves were in the basement, breaking into the vault. But the gang's luck proved short-lived. When they finally breached the wall against which the metal cabinet holding the safe-deposit boxes was standing, they were stopped because the cabinet was bolted to the ceiling and floor, and they could not dislodge it.

They left around 8 a.m., empty-handed. But they returned two days later, on Mr. Perkins's 67th birthday. On their second attempt, after a trip to the hardware store, the men managed to dislodge the cabinet, though Mr. Reader was not there to enjoy the moment, having apparently lost his nerve.

The men ransacked 73 safe deposit boxes, filling several bags and two large trash bins with jewels, gold, precious stones and cash. Prosecutors said the men struggled to carry the loot up the stairs to a fire escape. Mr. Collins, the lookout, was waiting nearby in the van. At 6:40 a.m. they sped away.

Another two days went by before the theft was discovered. Pictures of the gaping holes drilled through the wall were soon splashed in Britain's papers. Angry safe-deposit box owners, some of them uninsured, lashed out at the police and at the safety-deposit company for their perceived incompetence.

Mirza Baig, a jewelry dealer, said he had lost everything. "I don't have a penny's worth of stones left with me because they were all in the safe deposit—the safest place you can imagine," he told ITV News.

For several days the men reveled in the heist, but the police were closing in. The men had been identified from hours of surveillance footage, and electronic bugs, which had been placed in two of their cars, picked up their boasts, in cockney rhyming slang.

"The biggest cash robbery in history," Mr. Jones can be heard crowing in recordings played in court, "that's what they are saying."

The men continued to meet at the Castle, a traditional pub that serves heaping plates of bangers and mash. The police filmed them with hidden cameras and used lip readers to figure out what they were saying.

After the robbery, they argued over how to split the proceeds and launder the jewels, prosecutors say. Mr. Perkins was overheard saying he planned to melt down some of his gold. "That could be my pension," he said.

The men stashed some of the gold and jewels in their homes, behind baseboards and kitchen cabinets. On May 19, 45 days after the burglary, 200 police officers swept in as Mr. Jones and Mr. Collins were transferring some of the jewels to the home of Mr. Perkins's daughter. The police raided 12 addresses in North London and arrested seven suspects.

At Mr. Reader's house, the police discovered a diamond tester and a book on the diamond underworld. At the home of Mr. Perkins's daughter, they found vast quantities of sapphires and diamonds, and a brown leather bag stuffed with watches. Heat-resistant porcelain pots and tongs used for smelting gold were discovered hidden in a washing machine.

After his arrest, Mr. Jones agreed to show prosecutors where he had hidden one bag of loot, under the gravestone of a relative.

Mr. Jones wrote to a Sky News reporter from his jail cell, saying he had notified the police of the stash to "make amends to my loved ones and show I'm trying to change," and added, "It seems a bit late in my life, but I'm trying."

The police subsequently discovered that he had failed to mention a much larger haul from the Hatton Garden burglary at the same cemetery.

Hatton Safe Deposit has been forced into liquidation, and the building's new owner said he was considering turning the vault into a museum devoted to the heist.

The police have struggled to identify thousands of identical-looking chains and gems that have been recovered. Many millions of pounds worth of the loot still has not been found, prosecutors say, and at least some had probably been melted down, laundered or hidden before the arrests.

—December 13, 2015

CHAPTER 3

KIDNAPPINGS

"Dear Sir!

Have 50000$ redy 25000$ in
20$ bills 15000$ in 10$ bills and
10000$ in 5$ bills After 2-4 days
we will inform you were to deliver
the Mony."

—Misspelled text of a Lindbergh baby ransom note

NO ONE HOLDS A HERMIT HOSTAGE. Kidnappers act on the presumption that the person they take is loved, or at least valued, and that the horror of their loss will compel others to pay heavily, with money or action, for their return. Anyone who has ever briefly lost a child at the park understands the anguish that kidnappers inflicted on Charles Lindbergh and the mother of Jaycee Dugard. But just a bit of it.

OPPOSITE: Charles A. Lindbergh, center, leaves a Bronx courtroom after telling a grand jury his story of the payment of a $50,000 ransom for his son, 1934.

FRANKS SLAYERS GET LIFE IMPRISONMENT; YOUTH AVERTS NOOSE

Precisely 11 days after they had kidnapped and murdered 14-year-old Robert Franks, Nathan F. Leopold Jr. and Richard A. Loeb stood at the bar of justice today and heard with audible sighs of relief the sentence of life imprisonment passed on them by Chief Justice John R. Caverly of the Criminal Court of Cook County. In the sentence, in addition to the life term for murder, 99 years in prison was imposed for the kidnapping for ransom of the Franks boy prior to his slaying.

Justice Caverly made it plain that life imprisonment meant the full term of the natural life of the two boys and expressed the hope that any future attempt to obtain a commutation of sentence through the medium of the parole board would be futile.

Justice Caverly could find "no mitigating circumstances" in the kidnapping and murder of a 14-year-old boy, he said, as he pronounced the fate of the two wealthy, college-trained youths, but "in accordance with the progress of criminal law all over the world" and "the dictates of enlightened humanity," he saved them from death on the gallows.

Defendants Sigh Their Relief

There was a sigh of relief from the defendants' side of the courtroom when they heard "prison for life." Loeb gulped uneasily. Leopold smiled. Mr. Darrow, who, according to his own figures, has saved 102 persons from hanging, shed a few tears.

Guards stood at Justice Caverly's side as he pronounced the sentence. Other guards watched the prisoners and crowd inside the room and did sentry duty at the doors and hallways. They formed a cordon all about the building and jail, lest some of the hundreds of "cranks" who have written threatening letters to Justice Caverly try to do violence.

As soon as the two youths, happy and smiling, had been led back to their cells, the patrols outside the jail were doubled and Sheriff Hoffman made plans to hurry his prisoners to Joliet at 8 a.m. tomorrow to begin their double life terms.

Justice Caverly took his seat promptly at the appointed hour, carrying a bundle of papers, his decision and copies of it.

"Richard A. Loeb and Nathan P. Leopold Jr.," the clerk called. In from the hidden lockup outside the court room came the two boys, with guards before and behind them. They were white as ghosts, but they managed to smile to members of their families and their lawyers.

The justice settled his steel-rimmed glasses down toward the end of his nose and began to read slowly in a calm voice. The clicking of a battery of cameras interrupted him, but left him unruffled.

"When you are through," he said to the photographers, "I will go on."

White as They Hear Judge

The white faces of the two youths grew whiter. Nathan Leopold Sr., seated back of his son, gripped the arm of his bench. Jacob Loeb, Richard's uncle, and Allan Loeb, his brother, leaned forward.

The words that reached their ears told them that the court had found no mitigating circumstances in the crime. The defendants had pleaded guilty, but not in the usual way. There had been no agreement with the state's attorney, as is customary, and the state's labor had not been lessened by the plea. The fact that the murderers had admitted their guilt could not be considered a circumstance in their favor.

"It's hanging," one spectator whispered to another. The elder Leopold's face was like a death mask.

Justice Caverly went on. There was no evidence of insanity.

Young Leopold shifted his feet as the court paused. Loeb stared sullenly at the base of the judicial dais. There were no mitigating circumstances in all the ghastly record, they heard. But suddenly there was a change in the tenor of the words. Given by law the responsibility of fixing punishment, he was determined to be merciful, said the arbiter of their fate.

Leopold's head jerked upward a trifle.

"This determination," the justice continued, "appears to be in accordance with the progress of criminal law all over the world and with the dictates of enlightened, humanity. More than that, it seems to be in accordance, with the precedents hitherto observed in this state."

The tense crowd breathed faster.

"In the history of Illinois, only two minors have been put to death by legal process—to which number the court does not feel inclined to make an addition," was the sentence that ended all doubt.

There was a pause. Color returned in a rush to the elder Leopold's drawn face. Jacob Loeb sat up a little straighter. It was to be life, then. The next words confirmed the hope.

"Life imprisonment," said the justice, "may not at the moment strike the public imagination as forcibly as would death by hanging, but to the offenders, particularly of the type

Nathan Leopold (left) and Richard Loeb (right) with their defense attorney, Clarence Darrow, 1924.

they are, the prolonged suffering of years of confinement may well be the severer form of retribution and expiation."

There was a sudden shuffling of feet as messengers raced to their wires with the news. Before it had died down the court had ended. Life imprisonment for murder, 99 years for kidnapping—concurrent sentences, likely to keep Loeb and Leopold inside the walls of Joliet until they are old men, if not until they die.

The boys relaxed, smiled and reached over to shake the hands of their lawyers.

The justice rose and the spectators relaxed their taut attention, while eager men and women pressed forward with congratulations. But Loeb and Leopold had no time to receive them. Their guards pushed them through the crowd, and with waves of their hands they were gone.

More than 5,000 persons packed the streets around the criminal court building while sentence was being pronounced.

When the clock on a nearby building had passed 9:30, the hour when Judge Caverly was to go to the bench, half of those in the street took their watches in their hands. Ten minutes passed. Then a deputy sheriff popped out of the door and passed the word to the policemen guarding the entrance. A motorcycle policeman cupped his hands and shouted to a friend across the street:

"Rest o' natural life."

"Yeah, it's life," someone shouted down the line, and in a twinkling the news had gone around the block.

The crowd dispersed as quietly as it had gathered.

Leopold and Loeb will sleep in the county jail for the last time tonight. Tomorrow morning they will be conveyed to the penitentiary at Joliet.

"Go out," said Leopold, as soon as he and Loeb were returned to their jail cells, "and order us a big meal. Get us two steaks—that thick!" And he measured off a liberal three inches with a thumb and forefinger.

"Yes," said Loeb, "And be sure they are smothered in onions. And bring every side dish that you can find. This may be our last good meal."

"And," added Leopold, "bring chocolate éclairs for dessert."

Statements of Counsel and Parents

State's attorney Crowe issued the following statement after the sentence was announced:

"When the state's attorney arrested the defendants he solved what was then a mystery, by the thoroughness of his preparation compelled the defendants to plead guilty, presented a mountain of evidence to the court and made his arguments. His duty was fully performed.

"He is in no measure responsible for the decision of the court. The responsibility for that decision rests with the judge alone. Like all other law-abiding citizens, when the court presents his decision I must be content with it, because his decision in this case is final. While I do not intend and have no desire to criticize the decision of the court, I still believe the death penalty is the only penalty feared by murderers.

"Fathers and mothers in Cook County may rest assured that as long as I remain state's attorney I will always do everything within my power to enforce the law honestly, fearlessly and vigorously without regard to the status of the criminals."

"It was all we could have asked for," said Clarence Darrow of the defense counsel. "There will be no appeal."

"I do not regard it as a victory, except a victory for Justice," said Benjamin Bachrach, also of the defense.

Jacob M. Loeb, uncle of Richard A. Loeb, issued the following statement: "On behalf of the Leopold and Loeb families there is but little to say. We have been spared the extreme penalty. What have these families to look forward to?

"Nathan P. Leopold Sr. is 64 years old. He has lived in Chicago practically his entire life, coming here from Michigan as a boy. He has been an exemplary citizen. His youngest boy was his special pride. He justly believed that this boy was a genius, a most brilliant student and a loving son. He honored him with his own name. He hoped that this boy of 19 would make his mark in the world, would be a comfort and solace in his old age and accomplish tasks for the benefit of humanity. Now Mr. Leopold is crushed in spirit in his declining years.

"Albert Loeb, my brother, has spent his entire life of 56 years in the city of Chicago. He came from the ranks; he worked his way through college. He became a lawyer of repute; then a great businessman. He was always interested in every forward movement for the communal welfare. His one hobby has always been his wife and children. He considered 'Dickie,' the third boy, particularly talented. This son entered the University of Michigan at 14 and he was the youngest graduate of that college. He was always a most affectionate and loving son, never known in his home life to be disobedient but was always thoughtful and considerate of his parents and the members of the family until this terrible tragedy overtook them. It is pitiful that on account of illness, at a time like this, the father and mother are unable to be at the side of their son.

"Again I say what have these two families, whose names have stood for everything that was good and reputable in the community, to look forward to? Their unfortunate boys, 19 years of age, must spend the rest of their lives in the penitentiary. What is there in the future but grief and sorrow, darkness and despair?"

—September 11, 1924

NOTE: *The two suspects in the kidnapping and murder were said to be intellectuals, fascinated with the thought of committing the perfect crime. A fellow prisoner stabbed Loeb to death in the shower in 1936. After receiving parole in 1958, Leopold moved to Puerto Rico, where he died of a heart ailment in 1971.*

LINDBERGH BABY KIDNAPPED FROM HOME OF PARENTS ON FARM NEAR PRINCETON; TAKEN FROM HIS CRIB; WIDE SEARCH ON

Charles Augustus Lindbergh Jr., 20-month-old son of Colonel and Mrs. Charles A. Lindbergh, was kidnapped between 8:30 and 10 o'clock last night from his crib in the nursery on the second floor of his parents' home at Hopewell, near Princeton, N.J.

Apparently the kidnapping was carried out either while Colonel and Mrs. Lindbergh were at dinner, or soon afterward. The baby's nurse, Miss Betty Gow, visited the nursery about 8:30 and found everything in order. When she returned at 10 o'clock, however, the crib was empty.

Muddy footprints that trailed across the floor from the crib to an open window bore mute testimony as to how the baby had disappeared. Miss Gow dashed downstairs. "The baby's been kidnapped!" she shouted. Colonel Lindbergh raced to the nursery, followed by his wife. Mrs. Lindbergh recalled that earlier in the day she had tried to fasten a screen on the window that had been opened and had been unable to do so.

Portrait of Charles A. Lindbergh Jr., 1931, on his first birthday.

Colonel Lindbergh telephoned Chief of Police Charles Williamson at Hopewell. Williamson drove to the house accompanied by another officer. Outside the door they met the colonel. He wore an old black leather jacket such as he frequently wears on his flights.

Footprints under Window

Briefly he told Williamson what had occurred. The chief telephoned first to State Police Headquarters at Trenton. Then he, his fellow officer and the colonel began searching the grounds. Beneath the nursery window were marks where a ladder had stood and the footprints of one person. There were no shoe prints. The kidnapper, apparently, had worn socks or moccasins.

Sixty feet away, at the edge of a wood, the colonel and Chief Williamson found a makeshift ladder. Its rungs were caked with mud. Colonel Lindbergh thought it might have been left there by the builders while the house was being constructed during his flight to the Orient last summer with Mrs. Lindbergh.

The searchers had no difficulty in following the footprints across the muddy ground. A second set of smaller tracks joined them near the edge of the woods. The two officers thought they might be those of a woman.

The search was interrupted by the arrival of state troopers sent from the barracks at Lambertville. The tracks were followed to the main highway, half a mile from the house, where they disappeared. The kidnappers evidently had entered an automobile at that point.

Lindbergh Aids Search

Carrying a flashlight, Colonel Lindbergh stayed with the searching party until after midnight. Once or twice he returned to the house, but he declined to discuss the kidnapping with newspapermen. Instead, he referred them to Major Schoeffel of the state police, who told the story in detail.

"I hope you boys will excuse me," Colonel Lindbergh explained to the reporters, "but I would rather the state solice answered all questions. I am sure you understand how I feel." Mrs. Lindbergh, though greatly shocked by the baby's disappearance, was reported to be bearing up as well as could be expected.

Within a few minutes after word of the kidnapping reached state police headquarters at Trenton, all available troopers were ordered out to search automobiles along the highways and an alarm was flashed over the police teletype system in New Jersey and adjacent states.

When news got abroad that the Lindbergh baby had been kidnapped, George Jennings, a laborer, drove to police headquarters in Princeton and told the police how two men in a dark sedan bearing a New York license had stopped him in Washington Road, Princeton, yesterday afternoon and inquired the way to the Lindbergh home. An alarm for the car was sent out over the teletype.

When word reached New York, Police Commissioner Mulrooney, who was home in bed, was notified. He hurried to police headquarters to take personal charge of the hunt here. He ordered special guards posted at once at the entrance to the Holland Tube and the George Washington Memorial Bridge, as well as at all ferry terminals. He also mustered all available police department cars and sent them out with orders to search automobiles whose occupants looked suspicious.

Meanwhile the Lindberghs had notified Mrs. Dwight W. Morrow, mother of Mrs. Lindbergh, at her home in Englewood, N.J., and Mrs. Evangeline L. Lindbergh, Colonel Lindbergh's mother, at her home in Grosse Pointe, a suburb of Detroit.

Long after last midnight the Lindbergh home at Hopewell was ablaze with lights, while Colonel Lindbergh was kept busy discussing the kidnapping with officials of the state and county police. A trooper stood guard at the entrance of the lane that leads back from the highway to the house. Two more troopers guarded the entrance to the house, while at least a score of others were scattered over the vicinity hunting clues.

Report of a Ransom Note

The ladder was being carefully examined for fingerprints and the grounds searched for anything that might indicate the identity of the kidnappers. It was reported that a note demanding ransom had been left by the kidnappers in the nursery, but state police denied knowledge of it.

Colonel Lindbergh agreed with the police that the persons responsible for the kidnapping had been well acquainted with the layout of the house. Neither he nor Mrs. Lindbergh nor any other of the occupants of the house had heard any sounds of prowlers, he said.

Major Schoffel announced that he would obtain from the contractor who built the Lindbergh home a list of every man employed there during the building, and that all of these men would be questioned today by police.

—March 2, 1932

NOTE: *The Lindbergh family paid a $50,000 ransom for the return of the infant, an effort that proved futile. In May 1932, a truck driver discovered the baby's body in a wooded area near the family home. Police traced the bills used in the ransom to Bruno Hauptmann, a German immigrant who lived in the Bronx. Hauptmann was charged with murder and convicted in February 1935. He continued to profess his innocence until his execution in April 1936.*

BRONFMAN'S SON RESCUED IN CITY AFTER A PAYMENT OF $2.3 MILLION; MONEY RECOVERED, 2 SUSPECTS HELD

By PETER KIHSS

Samuel Bronfman 2d, the 21-year-old heir to the Seagram liquor fortune, was rescued at 4 a.m. yesterday on the ninth day of his kidnapping. He was freed without violence by 40 to 60 FBI agents and New York City policemen who surprised a captor in an apartment in the Flatbush section of Brooklyn.

Two men were arrested during the rescue and charged with extortion by use of the mails.

They were identified as Mel Patrick Lynch, 37, a city fireman, of East 19th Street, Brooklyn, where the victim was being held, and Dominic Byrne, 53, operator of a limousine service, of Foster Avenue, who led authorities to the Lynch apartment nearby.

Ransom Recovered

A ransom of $2.3 million, paid 25 hours earlier by his father, Edgar, was recovered by the federal agents yesterday afternoon from under a bed in an unoccupied apartment in the neighborhood.

The rescuers reported they had found young Mr. Bronfman sitting on a couch in Mr. Lynch's apartment, his hands bound in front of him, adhesive tape over his mouth and eyes. An agent removed the tape.

"Thank God," the kidnap victim said. "I want to call my father," he went on. When he got his father on the telephone, these were his words: "Dad, I'm all right. Thanks for everything, Dad."

Suspect Unarmed

Mr. Lynch had been sitting down, according to the police, but immediately stood and put his hands against the wall. He was unarmed. "What's going on?" he demanded. He was immediately handcuffed.

Mr. Byrne told the police and the FBI that he and Mr. Lynch had been dragooned into the kidnapping by two strange men. The strangers, he said, hired a Byrne limousine, and then, by gunpoint, forced Mr. Byrne to help abduct Mr. Bronfman from his home in Purchase, N.Y., in Westchester County, and Mr. Lynch to detain the victim in the Brooklyn apartment.

But after the ransom recovery, J. Wallace LaPrade, head of the FBI's New York office, said, "As far as we are concerned, all the individuals known to be involved have been arrested." He denied that any other suspect was being sought.

The original FBI announcement on the case Sunday night, Aug. 9, said that Samuel Bronfman had called his father to report a kidnapping by three men. There were reports yesterday that when he was interviewed by agents after the rescue, he had repeated this impression of having been abducted by three men.

Mr. LaPrade said he knew of no reason why Mr. Bronfman had been singled out for the kidnapping. But as to the kidnappers' plans for the huge ransom, a sum of money they assertedly reduced in half during negotiations, he said simply, "Spend it." Brooklyn neighbors described both suspects as hard workers and religious.

Mr. Lynch worked shifts as a fireman at Ladder Company 172 in Bensonhurst on Thursday and Friday. Mr. Byrne, who owned a liquor store below his apartment before going into the limousine business, was reported to have walked his dog every day last week, as usual.

Father-Son Reunion

Samuel Bronfman was rushed to the home of his father on Fifth Avenue by Mr. LaPrade, who had led the entry into the Brooklyn hideaway. The young man was spirited into a side entrance on East 77th Street, while Jonathan Rinehart, a family spokesman, was announcing the rescue at 4:28 a.m. outside the Fifth Avenue entrance.

Mr. Rinehart, a public relations consultant, said that the young man was "fine" and that "the family is, of course, just absolutely delighted to have him home."

Up at the Edgar Bronfman estate in Yorktown Heights, N.Y., a telephone call from Mr. Rinehart woke up Samuel Bronfman's closest friend, Peter Kaufman.

"I told him we had done a lot of wild things, but never a kidnapping,"

"I almost went through the ceiling," Mr. Kaufman recalled later. José Luís, the family butler, broke out a bottle of champagne, and Samuel's mother, the former Ann Margaret Loeb, who is divorced from his father, joined the celebration.

Then Samuel himself called Mr. Kaufman. "I told him we had done a lot of wild things, but never a kidnapping," Mr. Kaufman related. "I told him he wasn't worth $4.5 million"—the originally reported ransom sum.

Actually, Mr. LaPrade, the FBI director, said that the first ransom demand was for $4.6 million and this had been reduced, on the initiative of the kidnappers, to $2.3 million.

Victim Threatened

The FBI director said that Mr. Bronfman had been held under "exhausting, trying conditions, blindfolded and bound." Later he said there were "threats to his life throughout."

Other law-enforcement sources said that Mr. Bronfman had been tied to the couch in the Lynch apartment throughout his abduction, with his mouth taped and his eyes blindfolded. He was fed ham sandwiches and cola drinks, with an occasional hamburger.

Eventually the $2.3 million ransom was paid. It was delivered by Edgar Bronfman, who, Mr. LaPrade said, was alone at the time. The money, in brown paper bags stuffed inside two plastic garbage bags, was passed at 3 a.m. Saturday from "car to car," at an undisclosed site in Queens..

Funds from Seagram

The money was said to have been drawn from bank accounts of the Seagram Company, Ltd., the worldwide company with liquor, real-estate and oil and gas interests controlled by the Bronfman family.

The father returned to his Fifth Avenue home at 3:40 a.m., reporting to agents that "Sammy's OK." Hours went by.

Mr. LaPrade said that "the FBI maintained a waiting posture in the hope that the abductors would make good their promise to release Samuel Bronfman several hours after the demands were met."

"Inasmuch as the abductors failed to release their hostage, it became necessary to aggressively pursue investigate leads," Mr. LaPrade went on.

Det. Thomas Cerbone of the 70th Precinct said city detectives had been told "the money was passed in Lynch's car." Mr. LaPrade declined to say more than that "the ransom was given to one of the two suspects."

Police Get a Note

Det. Cerbone and a partner, James E. Schry, entered the case when Sgt. Frank Wueger, of the precinct, assigned them to check a note sent after Saturday midnight to the station-house by Mr. Byrne, who later was seized as a suspect.

Mr. Byrne's note, the officers related later, said he knew where the kidnap victim was. When Detectives Cerbone and Schry, joined by Sergeant Wueger, went to his apartment, they found FBI agents in an unmarked car parked across the street. The result, Mr. LaPrade and Police Commissioner Michael J. Codd reported, was that top officials of the federal and city forces pooled their information, and the move into Mr. Lynch's apartment and rescue was a joint operation.

The two suspects were questioned during the day at FBI headquarters, and then transferred to the Federal House of Detention. Today they are to be arraigned before a U.S. magistrate. Under Title 18, Section 876, of the U.S. Code, could involve, in the event of conviction, sentences of up to 20 years' imprisonment and a $5,000 fine. The federal government's so-called Lindbergh anti-kidnapping law applies only to kidnappings that involve the crossing of state lines. The federal charges in the Bronfman case involve the use of the mails to extort.

Every state has its own laws against kidnapping. New York State's law makes the crime a Class A felony, with a minimum penalty of 25 years to life imprisonment.

—August 8, 1975

NOTE: *At trial in 1976, lawyers for Lynch and Byrne argued that Bronfman, their abductee, had been the mastermind of the case, an assertion that Samuel Bronfman rejected. The pair was never convicted of kidnapping charges, only extortion.*

MISS HEARST IS CONVICTED ON BANK ROBBERY CHARGES

By WALLACE TURNER

Patricia Campbell Hearst was convicted of armed robbery today by a jury that refused to believe her story that she was an innocent victim forced into crime by the group of revolutionaries that had kidnapped her 10 weeks before.

Her lawyers said that they would appeal as soon as sentence is passed and judgment entered on April 19. The prosecutor called the verdict "entirely proper." The judge said the evidence supported it.

Miss Hearst's parents, Randolph A. and Catherine Hearst, made no substantive comment before private cars hustled them away from the federal courthouse.

Miss Hearst seemed to shrink and her pale face became ashen as the verdict was read. Her parents sat 10 feet away. She did not look at them.

Family's Reaction

Mrs. Hearst, who left the court in tears yesterday, dropped her gaze to the floor. Mr. Hearst stared into space. Their 20-year-old daughter, Anne, seated beside them, broke into tears. Two other sisters, Vickie and Mrs. Virginia Bosworth, were in court. A fourth, Catherine, was not present.

There were two counts to the indictment, and Miss Hearst was convicted on both, with the verdict so signed by the foreman, William Wright, a 55-year-old retired army colonel from Mill Valley. The seven woman and five men of the jury had deliberated for 12 hours.

The first count alleged that Miss Hearst had taken part in the armed robbery of the Sunset branch of the Hibernia Bank at about 9 a.m. on April 15, 1974. The second count, of which she would automatically have been acquitted had she not been convicted on the first, alleged the use of a firearm to commit a felony.

Maximum Sentences

Armed bank robbery involves a maximum sentence of 25 years in prison; the maximum term for the firearms charge is 10 years. A year ago, Federal District Judge Oliver J.

Carter, who presided at Miss Hearst's trial and will determine her punishment, sentenced a young woman in a similar case to 30 months in prison.

Miss Hearst still faces multiple felony charges in Los Angeles, ranging from kidnapping to auto theft. They grew out of events of May 16 and 17, 1974, when she emptied an automatic carbine into a street and storefront to enable William and Emily Harris, members of the self-styled Symbionese Liberation Army, which had kidnapped her on Feb. 4, 1974, to escape capture.

F. Lee Bailey, the chief defense attorney, asked if there was a possibility that Miss Hearst might be freed on bail before her trial in Los Angeles, replied: "Legally, it's possible. I'm not sure that we'll try."

He said the 22-year-old Miss Hearst was "disappointed," but that she "sort of half expected it, I guess, to the extent that a kid that age would have no prior trial experience." He added: "At least she's alive, and we're grateful for that."

J. Albert Johnson, Mr. Bailey's partner, who has spent many hours with Miss Hearst in the last six months, said: "She's just as beaten as the rest of us. She always thought the cards were stacked against her from the beginning. She said a lot of times, 'No, they'll never let me off.'"

Verdict Defended

James L. Browning Jr., the U.S. Attorney who prosecuted Miss Hearst, said the verdict "bears out what most Americans believe, that the American system of justice works very well."

Mr. Browning described himself as sympathetic to her family, and said, "Patricia Hearst can straighten out her life, and I hope she will. She got caught up in the rhetoric and voluntarily joined the SLA."

> *She got caught up in the rhetoric and voluntarily joined the SLA*

Mr. Browning said the crucial witnesses, in his estimation, were Zigurd Berzin, who said he saw Miss Hearst scrambling to pick up ammunition in front of the bank, and Dr. Joel Fort, a medical expert who testified for the government and whom Mr. Bailey tried to destroy in a bitter attack that portrayed him as a supplier of drug prescriptions to the late Lenny Bruce, the comedian.

Pressed to predict the sentence Miss Hearst would receive, Mr. Browning said the maximum could be 35 years and the minimum could be probation, with no jail time. "A lot will depend on the probation report," he said. Miss Hearst knows a great deal about others whom the government wants to prosecute—among them, those who helped her to hide as a fugitive for more than a year. Mr. Bailey said he believed the jury had been influenced by Miss Hearst's resort to the Fifth Amendment protection against self-incrimination when she testified. He also said he felt that some of the evidence about the shooting in Los Angeles and certain documents submitted against her had played a major role in the jury's verdict.

Role in Verdict

Mr. Bailey said he believed that the so-called "Tanya interview," a document that was partly in Miss Hearst's handwriting, had hurt the defense. Miss Hearst said she wrote the material under threats and the orders of the Harrises, the only survivors of the band of eight revolutionaries who had kidnapped her.

Miss Hearst's 39-day trial served to put some flesh on the bare bones of the sensational story of her kidnapping, alleged conversion to the doctrines of the self-styled Symbionese Liberation Army and life underground for 19 months as captive and then as fugitive.

Miss Hearst testified in her own defense. At first, it appeared that she was ready to tell all, to incriminate others without exception. It was not to be that way.

On Feb. 23, she took the Fifth Amendment 42 times to avoid being required to incriminate herself. Fundamentally, she was refusing to talk about anything that happened to her in the year from September 1974, when Jack Scott, the sports radical, dropped her off in Las Vegas, Nev., after an auto trip across country from Pennsylvania, to Sept. 18, 1975, when an FBI agent and a San Francisco policeman burst into her apartment on Morse Street here to arrest her and Wendy Yoshimura, another fugitive, who lived there with her and Steven Soliah, who now is on trial for bank robbery in Sacramento.

To understand the convolutions of the Patricia Hearst story, it is best to go back to the point where she became a figure for American folklore, the night that William Randolph Hearst's granddaughter was dragged in her nightclothes, screaming, to be held for ransom by a group of protest-maddened young people led by a half-crazed escaped convict.

The escaped convict, Donald DeFreeze, a black, had nothing in common with the others. All the others were white, the children of middle-class America, but also children of the Vietnam War, the draft that fed the war and the turmoil that gripped the nation in that time.

Mr. Harris was a Vietnam veteran. William Lawton Wolfe, son of a Pennsylvania doctor, was too young for that, but he had cut his teeth on organizing a black cultural association that the radicals sought to use to recruit a following among black convicts in the prisons they were allowed to visit.

Nancy Ling Perry had been a high school cheerleader and a Barry Goldwater backer. She became a drug user, a dealer at topless blackjack and a political misfit in the intellectual jungles around San Francisco Bay. Angela Atwood had been married, but her husband left. Emily Harris had written her parents that she was involved in something new in sexual relationships. There was "this wonderful black man" and her husband understood, she wrote.

Camilla Hall, a minister's daughter, had as her homosexual lover the militant lesbian, Patricia Soltysik, who called herself Mizmoon.

It was those eight who planned and brought off the successful abduction of Miss Hearst at about 9 p.m. on Feb. 4. 1974.

Miss Hearst had been living with her fiancé, Steven Weed, a 26-year-old onetime radical at Princeton University.

The prosecution psychiatrists sought to portray Miss Hearst as a young woman in the throes of disenchantment with her fiancé, willing to end their relationship, but not able at the time of the kidnapping to work out a way to do that gracefully.

The prosecution's medical and mental experts leaned heavily on this view of Miss Hearst's unhappiness, for it was a strong element of their assertion that Miss Hearst was "a rebel seeking a cause."

According to trial testimony, the kidnapping began when a young woman knocked at the door to ask to use the phone. Miss Hearst said that before she could tell Mr. Weed that she did not want him to open the door he opened it, and in burst the woman and two men. She said that one was Mr. DeFreeze.

Miss Hearst's Story

The other man, she said, was William Harris, and since he is alive and could be prosecuted, this aroused the expectation that Miss Hearst might be prepared to tell all.

Miss Hearst said she had been thrown into the trunk of a car, after being bound and gagged, driven a short way and thrown onto the floor of another car. She was driven for an hour or more in the second car, she said, and then led, blindfolded, into a house and put into a closet.

She said she stayed in there for weeks, and it was eventually estimated that she was in this closet in a little house in Daly City, a suburb, for three and a half weeks.

She told of being "interrogated" by Mr. DeFreeze and of making the early tape recordings that her captors used to tell her parents and the world that she was alive. The recordings were played to the jury, and the voices of Mr. DeFreeze and the others echoed through the oak-paneled courtroom.

The kidnapping soon became an attempt to make the Hearst family give millions of dollars worth of food to the poor. This became the "People in Need" program. In the trial it was disclosed that the group lived until late March in Daly City and then moved to another hideout on Golden Gate Avenue in San Francisco.

The government accepted Miss Hearst's story of being held in the closet at Daly City, although one of the government medical witnesses, Dr. Joel Fort, seemed to try to make it sound like a pleasant place to be. However, the government did not accept her statement of being held similarly in a tiny closet—one foot eight inches wide; five feet five inches long—in the Golden Gate apartment.

By the time of the move there, the government contended, Miss Hearst was already a member of the SLA.

Some tape recordings were made at the Golden Gate apartment, including one on April 1 in which Miss Hearst's voice announced to the world that although offered the door to freedom, she had decided to "stay and fight."

She testified that this was in fact a script written for her to read by Mrs. Atwood.

Miss Hearst's first foray outside the apartment was to the bank robbery. The bank guard, Eldon Shea, testified that Miss Hearst had told him to get on the floor and threatened to blow his head off if he did not.

On cross-examination, Mr. Bailey managed to becloud Mr. Shea's testimony. But the defense lawyer could not shake the identification made by a government witness, Zigurd Berzins, operator of a radio-equipment store across the street.

Mr. Berzins said he went into the bank that morning and saw a woman kneeling, a carbine projecting from beneath her coat. She picked up two ammunition clips for the carbine and some cartridges that had spilled, he said. He did not see her face, he said, but in looking at a crude, jerky film the government produced from the bank surveillance camera negatives, he pointed to the figure of Miss Hearst as the woman he saw.

"I don't care if it's Patricia Hearst or who it is," he said, "that's the woman I saw." This was strong medicine for the prosecution, for Miss Hearst had said in her testimony that she had not known if her gun was loaded.

The defense, including Miss Hearst's own statements, asserted that she had been told before the robbery that she would be covered by a gun of others in the group and "would be shot on the spot" if she did anything to frustrate the robbery.

In a photograph released by the Symbionese Liberation Army (SLA), Patty Hearst poses with a machine gun in front of a poster with the SLA seven-headed cobra emblem, 1974.

A few days later, she said, Mrs. Atwood wrote another script for her to read into the tape recorder. This one denied that Miss Hearst had been brainwashed or coerced, and contended that she was a willing participant in the bank robbery.

Shortly after that, Miss Hearst said, the group moved to another apartment, and then soon left for Los Angeles, about May 1, 1974. They drove down in three Volkswagen vans, she said, and lived first in a motel, then in a small empty house. On May 16, 1974, Miss Hearst went with Mr. and Mrs. Harris to a sporting goods store in Inglewood. Mr. Harris was accused by a clerk of shoplifting and a struggle ensued.

Miss Hearst, across the street in a parking lot, saw the Harrises struggling with the clerks and picked up Mr. Harris's M-1, which had been altered to make it automatic. She said she fired it, and the recoil knocked it out of her hand. She picked it up again and emptied it into the street. Then she picked up her own carbine and fired two shots from it.

The government told the jury that she did this because she had become a full-fledged member of the S.L.A. and was freeing her comrades. Her defense urged that she had acted because she had been so thoroughly indoctrinated and intimidated that the reaction was automatic.

She said that Mr. Scott and his parents, Mr. and Mrs. John Scott of Las Vegas, drove her east in the summer of 1974.

The Scotts took her to an apartment in New York City, she said, and then to a farmhouse in Pennsylvania, then to another farmhouse in upstate New York. It was in that period that she met Miss Yoshimura, she said.

Mr. Scott and she drove alone back to Las Vegas, where he left her. And that was where her story faded behind a constant response of Fifth Amendment claims.

But from other evidence in the trial, it is plain that Miss Hearst lived for a time in Sacramento.

There was a typed list that had Miss Hearst's fingerprints on it. It was headed "bakery" but really was plainly a detailed plan of the steps to take to rob a bank.

This and many other documents were put into evidence after being taken either from the Morse Street house where Miss Hearst lived with Mr. Soliah and Miss Yoshimura, or from the Precita Street flat where the Harrises lived.

One of these was the so-called Tania interview, which contained many things damaging to Miss Hearst, some of them written in her own hand. She testified that this was the product of the Harrises' desire to write a book and that her answers had been dictated by what they wanted her to say. If true, the "interview" described how Miss Hearst, the kidnapping victim, became Tania, the SLA member and bank robber.

—*March 21, 1976*

NOTE: *Hearst was sentenced to seven years in prison for her role in the bank robbery. She had served about 22 months when President Jimmy Carter granted her executive clemency in January 1979. President Bill Clinton pardoned Hearst in one of his final acts in office in 2001. Hearst married and had two daughters with her bodyguard, Bernard Shaw, who died in 2013. She has published a memoir and a novel and is active in the show-dog world.*

AGONY LINGERS, 20 YEARS AFTER THE MORO KILLING

By ALESSANDRA STANLEY

O n May 9, 1978, the bullet-riddled body of a former Italian prime minister, Aldo Moro, was found in the trunk of a car in central Rome, 55 days after he was kidnapped by members of the Red Brigades. Twenty years later, the anniversary is being marked with an orgy of national brooding.

"It has been 20 years, and still the deeper truth has not come out," said Marco Baliani, 47, an actor-playwright whose one-man show about the Moro case will be shown live on Italy's second largest state network on Saturday night. "How can we found a new republic if we cannot tell the truth to ourselves?"

Like the Kennedy assassination in the United States, the killing of so powerful a political figure remains an obsession for Italians, who view it both as a national trauma that marked the end of innocence for an entire postwar generation and as a dark conspiracy that remains veiled.

After hundreds of books, a parliamentary investigation that has dragged on for 10 years, five completed trials and a sixth that is about to begin, Italians are so bitterly consumed with the missing pieces that even on the 20th anniversary they overlook a larger irony that was unimaginable only five years ago.

Giulio Andreotti, 79, the wily, powerful politician who was prime minister seven times, including the period of the Moro crisis, is currently on trial in Perugia on charges that he conspired to order the killing of a journalist investigating, among other things, an alleged cover-up of the Moro case. Mr. Andreotti's refusal to negotiate with his colleague's captors is one of the more examined mysteries in the case.

All of the 23 Red Brigades terrorists who were convicted of collusion in Moro's slaying, and that of his five bodyguards, have either completed their sentences, or are in home-arrest or work-release programs. Mario Moretti, 52, the most senior Red Brigades leader, who admits he shot Moro, commutes four days a week from his Milan prison cell to a computer-programming job.

And Italian society, so torn in the hate-filled 1970s that the Andreotti government imposed special laws to combat terrorism and social unrest, is now united on at least one point: The full story behind the crime has not yet been told.

The only prominent dissenters are Mr. Andreotti and his closest aides, some former Red Brigades terrorists who still resist the notion that they were unwittingly manipulated

103

by sinister right-wing forces, and an American scholar, Richard Drake, who wrote a 1995 book concluding that there was no conspiracy.

The morning of his abduction on March 16, Aldo Moro, the leader of the Christian Democratic Party, was on his way to Parliament to usher in the first Italian government actively supported by the Communist Party—the so-called historic compromise that he had arranged.

Mr. Andreotti refused to make concessions to the terrorists to save Moro. The Italian police and secret services were unable to rescue him, and their stunning display of incompetence was quickly interpreted as deliberate. To this day, most Italians believe that Moro died because the powers-that-were had reasons not to keep him alive.

"On this anniversary I feel the need to in some way understand what really happened," said Alberto Franceschini, who, as one of the founders of the Red Brigades, should know. Arrested in 1974, he got out of prison in 1992 and now works at a foundation that distributes European grants to Italian unemployment programs.

Mr. Franceschini said that his comrades had definitely killed Moro, but that they might not have acted alone.

"I don't know whose hands were behind the scenes, Andreotti's or Nixon's," he said, "but I know we were part of a much larger game."

Italy has always been deeply attached to conspiracy theories. For the last 55 days, Italian radio, television, newspapers and magazines have overflowed with interviews, documentaries and debates about the Moro case. At least a dozen books about the case and its mysteries have been published this month. One reason for the media storm is that the generation of baby boomers who two decades ago wore Palestinian scarves, threw firebombs and for a while sided with the Red Brigades are now middle-aged network executives and publishers who shape public opinion.

"I didn't want to do another journalistic chronicle of the case," Mr. Baliani explained. "I wanted to tell the story thorough my own personal experience and that of so many people like me."

A counterculture actor at the time, he begins his tale by describing his feelings of "euphoria" over the news of Moro's kidnapping, and traces the bitter disenchantment and horror he felt at his death.

His televised tribute to the case on Saturday is viewed as so momentous that for the first time, the Italian Ministry of Culture permitted filming in one of Rome's most ancient ruins, the Forum of Augustus. The setting was irresistible.

"We wanted to make the connection to classical tragedy," Mr. Baliani said. "The death of Moro is the classic drama of our age—tragic, yet squalid."

—May 9, 1998

CAPTIVE'S OWN ACCOUNT OF 18 YEARS AS A HOSTAGE

By JESSE McKINLEY

A normal morning violently interrupted. Day after day of fear, sexual assault and loneliness. A desperate striving for normalcy in depraved surroundings.

Such are the scenes that emerge from testimony released this week in the case of Jaycee Dugard, who was kidnapped at age 11 and held against her will for 18 years.

On Thursday, Phillip and Nancy Garrido were sentenced to lengthy terms for Ms. Dugard's kidnapping, rape and imprisonment. After the sentencing, Judge Douglas C. Phimister of El Dorado County Superior Court released a redacted version of grand jury testimony Ms. Dugard gave in September, revealing new details about her captivity.

It offers a glimpse into the twisted thinking of Mr. Garrido, a convicted sex offender on parole for a 1976 attack on a Nevada casino worker, and his justification for his crime.

> *A desperate striving for normalcy in depraved surroundings.*

Ms. Dugard says, for instance, that she was raped shortly after she was kidnapped, and repeatedly thereafter during sessions that Mr. Garrido, who used methamphetamine, described as "runs." But Mr. Garrido told Ms. Dugard that she was simply "helping him" with a "sex problem."

He said "he got me so that he wouldn't have to do this to anybody else," Ms. Dugard recalls.

The accounts also include a chilling description of the morning of Ms. Dugard's kidnapping—June 10, 1991—near her home in South Lake Tahoe, Calif. Ms. Dugard said she had been walking to a bus stop when she was spotted by the Garridos, who had been hunting for a young girl.

"This car comes up behind me," Ms. Dugard said in her testimony. "I didn't feel it was weird at the time, but it kind of pulled in close," adding that she thought that the person was going to ask for directions.

Suddenly, however, Ms. Dugard said she felt a shock through her body—the Garridos used a stun gun—and she fell into a bush. It was then she saw Phillip Garrido for the first time.

"He gets out and I stumble back into the bushes," Ms. Dugard recalled.

She was thrown into the back seat and covered by a blanket. "And then I heard voices in the front, and the man said, 'I can't believe we got away with it,' and he started laughing," Ms. Dugard said.

Later, Ms. Dugard describes being taken to the Garridos' home outside Antioch, Calif., a Bay Area suburb, where she pleaded for her release.

"I just wanted to go home," she said. "I kept telling him that, you know, 'I don't know why you're doing this. If you're holding me for ransom, my family doesn't have a lot of money.'"

When the Garridos were arrested in August 2009, the authorities discovered a hidden backyard compound made up of ramshackle tents and sheds, including a sparsely furnished two-room building where Ms. Dugard said she was held.

Jaycee Dugard, c. 1990, before her kidnapping by Phillip and Nancy Garrido.

Ms. Dugard spent most of the first year alone—except during Mr. Garrido's sexual assaults—though Mr. Garrido gave her a cat to keep her company.

Ms. Dugard was eventually introduced to Ms. Garrido, who took over feeding their captive, and the Garridos moved into the shed themselves. "Basically, we were all sleeping in the same room," she said. "We watched TV together. I didn't feel as lonely anymore." They also gave her Barbie dolls to play with.

But there was also intimidation from Mr. Garrido, including attack dogs and threats to use the stun gun.

"He would turn it on and say something like, you know, 'You don't want it to happen again. You should be good.'" In 1993, Mr. Garrido returned to prison for a short time for a parole violation, a period during which Ms. Dugard remembers asking Ms. Garrido where he was. She said "he was on this island for a little vacation," Ms. Dugard said. "And he came back with an ankle bracelet."

Ms. Dugard was glad not to suffer any more sexual attacks during that period, and the rapes were less frequent after Ms. Dugard got pregnant at age 13. She gave birth to a daughter in 1994 in the building where she was held, with Ms. Garrido helping with the delivery.

"He knew I was really scared about getting pregnant again," Ms. Dugard said. "He said he just couldn't help himself, but he was really trying to stop."

Ms. Dugard did eventually get pregnant again, giving birth to a second daughter in 1997, a result of a final attack by Mr. Garrido.

Soon after, they just started "acting like a family," celebrating birthdays, and "just trying to be normal, I guess." There was a backyard pool and a family printing business.

At one point during her testimony, Ms. Dugard was shown a journal she kept, including entries in which she called herself a coward for not trying to escape. But, she said, "I couldn't leave. I had the girls."

Near the end of the testimony, Ms. Dugard describes the final days of her ordeal, in August 2009, after Mr. Garrido had been brought in by parole officers for questioning after a campus officer at the University of California, Berkeley, had raised their suspicions.

Ms. Dugard, who went with Mr. Garrido to the meeting, had been told to lie for him and to give her name as "Alissa," but parole officers soon began peppering her with questions about her identity, flustering her. Moments later, an officer came in and said Mr. Garrido had confessed to the kidnapping.

"I started crying," Ms. Dugard said. "And she said, 'You need to tell me your name.'"

"And I said that I can't because I hadn't said my name in 18 years," Ms. Dugard said. But then, she said, "I wrote it down."

—June 4, 2011

CHAPTER 4

MASS MURDER

"Any death of this sort is a tragedy. Any shooting involving multiple victims is a tragedy. There is something particularly heartbreaking about the death happening in a place in which we seek solace and we seek peace, in a place of worship."

—President Barack Obama in June 2015, after a deadly shooting at the Emanuel African Methodist Episcopal Church in Charleston, S.C.

THERE IS SO OFTEN a randomness to the killing done by mass murderers, and the pain is somehow deepened by the indiscriminate nature of it all. Even those who target a particular group don't single out the persons they shoot. Their victims are just there, by chance—not the vital, unique individuals they are, but props in a twisted, convulsive statement that ignores the value of life and frightens us all.

OPPOSITE: Flowers and balloons were left at the gate of the Emanuel African Methodist Episcopal Church in Charleston, South Carolina, on June 20, 2015, in honor of the nine victims of the mass shooting there three days prior.

SCHOOL DYNAMITER
FIRST SLEW WIFE

S till stunned by the deed of the madman Andrew Kehoe, who yesterday killed his wife and then blew up the consolidated school here and his own automobile, causing the death of 43 persons, including himself, the little community of Bath, Michigan, today was groping its way through tears trying to meet the awful consequences of the tragedy.

Sad-faced parents of the 37 children killed in the school came to console one another in their grief, but funeral arrangements were left until tomorrow.

Governor Fred W. Green issued a proclamation appealing to the people of Michigan to raise funds to rebuild the school and provide relief to families.

The little village of 300 inhabitants is virtually bankrupt as a result of the disaster.

The deaths of Mrs. Blanche Hart, 30, a teacher, and Oleo Clayton, 8, a pupil, in a Lansing hospital today brought the total dead to 44.

Kehoe's Wife Slain and Burned

The finding of the body of Kehoe's wife this morning by deputy sheriffs was not entirely unexpected. State troopers had combed the state last night, following clues that she was in a sanatorium. When this inquiry failed, attention was directed to the ruins of the home, which Kehoe blew up yesterday before he set off the blast at the school.

Though charred beyond recognition, the body was found in plain sight on a milk cart, near a hen coop, the only building on the farm that was not destroyed. Dynamite was found under some straw.

State troopers had combed the state last night, following clues that she was in a sanatorium.

It is the belief of prosecuting attorney William C. Searl that Kehoe either cut his wife's throat or beat in her skull and then tied her to the cart and set it afire. Piled around the cart were silverware, jewels, a metal cash box and the ashes of several bank notes.

Officers were unable to account for the burning during the night of a davenport, a small table and three chairs that members of a Consumers Power road crew had taken out of the burning house yesterday morning. All this was intact last night, but in ashes this morning.

Narrow Escape from Death

G. H. Buck, foreman of the road crew, gave the following account of what happened:

"Arriving near the Kehoe place, we saw that the buildings were afire and speeded up. The south side of the house was in flames when we got there. We ran around to the north windows and two of us crawled in. We shoved out a davenport, a table and some chairs.

"Then, in a corner of the room, I found a pile of dynamite. Without thinking much about what I was doing. I picked up an armful and handed it to one of the men. The room was filled with smoke, so we got out.

"Then I heard a woman across the road yelling that the school had been blown up. We started for our car and had just arrived there when a terrific blast let go in the house behind us. I was slammed against the car.

"We got in and drove rapidly to Bath. A tragic scene confronted us at the school. The north half of the building was a jumble of debris. Several men were digging into the wreckage. We could hear the voices of the imprisoned children calling for help. I ran across the lawn and began helping.

"I had no more than started when I was bowled over by an explosion at the roadside. I got up and looked around. A great cloud of black smoke was rolling up. Under it I saw the tangled remains of a car. Part of a human body was caught in the steering wheel. Three or four other bodies were lying on the ground near by."

Seemed Like End of the World

"I began to feel as though the world was coming to an end. I guess I was a bit hazy. Anyway, the next thing I remember I was out on the street. One of our men was binding up the wounds of Glenn Smith, the postmaster. His leg had been blown off. I went back to the building and helped with the rescue work until we were ordered to stop while a search was made for dynamite."

The placard "criminals are made, not born," found wired to a fence on the Kehoe farm, may give an inkling to the psychology of the man who, it is believed, attempted to wreak vengeance on the community for what he felt was the high tax imposed on him and other financial troubles.

Evidence disclosed today indicates that he mapped out his plans months ago. He was notified last June that the mortgage on his farm would be foreclosed, and that may have been what started the clockwork of anarchy and madness in his brain.

M. W. Keyes, superintendent of the school board, said Kehoe appeared to have a tax mania and fought the expenditure of money for the most necessary equipment.

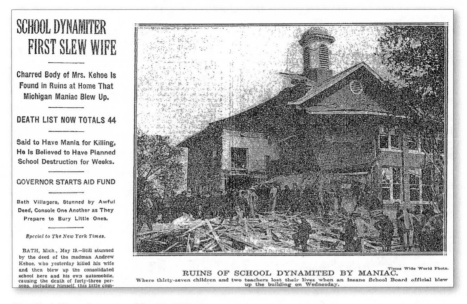

SCHOOL DYNAMITER FIRST SLEW WIFE

Charred Body of Mrs. Kehoe Is Found in Ruins at Home That Michigan Maniac Blew Up.

DEATH LIST NOW TOTALS 44

Said to Have Mania for Killing, He Is Believed to Have Planned School Destruction for Weeks.

GOVERNOR STARTS AID FUND

Bath Villagers, Stunned by Awful Deed, Console One Another as They Prepare to Bury Little Ones.

Special to The New York Times.

BATH, Mich., May 19.—Still stunned by the deed of the madman Andrew Kehoe, who yesterday killed his wife and then blew up the consolidated school here and his own automobile, causing the death of forty-three persons, including himself, this little com-

RUINS OF SCHOOL DYNAMITED BY MANIAC.
Where thirty-seven children and two teachers lost their lives when an insane School Board official blew up the building on Wednesday.

New York Times front page, May 20, 1927.

Chance to Prepare for Dynamiting

"I have no doubt that he made his plans last fall to blow up the school," Keyes declared. "He was an experienced electrician, and the board employed him in November to make some repairs on the school lighting system. He had ample opportunity then to plant the explosives and lay the wires for touching it off."

Prosecutor Searl revealed that a shattered alarm clock had been found in the basement of the school, connected with a battery and wires leading to caches of dynamite and gunpowder. The face of the clock was intact. The hands pointed to 8:45.

Bernice Sterling, a first grade teacher who escaped injury, said she telephoned Kehoe yesterday morning and asked permission to use his grove for a picnic for her class. He told her that if she "wanted a picnic she would better have it at once."

Evidence that Kehoe was planning his scheme early in April was brought out at the inquiry before State Fire Marshal Charles V. Lane and the Clinton County prosecutor today. Neighbors testified that he was wiring the buildings at his farm about that time and that he evaded questions regarding his purpose.

Numerous witnesses declared that Kehoe had an ungovernable temper and that he developed a mania for killing things. He beat one of his horses to death last spring, it was stated.

The man was known through the countryside as a "dynamite farmer." Neighbors detailed how he was continually setting off blasts on his farm, blowing up stumps and rocks.

Pyrotol Found in School Debris

The wiring for the explosions in Kehoe's house and outbuildings was complicated. A timing apparatus was found in the chicken coop. Wires were found leading to the house and barns from the telephone lines on the road in front of the house. Kehoe evidently intended to tap the lines for current to set off the dynamite. The explosion destroyed only the small part of the house; fire did the rest.

A rescue worker digging in the debris of the school found a quantity of Pyrotol, a war salvage explosive distributed to farmers by the federal government, between a floor and a ceiling above the coal bin in the part of the building left standing. Two bushels of sticks were removed.

In the basement state troopers found a container filled with gasoline, so fitted that the natural expansion of the gas would force the inflammable vapor through a tube to a spark gap. When this point had been reached, the gas could have been exploded by one pressing an electric button and burning gasoline would have been scattered throughout the basement.

It is the belief of investigators that Kehoe meant to burn the building if the dynamiting failed.

—May 20, 1927

SUSPECT SEIZED IN CHICAGO
IN SLAYING OF EIGHT NURSES

By AUSTIN C. WEHRWEIN

Richard Franklin Speck, the 24-year-old ex-convict sought in the slaying of eight nurses last Thursday, was seized by police about 2 a.m. today bleeding from his right wrist and left elbow in a transient hotel on West Madison Street.

Speck, the object of a nationwide search, was taken by police to Cook County Hospital under guard.

Sergeant John Griffith, of the homicide squad, said, "There is no doubt that this is Speck."

He said the man had the same tattoo marks described by the FBI. The sergeant said blood was flowing heavily from knife wounds in the man's arms and that he apparently had attempted suicide.

—*July 17, 1966*

Identified by Police

A murder warrant was sworn out today for the arrest of Richard Franklin Speck, a tattooed 24-year-old casual laborer and seaman, in the slaying of eight nurses last Thursday.

"I feel that we have enough information to be absolutely positive that this man is the murderer," Superintendent of Police O. W. Wilson told reporters.

Mr. Wilson's office said that a Cook County warrant for murder "collectively" had been issued by James L. Staring, a circuit court magistrate.

Within minutes, Judge Julius J. Hoffman of U.S. District Court signed a complaint against Speck for unlawful flight to avoid prosecution for murder. This gave the FBI authority to enter the case in a nationwide search.

The Chicago police were checking a report that Speck might be near Monmouth in eastern Illinois. There his 35-year-old brother, a carpenter, said Speck had done odd jobs around Monmouth a month and a half ago, then departed for Dallas.

Speck was once convicted in Dallas for burglary and forgery and sentenced to three years in prison.

Speck was last seen leaving a hotel on North Dearborn Street at 9 p.m. yesterday when the Chicago police already had 140 men on the case. The police said he left

32 fingerprints on the door of the second-floor bedroom of the garden apartment that served as a nurses' dormitory, the scene of the crime.

Identified by Nurse

Mr. Wilson said Speck, also known as Richard Benjamin Speck, was described by the FBI much as Corazon Amurao, the only survivor of the slayings, had pictured him.

He is 6 feet 1 inch tall and weighs 160 pounds, with blue eyes and short brownish-blond hair, which the Chicago police described as "dishwater blond." On his upper left arm is a tattoo that says "Born to Raise Hell," and on his right forearm are tattoos of a dagger and snake and a skull with a hat and goggles.

Miss Amurao, a 23-year-old Filipino exchange program nurse who escaped by hiding under a bunk bed, made a positive identification from a National Maritime Union passport-size picture after looking at nearly 200 photographs in her guarded room at the South Chicago Community Hospital, where she is being treated for shock.

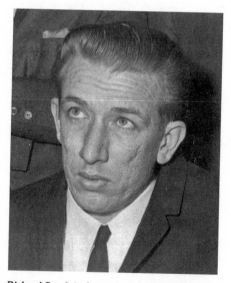

Otto Kreuzer, chief of Chicago detectives, said Speck would probably become the "most wanted" criminal on the FBI's list. Mr. Kreuzer declared that it would be impossible for Speck to escape from the county from this point on.

Mr. Kreuzer said that stakeouts had been placed at all airline, bus and railroad terminals. He said that if Speck intended to go back to Dallas it might have been "reasonable" for him first to work his way to New Orleans.

Richard Speck is shown during a December 19, 1966, court appearance in Chicago.

This was a reference to the statements the killer made to the girls before he killed them that he wanted money to go to New Orleans. Miss Amurao told the police that he had told the girls he would not harm them if they complied with his request. Then he took them to other parts of the building, one by one, where he strangled five and fatally stabbed three.

Seen Leaving Hotel

Francis Flanagan, commander of the homicide unit, who is in charge of the manhunt, said that Speck was seen leaving the North Dearborn Street hotel last night. Commander Flanagan added, however, that Speck did not check out of the hotel. He said that Speck was believed to have been in Chicago previously, but it would be "virtually impossible" to trace his movements.

Mr. Wilson said that Speck was seen last Monday and Tuesday at the National Maritime Union hiring hall, close to the murder site. Mr. Wilson said Speck was trying to get employment on a boat going to New Orleans.

Meanwhile, services were held for one of the victims, Gloria Jean Davy, 22, in Dyer, Ind.

The bodies of the two Filipino victims—Valentina Pasion, 23, and Merlita Gargullo, 23, were to be returned to the Philippines.

Services were planned Monday for Suzanne Bridget Farris, 21, Chicago; Mary Ann Jordan, 20, Chicago; Patricia Ann Matusek, 20, Chicago; Nina Jo Schmale, 24, Wheaton, Ill., and Pamela Lee Wilkening, 20, Lansing, Ill.

—*July 16, 1966*

NOTE: *In 1967, Speck was convicted of murder and sentenced to death. The U.S. Supreme Court in 1971 upheld his conviction but struck down the sentence because potential jurors who opposed capital punishment had been excluded from the panel. After the Supreme Court ruled in 1972 that the death penalty as then administered was unconstitutional, an Illinois judge resentenced Speck to eight consecutive terms of 50 to 150 years. Speck died in prison in 1991.*

TERROR IN LITTLETON: THE OVERVIEW; 2 STUDENTS IN COLORADO SCHOOL SAID TO GUN DOWN AS MANY AS 23 AND KILL THEMSELVES IN A SIEGE

By JAMES BROOKE

In the deadliest school massacre in the nation's history, two young men stormed into a suburban high school here in Littleton, Colorado, at lunch time today with guns and explosives, killing as many as 23 students and teachers and wounding at least 20 in a 5-hour siege, the authorities said.

The two students believed to have been the gunmen, Eric Harris and Dylan Klebold, who were students at Columbine High School, were found dead of self-inflicted gunshot wounds in the library, said Steve Davis, the spokesman for the Jefferson County Sheriff's Department.

Beginning about 11:30 a.m., the gunmen, wearing ski masks, stalked through the school as they fired semiautomatic weapons at students and teachers and tossed explosives, with one student being hit nine times in the chest by shrapnel, the authorities said. Gunshots continued to ring out at the school for hours. One bomb exploded in the library and one in a car outside. Two more cars were rigged with bombs.

One bomb exploded in the library and one in a car outside.

About 3 p.m., hundreds of police officers evacuated the building and searched for the gunmen. Their bodies and those of several of their victims appeared to have been wired with explosives.

Sheriff John Stone said, "It appears to be a suicide mission."

Mr. Davis said that as many as 25 people were dead, "a mixture of students and faculty." He said that most of the bodies were found in the school's entrance, the library and the commons cafeteria. No precise death toll was available.

Kaleb Newberry, 16, said: "I was in class and one teacher came in and basically told us to run for our lives, I saw a girl maybe five paces behind me fall. She was shot in the leg, but a teacher helped her."

Students said the gunmen were part of a group of misfits who called themselves the trench coat mafia, which expressed disdain for racial minorities and athletes. Members of

117

Eric Harris, left, and Dylan Klebold are shown in this image made from video, released by the Jefferson County Sheriff's department, as they walked the hallway at Columbine High School in Littleton, Colorado, wearing trenchcoats. The video was made by Harris and Klebold as part of a school project, prior to the killings at Columbine.

the group dressed in dark gothic-style clothing including long black coats. They became easy to notice among the 1,870 students at the school, since every day, regardless of the weather, they wore their coats.

Today the gunmen appeared to aim at minority members and athletes at the 1,800-student school, as well as peers who had poked fun at the group.

Fourteen-year-old Katie Corona said she was trapped in a classroom with her teacher and about 30 classmates for hours.

"I thought I was going to die," she said. "I really didn't think I was going to make it. We would hear shots, then we heard crying. We had no clue what was going on."

"Everyone around me got shot, and I begged him for 10 minutes not to shoot me," one young woman said tonight in an interview broadcast on the Cable News Network. "And he just put the gun in my face and started laughing and saying it was all because people were mean to him last year."

The mass shooting was the first at an American school during this academic year, but revived memories of similar tragedies that struck six different communities last year and set off national alarms about teen-age violence.

President Clinton immediately dispatched a crisis-response team to aid the school community and the victim's families.

"We don't know yet all the how's or why's of this tragedy; perhaps we will never fully understand it," the president said in a nationally televised news conference just before 8 p.m. "St. Paul reminds us that we all see things in life darkly, that we only partly understand what is happening."

He added, "We do know that we must do more to reach out to our children and teach them to express their anger and to resolve their conflicts with words, not weapons."

A sunny spring day turned into a bloody nightmare for this suburb of 35,000 people southwest of Denver, as ambulances ferried the injured from the high school, past tennis courts, a baseball diamond and a student parking lot.

"I hope we can all pull together, because we will need all our strengths," Jane Hammond, Jefferson County superintendent of schools, said tonight. Tonight at least three church vigils were held for the dead and injured.

About 3 p.m., SWAT teams police officers used a fire truck and an armored car to get close to the building, dozens of students raced out of the two-story building, some slipping in the mud, others holding up their hands in the air or behind their heads. Police said they feared that the gunmen would try to escape by mingling with the trapped students.

One student, bloodied from an injury, broke out a second-story window, and climbed down into the hands of the police.

As fire alarms rang in the halls, students who had seen the gunmen trampled each other to get out of the building, running through one exit where three bodies lay on a staircase. Trapped inside, others took refuge in classrooms, bathrooms and a choir room, frantically barricading doors with desks and file cabinets.

One cafeteria worker who barricaded herself in a women's bathroom said, "We could hear them blowing the heck out of the place."

The trench coat mafia is a small band of a dozen juniors and seniors at Columbine who are easily recognized yet little feared, according to people who live in the neighborhood near the school. Regardless of the weather, they favor long black coats and Gothic makeup.

"It was that devilish, half-dead, half-alive look," said Bret, a sophomore who spoke on the condition only his first name be used.

The group often gathered in the cafeteria after school. Chris McCaffrey, manager of Angie's Restaurant a few blocks from Columbine, said that residents had known about the group for about five years and that no one considered it a threat.

"Mostly it was just kids who nobody wanted to have anything to do with," Mr. McCaffrey said. "They weren't particularly feared. They were just a bunch of punks who kind of hang around the school."

Students said the group was mostly boys, but that some girls appeared to be closely associated with it. One student described the group as "nerds, geeks and dweebs trying to find someplace to fit in."

Bret suggested that the mafia might have targeted athletes out of resentment for their own lack of popularity and success at school.

The students "weren't really accepted as younger kids and as they got older they were accepted by this group," Bret said. "They got their fair share of being picked on. I could understand that they might have targeted some of the more popular kids."

In an age when cellular telephones are increasingly common among high school students, several trapped students called television stations when they could not get through on 911 lines.

"I hear a couple of gunshots, people running up and down," a student said in a frightened whisper to KUSA-TV, a Denver television station. Identifying himself only as James, he added, "There are a bunch of kids downstairs, I can hear them crying."

Aware that the gunmen might be watching on a classroom television set, he said, "I am staying upstairs," and then hung up.

"This is a cultural virus," Gov. Bill Owens of Colorado said before hurrying to the scene. Noting that he felt particularly affected by the tragedy because his 16-year-old daughter goes to a suburban Denver high school, he said, "We have to ask ourselves what kind of children we are raising."

—April 21, 1999

NOTE: *Harris and Klebold killed 12 students and one teacher before committing suicide.*

MASSACRE IN VIRGINIA; DRUMBEAT OF SHOTS, BROKEN BY PAUSES TO RELOAD

By SHAILA DEWAN

The gunshots were so slow and steady that some students thought they came from a nearby construction site, until they saw the police officers with rifles pointed at Norris Hall, the engineering building at Virginia Tech.

Bang. Bang. Bang.

They went on and on, for what seemed like 10 or 15 or 20 minutes, an eternity with punctuation.

Bang. Bang. On the third floor of Norris Hall, Scott L. Hendricks, a professor, looked out the window of his office and saw students crawling away from the building.

Bang. Tiffany Otey's accounting class crammed into an office and locked themselves in, crying in fright.

Every so often, the shots paused for a minute or so. That was the gunman, who was in the midst of the worst shooting rampage in American history, stopping to reload. When it was over, 33 people, including the gunman, were dead and at least 15 more were injured.

"I was terrified," said Ms. Otey, a junior whose class met in the room above the one where much of the shooting took place.

One student finished the day's assignment and tried to leave, but returned to tell the others that the hall was full of smoke and there were police officers everywhere. The class decided to go into a room with a lock. Dr. Hendricks, an engineering and mechanics professor on the same floor, barricaded himself in his office, pushing a bookcase in front of the door. Some students took refuge in the library, searching the Web to find out what was happening. No one knew.

The violence began in the morning in Ambler Johnston, the largest dormitory at Virginia Tech, where two people were killed, officials said. But when the first class started two hours later, at 9:05 a.m., many on campus remained unaware of any danger.

"I woke up and I didn't know anything was wrong," said Sarah Ulmer, a freshman who lives in the east wing of the dorm. "I went to my first class and my teacher was talking about how some people weren't coming because there was a gun threat at West A. J. and they were blocking it off."

The school did not notify students by e-mail of the first shootings until 9:26 a.m., said Matt Dixon, who lives in the dorm. Mr. Dixon did not receive the e-mail message until he returned from his 9:05 class. When he left for that class, he said, a resident adviser told him not to use the central stairs, so he left another way.

Other students and faculty members said they had only a vague notion that there had been a shooting at the dorm. Several faculty members said they had reached campus during or just after the Norris Hall shooting and had gone unimpeded to their buildings.

Many were bewildered or angry that the campus had not been locked down after the first shooting.

"I am outraged at what happened today on the Virginia Tech campus," wrote Huy That Ton, a member of the chemical engineering faculty, in an e-mail message. "Countless lives could have been saved if they had informed the student body of the first shooting. What was the security department thinking?!"

Campus officials said they believed the first incident was confined to a single building and was a domestic dispute, and had no idea that the violence would spread elsewhere.

He peeked into the German class in Room 207, witnesses said, then pushed his way in.

The gunman in Norris Hall was described as a young Asian man with two pistols who calmly entered classrooms and shot professors and students. He peeked into the German class in Room 207, witnesses said, then pushed his way in.

Gene Cole, who works in Virginia Tech's housekeeping services, told *The Roanoke Times* that he was on the second floor of Norris Hall on Monday morning and saw a person lying on a hallway floor. As Mr. Cole went up to the body, a man wearing a hat and holding a gun stepped into the hallway. "Someone stepped out of a classroom and started shooting at me," he said. Mr. Cole fled down the corridor, then down a flight of steps to safety. "All I saw was blood in the hallways," Mr. Cole said.

Elaine Goss of Waynesboro, Va., said she first spoke to her son, Alec Calhoun, a student, about 9:30 a.m., after he had leapt from a second-story classroom window as the gunman entered. "I couldn't understand him. It was like gibberish," Ms. Goss said. "It took a while to figure out shootings, lots of shootings, and that his whole class had jumped out the window." As word spread of the shootings, there were first reports of one dead, then 20, then more than 30.

"Every time we turned our heads, the total just kept going up," said Stuart Crowder, 22, a building and construction major.

Students, parents and professors jammed phone lines trying to check on loved ones and friends. There were frantic e-mail and text messages, clogged voice mails and busy signals. Kathryn Beard, an education professor at Virginia Tech whose daughter is a student there, said she became frantic when she was barred from entering. "The teacher in me was panicking, and the mother in me was panicking," she said. "I can't imagine something like this happening on my campus."

—April 17, 2007

NOTE: *The shooter was identified as a student named Seung-Hui Cho. He fatally shot 32 people and wounded 17 before killing himself.*

GUNMAN KILLS 12 AT COLORADO THEATER; SCORES ARE WOUNDED, REVIVING DEBATE

By DAN FROSCH AND KIRK JOHNSON

Anticipation built in the packed, darkened movie theater. Life and its cares began to recede.

Then, just after midnight on Friday, fantasy became nightmare, and a place of escape became a trap, when a man strode to the front in a multiplex near Denver and opened fire. At least 12 people were killed and 58 wounded, with witnesses describing a scene of claustrophobia, panic and blood. Minutes later, the police arrested James Holmes, 24, in the theater's parking lot.

"It was just chaos. You started hearing screaming. You looked up and people were falling. It was like a dream," said Jamie Rohrs, 25, who was there with his fiancée,

James Holmes appears in Arapahoe County District Court in Centennial, Colorado, July 23, 2012.

cradling his 4-month-old son, Ethan, in his arms as the movie began. It was the midnight premiere of *The Dark Knight Rises,* the latest Batman sequel, at the Century 16 multiplex in Aurora, about 10 miles from downtown Denver.

Mr. Rohrs jumped between the seats for cover, still holding the baby. He stumbled and crawled trying to figure out what to do, clutching his son to his chest as he went. "Do I run out the door? Is he going to shoot the baby?" Mr. Rohrs said, his voice quavering. But he, his fiancée and the baby eventually made it out.

And so once again, with a squeeze of a trigger, just 20 miles from Columbine High School, scene of the 1999 student massacre, the nation was plunged into another debate about guns and violence.

Some survivors thought at first they were witnessing a promotional stunt. The gunman, wearing what Aurora Police Department officials described as nearly head-to-toe "ballistic gear," including a throat protector and leggings, plus a gas mask and a long black coat, came in through a parking lot exit door near the screen of Theater 9.

"He walked in so casually," said a witness, Jordan Crofter, 19, a Batman fan who had gone with a group of friends and had a seat in the front row. The gunman then released two devices down the theater aisles emitting what the police said was smoke or some sort of irritant.

Witnesses told the police that Mr. Holmes said something to the effect of "I am the Joker," according to a federal law enforcement official, and that his hair had been dyed or he was wearing a wig. Then, as people began to rise from their seats in confusion or anxiety, he began to shoot.

Mr. Holmes was detained by the police soon afterward, standing by his white Hyundai. He was identified by the authorities as a former Ph.D. student at

> *Some survivors thought at first they were witnessing a promotional stunt.*

the University of Colorado in Denver, and an honors graduate in neuroscience from the University of California, Riverside. He had in the car an AR-15 assault rifle, a Remington 12-gauge shotgun, and a .40 caliber Glock handgun, said Chief Dan Oates of the Aurora police, and all three were believed to have been used inside the theater. Another Glock .40 caliber handgun was recovered inside the theater. Chief Oates said that "many, many" rounds were fired.

In the last 60 days Mr. Holmes had purchased four guns at local gun shops, Chief Oates said. And through the Internet, he bought more than 6,000 rounds of ammunition. The guns were all bought legally, a federal law enforcement official said.

Mr. Holmes also purchased online multiple magazines for the assault rifle, including one 100-round drum magazine. "With that drum magazine, he could have gotten off 50, 60 rounds, even if it was semiautomatic, within one minute," Chief Oates said.

After the chaos—the evacuation, the rush of 911 calls beginning at 12:39 a.m., the mass casualties rushed to area hospitals, the images that witnesses described to authorities of dead or dying friends or loved ones left inside—the emerging details got more mysterious and in some ways more horrifying.

"Our investigation determined his apartment is booby trapped with various incendiary and chemical devices and apparent trip wires," Chief Oates said. "We have an active and difficult scene. It may be resolved in hours or days. We simply don't know how we're going to handle that."

Federal law enforcement officials said that the apartment had been so extensively booby-trapped that the devices could not be safely defused and that a robot would be sent to trigger them.

"It is a very vexing problem how to enter that apartment safely," Chief Oates said. "Personally I've never seen anything like what the pictures show us is in there. I'm a layman when it comes to bomb stuff. I see an awful lot of wires. Trip wires. Jars full of ammunition. Jars full of liquid. Some things that look like mortar rounds. We have a lot of challenges to get in there safely."

In the suspect's neighborhood of red-brick apartment buildings and dusty lots, not far from Children's Hospital Colorado, where some of the victims were taken, neighbors shook their heads in disbelief as the police and bomb squad vehicles cordoned off the area.

At one point, as children played in an overgrown front yard and day laborers stared in disbelief, firefighters in a hook and ladder truck smashed a window in the third story of the building where the police said Mr. Holmes lived.

Whether a violent movie had inspired violence or was merely the coincidental setting, police authorities in some other cities said they were taking no chances and had increased security at theaters showing the movie.

In Paris, Warner Bros. canceled a premiere of *The Dark Knight Rises*, along with other promotional events. On Friday afternoon workers removed a giant Batman mask that had been mounted on the front of a theater along the Champs-Élysées, where the screening was to take place.

Warner Bros., which is owned by Time Warner, released a statement Friday, saying that the company and the filmmakers were "deeply saddened" and "extend our sincere sympathies to the families and loved ones of the victims at this tragic time."

The shooting inevitably stirred memories of Columbine High School and the murders there in April 1999, when two armed students stalked through the hallways, killing 12 students and a teacher as they went, before shooting themselves.

And the psychological echo and the similar feel of the two massacres was palpable: Theater 9 was a place of seeming safety, not unlike Columbine's library, where some of the killings occurred. Both were ordinary settings that became death traps.

Mr. Holmes seemed ordinary too, said Billy Kromka, a premed student at the University of Colorado, Boulder, who worked with Mr. Holmes last summer as a research assistant.

"There was no way I thought he could have the capacity to commit an atrocity like this," said Mr. Kromka, who is from Aurora. Mr. Kromka said that Mr. Holmes's "disposition was a little off" and that he could be socially awkward. He spent much of his time immersed in his computer, often participating in role-playing online games.

His criminal history with the Aurora Police Department consisted before Friday of one traffic summons, for speeding, in October.

A spokeswoman for the University of Colorado Denver-Anschutz Medical Campus, Jackie Brinkman, said Mr. Holmes was in the process of dropping out of school because of academic problems. She said the university was unaware of any incidents with campus police or disciplinary problems involving Mr. Holmes while he was enrolled.

Mr. Holmes grew up in a quiet, middle-class community at the edge of San Diego, where his parents still live. Two-story, Spanish-style tract homes line the street, all white stucco with red-tile roofs and well-kept lawns. His mother, Arlene Rosemary Holmes, is a nurse.

One neighbor, Margie Aguilar, said she knew the Holmes family, who she said had lived in the area for at least 10 years. Her son was a little younger than Mr. Holmes and attended the same high school, Westview.

"The parents are really, really nice people," Ms. Aguilar said. "This is the last thing you'd expect."

One of the victims, Jessica Ghawi, was a 25-year-old college student and sports broadcaster active on social media under the name Jessica Redfield, a tribute to her red hair. She posted early Friday that she was at the movie screening after convincing a friend to go with her.

Her brother, Jordan Ghawi, said in a blog post on Friday that when the gunfire began, Jessica took two rounds. "My sister took one round followed by an additional round which appeared to strike her in the head," he wrote.

Her last tweet said the movie would start in 20 minutes.

—July 21, 2012

NOTE: *In 2015, a jury rejected the defense's claims that Holmes was insane at the time of the shootings, and found him guilty of killing 12 people and injuring 70. A judge sentenced Holmes to 12 life terms plus 3,318 years.*

NORWEGIAN MASS KILLER GETS MAXIMUM SENTENCE: 21 YEARS

By MARK LEWIS AND SARAH LYALL

Convicted of killing 77 people in a horrific bombing and shooting attack in July last year, the Norwegian extremist Anders Behring Breivik was sentenced Friday to 21 years in prison—fewer than four months per victim—ending a case that thoroughly tested this gentle country's collective commitment to values like tolerance, nonviolence and merciful justice.

Mr. Breivik, lawyers say, will live in a prison outside Oslo in a three-cell suite of rooms equipped with exercise equipment, a television and a laptop, albeit one without Internet access. If he is not considered a threat after serving his sentence, the maximum available under Norwegian law, he will be eligible for release in 2033, at the age of 53.

However, his demeanor, testimony and declaration that he would have liked to kill more people helped convince the judges that Mr. Breivik is unlikely ever to be released from prison. He could be kept there indefinitely by judges adding a succession of five-year extensions to his sentence.

The relative leniency of the sentence imposed on Mr. Breivik, the worst criminal modern Scandinavia has known, is no anomaly. Rather, it is consistent with Norway's general approach to criminal justice. Like the rest of Europe—and in contrast with much of the United States, whose criminal justice system many Europeans consider to be cruelly punitive—Norway no longer has the death penalty and considers prison more a means for rehabilitation than retribution.

Even some parents who lost children in the attack appeared to be satisfied with the verdict, seeing it as fair punishment that would allow the country, perhaps, to move past its trauma.

"Now we won't hear about him for quite a while; now we can have peace and quiet," Per Balch Sørensen, whose daughter was among the dead, told TV2. He felt no personal rancor toward Mr. Breivik, he was quoted as saying.

"He doesn't mean anything to me," Mr. Sørensen said. "He is just air."

Even more than a year later, the events of that day are still almost impossible to fathom, so brutally, methodically and callously was the attack carried out. After setting off a series of bombs in downtown Oslo that killed eight people, Mr. Breivik made his way to tiny Utoya Island, where, dressed as a police officer and toting a virtual arsenal of weapons, he calmly and systematically hunted down and shot dead 69 others, most of them young people attending a summer camp run by the Labor Party. Hundreds were wounded.

Norway's soft-touch approach, which defers to the rights of the accused and the rights of victims as much as it gives weight to the arguments of prosecutors, informed every aspect of Mr. Breivik's trial. He was given ample time to speak of his rambling, anti-Muslim, anti-multicultural political views, which included a rant about the "deconstruction" of Norway at the hands of "cultural Marxists."

He interrupted witnesses freely, smiled when the verdict was announced and entered court on Friday making a fascist salute.

"The thoughts of murder were evidently stimulating for the defendant," Judge Arne Lyng said, reading from the 90-page judgment. "This was clear when he talked about decapitating ex-Prime Minister Gro Harlem Brundtland." It is hard to imagine, the judgment continues, "that such a term-limited sentence is sufficient to protect this country from this man."

Even more than a year later, the events of that day are still almost impossible to fathom . . .

As the court listened to the killer, so it listened to his victims, who were treated in the proceedings with care, even tenderness. The court heard 77 autopsy reports, listened to biographies describing the lives of each of the dead, and allowed the survivors to describe in detail what happened and how it has affected them.

"At first I was shot in the arms and I thought, 'O.K., I can survive this; it's O.K. if you're shot in the arms,' " Ina Rangones Libak, 22, said in May in testimony that had spectators laughing and crying by turns. "Then I was shot in the jaw. I thought, 'O.K., this is a lot more serious.' Then I was shot in the chest and I thought, 'O.K., this is going to kill me.'"

But as she lay there, she heard a friend say, "We can't leave Ina here," and she was then cradled by a group who hid together even as Mr. Breivik shot others nearby, taking off their clothes to use as tourniquets. In the end, Ms. Libak told the court, "We are stronger than ever."

The sense that Mr. Breivik's hateful beliefs should not be allowed to fill Norway with hate, too, was part of the country's response to the attacks. In April, tens of thousands of people around the country gathered for a mass sing-along of "Children of the Rainbow," a song Mr. Breivik denounced in court as Marxist propaganda, to show that he had not shattered their commitment to tolerance and inclusiveness.

Mr. Breivik's guilt was never at issue in the 10-week trial, which ended in June; the question was whether he was sane, as he claimed, or insane, as the prosecutors argued. On Friday, a five-panel judge ruled him sane and gave him what he had sought: incarceration in a regular prison, not a mental hospital.

Many said they did not mind that Mr. Breivik prevailed in his argument, since the court's declaration that he was not insane forced him to be accountable for what he had done.

"I am relieved to see this verdict," said Tore Sinding Beddekal, who survived the shootings by hiding in a storeroom. "The temptation for people to fob him off as a madman has gone. It would have been difficult to unite the concept of insanity with the level of detail in his planning."

Bjorn Magnus Ihler, another survivor, said that Norway's treatment of Mr. Breivik was a sign of a fundamentally civilized nation.

"If he is deemed not to be dangerous any more after 21 years, then he should be released," Mr. Ihler said. "That's how it should work. That's staying true to our principles, and the best evidence that he hasn't changed our society."

—August 25, 2012

SANDY HOOK PUPILS WERE ALL SHOT MULTIPLE TIMES WITH A SEMIAUTOMATIC, OFFICIALS SAY

By JAMES BARRON

The gunman in the Connecticut shooting blasted his way into the elementary school and then sprayed the children with bullets, first from a distance and then at close range, hitting some of them as many as 11 times, as he fired a semiautomatic rifle loaded with ammunition designed for maximum damage, officials said Saturday.

The state's chief medical examiner, H. Wayne Carver II, said all of the 20 children and 6 adults gunned down at Sandy Hook Elementary School in Newtown, Conn., had been struck more than once.

"This is a very devastating set of injuries," he said at a briefing in Newtown. When he was asked if they had suffered after they were hit, he said, "Not for very long."

The disclosures came as the police released the victims' names. They ranged in age from 6 to 56.

The children—12 girls and 8 boys—were all first-graders. One little girl had just turned 7 on Tuesday. All of the adults were women.

The White House announced that President Obama would visit Newtown on Sunday to meet with victims' families and speak at an interfaith vigil.

On Saturday, as families began to claim the bodies, some sought privacy. Others spoke out. Robbie Parker, whose six-year-old daughter, Emilie, was among the dead, choked back tears as he described her as "bright, creative and very loving."

But, he added, "as we move on from what happened here, what happened to so many people, let us not let it turn into something that defines us."

On a day of anguish and mourning, other details emerged about how the devastating attack had happened, turning a place where children were supposed to be safe into a national symbol of heartbreak.

The Newtown school superintendent said the principal and the school psychologist had been shot as they tried to tackle the gunman in order to protect their students.

That was just one act of bravery during the maelstrom. There were others, said the superintendent, Janet Robinson. She said one teacher had helped children escape through a window. Another shoved students into a room with a kiln and held them there until the danger had passed.

It was not enough: First responders described a scene of carnage in the two class-rooms where the children were killed, with no movement and no one left to save.

The gunman, identified as Adam Lanza, 20, had grown up in Newtown and had an uncle who had been a police officer in New Hampshire. The uncle, James M. Champion, issued a statement expressing "heartfelt sorrow," adding that the family was struggling "to comprehend the tremendous loss we all share." It was unclear why Mr. Lanza had gone on the attack. A law enforcement official said investigators had not found a suicide note or messages that spoke to the planning of such a deadly attack. And Ms. Robinson, the school superintendent, said they had found no connection between Mr. Lanza's mother and the school.

Dr. Carver said it appeared that all of the children had been killed by a "long rifle" that Mr. Lanza was carrying; a .223 Bushmaster semiautomatic rifle was one of the several weapons police found in the school. The other guns were semiautomatic pistols, including a 10-millimeter Glock and a 9-millimeter Sig Sauer.

The bullets Mr. Lanza used were "designed in such a fashion the energy is deposited in the tissue so the bullet stays in," resulting in deep damage, Dr. Carver said. As to how many bullets Mr. Lanza had fired, Dr. Carver said he did not have an exact count. He said that parents had identified their children from photographs to spare them from seeing the gruesome results of the rampage.

"This is probably the worst I have seen or the worst that I know of any of my colleagues having seen," said Dr. Carver, who is 60 and has been Connecticut's chief medical examiner since 1989.

He said that only Mr. Lanza and his first victim—his mother, Nancy Lanza—remained to be autopsied. Officials said the killing spree began early on Friday at the house where the Lanzas lived. There, Mr. Lanza shot his mother in the face, making her his first victim. Then, after taking three guns that belonged to her, they said, he climbed into her car for the short drive to the school.

Outfitted in combat gear, Mr. Lanza shot his way in, defeating a security system requiring visitors to be buzzed in. "He was not voluntarily let into the school at all," said Lt. J. Paul Vance, a spokesman for the state police. "He forced his way in."

The lieutenant's account was consistent with recordings of police dispatchers who answered call after call from adults at the school. "The front glass has been broken," one dispatcher cautioned officers who were rushing there. "They are unsure why."

The dispatchers kept up a running account of the drama at the school. "The individual I have on the phone indicates continuing to hear what he believes to be gunfire," one dispatcher said.

Soon, another dispatcher reported that the "shooting appears to have stopped," and the conversation on the official radios turned to making sure that help was available.

"What is the number of ambulances you will require?" a dispatcher asked.

The answer hinted at the unthinkable scope of the tragedy: "They are not giving us a number."

Another radio transmission, apparently from someone at the school, underlined the desperation: "You might want to see if the surrounding towns can send E.M.S. personnel. We're running out real quick, real fast."

Inside the school, teachers and school staff members had scrambled to move children to safety as the massacre began. Maryann Jacob, a library clerk, said she initially herded students behind a bookcase against a wall "where they can't be seen." She said that spot had been chosen in practice drills for school lockdowns, but on Friday, she had to move the pupils to a storage room "because we discovered one of our doors didn't lock."

Ms. Jacob said the storage room had crayons and paper that they tore up for the children to color while they waited. "They were asking what was going on," she said. "We said: 'We don't know. Our job is just to be quiet.'" But she said that she did know, because she had called the school office and learned that the school was under siege.

It was eerily silent in the school when police officers rushed in with their rifles drawn. There were the dead or dying in one section of the building, while elsewhere, those who had eluded the bullets were under orders from their teachers to remain quiet in their hiding places.

The officers discovered still more carnage: After gunning down the children and the school employees, the authorities said, Mr. Lanza had killed himself.

The principal, Dawn Hochsprung, 47, and the psychologist, Mary Sherlach, 56, were among the dead, as were the teachers Rachel D'Avino, 29; Anne Marie Murphy, 52; and Victoria Soto, 27. Lauren Rousseau, 30, had started as a full-time teacher in September after years of working as a substitute. "It was the best year of her life," *The News-Times* quoted her mother, Teresa, a copy editor at the newspaper, as saying.

Ms. Soto reportedly shooed her first graders into closets and cabinets when she heard the first shots, and then, by some accounts, told the gunman the youngsters were in the gym. Her cousin, James Willsie, told ABC News that she had "put herself between the gunman and the kids."

"She lost her life protecting those little ones," he said.

—December 16, 2012

NOTE: *The Newtown School District opted to tear down and replace Sandy Hook Elementary. A new school building opened on a different section of the property in August 2016.*

A HECTIC DAY AT CHURCH, AND THEN A HELLISH VISITOR

By RICHARD FAUSSET, JOHN ELIGON,
JASON HOROWITZ AND FRANCES ROBLES

Wednesday was a busy day at the Emanuel African Methodist Episcopal Church.

The pastor, the Rev. Clementa C. Pinckney, a tall, rangy man with a deep voice, would normally have stayed in Columbia, the capital, for his job as a state senator. But he had returned to his congregation here for an important meeting with the presiding elder of the district. There was the matter of the church elevator, long under construction. The budget needed review. And three congregants were officially received as new preachers. One by one, they stepped before the group to receive a certificate and applause.

The meeting in the church basement ended around 8 p.m., and the crowd of about 50 dwindled to 12 of the congregation's most devout members, who would remain for the Wednesday night Bible study.

Dylan Roof is escorted from the Shelby, North Carolina, police department, June 18, 2015.

That was when the visitor, a young white man, came to the door, asking for the minister. It was unusual for a stranger, much less a white one, to come to the Wednesday night session, but Bible study was open to all, and Mr. Pinckney welcomed him. They sat together around a green table, prayed, sang and then opened to the Gospel of Mark, 4:16–20, which likens the word of God to a seed that must fall on good soil to bear fruit.

At about 9, gunfire and terrified cries shattered the evening calm. In the pastor's office, Mr. Pinckney's wife, who had been waiting patiently with their younger daughter, turned off the lights, locked the door, hugged her child close and called 911.

When the shooting was over, nine congregants were dead, including Mr. Pinckney and two of the newly ordained ministers, each shot multiple times with a .45-caliber handgun. The stranger—identified by the police as Dylann Roof, 21, a high school dropout and sometime landscaper—has been charged with nine counts of murder.

"You are raping our women and taking over our country," Mr. Roof said to the victims, all of them black, before killing them, witnesses told the police.

In a matter of moments, the future of the Emanuel A.M.E. Church and its 350 active members would be changed forever. Church leaders were lost, along with worshipers young and middle-aged. Children were left motherless. A girls' track team lost its coach; a university its admissions coordinator. And residents of all races in Charleston, a city that places such value on its houses of worship that it calls itself the Holy City, recoiled in horror as one of its most storied buildings was desecrated by intolerant rage and briefly transformed into a charnel house.

The massacre has reverberated far beyond Charleston, prompting fierce new debate about race relations in a nation already grappling with protests over police conduct toward African-Americans.

President Obama spoke Thursday of "the heartache and the sadness and the anger" the shootings had elicited. In Columbia, where Mr. Pinckney's empty desk in the legislature has been adorned with a black cloak and flowers, lawmakers were once again grappling with the question of whether the Confederate battle flag should fly on the grounds of the statehouse.

But the deepest pain was at the handsome, whitewashed old church in Charleston, now cordoned off with yellow police tape, and along the intimate tendrils that connected its members to friends and family.

The "Itinerant Pastor"

Mr. Pinckney, 41, was a busy man. But when he was talking to you, said Sylvia Johnson, his cousin, he locked eyes intently and listened carefully. He was especially tender toward Ms. Johnson's blind daughter. His voice could move into a more stern, but still loving, register when he addressed his own daughters, Eliana and Malana.

With his flock in Charleston, his home in Jasper County, at South Carolina's southernmost tip, and his job up in Columbia, Mr. Pinckney had to work to spread his love around. He called himself the "itinerant pastor." On Wednesday morning in Columbia, he was dressed, sharp as always, in a dark suit and sitting in his office with his back to a view of the capitol dome, preparing for a Senate Finance Committee meeting. He was surrounded by framed newspaper spreads ("Leading from the Pulpit"; "Under 30 and on the Move"), recognitions of achievement (Prestigious Jaguar Award, Jasper County High School, 1991), volumes of Bibles and a poster of the Rev. Dr. Martin Luther King Jr. Next to a refrigerator bearing a "Yes! I Love My Library" sticker given to him by his wife, Jennifer, a librarian, he had rolled up a bunch of posters depicting African-American life in the South Carolina Lowcountry. He planned to take them home that day.

> *He had dropped out of the lives of many of his oldest friends some years ago.*

But first, another day of work. Mr. Pinckney, elected to the South Carolina House at age 23, had always had a sense of purpose. In seventh grade, he endured the taunts of his classmates in Jasper County, a depressed angle of what Senate colleagues called the Forgotten Triangle, for wearing a starched shirt and tie and carrying a briefcase instead of a backpack. He thought you needed to dress like someone to be someone.

He quickly became someone. He had begun preaching sermons in his teens. An ambitious intern unafraid to ask his bosses to look at the county budget, he became a page in the State House of Representatives and ultimately a member, and then a senator.

Now, 12 hours before he was killed, he took the elevator down to Room 105 for another meeting on the budget, where he again pushed, in the face of an overwhelming Republican majority, for funding to fix the roads in his deprived district.

Later, he rode an escalator up from the parking lot to the statehouse. He walked between marble columns and up a mahogany staircase lined with paintings of the Revolutionary War, and greeted friends in a lobby presided over by a statue of John C. Calhoun. In the stately Senate chamber, he greeted more friends on the floor and took a seat next to Senator Vincent A. Sheheen, a fellow Democrat.

It was here that Mr. Pinckney made his mark that day.

When Mr. Sheheen nervously prepared to voice his opposition to a compromise reached with Republicans on their effort to introduce a voter ID bill, he was shocked to hear Mr. Pinckney's booming voice call out, "No."

"When I heard him voting no, loud and clear, I knew I was doing the right thing," Mr. Sheheen said. They were the only two to vote in dissent.

Mr. Pinckney left another meeting early, telling colleagues that he had an appointment at his church back in Charleston.

A Wild-Talking Suspect

It is not clear where or how Mr. Roof spent his Wednesday morning. Even to his friends, there were unexplained gaps.

He had dropped out of the lives of many of his oldest friends some years ago. But he resurfaced about a month ago, telling them that he had gone to a public library in Columbia to open a Facebook account for the express purpose of finding them.

As a younger man, Mr. Roof had a rocky academic career, attending ninth grade twice at two schools, but possibly not making it any further. Friends recalled him as painfully shy.

Recently, however, he had been showing a new side, his friends said: spouting racist comments, praising segregation and talking wildly of setting off a race war. He had also been arrested twice: once in February for possession of Suboxone, a drug used to treat opiate addiction, and a second time in April for trespassing at a mall where he had been banned for a year after the first arrest.

On the day Mr. Roof contacted his old friends through Facebook, he went to the family trailer home of one of them, Joseph C. Meek Jr., in Red Bank, in suburban Lexington County. Soon he was sleeping there as often as four times a week. He had a cellphone, his friends said, but no phone service. To communicate, he used Wi-Fi to send messages via Facebook, or he showed up in person.

Mr. Roof told his friends that he had quit a landscaping job because he could not bear working in the Southern heat. He spent his days loafing around the place, watching television and sometimes calling his father, pretending to be at work, said Jacob Meek, 15, Joseph's brother. "He said his parents kept pressuring him to get a job," Jacob said.

He was fond of vodka and usually kept a stash around. He went to the Platinum Plus strip club recently, Jacob said, and threw dollar bills at the dancers.

But amid his aimlessness, Joseph Meek, 20, and other friends said, Mr. Roof talked wildly about hurting African-Americans, about doing something "crazy." Joseph, worried, hid the .45-caliber handgun Mr. Roof had bought with money his parents gave him for his 21st birthday. But Joseph eventually returned the gun because he was on probation and feared having it around.

At one point, Jacob said, Mr. Roof's parents took the gun, too. "I guess he stole it back," he said.

On Tuesday, Mr. Roof agreed to drive his friends to Lake Murray. He said he wanted to make the 2 p.m. showing of *Jurassic World* at the AMC theater. He showed Jacob the movie coupon he had in his car. He wore a gray shirt with a Border Patrol logo on one side and a sleeve stained with battery acid. He wore that shirt all the time, Jacob said.

He was not acting jumpy or out of the ordinary, his friends recalled. He was acting like a guy who had a movie to catch.

The Massacre

The Bible study group was wrapping up when the first gunshots sounded.

Felicia Sanders, who was in the room, heard the gunfire before seeing who the gunman was, she later told a friend, Ms. Johnson, Mr. Pinckney's cousin.

Ms. Sanders dropped to the ground with her five-year-old granddaughter. She saw blood everywhere. The white visitor was doing the shooting, and he reloaded his weapon five times.

Ms. Sanders's son, Tywanza Sanders, tried unsuccessfully to shield his aunt, Susie Jackson, 87, and talk sense to the gunman.

"That's when the gunman said: 'Y'all are raping our women and taking over the country. This must be done,'" Ms. Johnson recalled Ms. Sanders telling her.

Then he shot Tywanza. At one point, he asked a woman if she had been shot yet. When she said no, he said: "Good. Someone has to live to tell the story, because I'm going to kill myself, too." Ms. Sanders survived only by playing dead, Ms. Johnson said.

Soon the gunman was gone, fleeing in his Hyundai Elantra and leaving nine church-goers dead or dying.

Mr. Sanders, 26, who recently graduated from college, had been cutting hair and hoping to get a better job. In his final Instagram post, he quoted Jackie Robinson: "A life is not important except in the impact it has on other lives."

Ethel Lance, 70, was a mother of five. She was a sexton at the church and had worked as a custodian at Charleston's Gaillard Center for 35 years until her retirement.

A fan of gospel music, Ms. Lance was in charge of the backstage area there, including the dressing rooms, a job she loved because of the procession of performers who filed in and out. "She got a kick of that," said Cam Patterson, a former co-worker.

Cynthia Graham Hurd, a Charleston County librarian, had spent much of her last day in meetings at work before going to church. One of the presentations had been about civility, said her colleague Cynthia Bledsoe.

"She was so vocal and excited and happy about what was going on," said Darlene P. Jackson, the manager of the main county library. "She was happy about how we were going to set policies to help people."

In a 2003 feature in the local newspaper, *The Post and Courier*, Ms. Hurd said marrying her husband, Steve, had been one of the greatest joys of her life. Mr. Hurd, a merchant seaman, was making his way back from Saudi Arabia when Ms. Hurd was killed. Sunday would have been her 55th birthday, and Mr. Hurd had arranged a surprise, a delivery of pizza and cake.

For another victim, the Rev. Daniel Lee Simmons Sr., 74, the church had been a second home. He was a war veteran who rarely missed Wednesday Bible study, which he usually led.

On this Wednesday, as the business meeting broke up and congregants began gathering for the study group, Mr. Simmons urged Leon Alston, a steward at the church, to join. He did that almost every week. And almost every week, Mr. Alston declined.

"You need to start coming to Bible study a lot more," Mr. Simmons said.

"Maybe the next meeting," Mr. Alston replied.

A Suspicion Confirmed

Up in Red Bank on Wednesday night, the Meek brothers heard the news about a mass killing in Charleston. Mr. Roof immediately came to mind, Jacob said. They waited until they saw the surveillance photos to be sure.

There was a familiar figure, wearing a recognizable Border Patrol shirt stained in black.

They called the FBI. The authorities quickly arrived at the trailer and went through Mr. Roof's things, Joseph Meek said.

The Charleston police say Mr. Roof's father also called the authorities that night when he saw photographs of the suspect. He told them his son owned a .45-caliber handgun. Law enforcement officials had found .45-caliber casings at the scene.

At home in Summerville, half an hour northwest of Charleston, Ms. Johnson received a call Wednesday evening from Mr. Pinckney's wife, who told her that there had been a shooting.

"I said, 'Where's Clementa?'" Ms. Johnson recalled.

Her cousin's wife, distraught, replied: "I don't know. I don't know."

—June 21, 2015

NOTE: *Roof was charged with both federal and state crimes, including federal hate crimes. In December 2016 he was convicted on federal charges in the nine deaths. A federal jury in Charleston voted for the death penalty on January 10, 2017. State penalties are pending as of this writing.*

PRAISING ISIS, GUNMAN ATTACKS GAY NIGHTCLUB, LEAVING 50 DEAD IN WORST SHOOTING ON U.S. SOIL

By LIZETTE ALVAREZ AND RICHARD PÉREZ-PEÑA

A man who called 911 to proclaim allegiance to the Islamic State terrorist group, and who had been investigated in the past for possible terrorist ties, stormed a gay nightclub here Sunday morning, wielding an assault rifle and a pistol, and carried out the worst mass shooting in United States history, leaving 50 people dead and 53 wounded.

The attacker, identified by law enforcement officials as Omar Mateen, a 29-year-old who was born in New York, turned what had been a celebratory night of dancing to salsa and merengue music at the crowded Pulse nightclub into a panicked scene of unimaginable slaughter, the floors slicked with blood, the dead and the injured piled atop one another. Terrified people poured onto the darkened streets of the surrounding neighborhood, some carried wounded victims to safety, and police vehicles were pressed into service as makeshift ambulances to rush people to hospitals.

Joel Figueroa and his friends "were dancing by the hip-hop area when I heard shots, bam, bam, bam," he said, adding, "Everybody was screaming and running toward the front door."

Pulse, which calls itself "Orlando's Latin Hotspot," was holding its weekly "Upscale Latin Saturdays" party. The shooting began around 2 a.m., and some patrons thought at first that the booming reports they heard were firecrackers or part of the loud, thumping dance music.

Some people who were trapped inside hid where they could, calling 911 or posting messages to social media, pleading for help. The club posted a stark message on its Facebook page: "Everyone get out of Pulse and keep running."

Hundreds of people gathered in the glare of flashing red lights on the fringes of the law enforcement cordon around the nightclub, and later at area hospitals, hoping desperately for word on the fates of their relatives and friends.

More than 12 hours after the attack, anguished relatives paced between Orlando Regional Medical Center and a nearby hotel as they waited for word. They were told that so many were gunned down that victims would be tagged as anonymous until the hospital could identify them.

"We are here suffering, knowing nothing," said Baron Serrano, whose brother, Juan Rivera, 36, had been celebrating a friend's birthday with his husband and was now unaccounted for. "I cannot understand why they can't tell me anything because my brother is a very well-known person here in Orlando. He is a hairstylist, and everybody knows him."

A tally of victims whose relatives had been notified began building on a city website; by 6 p.m., it had six names. Among them was Juan Ramon Guerrero, a 22-year-old man of Dominican descent who had gone to the club with his boyfriend, Christopher Leinonen, who goes by the name Drew, because they wanted to listen to salsa. A friend, Brandon Wolf, watched people carry Mr. Guerrero outside, his body riddled with gunshot wounds.

But no one knew what had become of Mr. Leinonen. His mother, Christine, anxious because of health problems, had woken at 3 a.m. to news of the shooting, and learned from Mr. Wolf that her son had been inside.

A three-hour standoff followed the initial assault, with people inside effectively held hostage until around 5 a.m., when law enforcement officials led by a SWAT team raided the club, using an armored vehicle and explosives designed to disorient and distract. Over a dozen police officers and sheriff's deputies engaged in

"Everyone get out of Pulse and keep running."

a shootout with Mr. Mateen, leaving him dead and an officer wounded, his life saved by a helmet that deflected a bullet.

At least 30 people inside were rescued, and even the hardened police veterans who took the building and combed through it, aiding the living and identifying the dead, were shaken by what they saw, said John Mina, the Orlando police chief. "Just to look into the eyes of our officers told the whole story," he said.

It was the worst act of terrorism on American soil since Sept. 11, 2001, and the deadliest attack on a gay target in the nation's history, though officials said it was not clear whether some victims had been accidentally shot by law enforcement officers. The toll of 50 dead is larger than the number of murders in Orlando over the previous three years. Of an estimated 320 people in the club, nearly one-third were shot. The casualties far exceeded those in the 2007 shooting at Virginia Tech, where 32 people were killed, and the 2012 shooting at an elementary school in Newtown, Conn., where 26 people died.

"In the face of hate and violence, we will love one another," President Obama said in a special address from the White House. "We will not give in to fear or turn against each other. Instead, we will stand united as Americans to protect our people and defend our nation, and to take action against those who threaten us."

As he had done after several previous mass shootings, the president said the shooting demonstrated the need for what he called "common-sense" gun measures.

"This massacre is therefore a further reminder of how easy it is for someone to get their hands on a weapon that lets them shoot people in a school or a house of worship or a movie theater or a nightclub," Mr. Obama said. "We have to decide if that's the kind of country we want to be. To actively do nothing is a decision as well."

Fears of violence led to heightened security at lesbian, gay, bisexual and transgender events and gathering places around the country. The FBI investigated Mr. Mateen in 2013 when he made comments to co-workers suggesting he had terrorist ties, and again the next year, for possible connections to Moner Mohammad Abusalha, an American who became a suicide bomber in Syria, said Ronald Hopper, an assistant agent in charge of the bureau's Tampa Division. But each time, the FBI found no solid evidence that Mr. Mateen had any real connection to terrorism or had broken any laws. Still, he is believed to be on at least one watch list.

Mr. Mateen, who lived in Fort Pierce, Fla., was able to continue working as a security guard with the security firm G4S, where he had worked since 2007, and he was able to buy guns. The Federal Bureau of Alcohol, Tobacco, Firearms and Explosives said Mr. Mateen had legally bought a long gun and a pistol in the past week or two, though it was not clear whether those were the weapons used in the assault, which officials described as a handgun and an AR-15-type of assault rifle.

A former co-worker, Daniel Gilroy, said Mr. Mateen had talked often about killing people and had voiced hatred of gays, blacks, women and Jews.

Around the time of the massacre, Mr. Mateen called 911 and declared his allegiance to the Islamic State, Agent Hopper said. Other law enforcement officials said he called after beginning his assault.

Hours later, the Islamic State, also known as ISIS or ISIL, claimed responsibility in a statement released over an encrypted phone app used by the group. It stated that the attack "was carried out by an Islamic State fighter," according to a transcript provided by the SITE Intelligence Group, which tracks jihadist propaganda.

But officials cautioned that even if Mr. Mateen, who court records show was briefly married and then divorced, was inspired by the group, there was no indication that it had trained or instructed him, or had any direct connection with him. The Islamic State has encouraged "lone wolf" attacks in the West, a point reinforced recently by a group spokesman, Abu Muhammad al-Adnani, in his annual speech just before the holy month of Ramadan. In past years, the Islamic State and Al Qaeda ramped up attacks during Ramadan.

American Muslim groups condemned the shooting. "The Muslim community joins our fellow Americans in repudiating anyone or any group that would claim to justify or excuse such an appalling act of violence," said Rasha Mubarak, the Orlando regional coordinator of the Council on American-Islamic Relations.

—June 13, 2016

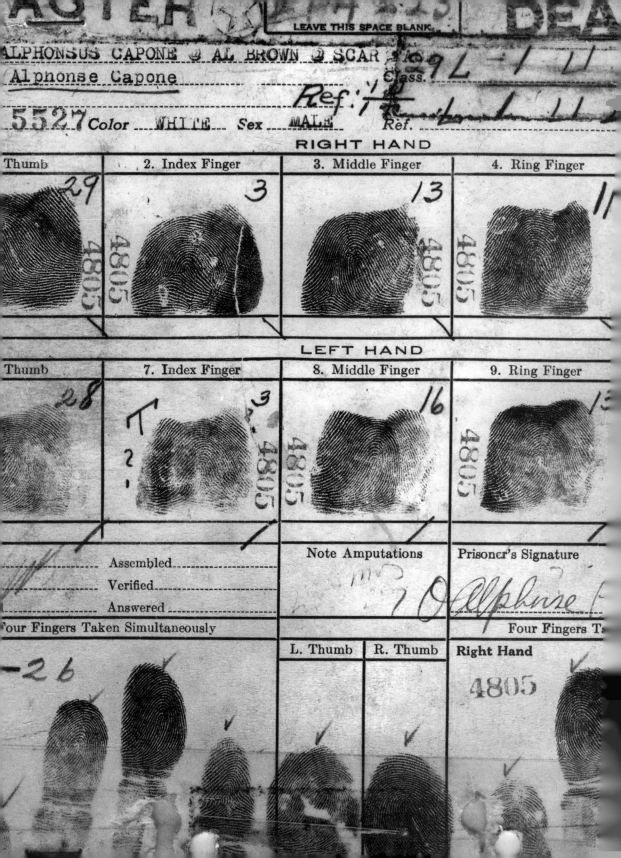

CHAPTER 5

THE MOB

"Know why he's dying? He's gonna die because he refused to come in when I called. He didn't do nothing else wrong."

—Mafia crime boss John Gotti, captured on a 1989 wiretap talking about his intention of murdering an underling who had not reported after being summoned

THEY ARE VILLAINOUS GROUPS that use fear as a weapon, prey on society and collapse at times from internal rivalries that lead to betrayal and bloodshed. But mob families have long captivated Hollywood scriptwriters and newspaper readers because of their allure as secret societies with formal hierarchies, an oft-ignored internal code and an initiation rite that features blood and the burning image of a saint. Over the decades, *Times* readers have seen inside the social clubs, admired the cut of John Gotti's suits and witnessed the death of Carmine Galante, his cigar still dangling from his lips.

OPPOSITE: Al Capone's federal fingerprint card, 1932.

7 CHICAGO GANGSTERS SLAIN BY FIRING SQUAD OF RIVALS, SOME IN POLICE UNIFORMS

Chicago gangland leaders observed Valentine's Day with machine guns and a stream of bullets and as a result seven members of the George "Bugs" Moran–Dean O'Banion, North Side Gang are dead in the most cold-blooded gang massacre in the history of this city's underworld.

The seven gang warriors were trapped in a beer-distributors' rendezvous at 2122 North Clark Street, lined up against the wall by four men, two of whom were in police uniforms, and executed with the precision of a firing squad.

The killings have stunned the citizenry of Chicago as well as the police department, and while tonight there was no solution, the one outstanding cause was illicit liquor traffic.

The dead, as identified by the police were:

CLARK, JAMES, aliases Frank Meyer and Albert Kashellek, convicted robber and burglar; brother-in-law of George Moran, the gang leader.

GUSENBERG, FRANK, who died after the others were killed, but refused to talk.

GUSENBERG, PETER, brother of Frank, a notorious gunman for [Moran's faction].

MAY, JOHN, auto mechanic, thought to be a safe-blower before joining the Moran gang.

SCHWIMMER, REINHARDT H., a resident of Hotel Parkway, an optometrist, with offices in the Capitol Building, known as a companion of gangsters, but lacking a criminal record.

SNYDER, JOHN, aliases Arthur Hayes, Adam Hoyer, Adam Hyers; convicted robber and confidence man.

WEINSHANK, ALBERT, henchman of Moran and strong-arm agent of Chicago cleaning and dyeing industry.

The dead, the greatest in point of numbers since Chicago gang killings began in 1924 with the assassination of Dean O'Banion, were remnants of the "mob" organized by O'Banion, later captained by Hymie Weiss and Peter Gusenberg and recently commanded by George "Bugs" Moran.

Bodies of slain Chicago North Side gang members, after the Valentine's Day Massacre of February 14, 1929.

Capone's Name Is Mentioned

One name loomed in the police investigation under way this afternoon and tonight. It was that of Alphonse "Scarface" Capone, gang leader extraordinary.

Six of the slain gangsters died in their tracks on the floor of the North Clark Street garage, a block from Lincoln Park and its fine residential neighborhood. A seventh, with 20 or more bullets in his body, died within an hour.

The police found more than 160 empty machine gun shells strewing the floor of the execution room, and there was a report that Moran had been taken out alive by the marauders.

Police Commissioner William F. Russell and his First Deputy Commissioner, John Stege, were bewildered tonight over the fact that the ambush was arranged by two men in police uniforms, wearing police badges, and the fact that the other killers arrived at the scene in an automobile resembling a detective bureau squad car.

Police Declare "War to the Finish"

Tonight an underworld roundup unparalleled in the annals of the police department is underway.

"It's a war to the finish," Commissioner Russell said. "I've never known of a challenge like this—the killers posing as policemen—but now the challenge has been made, it's accepted. We're going to make this the knell of gangdom in Chicago."

Al Capone at a football game, January 19, 1931.

Reconstructing the massacre as it occurred, police and prosecuting officials were of the opinion that the men were victims of their own cupidity as well as the wrath of their enemies, for they had been stood up against the brick wall of the garage, their backs, rather than their faces, toward the executioners.

This morning about 10 o'clock seven men were sitting about the garage, two in the front, five others behind a wooden partition in the garage proper, according to the investigators' theory.

Four of the men were gathered about an electric stove on which bubbled a pot of coffee. A box of crackers and a half-dozen cups completed the breakfast layout. The men munched away in between telephone calls.

The fifth man, John May, the mechanic, is believed to have been puttering about the trucks, one of which was loaded with a new wooden beer bat.

There was a noise outside that rose above the clatter of Clark Street traffic, sounding like a police gong. The front door of the garage opened.

In marched two men wearing the uniforms of policemen, their stars gleaming against the blue of the cloth. Two men in civilian attire followed them. All were armed, the first two with sub-machine guns, the last two with sawed-off shotguns.

Swift Execution Accomplished

The two men in the front office threw up their hands, apparently believing a regular police raid was in progress, and marched to the rear. There was a scramble among the men about the improvised breakfast tables as they saw the police uniforms.

One of the men in police uniform probably gave the order to line up, face to the wall, and sighting May, made him join the others. As the seven stood staring at the white-washed wall, they were swiftly deprived of their weapons.

Then, it is believed, came the order to "give it to them" and the roar of the shotguns mingled with the rat-a-tat of the machine gun, a clatter like that of a gigantic type-writer.

Evidently May, incredulous that he, an ordinary mechanic, should be included, made a mad leap only to drop within six inches of a man wielding a shotgun.

The machine-gunners probably sprayed the heap of dead on the floor and then the four executioners marched out.

A tailor glanced up from his pressing iron next door, and a woman living nearby ran to the street. They saw what appeared to be two men under arrest, their hands in the air, followed by two policemen.

The four climbed into what looked like a police squad car, a fifth man sitting at the wheel, the motor humming. The car roared south in Clark Street, sweeping around the wrong side of a streetcar, and was lost in the traffic.

When police arrived upon the scene they found six of the men dead. The seventh, Frank Gusenberg, was crawling on the floor toward Police Lieutenant Tom Loftus. Gusenberg died within an hour at the Alexandrian Hospital.

The majority of the victims were dangerous men, with reputations equal to the worst, Deputy Commissioner Stege said.

"Where is 'Bugs' Moran?" Stege asked when his officers discovered the automobile that Moran was supposed to own.

Then came the story that perhaps he was one of the men who walked out of the garage, hands high above his head, followed by the pseudo policemen.

Squads were dispatched to seek Moran. Others were sent after information concerning "Scarface" Al Capone's whereabouts. The latter group came back with word that Capone was at his winter home in Miami, Fla.

The police recalled that the Aiello brothers' gang of North Side Sicilians had a year or so ago affiliated themselves with the Moran gang, and that the Aiellos and the Caponites were deadly enemies. But no Aiellos were found.

Coroner Herman N. Bundesen reached the garage within a half hour after the fusillade. The bodies were photographed and searched.

Cash and Diamond Rings on Bodies

Lieutenants John L. Sullivan and Otto Erlanson of the Homicide Bureau checked the identifications and kept records of search results.

Peter Gusenberg had a large diamond ring and $447 in cash.

Albert Weinshank proved to be the cousin of a former state representative of the same family name. Weinshank, who recently took an "executive position" with the Central Cleaners and Dyers Company, had only $418 in cash, but he had a diamond ring and a bankbook showing an account in the name of A. H. Shanks.

Then a body was identified as that of John Snyder, alias Adam Meyers, alias Adam Hyers, alias Hayes. It was said that Snyder was owner of the Fairview Kennels, a dog track rivaling Capone's Hawthorne course. Chief Egan was told that Snyder was the "brains" of the Moran "mob." Snyder had $1,399.

The body of May, the overall-clad mechanic, had only a few dollars in the pockets. He was the father of seven children. A machine gun bullet had penetrated two medals of St. Christopher.

The fifth of the five bodies in the row, flat on their backs with their heads to the south, was recorded as that of Reinhardt H. Schwimmer, an optometrist. Despite his having no police record, it is said that he recently boasted that he was in the alcohol business and could have any one "taken for a ride."

Closer to the door, face down, with his head to the east, lay James Clark, brother-in-law of Moran, and rated as a killer with many notches in his guns. His clothes contained $681.

Women's Story Aids Police

"Bullet marks on the wall," Captain Thomas Condon observed, and it was seen that few of the pellets missed their marks, for there were only seven or eight places where the detectives were sure bullets had struck.

Each victim had six to ten bullets shot through him. A high-powered electric bulb overhead flooded the execution chamber with a glare of light. Chained in a corner was a huge police dog, which snarled at the detectives.

The police expressed amazement that the seven gangsters had been induced to face the wall and certain death without a struggle.

"That bunch always went well armed," a police captain said.

An explanation was seen in the story of Mrs. Alphonsine Morin, who lives across the street from the garage. She told of seeing men she thought were policemen coming out after hearing the shooting.

"Two men in uniforms had rifles or shotguns as they came out the door," she said, "and there were two or three men walking ahead of them with their hands up in the air. It looked as though the police were making an arrest and they all got into an automobile and drove away."

Each victim had six to ten bullets shot through him.

"Quite simple," chief Egan commented. "They would never have got that gang to line up unless they came in police uniforms."

Typical of his life, Frank Gusenberg refused during his last hour to tell the police anything. He was conscious, but he kept defying the police who sought names from him.

Assistant State's Attorney David Stansbury was put in charge of the investigation tonight by State's Attorney John A. Swanson. The police, prosecutor and the federal authorities were all working together to get trace of the slayers.

Theories about who plotted and carried out the execution were numerous.

"Hijackers, no doubt," Chief of Detectives John Egan termed the dead men. Other theories were:

- That the victims had been "hoisting" trucks of booze, Canadian beer, alcohol and fine liquors en route from Detroit, and the "Purple Gang" of Detroit had sallied out for vengeance.
- That they were involved in the bitter competition of rival organizations of cleaning and dyeing establishments, the Moran gang protecting the North Side concerns and the Capone outfit the Becker system.
- That it was a sequel to the sentencing of Alderman Titus Haffa yesterday to two years in Leavenworth Prison for violating the prohibition law. Haffa's ward adjoins the domain that Moran had ruled.

Other detectives said the killing was the work of the Capone "mob."

"It is the answer of the Sicilians for the killing of Tony Lombardo, and it is a logical sequel to the series of murders starting five years ago with the mowing down on O'Banion," one declared.

James D. Cunningham, president of the Illinois Manufacturers' Association, representing more than 2,000 industrial concerns centering around Chicago, issued an appeal tonight to "all law-abiding citizens" to assert themselves upon the issue of gang warfare as a result of today's "massacre."

Asserting that the story would be "broadcast internationally as the culminating blot" on the city's name, he concluded: "Would it not be appropriate for the city and state authorities to call a mass meeting and take steps to instill terror in the hearts of these organized murderers?"

North Side Gang "Dynasty" Falls

Gang warfare in Chicago began with the slaying of Dean O'Banion in November, 1924. In the 50 months since then, 38 murders, most of them attributed to the enmity between the North Side band founded by O'Banion and the West Side syndicate established by John Torrio and turned over to Al Capone, have been recorded.

Today's massacre marked the end of the proud North Side dynasty, which began with O'Banion. O'Banion yielded to Hymie Weiss, who was replaced by "Schemer" Drucci, who was succeeded by "Bugs" Moran. And Moran tonight was missing, while seven of his chief aids lay dead.

—February 15, 1929

NOTE: *Al Capone was in Florida at the time of the killings but is widely believed to have ordered them. They cleared the way for him to assume the role of undisputed kingpin of Chicago's under-world. When he ultimately went to jail, though, in 1931, it was not for murder but for tax evasion.*

THE CRIME HEARINGS: TELEVISION PROVIDES BOTH A LIVELY SHOW AND A NOTABLE PUBLIC SERVICE

By JACK GOULD

Last week's all-star television revue with Frank Erickson, Joe Adonis and Frank Costello, the man with the fascinating hands, marked an epoch for television and gangsterdom alike.

The reluctant trio from the underworld were forced to leave the privacy of their favorite restaurants and barbershops and let millions watch them try to get off the spot. The big boys who always preferred to stay in the background suddenly found themselves in the center of the stage, the most popular act in town.

In turn, television displayed a social impact of such enormous potentialities that undoubtedly the politicians, broadcasters and educators will be studying and debating its implications for days to come. Housewives have left the housework undone and husbands have slipped away from their jobs to watch. The city has been under a hypnotic spell, absorbed, fascinated, angered and amused.

Timely

From the standpoint of public enlightenment the union of television and the Senate Crime Investigating Committee, headed by the soft-spoken Southerner, Senator Estes W. Kefauver, Democrat of Tennessee, has been uniquely timely and beneficial.

In the committee there has been the will to bring into the open the seamy side of the shadowy figures who live on both sides of the law and permeate even the highest levels of society. In television there has been the means to make the story come alive in the minds of millions.

An almost incredible cast of characters have made their entrance on the screen. The poker-faced Erickson, the suavely arrogant Adonis, the shy Costello and the jocose Virginia Hill might have been hired from Hollywood's Central Casting Bureau. The committee's counsel, Rudolph Halley of the flat sandpaper voice, has been the relentless inquisitor of tradition.

Both principals and bit players have made a capital show and the hearings have had all the elements of drama—suspense, conflict, varied motivation and contrasting personalities—so dear to the impresario's heart. Yet underneath has lain the hard core of harsh reality, which has kept one glued to the screen.

Narcotic

Watching personalities who were real yet had all the appeal of characters straight out of a mystery thriller had a narcotic fascination on the viewer at home.

But to conclude that television by itself was responsible for the theatrical overtones to the hearings would be a mistake. With such a list of witnesses the hearings would have been just as dramatic had the cameras not been there, as was true of any number of similar investigations before the day of TV. Television is a new and complementary medium of mass communication, which in the case of actuality broadcasts, such as last week's hearings, mirror the scene as it exists. The committee and the witnesses put on the show. For years the press has had to cope with those who could not or would not see the distinction between making news and reporting news. If television is to have its rightful freedom as a reportorial medium, it now faces the same task.

Frank Costello answering questions put to him by Rudolph Halley, chief counsel of the committee, March 19, 1951.

Certainly, it is of the utmost importance that such hearings be conducted with scrupulous regard for the rights of a witness, but Costello's objections first to having his face shown on camera and then to the lighting, were tenuous to say the least.

Veteran reporters at the hearing say that the lighting is far less troublesome than is experienced at national political conventions. The members of the committee and in particular Mr. Halley, who has been "on camera" more than any other individual, also have not appeared bothered.

What is so new and strange to Costello—and many others who have not yet thoroughly grasped the true meaning of television's advent—is that video takes away the walls around the hearing room. It makes the public hearing more public than ever before.

In this fact lies the true measure of the importance of television's coverage of the hearings. It has shown that it can arouse public interest to a degree that virtually beggars immediate description.

Participation

Through the medium of the camera's perceptive eye the individual has had a liberal education in government and morality. Television's qualities of intimacy and immediacy have made the experience so personal that the TV viewer actually is closer to the scene that the spectator in the courtroom.

What television has done is to provide the implementation for the goal of Senator Kefauver's committee. Once the set has been tuned in to the proceedings in the federal building, it has taken extraordinary will power to turn the receiver off. Whether sitting at home, in an office or at a bar, the viewer becomes a participant to see with his own eyes, to hear with his own ears, and to form his own opinion at first-hand.

The power to elicit this public participation is a priceless asset at a time when democracy is facing one of its severest tests. To employ the power wisely and progressively can bring benefits and gains far transcending television itself.

The hearings of Senator Kefauver's committee have provided a wonderful show. But as they draw to a close the telecasts also should make the public, broadcasters and legislators a little humble. The last week has demonstrated with awesome vividness what television can do to enlighten, to educate and to drive home a lesson. It will take the best efforts of all of us to see that TV truly rises to its own opportunity.

—March 18, 1951

NOTE: *The Kefauver hearings (run by the Senate's Special Committee on Organized Crime in Interstate Commerce) of 1950–51 did not lead to groundbreaking legislation to combat crime. But the sessions, televised live and held in cities across the country, gave many Americans their first detailed exposure to the power of organized crime.*

65 HOODLUMS SEIZED IN A RAID
AND RUN OUT OF UPSTATE VILLAGE

State policemen and federal agents rounded up today 65 men whom they described as hoodlums attending a meeting of the "hierarchy of the Eastern Seaboard criminal world."

The men were released because the police said they had "nothing to hold them on." But they were told "to get out of town and stay out of town from now on."

The men, almost all with criminal records of one kind or another, had come from places as far as New Jersey, Ohio, California, Buffalo and Puerto Rico. They drove out of town in a variety of expensive cars, the oldest of which was a 1956 Cadillac.

Among those attending the meeting in this small town of less than 1,000 persons was Vito Genovese, 60 years old, a close associate of Albert Anastasia, the slain boss of Murder Inc. Another was John Anthony DeMarco, 54, of Shaker Heights, Ohio, who has been arrested on charges of murder, bombing and blackmail.

The hoodlums were expensively dressed, some with diamonds in their belt buckles and most with gold watches on their wrists. The police said that the lowest amount of money found on an individual was $450 and the largest $10,000.

"It looked like a meeting of George Rafts," Sgt. Edgar Croswell, of the state police said. "In fact we would have had a harder time getting them if it weren't for the fact they were such city slickers."

Sgt. Croswell was referring to the fact that when the police surrounded the house where the men were meeting, about 15 of them tried to run away into the woods. "Those city boys didn't have a chance," he said. "With their fancy shoes and their hats and coats snagging on tree branches, we could grab them easy."

This day started quietly for Apalachin, a hamlet 15 miles west of Binghamton, although the state police had an inkling there would be trouble. This town itself has no police force.

Gangsters had met here back in 1956. The host on that occasion had been Joseph Barbara, a man who owns a big house on a hill back in the woods in Apalachin. Barbara has been arrested three times on homicide charges, but never convicted.

The police noted that Barbara was putting out calls to motels near the town making reservations for his guests. He asked for the best and "never mind the price."

Their suspicions that trouble was in the offing were confirmed when yesterday the procession of expensive fare began to park in front of the motels. By this morning the flow became a flood.

The police even noted that one of those arriving was Lewis Santos, the manager of the Sans Souci nightclub in Havana. The police knew that reinforcements were needed, and additional state police were sent to Apalachin so that the force was augmented to 15 men. Two agents from the Alcohol Tax unit of the Treasury Department also arrived in case any illegal liquor was discovered.

The police said that between 12 and 15 of them began to make a break for the woods.

The police noted that about midday cars began to drive to Barbara's house in Apalachin. The parking area next to the house became jammed.

The police did not have warrants to search the house. But they set up a road-block to prevent the cars from leaving. Then they began to check the license numbers of the cars parked in the lot.

That was enough to panic some of the gangsters. The police said that between 12 and 15 of them began to make a break for the woods. "They poured out of the doors, windows—everywhere," one policeman said.

The policemen followed in hot pursuit. No shots were fired in the race through the forest. But the forest began to wear down the gangsters and in groups of two or three they were picked up by the police.

Back at the house, others gave themselves up, some stripping themselves of all identifying cards before surrendering.

Meeting: A Mystery

All of them were brought back to the state police barracks where the police wrung the identities from each. But no one would say what the meeting was all about.

"If we knew why they were meeting," Sgt. Croswell said, "we wouldn't have to let them go. We gave them a rough time in the station house. But we couldn't even make them commit disorderly conduct there."

Sgt. Croswell, 42 years old, is a big man—six feet tall, weighing about 200 pounds—who rarely smiles and makes few friends.

"He'd probably be the only cop in the state who would do it," a friend said, commenting on the sergeant's exploit in Vestal. "He's the antithesis of the kind of cop who would take a free meal on his beat."

He has been in the state police for 12 years, the last 12 years in criminal investigation.

There was speculation why the men were meeting, however. The investigation by Senate Select Committee on Improper Activities in Labor or Management into the matter of the garbage-hauling racket was one of them. The murder of gang boss Anastasia was another.

Sgt. Croswell, divorced from his wife, lives in police barracks, where he keeps pretty much to himself. His most striking physical characteristic, apart from his size, is his eyes. They are gray and cold.

In 1947, when the state police were cracking down on lotteries all over the mid-state area, Sgt. Croswell was detailed to pick up a suspect. The man was said to have had $50,000 in cash and to have offered the sergeant a large chunk of it to let him go. Sergeant Croswell turned the man in.

—November 15, 1957

NOTE: *The enclave, attended by crime figures from as far away as Cuba and Italy, was very much an underworld summit. Authorities charged some of the attendees criminally after they refused to describe the purpose of the meeting. (Some said they were there to visit Barbara because he was sick and it was a coincidence that so many had arrived at the same time.) But the convictions were later overturned.*

VALACHI NAMES 5 AS CRIME CHIEFS IN NEW YORK AREA

By EMANUEL PERLMUTTER

Joseph M. Valachi calmly recited today the bloody history of a war for control of the Cosa Nostra crime syndicate. From this war, he said, five men emerged as leaders of the New York underworld and administrators of its code.

He identified the leaders of New York's five Cosa Nostra "families" as Vito Genovese, Carlo Gambino, Joseph Magliocco, Joseph Bonanno and Thomas Lucchese. Genovese is in prison.

The 60-year-old Valachi, himself a convicted murderer, also gave the Senate Permanent Subcommittee on Investigations the names of two men, still alive, who he said had participated in the still unsolved slayings of four syndicate members in the 1930s. He testified at the open hearing that he had driven the getaway car in one of the assassinations.

Describes Initiation

The committee and an overflow crowd of more than 500 spectators listened intently as Valachi described his secret initiation into Cosa Nostra in 1930.

The witness told of his induction by ritual oath, bloodletting and the ceremonial burning of paper in his cupped hands to illustrate how he would burn if he betrayed the organization.

Valachi's testimony was often rambling. It was told in an illiterate diction that sometimes left his hearers confused. But the sinister story held his listeners in its grip.

The men named by Valachi as killers who are still alive were Girolamo Santuccio, alias Bobby Doyle, and Salvatore Shillitani, also known as Solly Shields.

He said Santuccio whose alias, "Doyle," he pronounced in Brooklynese as "Derl"— was the slayer of Joseph Pinzolo, a syndicate chief found dead of gunshot wounds on Sept. 9, 1930, in Pinzolo's fruit-importing office on Broadway. The suite had been leased in the name of Luchese.

Valachi testified also that Santuccio and two other men, known to him only as "Buster from Chicago" and the other called Nick Capuzzi, had killed Alfred Mineo and Steve Ferrigno in an apartment on Pelham Parkway in the Bronx on Nov. 5, 1930.

Valachi said the last information he had had on Santuccio was in 1960, when the latter was living in Stamford, Conn., the owner of a restaurant and "mixed up in numbers and bookmaking."

Valachi said Buster, whom he characterized as a "collegiate type," had been brought by the mob from Chicago, where he had fled from Al Capone.

"He looked like a college boy," the witness said of Buster. "He was 23 years old, about 6 feet tall, weighed 200 pounds. He always carried a violin case."

"What did he carry in the violin case?" asked Jerome S. Adlerman, the subcommittee's general counsel.

"A machine gun," Valachi replied.

"Buster later got killed in an argument at a crap game." Valachi said. "This was in peacetime." He added that Capuzzi had subsequently died of natural causes.

The witness said Shillitani, together with Buster and Capuzzi, had fatally shot Joseph Catania, alias Joseph Baker, outside an apartment house on Crescent Avenue, the Bronx, on Feb. 3, 1931.

Shillitani is now out on parole, Valachi said.

However, the police in New York said Shillitani was still in prison.

Valachi testified that he had driven the getaway car in the Catania murder and had been involved in two unsuccessful attempts to kill Mineo and Ferrigno before they were slain while he was away from the scene of the shootings.

First Slaying "Contract"

Valachi said his involvement in the Catania murder had been the first "contract" he performed for the syndicate after his initiation into it. During the Mineo-Ferrigno incidents, he explained, he was only on trial.

"Did you get paid for this contract?" asked Senator Edmund S. Muskie, Democrat of Maine.

"No," Valachi replied. "If the organization finds out that any member gets paid for murder for the organization, he's in trouble."

"Did you have to take this contract?" Senator Muskie continued.

Valachi shrugged. "We were in a war, senator," he replied. "We were working like a team, like an army would."

"You mean killing for the organization was like breathing for you?" the senator asked.

"It was like breathing," the witness replied.

"Moonlighting" Gangster

When Senator Henry M. Jackson, Democrat of Washington, asked Valachi whether he and the other soldiers had received any pay from the organization in this period, the witness responded, "About $25 a week."

"I went out on a couple of burglaries so that I could have some money for myself," Valachi added.

"Something like moonlighting, wasn't it?" Senator Jackson commented.

"Well, $25 wasn't a lot of money," the witness said.

The story that Valachi told of the underworld war that has flared intermittently since 1930 was complicated, with gang members and leaders frequently changing sides.

In essence it added up to the following:

Peter Morello, alias "The Clutching Hand," was the "boss of bosses" of Cosa Nostra until his assassination on Aug. 15, 1930, at his office on East 116th Street. Valachi testified that Buster had shot Morello.

After Morello's death, a war for dominance developed between one faction headed by Giuseppe "Joe the Boss" Masseria and another led by Salvatore Maranzano. Masseria has as an ally the "family" headed by Mineo and Ferrigno. Maranzano had a group headed by Gaetana Reina as his ally. Most of the Masseria forces were of Neapolitan origin. The Maranzano "soldiers," or underlings, came mainly from Sicily, especially the area of Castel del Mar.

Gang Short of Men

On Feb. 26, 1930, Retina was killed by an unidentified member of the Masseria mob. Masseria installed Pinzolo as Reina's successor, but Reina's old followers then had Pinzolo murdered. Gaetano Gagliano, one of Reina's underbosses, then took over the combine. It was at this juncture that the Gagliano group, in need of manpower, recruited Valachi.

In this war for dominance, Masseria had the support of Al Capone and of Arthur Flegenheimer, known as "Dutch Schultz," the leader of a non-Italian gang, according to Valachi.

After the murder of Mineo and Ferrigno, the stifle flared into the open, with Masseria and his followers declaring "death to all Castellamarese" (those from Castel der Mar) throughout the United States, Valachi testified.

The tide of battle soon swung to Maranzano and his allies. At this point, Valachi said, the Maranzano forces numbered 600 men, while Masseria had only a few.

Masseria was assassinated on April 20, 1931, in a Coney Island restaurant. Valachi said Charles "Lucky" Luciano and Vito Genovese, Masseria's deputies, had lured Masseria to his death.

Although Valachi's testimony today did not go beyond this point in the struggle, he said the war had ended with Masseria's murder and Maranzano's ascension to top leadership.

A chart of the warfare, introduced by the subcommittee, showed that Maranzano was killed on Sept. 11, 1931, and that four families then took over, one headed by Luciano, one by Philip and Vincent Mangano, another by Joseph Profaci and the fourth by Gagliano. Ultimately, the control passed to the five leaders named by Valachi today.

Valachi's story of his introduction into Cosa Nostra in 1930 had the quality of a movie melodrama. He said he and three others had driven to a private house "90 miles upstate." There were about 40 men in the place, he said; Maranzano, the leader was among them.

"The purpose was to make us new members and to meet the others for the first time," he said.

Valachi said he had been take into a large room, where 30 or 35 men were sitting at a long table.

"There was a gun and a knife on the table," Valachi testified. "They sat me down next to Maranzano, I repeated some words in Sicilian after him."

"What did the words mean?" asked Senator John J. McClellan, Democrat of Arkansas, the subcommittee chairman.

"You live by the gun and knife, and die by the gun and knife," Valachi said.

The witness said Maranzano had then given him a piece of paper that was set afire in his hand.

"I repeated in Sicilian, 'This is the way I burn if I betray the organization,'" he continued.

"Godfather" Selected

Valachi said the men at the table then "threw out a number," with each man holding up fingers from one to five. The total was taken. Starting with Maranzano, the sum was then counted off around the table. The man on whom the final number fell was designated as Valachi's "godfather" in the family. Valachi said the lot had fallen to Bonanno.

The witness said that he had then had his finger pricked by a needle by Bonanno to show he was united to Bonanno by blood. Afterward, all those present joined hands in a bond to the organization.

Valachi said he was given two rules in Cosa Nostra that night—one concerning allegiance to it and another a promise to never possess another member's wife, sister or daughter.

For the first time, the witness grew grim. "This is the worst thing I can do, to tell about the ceremony," he said. "This is my doom, telling it to you and the press."

The witness started his day's testimony by telling of his life as a member of burglary gangs in East Harlem before he became involved with Cosa Nostra. He said he had first been a member of a neighborhood burglary gang consisting mainly of Italians, who broke store windows to commit thefts. After a while, he said, he joined a burglary combine known as "the Irish gang."

Valachi said rivalry had erupted between the two gangs and that Vincent Rao, still a Harlem underworld figure, had asked him to double-cross the Irish gang. That was in 1924.

"I turned it down," Valachi said. "I told Rao, 'You guys gave me only a contract a dog would do, to double-cross your own friends.'

"I was thinking of my own principles," he explained to the committee.

Valachi testified that he was sent to Sing Sing in 1925 for a burglary and served 44 months. On his return, he learned that Frank La Puma, one of the Irish gang, had been murdered and that he himself was marked for death.

The witness said he was told that a thug named "Bum" Rogers got "$100 from Ciro Terranova to do the job."

Valachi said that he then had gone to see Frank Livorsi, Terranova's chauffeur and bodyguard, to plead his own case and that his life had been spared. Terranova, known as "the artichoke king," was a former henchman of Al Capone, and a long-time power in the underworld.

"Why was Terranova called the artichoke king?" Mr. McClellan continued.

"He had all the artichokes that came into the city tied up," Valachi said. "The artichokes could keep and then he would make his own price."

"Were artichokes so important?" the Senator asked.

"An artichoke is something an Italian must have for dessert," Valachi explained.

—*October 2, 1963*

NOTE: *At a time when some U.S. law enforcement officials were still skeptical of the Mafia's reach, Valachi became the first mob member to admit the existence of an elaborate crime organization operating in America. He died in prison in 1971.*

GALANTE AND 2 SHOT TO DEATH IN A BROOKLYN RESTAURANT

By ROBERT D. McFADDEN

Carmine Galante, the reputed organized-crime leader, was slain in a barrage of gunfire and shotgun blasts in an apparent underworld execution yesterday afternoon as he dined on the patio of a quiet, sunlit garden in a small Brooklyn restaurant.

Two other men—a Galante bodyguard and the owner of the restaurant—also were killed. The 17-year-old son of the restaurateur was seriously wounded in the attack by three ski-masked gunmen at Joe and Mary's Italian-American Restaurant at 205 Knickerbocker Avenue in the Bushwick section.

All three of the slain men were unarmed. They were shot at point-blank range as they sat with an unknown companion at a small table on the concrete patio. The fourth diner, whose identity was being sought, was unharmed. He was said to have hurried away after the shooting, and investigators said his role in the execution scheme was unclear.

Mr. Galante, a short, baldish 69-year-old man, was blown backward by the force of a shotgun blast that struck him in the chest and by bullets that pierced his left eye and riddled his chest.

Son of Restaurateur Shot

He and his bodyguard, Leonardo Coppolla, 40, who was shot in the head, died instantly. The restaurant owner, Giuseppe Turano, 48, was shot in the head and shoulder and died later en route to Wyckoff Heights Hospital; his son, John, 17, was shot twice in the back in another part of the restaurant as he ran toward the patio when the shooting there began.

The killers, believed to be underworld "hit" men fulfilling a contract, ran out, joined several armed accomplices who had acted as lookouts and sped away in two or three cars. Three stunned diners fled ahead of the killers, whose getaway was witnessed by storekeepers in nearby shops and neighbors gaping from the windows of three-story tenements overlooking the street.

"I was walking down the stairs when I heard sounds like cherry bombs going off," said Lisa Santiago, whose apartment overlooks the patio. She said she had counted six blasts.

"There was no warning whatsoever," said one police officer. "They just walked in calmly and began shooting."

Body of Carmine Galante on the patio of a Brooklyn restaurant, July 12, 1979.

Indicative of the surprise with which the killers struck, a cigar Mr. Galante was puffing when the barrage erupted was still clenched in his teeth when the police arrived at the blood-spattered patio.

Near the three sprawled and bloody victims, a half-finished lettuce and tomato salad, some rolls, a peach and a half-finished carafe of red wine were still standing atop the floral-pattern oilcloth on the table.

The patio was littered with double-0 buckshot, a large-size shotgun pellet, and a number of .45-caliber shell casings. The police said shotguns had definitely been used in the attack, but they said they were unsure whether the bullets had been fired from pistols or automatic rifles.

Law-enforcement sources said that Mr. Galante, whom many authorities considered one of the nation's most powerful organized crime figures, had been marked for a gangland slaying for a year or more because of his alleged aspirations to succeed the late Carlo Gambino, the underworld figure once known as "the boss of all bosses."

Lt. Remo Franceshini, the head of the Queens district attorney's detective squad and former head of the police department's organized-crime squad, said he believed that Mr. Galante had been executed on orders from a rival for power in the underworld, Frank

Tieri, who is described by law-enforcement authorities as the head of a crime "family" organized by the late Vito Genovese.

Mr. Galante, who had served 12 years in prison on a narcotics charge and an additional 17 months for parole violation, had been free on $50,000 bail since March 23 pending a parole hearing. He has been described by the police as the head of the 200-member crime "family" formerly headed by Joseph Bonanno.

Apartment in Little Italy

The owner of a dry-cleaning shop in Little Italy, Mr. Galante lived officially in an apartment on Waverly Place in Greenwich Village, but law-enforcement sources said he had lived for years with a woman friend on East 38th Street. The superintendent of the Waverly Place building said that in the eight years he had worked there he had never seen Mr. Galante.

The shooting yesterday was the most sensational underworld slaying in New York since Joseph Gallo was gunned down on April 7, 1972, in a restaurant in Little Italy.

The slayings yesterday occurred at 2:50 p.m., according to accounts provided by the police and eyewitnesses in nearby shops and tenements on the block, Knickerbocker Avenue between Jefferson and Troutman Streets, in a predominantly Italian and Hispanic section.

Although witnesses were believed to have seen portions of what happened, many were reluctant to talk about the slayings and there were conflicting accounts about how many assassins were involved and how many cars they used. At least five, and perhaps seven or more men, were involved, authorities said, although only three were believed to have fired the fatal shots.

The police said the slaying had been carried out with swift precision. By one account, two men used a black limousine to block off traffic on nearby Jefferson Street, apparently to insure a smooth getaway, while five others pulled up outside the restaurant in one or two cars.

Deputy Inspector Martin Hayes said that three gunmen entered the restaurant while two others stayed at the front door, standing lookout and waving guns at passersby.

Only three customers, in addition to Mr. Galante and his companions, were dining in the restaurant, which has two indoor dining rooms, one behind the other, in addition to the outdoor patio in the rear. Yellow curtains hung across the front windows and just inside the door hung a picture of *The Last Supper*.

In the first room, the killers encountered John Turano, a high school student who has often worked at the restaurant, standing behind a counter and talking on a telephone. They ordered him to hang up and hurried toward the back, passing the mother and a

16-year-old daughter of the owner and a cook-counterman. In the second dining room, they passed three diners and rushed out onto the patio.

Open Fire at Close Range

There, Mr. Galante, carrying $860 in cash and wearing blue slacks and a white shirt open at the neck, was seated with Mr. Coppolla, Mr. Turano and the unidentified diner in a modest but pastoral setting. Grape vines hung near the dining table and tomato plants sprouted from a small patch of ground nearby. Chest-high wire fences separated the patio from adjacent backyards.

The gunmen opened fire from a range of less than six feet, the police said.

Mr. Galante, struck in the eye and chest, was hurled backward onto the patio and fell on his back, his left arm slung across his chest and his right hand at his belt. A short black cigar protruded from his mouth, and blood streaked his face.

Half of Mr. Coppolla's face was blown away by a shotgun blast, the police said, and he also died instantly. Mr. Turano had part of the right side of his head and his right shoulder blown off, according to a witness in the hospital emergency room where he was pronounced dead.

"They Got My Father!"

As the shooting on the patio erupted, the police said, Mr. Turano's son, ignoring the gunmen's warnings to stay put, began running toward the garden and was shot in the back twice, either by a lookout man at the front or by the departing killers, who raced out and sped away.

A neighbor several doors away said he ran into the restaurant after the killers fled and found the wounded teenager. "He shouted to me, 'They got my father! They got my father!' I looked at him and saw he had a big bullet hole in his side."

Other neighbors said that Mr. Turano's wife and daughter were in Italy on vacation and that Mr. Turano had planned to leave this weekend to join them. The police said they were told Mr. Galante had gone to the restaurant to have a "bon voyage" luncheon with the owner.

—*July 13, 1979*

NOTE: *Anthony Indelicato was convicted in 1986 of being one of the three masked men who shot Galante, a killing said to have been ordered by a mob rival and sanctioned by the Mafia's ruling commission.*

THE MAFIA OF THE 1980s: DIVIDED AND UNDER SIEGE

By ROBERT D. McFADDEN

The old images seem like a caricature now: the shadowy world of secret rituals, the aging dons behind high-walled estates, the passion for vengeance and power over other men. For years, the Mafia was the stuff of novels and movies and whispers on Mulberry Street.

But in the past year, a series of federal trials featuring turncoat underworld informers and agents who risked their lives to penetrate and expose the Mafia has crippled its leadership and inflicted damage that would have been unthinkable only a few years ago. The evidence has also raised major questions about the underworld's structure and future activities.

Like a Business Cartel

The underworld's inner workings have been laid open as never before, disclosing a Mafia split by generation and divided psychologically—its hand in the corporate glitz of the 1980s, its heart in the sentimental sepia of a bygone era.

The trials—the "pizza connection," the mob "commission," the cases of John Gotti, Philip Rastelli and others—reveal a Mafia with all the accouterments of a global business cartel, with sophisticated operations to move drugs and swallow enterprises, with Swiss accounts to launder money and elaborate legal, financial and technical adjuncts.

But the thousands of hours of testimony by agents and informants and the secretly recorded conversations among hoodlums in their homes, cars and social clubs have also yielded a close-up picture of the criminals themselves.

The Value of Honor

Behind the facades of respectability, family life and surprisingly modest homes lay the profiles of fathers who hate drugs but sell tons of heroin, gambling czars who lose heavily on the horses, murderers who take offense at off-color language around women, and Runyonesque characters with funny nicknames who beat people to death with hammers.

The evidence documents what has long been suspected: the generation gap pitting younger, reckless, flamboyant mobsters who talk glibly of killing and big money, and elders who still value honor above all else, who speak solemnly of "friendship" and "respect," who would rather die than break the code of silence known as *omerta*.

But looking back on a year of criminal prosecutions and relentless surveillance, federal prosecutors, organized-crime experts and other law-enforcement officials also say that the problems of the Mafia now go well beyond generational conflicts and reach into the mob's organization and criminal pursuits.

"This has been the Mafia's worst year," said Rudolph W. Giuliani, the U.S. attorney in Manhattan. "We keep making gains and they keep getting moved backward. If we take back the labor unions, the legitimate businesses, eventually they become just another street gang."

The Picture in U.S. Court

The damage to the Mafia and its five New York families—known by the names of former leaders: Gambino, Genovese, Lucchese, Bonanno and Colombo—has been extensive and has largely been inflicted from within.

Undercover agents posing as thieves and thugs have infiltrated the Mafia and have provided a wealth of information on murder contracts, leadership plots and everyday life in the mob. Among the countless things they learned was that the Mafia does not work on Mother's Day.

Using the lure of a witness-protection program and the threat of heavy prison sentences, the authorities have also persuaded Mafiosi to break the once-sacred code of silence and testify against former friends.

The officials have also made extensive use of modern electronic eavesdropping and surveillance techniques and have effectively employed the Racketeer Influenced and Corrupt Organizations Act.

Gotti Jury Still Out

While the crackdown has been underway for years, the results have emerged only in the last year at a series of major criminal trials in Manhattan and Brooklyn:

· The mob commission case: Eight men, including Anthony Salerno, Anthony Corallo and Carmine Persico—bosses of the Genovese,

Lucchese and Colombo groups—were convicted in Manhattan Nov. 19 of being part of the Mafia's ruling commission.

· The pizza connection case: After 17 months in court, a former chief of Sicily's Mafia and 16 other men were convicted on March 2 in Manhattan of running an international ring that distributed tons of heroin, with a street value that federal authorities estimated at $1.6 billion, using pizza parlors to disguise drug meetings and money laundering.

· The John Gotti case: The jury is still out in the case against Mr. Gotti, listed by authorities as the head of the Gambino family, and six other reputed mob figures, charged with racketeering.

· The Philip Rastelli case: Mr. Rastelli, who authorities identify as head of the Bonanno family, and eight others were convicted last Oct. 15 of labor-racketeering.

While the trials have left the Mafia's leadership and some of its most lucrative rackets in disarray, organized crime continues to reap enormous profits from its enterprises, and even the most optimistic law-enforcement officials do not contend that the Mafia's death knell has already rung.

There have always been fascinating glimpses of the Mafia: news of shootings and shakedowns, pictures of bullet-riddled bodies, occasional arrests and trials, and fictionalized accounts of godfathers and their ring-kissing coteries. But the trials of the past year have provided an orgy of revelations about how the mob is organized, how it works in the 1980s and what its members are really like.

The trials have also provided an unusual behind-the-scenes look at modern investigatory methods and personnel. From bold undercover agents to parabolic microphones, they present an array of characters and technology that could fill a novelist's head with tales of danger, suspense and high-tech marvels.

How the Mob Is Organized

With elaborate charts and extensive testimony, prosecutors in the various trials showed that there is a Mafia commission that rules mob activities in the country. The leaders of New York's five families are among the most powerful commission members.

There are indications that a second commission operates out of Chicago and has jurisdiction over the western part of the country, but the consensus among law-enforcement officials is that the New York commission is the nation's supreme mob authority.

According to the prosecutors, the commission is composed of the family leaders and constitutes the policy-making body that carves up territory, decides what rackets to pursue and parcels them out among member families. It also resolves disputes between families and sometimes orders the executions of those who refuse to cooperate.

Below the commission level, each family is organized along fairly simple military lines to facilitate secrecy, communication and action: there is a boss, an underboss, a "consigliere" or counselor, a small number of captains and lieutenants followed by scores or even hundreds of "made" members called soldiers. Below these are "associates" who wish to become "made" members.

"Not Fit" to Be Boss

Among many tape recordings played at the commission trial was one that dramatically illustrated the leaders' supremacy. In it, Mr. Salerno told mobsters from Buffalo and Cleveland that the commission would settle a dispute over mob control in Buffalo.

"The commission wants it straightened out," Mr. Salerno, known as "Fat Tony," told two visitors at his Manhattan headquarters, the Palma Boys Social Club, in 1984.

"Tell him he's dealing with the big boys now."

One, Joseph Pieri, counselor of the Buffalo mob, was bitter about his family's boss, Joseph Todaro. "I killed a few guys who were against him," Mr. Pieri said. "And he got to be boss. He's not fit to be boss. He started neglecting me."

Supporting Mr. Pieri, John Tronolone, of Cleveland, said the Todaro faction was heavily armed and ready for trouble. "They were walking around with machine guns, these guys," he said. "Suppose we walk around with machine guns."

"No—I'll send word to Junior to straighten this thing out," Mr. Salerno said, referring to Mr. Persico. As for the Buffalo boss, Mr. Salerno said: "Give him the word from the commission."

"Tell him," Mr. Salerno said, "the commission from New York—tell him he's dealing with the big boys now."

New Look of the 1980s

"They have gone the way of sophisticated corporate America, and they've done it success-fully," said Thomas L. Sheer, head of the FBI's New York office and an expert on orga-nized crime. "It has enabled them to move swiftly into more profitable money-making areas, into legitimate businesses and unions."

With global contacts, with top financial and legal advisers, with control over trans-portation and labor unions, with vast amounts of cash to arrange deals and bribe officials, the Mafia has moved into a host of legitimate businesses in the 1980s to supplement income from its more traditional criminal enterprises. But in the competitive corporate world of the 1980s, the mob has yet another big advantage: muscle.

"They move into a legitimate business," Mr. Sheer explained, "and they take it over and compete with other businesses, but if they feel they are losing out, they will revert to breaking legs. True American corporate competition does not include breaking legs."

The Importance of Drugs

Often, as shown in the commission trial, the Mafia's route to control of an industry is through a labor union. Prosecutors said one defendant, Ralph Scopo, the president of the District Council of Cement and Concrete Workers, served as a conduit for extorting payoffs from the heads of companies involved in concrete construction work in New York.

Threats of physical harm or labor disruption that could ruin their companies were sufficient, two company owners testified, to make them join a "club" operated by the Mafia to allocate all contracts that cost more than $2 million and to extort 2 percent from the contractors.

In the 1980s, drugs became a major enterprise of the mob, as the pizza connection case demonstrated.

Presenting hundreds of witnesses and wiretapped conversations, prosecutors showed the Mafia smuggled tons of heroin and cocaine into the country between 1979 and 1984. It obtained morphine base in Turkey, processed it into heroin in Sicily and shipped it to the United States. Many of the wiretapped conversations were recorded in telephone booths near pizzerias owned by defendants. Wiretapped conversations showed that drug orders were often given in code. For example, Gaetano Badalamenti, former head of Sicily's Mafia, who was in Brazil, and another defendant, Salvatore Mazzurco, at a Queens phone booth, referred to "shirts," meaning cocaine, and "22 parcels" for 22 kilograms, "pure cotton" for undiluted drugs and "10 percent acrylic" for 90 percent pure heroin, prosecutors said.

The Men of the Mafia

The myths die hard, especially within the Mafia, and perhaps most difficult of all for those on trial was the spectacle of former associates on the stand, telling secrets, breaking the hallowed vows of silence.

One informer, James Cardinali, an admitted murderer who worked for John Gotti from 1979 to 1981, said he was taught the ways of the mob by Mr. Gotti, who the authorities say is head of the Gambino family.

"You don't get released from John Gotti's crew," Mr. Cardinali said. "You live with John Gotti, you die with John Gotti."

Gotti's Small Talk

Unlike the dons of fiction who live on grand estates surrounded with shotgun-toting bodyguards, Mr. Gotti, Mr. Persico and most of the other leaders of organized crime today lead surprisingly modest lives.

Mr. Persico, who acted as his own lawyer at the commission trial, once spent weeks hiding at the Wantagh, L.I., home of a cousin, Catherine DeChristopher. Explaining his routine, she recalled that he slept until 2 p.m., had coffee, read newspapers, watched television, played board games and went to bed.

Mr. Gotti, a 45-year-old grandfather, has lived for years in Howard Beach, Queens. Like most of the leaders, he has spent nearly all his time at a favorite hangout, in his case the Bergin Hunt and Fish Club in nearby Ozone Park.

Wiretaps at the club were filled with Mr. Gotti's small talk about his gambling losses, about petty disputes with his friends and fatherly advice on how a thug ought to act.

Mr. Cardinali, who savagely beat a man in 1982 as a favor to Mr. Gotti, recalled that Mr. Gotti once angrily told a mobster that he should not have visited the wife of a Gotti associate while the man

> *"If you ever go to a guy's house while he's in jail, I will kill you."*

was in jail. "If you ever go to a guy's house while he's in jail, I will kill you," Mr. Gotti was quoted as saying.

One witness at the pizza connection trial, Luigi Ronsisvalle, described the workmanlike way he committed 13 contract murders. Asked if he ever drank before killing someone, he seemed affronted. "That was a job," he said of the murders.

Thousands of hours at the trials were spent listening to wiretap recordings and the testimony of government agents, much of it touching rather on small but telling details about Mafiosi and their everyday activities.

Joseph Pistone, an undercover agent who posed as a thief to infiltrate the Bonanno family, said that as his initiation neared, a Bonanno member, Benjamin Ruggiero, told him to shave off his mustache, cut his hair and "keep a neat appearance at all times" because "a wise guy doesn't have a bushy mustache and long hair."

The erosion of respect was voiced by Aniello Dellacroce, the late Gambino underboss, in a secretly recorded 1985 berating of an underling who had gone over his head to the boss about some matter.

"I'm through with you," he said. "You understand? I don't want to say hello to ya." Later, he told the man he had got off easy. "Twenty years ago, youse woulda found yourself in some [expletive] hole someplace."

—March 11, 1987

JOHN GOTTI DIES IN PRISON AT 61; MAFIA BOSS RELISHED THE SPOTLIGHT

By SELWYN RAAB

John J. Gotti, who seized control of the Gambino crime family in a murderous coup, flaunted his power during a flamboyant reign as a Mafia boss, and then spent the last years of his life locked away in a maximum security penitentiary, his gang in shambles, died yesterday at the federal prison hospital at Springfield, Mo. He was 61.

The cause was cancer. In 1998, Mr. Gotti was operated on for neck and head cancer. He had been re-admitted to the hospital several times since then for treatment.

Traditional Mafia leaders led publicity-shy lives. Not so Mr. Gotti, who reveled in media attention as the boss of the nation's largest and most influential organized crime group. He cut a colorful figure in New York City, wining and dining in elegant restaurants and nightspots surrounded by a coterie of bodyguards.

From late 1985, when Mr. Gotti engineered the assassination of his predecessor, Paul Castellano, to 1992, when he was sent to a federal prison for life, Mr. Gotti's swagger and seeming immunity from punishment earned him mythic gangster status.

In tabloid argot, he was the Teflon Don, evading successful prosecution, or the Dapper Don, for his smart appearance. At the peak of his power, his silvery hair was styled in a swept-back coiffure, and

> *"He never tried to hide the fact that he was a superboss."*

he favored $2,000 double-breasted suits accessorized by $400 hand-painted floral silk ties.

Salvatore Gravano, the right-hand man to Mr. Gotti as the underboss of the Gambino crime family before he defected to become a government witness and helped bring down his boss, said Mr. Gotti viewed himself as Robin Hood, admired and respected by the world. Mr. Gravano, known as Sammy the Bull, once asked him if he disliked people staring at him. "No, no," Mr. Gotti replied. "This is my public, Sammy. They love me."

"He was the first media don," said J. Bruce Mouw, a former FBI agent who supervised the unit that uncovered the evidence that ultimately convicted Mr. Gotti. "He never tried to hide the fact that he was a superboss."

But when he was put on trial, Mr. Gotti never acknowledged that he was a Mafia leader. Outside the courtroom he responded to questions about being a mob kingpin by replying with a grin, "I'm the boss of my family, my wife and kids."

Mr. Gotti's penchant for public contradiction—the image of the hard-working family man who nonetheless seemed to lead the life of a Hollywood celebrity—was famously transparent. He claimed his income derived from a $100,000-a-year salary as a plumbing supply salesman and a job with a garment accessories firm.

Mob turncoats and investigators asserted that Mr. Gotti received $10 million to $12 million in cash every year as his share of the proceeds from the Gambino family's criminal activities. Mr. Gravano testified that he personally gave Mr. Gotti more than $1 million a year from shakedowns in the construction industry.

Mob defectors said that Mr. Gotti boasted that his role model was Albert Anastasia, the founder of Murder Incorporated, a group of killers used by the Mafia in the 1930s and '40s to carry out gangland executions. Mr. Gotti, according to Mr. Gravano, said that he had acquired his gift for guile and ruthlessness by reading Machiavelli's *The Prince*.

In contrast to the amiable personality Mr. Gotti displayed in public, secretly recorded tapes and testimony from former mobsters painted a picture of a narcissistic tyrant with a furious temper who betrayed allies and ordered the slayings of Gambino loyalists he suspected of being informers or who he thought had not shown him proper respect.

Those who prosecuted him said Mr. Gotti's need for absolute authority and his lust for vast wealth led to a recklessness that contributed to his downfall and undermined the entire Gambino family. By insisting that his lieutenants meet frequently and directly with him, he provided prosecutors with evidence to obtain court-authorized bugs that helped to convict the entire Gambino hierarchy in the 1990s.

On the day of Mr. Gotti's conviction for murder and racketeering, James M. Fox, the head of the FBI office in New York, proclaimed: "The Teflon is gone. The don is covered with Velcro, and all the charges stuck."

A Strapping Adolescent with Fast Fists

John Joseph Gotti was born in the South Bronx on Oct. 27, 1940, the fifth of 13 children raised by his father, John, and his mother, Fannie, both children of immigrants. Mr. Gotti's father, an often-unemployed day laborer, led a hardscrabble life. The Gottis moved often before settling in the blue-collar East New York section of Brooklyn when John was 12.

East New York was then a battleground for rival youth gangs. Mr. Gotti, a strapping adolescent with fast fists, became the leader of a gang called the Fulton-Rockaway Boys. During his teenage years in the 1950s, storefronts in the neighborhood were hangouts for mobsters, and Mr. Gotti ran errands for members of an underworld club in the neighborhood headed by Carmine Fatico, a capo (captain) of a crew in the Gambino family. Through club members, Mr. Gotti was introduced to Aniello Dellacroce, his future mentor in the Gambino family. A poor student with disciplinary problems, Mr. Gotti dropped out of Franklin K. Lane High School in Queens when he was 16. By 18, he was ranked by the police department as a low-level associate in the Fatico crew.

In the next eight years, Mr. Gotti's arrest record described a path of petty crimes from street fighting to stealing cars. Several of his nine arrests in that period were in the company of a boyhood friend, Angelo Ruggiero, a nephew of Mr. Dellacroce. None led to penalties of more than six months in a county jail.

Mr. Gotti's first major arrest came in 1968, when he, his brother Gene and Mr. Ruggiero were charged by the FBI with committing three cargo thefts and truck hijackings near Kennedy International Airport. The three men pleaded guilty to reduced counts and John Gotti served a three-year sentence.

The Bergin Hunt and Fish Club

While Mr. Gotti was in prison, the Fatico gang moved from East New York to a storefront in Ozone Park, Queens. The new headquarters was incorporated—perhaps sardonically—as a nonprofit association, and named the Bergin Hunt and Fish Club, apparently a misspelling of Bergen Street in East New York.

Soon after Mr. Gotti's release in 1972 on the hijacking conviction, his underworld career got some help. Mr. Fatico, facing a prison sentence for loan-sharking, decided on temporary retirement and designated Mr. Gotti to run the gang temporarily.

As an acting crew chief, Mr. Gotti met frequently with Mr. Dellacroce, the underboss of the Gambino crime family, who took a shine to him. In 1973, a nephew of Carlo Gambino, the family leader, was abducted and murdered. The family's intelligence network determined that a stick-up man, James McBratney, had been one of the kidnappers. According to investigators and informers, Mr. Gotti was handed the important assignment of exacting revenge.

Mr. McBratney was shot dead outside a Staten Island bar in an ambush by three men. But it was hardly a flawless crime; witnesses picked out two of the men, Mr. Gotti and Mr. Ruggiero, from photographs. Mr. Gotti was arrested in 1974 after evading capture for a year.

Carlo Gambino hired Roy M. Cohn to represent Mr. Gotti and Mr. Ruggiero. Although both defendants had been indicted on murder charges and identified by witnesses, Mr. Cohn negotiated a remarkable deal with the Staten Island district attorney's office. In exchange for reduced charges of attempted manslaughter, Mr. Gotti and Mr. Ruggiero pleaded guilty, and each received a prison term of four years.

Mr. Gotti spent the term lifting weights and obtaining unusual perquisites. He was taken from prison in upstate New York for visits to his new home in Howard Beach, Queens, and to restaurants in New York City, where he met with criminal friends. State investigators later determined that prison authorities and guards had been bribed.

In 1976, while Mr. Gotti was still in prison, Carlo Gambino died. By normal rights of succession, the family's underboss, Mr. Dellacroce, should have been elevated. But Mr. Gambino had anointed his brother-in-law, Paul Castellano, as heir. As a consolation prize, Mr. Castellano allowed Mr. Dellacroce to remain as underboss and to control 10 of the gang's 23 crews. By creating two factions, Mr. Castellano planted the seeds of his own destruction.

Paroled in 1977, Mr. Gotti left prison a muscular, barrel-chested figure, 5 feet 10 inches tall and weighing about 200 pounds. Returning to the city, he was promoted by Mr. Dellacroce to full-fledged capo of the Bergin crew.

Mr. Gotti was a popular figure in Howard Beach, where he lived with his wife, Victoria, and their five children. In March 1980, one of his children, 12-year-old Frank, steered his bicycle into the road and was killed by a car driven by a neighbor, John Favara. Frank's death was ruled accidental, but four months later, while Mr. Gotti and his wife were in Florida, witnesses saw Mr. Favara being clubbed over the head and then shoved into a van that sped away. Mr. Favara is presumed to have been murdered. Mr. Gotti denied any knowledge of Mr. Favara's disappearance.

Becoming a Target

By the early 1980s, Mr. Gotti's prominence in the Gambino family had turned him into a major target for federal and city prosecutors. The Queens district attorney's office installed a concealed microphone and a telephone tap in the Bergin club in 1981.

The eavesdropping revealed Mr. Gotti's ruthless control over a crew that included his younger brother, Gene, and Angelo Ruggiero.

In 1985, major federal indictments exploded against Mr. Gotti and his closest associates. He and Mr. Dellacroce were accused of racketeering charges that carried penalties of life sentences. Gene Gotti and Mr. Ruggiero were indicted on heroin trafficking charges. The narcotics charge infuriated Mr. Castellano, who as the Gambino family boss prohibited drug deals. Mr. Castellano feared such deals would unleash government crackdowns and result in long prison sentences that might induce convicted traffickers to become informers. Under Mr. Castellano's rules, John Gotti was responsible for the misdeeds of his crewmembers.

Mr. Gotti asked Mr. Dellacroce to intervene with Mr. Castellano, but before any resolution was made, Mr. Dellacroce died of cancer in December 1985. Two weeks later, on Dec. 16, 1985, Mr. Castellano and his new underboss, Thomas Billotti, were gunned down by a team of assassins in front of Sparks Steak House on East 46th Street in Manhattan.

Mr. Gravano later testified that he and Mr. Gotti had watched the shootings from a parked car. He said Mr. Gotti had arranged the killings to prevent Mr. Castellano from killing him and his allies.

As the new head of the Gambino family, Mr. Gotti immediately faced two trials from old criminal complaints. In 1984, a refrigerator repairman, Romual Piecyk, accused Mr. Gotti of taking $325 in cash from him during a parking dispute in Queens. When he identified Mr. Gotti, Mr. Piecyk was unaware of his reputation as a mobster. On the witness stand, a tense Mr. Piecyk could no longer recognize Mr. Gotti, and a state judge dismissed the charges.

The second trial began in August 1986 in Brooklyn, with Mr. Gotti, his brother Gene and five others accused of federal charges that they had violated the Racketeer Influenced and Corrupt Organizations Act by being members of a criminal enterprise. Mr. Gotti was defended by Bruce Cutler, a former assistant district attorney in Brooklyn.

The jury acquitted Mr. Gotti and the other defendants on all counts of racketeering and conspiracy. Gene Gotti, however, was subsequently convicted of the charges that he had trafficked in heroin, the allegation that had so angered Mr. Castellano.

The verdict against John Gotti may have been tainted. The foreman of the jury was later convicted of accepting a $60,000 bribe to vote for acquittals and to prevent a unanimous verdict, as required for convictions.

Appearing Invincible

Law enforcement officials grudgingly conceded that Mr. Gotti's back-to-back legal victories had wrapped him in a cloak of invincibility. Mr. Gotti became organized crime's most significant symbol of resistance to law enforcement since Al Capone in Chicago 60 years earlier. If he spotted detectives on stakeouts, he was known to taunt them by rubbing one index finger against another and mouthing the words: "Naughty, naughty."

John Gotti, during his trial in New York Supreme Court Manhattan on charges in the shooting of a carpenters' union president, January 23, 1990.

Usually, he began his working day at noon at the Bergin club. He installed a barber's chair where he sat while his hair was cut, washed and blow-dried every day.

In late afternoon, he was driven to his main headquarters in Little Italy, the Ravenite Social Club on Mulberry Street, which had been Mr. Dellacroce's base. The top members of the Gambino hierarchy were required to report to him several times a week. Mr. Gotti assumed command of the family when it had 23 active crews, about 300 made (inducted) members and more than 2,000 associates (men who hoped to become made members and who cooperated in criminal enterprises). The Gambino organizational structure was similar to that of New York City's four other longstanding Mafia groups: the Bonanno, Colombo, Genovese and Lucchese factions.

Mr. Gotti found himself at the center of a cornucopia of illegal profits, with all members and associates funneling shares of their loot to him.

Investigators estimated that the Gambino family in the mid-1980s grossed about $500 million a year, primarily from illegal activities in the New York area and Florida. Under the direction of Carlo Gambino and Paul Castellano, the family had expanded from a gang specializing in gambling, loan-sharking and stealing into more sophisticated operations, like extorting money from unions, garment manufacturers and garbage-carting companies. Unlike Mr. Gambino and Mr. Castellano, Mr. Gotti also met openly with known narcotics traffickers.

Mr. Gotti found himself in court again in 1990. He was tried in Manhattan on a New York State indictment charging that he had ordered the shooting of a carpenters' union president after a labor dispute. Again, he was acquitted despite evidence from tapes in which he was heard discussing preparations for the shooting.

In early 1990, while the state trial was proceeding in Manhattan, FBI technicians in a separate investigation installed eavesdropping equipment in an apartment above the Ravenite Social Club. For months, the bugs recorded conversations that implicated Mr. Gotti, Mr. Gravano and the family's consigliere, Frank Locascio, in crimes like murder, bribery, loan sharking, gambling and obstruction of justice.

A Final Trial as Boss

Mr. Gotti and his co-defendants were arrested at the Ravenite Club in December 1990. This time the authorities had a trump card. Mr. Gravano had made a deal with the prosecution to testify.

On April 2, 1992, Mr. Gotti and Mr. Locascio were convicted by a jury in federal court; Mr. Gotti on all 13 counts against him, including a racketeering charge that cited him for five murders, and related charges of murder, conspiracy, gambling, obstruction of justice and tax fraud.

Arms folded and smirking, Mr. Gotti declined to say anything before he was sentenced to life imprisonment. Mr. Gravano received a five-year sentence.

The day he was sentenced, Mr. Gotti was put aboard a plane and flown to the maximum-security federal prison in Marion, Ill.

Soon after his conviction, Mr. Gotti, according to federal prosecutors, appointed his eldest son, John A. Gotti, known as Junior, the acting boss of the Gambino family. In 1999, his son pleaded guilty to federal racketeering charges involving the Gambino family and was sentenced to six years and five months in prison.

Mr. Gotti is survived by his wife, the former Victoria DiGiorgio; his son John A.; and his brothers, Gene, who is serving a 50-year sentence for heroin trafficking, and Peter. Mr. Gotti is also survived by another son, Peter; two daughters, Victoria, an author of mysteries, and Angel Gotti Forca; and three other brothers, Richard, Vincent and Dominick.

From 1992 until 2000, Mr. Gotti was kept in virtual solitary confinement, restricted to his cell except for an hour of daily exercise.

"He was obsessed with his own importance," Mr. Mouw said of Mr. Gotti and his fall. "He gave his own status a higher priority than Cosa Nostra. He was convinced that no jury would ever convict him because he was John Gotti, a caesar, an emperor."

—June 11, 2002

A MAFIA BOSS BREAKS A CODE IN TELLING ALL

By WILLIAM K. RASHBAUM

t was a straightforward question, but not one usually answered by the likes of Joseph C. Massino. At least not with such candor.

The longtime boss of the Bonanno crime family was asked by a prosecutor, "What powers did you have?"

Mr. Massino, seated at the witness stand, offered a quick, matter-of-fact reply.

"Murders, responsibility for the family, made captains, break captains," he said.

And so it was that Mr. Massino, 68, the only official boss of a New York crime family ever to cooperate with federal authorities, appeared in federal district court in Brooklyn on Tuesday and became the first to testify against a former confederate.

For nearly five hours, Mr. Massino cataloged his misdeeds, recounting murders and other acts of varying criminal scope.

Mr. Massino would tell the jury that the man on trial, Vincent Basciano, the family's former acting boss, had spoken to him about ordering the 2004 killing of Randolph Pizzolo, a Bonanno associate, a conversation Mr. Massino secretly recorded. Mr. Basciano is charged with ordering Mr. Pizzolo's murder.

But for much of the day, Mr. Massino established his credentials and gave the jury his view from the top, his philosophy of mob management and his personal history—all larded with a steady stream of culinary metaphors and references.

"If you need somebody to kill somebody, you need workers—it takes all kinds of meat to make a good sauce," said the onetime restaurateur, catering consultant and coffee-truck owner, referring to what he said were Mr. Basciano's skills both as a killer and as an earner for the crime family.

He recounted turning to crime early as a 12-year-old, stealing some homing pigeons. By the time he was 14, he had run away from home; he said he hitchhiked to Florida and worked as a lifeguard in Miami. By the 1960s, he said, he had progressed to murder, and he testified that he was involved in about a dozen killings.

Mr. Massino's testimony also highlighted his underworld executive acumen in addition to his lifetime of crime, much of it in service of the Bonanno family, with which he said he had been affiliated for 33 or 34 years.

182

His unassuming appearance, with heavy jowls, drooping eyelids and an expansive midsection, was belied by his authoritative-sounding responses to the prosecutor, Assistant U.S. Attorney Taryn A. Merkl, who took him through his personal and professional history.

Mr. Massino began cooperating with the authorities after he was convicted of seven murders in 2004, for which he faced life in prison, and was set to go to trial for an eighth, for which he could have faced the death penalty. In 2005, he pleaded guilty to the eighth killing, and Judge Nicholas G. Garaufis of the federal district court, who is presiding over Mr. Basciano's trial, sentenced him to two consecutive life terms.

By testifying for the government, he is seeking a sentence reduction, though he told the jury that none had been promised. In his words: "I'm hoping to see a light at the end of the tunnel."

Dressed in a jogging suit with a white T-shirt visible beneath, he answered questions about his early crimes, his rise in the Bonanno family and his management of hundreds of members and associates after he became boss in 1991.

> "I'm hoping to see a light at the end of the tunnel."

The jurors at times appeared rapt, but at times seemed to fade as photograph after photograph of Bonanno crime family figures were introduced into evidence.

He presented himself as a master of the deft bureaucratic maneuver, both in his dealings with internal family rifts and with other crime clans, and in his efforts to thwart law enforcement.

He described going to the bosses of the Gambino and Colombo families—Paul Castellano and Carmine Persico, respectively—in 1981 before taking preemptive action against three senior Bonanno figures who were moving against his faction in a brewing power struggle. After securing approval to kill the men, Mr. Massino and several others shot them to death in an ambush in the basement of a social club.

He also testified about codes that he and his confederates worked out—to discuss murder plots and once to determine if a social club had been bugged—without alerting law enforcement. He described changes he put into effect after becoming boss that were meant to reduce the risk that members of his family could incriminate themselves or one another.

For example, Mr. Massino closed all the family's social clubs, saying that if crime family members hung out in these storefront establishments, they made the FBI's job easy, because one agent conducting surveillance outside could see everyone come and go. "If you close the club," he explained, "it takes 50 FBI agents to watch 50 people."

He was, he said, extremely careful about where and when he talked about mob business.

"You never talk in a club, you never talk in a car, you never talk on a cellphone, you never talk on a phone, you never talk in your house," he testified, saying that so called walk-talks, where two or more crime figures spoke as they strolled the streets, were safest.

Indeed, Mr. Massino said he discussed mob business in a walk-in refrigerator at a catering business where he worked to avoid electronic eavesdropping.

His efforts to thwart investigators, he said, were aided by at least four unnamed law officers: two New York Police Department detectives in the 1960s; an FBI agent who warned him of a pending arrest in the 1980s; and a Pennsylvania State trooper who destroyed copies of his fingerprints.

—April 13, 2011

NOTE: *Basciano was convicted at trial in Pizzolo's murder and is serving a life sentence in federal prison. Massino's sentence of two life terms was commuted in 2013; he is believed to be living under supervised release in the witness protection program.*

LONG ELUSIVE, IRISH MOB LEGEND ENDED UP A CALIFORNIA RECLUSE

By ADAM NAGOURNEY AND ABBY GOODNOUGH

Charlie and Carol Gasko seemed to be just another fading elderly couple enjoying retirement in a modest apartment building a few blocks from the Pacific in Santa Monica. He told a neighbor he had emphysema and spent his days lying on the couch watching television. Carol would venture out for strolls on the nearby Third Street Promenade, stopping by the Saturday farmers' market or feeding a neighborhood stray cat. Often, he tagged along.

But they were reclusive and a little odd, neighbors said. Charlie would often wear a baseball cap or fedora that shadowed his face. He would bark at neighbors when Carol lingered too long to speak to them, said one neighbor; Carol explained that he was suffering from dementia. In recent months, another neighbor said, a note was taped to their door reading, "Please do not Knock at Any Time."

But the couple who led this quiet life for more than a decade were not who they said they were.

Charlie Gasko was a notorious gangster—James "Whitey" Bulger, once Boston's most fearsome crime boss, a fixture on the FBI's 10 Most Wanted list—and she was his girl-friend, Catherine Greig, 60. They fled more than 16 years ago after Mr. Bulger, a sometime bureau informer, learned from a retired FBI agent that he was about to be arrested.

The long manhunt—which had produced Elvis-like Bulger sightings around the world, rumors of his death and considerable embarrassment for the FBI—ended shortly after 5 p.m. Wednesday when agents lured them out of their apartment and put them under arrest. Mr. Bulger, 81, offered no resistance as his long run as a fugitive ended and he came face to face with accusations of killing 19 people and other crimes, authorities said.

Appearing in federal district court in Los Angeles on Thursday, Mr. Bulger and Ms. Greig waived their right to fight their return to Boston and agreed to go back. Mr. Bulger—wearing a white shirt and blue jeans, and sporting a thick white beard—sat at the front, grinning as he surveyed the scene. Ms. Grieg appeared spectral, with short white hair and sunken cheeks.

When Magistrate John McDermott asked Mr. Bulger if he had read the indictment, he responded in a thick Boston accent. "I got them all here," Mr. Bulger said. "It will take me quite a while to finish these. But I know them all pretty much."

The end came just days after the FBI, frustrated at the elusiveness of Mr. Bulger—who had a $2 million bounty on his head—decided the best way to find the mobster was through his girlfriend. There had been no sightings of Ms. Greig, a former dental hygienist, since her disappearance, leading FBI officials to assume she was at his side. And she was a person with the kind of idiosyncrasies—a devotion to animals, the beauty parlor and monthly teeth cleanings—that might make her easier to find, they figured, especially given the assumption that the couple had altered their physical appearance with plastic surgery.

The FBI doubled the reward for her capture—to $100,000—and began broadcasting public service advertisements this week in 14 cities, during daytime television shows favored by older women.

The improbable end to a hunt that many people had long assumed had turned cold riveted his neighbors in Santa Monica, but even more so the people back in his old haunts in South Boston, where Whitey had been a legendary mobster—a hero to some, but loathed by many—who had helped define a Boston of old. The news that he had been caught, that he was still alive, was, for Boston, a hometown version of the killing of Osama bin Laden.

"I was shocked," said Mary Child, 75, who grew up around the corner from Mr. Bulger in the Old Harbor Housing Project in South Boston. "It's the end of an era."

Paul McGrath, 47, a union stagehand and Teamsters member, said he hoped Mr. Bulger's capture would remove what he believes to be a stain on the neighborhood where he was raised.

"A lot of honest blue-collar people built South Boston," Mr. McGrath said. "Not everyone here is a gangster. As soon as you say you're from South Boston, the conversation stops because everyone, including the FBI, thinks you have the back of Whitey Bulger."

Renown in South Boston

It is difficult to overstate the role of Mr. Bulger and his vanishing act in Boston culture and lore. People in Boston learn his name and story in childhood; many can point out the landmarks associated with his criminal reign, like the liquor store on Old Colony Avenue in South Boston that served as his longtime headquarters.

He was an inspiration for Jack Nicholson's Irish mob boss in the movie *The Departed*, set in Boston. And books on Mr. Bulger continue to be published.

Southie, as the neighborhood is known, was Mr. Bulger's home since childhood, when his shock of white-blond hair earned him the nickname that would stick—to his annoyance, it was said. Many were terrified of Mr. Bulger, known for his violent temper; others considered him a Robin Hood figure who looked out for neighbors.

Whitey Bulger's Alcatraz mug shot of November 11, 1959.

A troublemaker from an early age, Mr. Bulger joined the air force in 1949, when he was 20, but was discharged three years later after going absent without leave. He returned to Boston and began a life of crime; by 1956, he had been sentenced to prison for his involvement in a string of bank robberies. He spent part of his sentence on Alcatraz Island.

Back in Boston, he joined the infamous Winter Hill Gang, which came to dominate organized crime in Southie and the city's other Irish neighborhoods. He ultimately became a leader of the gang along with Stephen "the Rifleman" Flemmi.

Prosecutors would later describe the pair as the kind of territorial bosses who would demand protection money from bookmakers, loan sharks and other petty criminals, and who were also involved in illegal gambling enterprises and loan sharking themselves. Mr. Bulger was known for his almost maniacal cruelty, like strangling the girlfriends of two of his lieutenants.

"The saying in Southie used to be that when Whitey walked down the street, the sidewalk shook," said Robert Stutman, who headed the Boston office of the Drug Enforcement Agency in the 1980s. Mr. Bulger's already outsize life took on another surreal dimension in the mid-1970s, when the FBI recruited him as an informer in its mission to close down a rival criminal organization: the New England branch of the Mafia. Agents who worked with Mr. Bulger allowed him to continue his criminal activities, ostensibly as long as no violence was committed.

But evidence later emerged that Mr. Bulger and Mr. Flemmi were involved in gruesome murders while serving as informers. Other law enforcement agencies, including the D.E.A. and the Massachusetts State Police, opened investigations into Mr. Bulger's criminal activities while he was an FBI informer, but it was later revealed that he had been tipped off or protected by his FBI allies.

Such actions, revealed in a racketeering case against Mr. Bulger in the late '90s, became a huge embarrassment for the FBI. In 2003, a report by a congressional committee called it "one of the greatest failures in the history of federal law enforcement."

The FBI agent whom Mr. Bulger had worked with most closely, John Connolly Jr., tipped him off about his imminent arrest in December 1994, according to court testimony. Mr. Bulger fled to New York that night.

When revelations of his arrangement with Mr. Connolly emerged, the FBI's role in Mr. Bulger's disappearance became almost legend in Boston. Many residents believed the FBI had chosen not to catch Mr. Bulger out of fear he would reveal more embarrassing secrets about its dealings with him.

But most of the agents from Mr. Bulger's days in Boston are retired or dead now. Dick Lehr, a former *Boston Globe* reporter who was an author of a book about Mr. Bulger, *Black Mass: The True Story of an Unholy Alliance Between the FBI and the Irish Mob*, said the newer generation of FBI agents had been determined to catch him.

"In recent times, they really wanted him," Mr. Lehr said. "There's been this cloud over the Boston office."

Federal officials appeared eager to remove that cloud on Thursday. "Although there are those that have doubted our resolve at times over the years," said Richard DesLauriers, the special agent in charge of the FBI's Boston office, "we have never wavered."

A Sunny Hideout

Santa Monica was a place where the couple could disappear into a backdrop of palm trees, skaters and endless beach, a diverse community that includes many transplanted people from the East Coast. Their building was just off the corner of Third Street and Washington Avenue, an easy walk to the park overlooking the ocean, Santa Monica Beach and the farmers' market.

Their apartment—a 1,000-square-foot two bedroom on the third floor—cost them $1,145 a month, which they always paid in cash. Joshua Bond, the building manager, said they had lived in the building since at least 1996.

Barbara Gluck, a neighbor, described Ms. Greig as a "lovely person," but added: "He, on the other hand, when we talked too long, would shout, 'Stop talking, let's go.'" Janus

Goodwin, 61, said she visited them in the apartment. "When I would be invited in, he would always be lying on the sofa, watching TV," she said. "He was very proud of his little art pieces, which were cheap knockoffs of Monet and Van Gogh."

Ms. Goodwin said Ms. Grieg had blond hair and was always nicely dressed; Mr. Bulger would appear in dress shirts and dark pants, and had dark hair, which she assumed was dyed.

An Ad Campaign Pays Off

Mr. DesLauriers, the special agent, said that the tip that led to the arrest came into the FBI just after 11 p.m. Tuesday, and that it was a "direct result" of the campaign that began Monday aimed at drawing attention to Ms. Greig.

On Wednesday morning, he said, agents from the FBI's fugitive task force in Los Angeles opened a surveillance operation at the apartment on Third Street. By 4 p.m., the FBI concluded the tip was correct, after agents observed a couple who resembled Mr. Bulger and Ms. Greig leaving the building. Agents lured Mr. Bulger out of the apartment using a ruse at about 5:45 p.m., Mr. DesLauriers said. Inside the apartment, they found more than $800,000 and more than 20 firearms, including handguns and several longer guns. They also found knives and false IDs.

Carmen Ortiz, the U.S. attorney in Boston, said Mr. Bulger could get life in prison in the federal case here but that he could face the death penalty in two separate pending cases in Oklahoma and Florida. Within hours of his capture, Katherine Fernandez Rundle, the Miami-Dade state attorney, said she was eager to try him on charges of orchestrating a 1982 murder of a gambling executive at Miami International Airport. If convicted, Mr. Bulger could face the death penalty.

Back in Boston, family members of others believed to be Mr. Bulger's victims were still absorbing the events taking place 3,000 miles away. "I never thought I'd see this day," said Patricia Donahue, whose husband, Michael, was a bystander in a killing Mr. Bulger is accused of committing in 1982. "I have satisfaction and despair, because it brings back so many old memories. But satisfaction that they have him."

—June 24, 2011

NOTE: *In 2013, Bulger was convicted of multiple crimes, including his involvement in 11 murders. He was sentenced to two consecutive life terms in prison.*

CHAPTER 6

MURDER

"He deserved it. I can prove it. He ruined my life and then deserted the girl."

—Harry Kendall Thaw reported to have said to the police officer
who apprehended Thaw after he shot Stanford White

JEALOUSY. GREED. RACISM. For prosecutors, explaining the motivation for murder is often crucial to obtaining a conviction. Sometimes there seems to be no solid sense of what provoked the crime, or the motivation is simply madness. Mark David Chapman gave several rationales for shooting John Lennon: one was that he knew the crime would make him a celebrity. In the case of JonBenét Ramsey, as covered in *The Times*, the mystery surrounding her murder remains not only the matter of who killed her, but why.

OPPOSITE: Model and chorus girl Evelyn Nesbit, c. 1903; Nesbit's former relationship with famed architect Stanford White was the motivation that drove her husband, Harry Kendall Thaw, to murder White in 1906.

THAW MURDERS STANFORD WHITE: SHOOTS HIM ON THE MADISON SQUARE GARDEN ROOF

Harry Kendall Thaw of Pittsburg, husband of Florence Evelyn Nesbit, former actress and artist's model, shot and killed Stanford White, the architect, on the roof of Madison Square Garden at 11:05 o'clock last night, just as the first performance of the musical comedy *Mamzelle Champagne* was drawing to a close. Thaw, who is a brother of the countess of Yarmouth and a member of a well-known and wealthy family, left his seat near the stage, passed between a number of tables, and, in full view of the players and of scores of persons, shot White through the head. Mr. White was the designer of the building on the roof of which he was killed. He it was who put Miss Nesbit, now Mrs. Thaw, on the stage.

Thaw, who was in evening clothes, had evidently been waiting for Mr. White's appearance. The latter entered the Garden at 10:55 and took a seat at a table five rows from the stage. He rested his chin in his right hand and seemed lost in contemplation.

Thaw had a pistol concealed under his coat. His face was deathly white. According to A. L. Belstone, who sat near, White must have seen Thaw approaching. But he made no move. Thaw placed the pistol almost against the head of the sitting man and fired three shots in quick succession.

Body Fell to the Floor

White's elbow slid from the table, the table crashed over, and the body then tumbled from the chair. On the stage a character was singing a song entitled "I Could Love a Million Girls." The refrain seemed to freeze upon his lips. There was dead silence for a second, and then Thaw lifted his pistol over his head, the barrel hanging downward, as if to show the audience that he was not going to harm anyone else.

With a firm stride Thaw started for the exit, holding his pistol as if anxious to have someone take it from his hand. A woman jumped to her feet and screamed. Many persons followed her example, and there was wild excitement.

L. Lawrence, the manager of the show, jumped on a table and above the uproar commanded the show to go on.

"Go on playing!" he shouted. "Bring on that chorus!"

The musicians made a feeble effort at gathering their wits and playing the chorus music, but the girls who romped on the stage were paralyzed with horror, and it was impossible to bring the performance to an orderly close.

Then the manager shouted for quiet, informed the audience that an accident had happened, and begged the people to leave quietly.

In the meanwhile Thaw had reached the elevators. On duty was fireman Paul Brudi. He took the pistol from Thaw's hand, but did not attempt to arrest him. Policeman Debes of the Tenderloin Station appeared and seized his arm. "He deserved it," Thaw said to the policeman. "I can prove it. He ruined my life and then deserted the girl."

A Woman Kissed Thaw

Just as the policeman started into the elevator with Thaw a woman described as dark-haired and short of stature reached up to him and kissed him on the cheek. This woman some witnesses declare was Mrs. Thaw.

The crowd was then scrambling wildly for the elevators and stairs. The employees of the Garden who knew Thaw, and nearly all of them did, as he visited the place often, did not seem greatly surprised at the tragedy. When Thaw entered the Garden in the early part of the show he seemed greatly agitated. He strolled from one part of the place to another, and finally took a seat in a little niche near the stage.

He was half hidden from the audience, but could see any one who might enter. It is believed that he knew just where White would sit, and had picked out this place in order to get at him without interference.

Henry Rogers was seated at the table next to White and said Thaw fired when the muzzle of his pistol was only a few inches from White's temple.

Another witness said that after firing three shots and looking at White as if to be sure that he was stone dead, Thaw uttered a curse and added: "You'll never go out with that woman again."

A Woman Sat Near White

At another table adjoining that at which White was killed sat a woman dressed in white. It was believed for a time that she was a companion of White's, but this could not be verified, and it is positive that White was alone when he entered the Garden.

Someone in the audience hurried to the fallen man to see if assistance was needed. A great pool of blood had formed on the floor. The tables had been pulled back, and in the glare of thousands of electric lights it was quickly seen that White was beyond any earthly help.

Thought It a Stage Trick

Two of the cast members said that the reason the fright of the audience was not worse when the shots rang out was that just before the tragedy a dialogue concerning a burlesque duel had begun carried on by two of the characters, and many people thought that the old trick of playing in the audience had been tried again.

As the lights of the Garden were dimmed, the body of White was straightened out, the arms brought to the sides, and the legs placed together. A sheet was obtained in one of the dressing rooms, and this was stretched over it.

While all of this was going on, Policeman Debes and his prisoner had reached the street entrance. Thaw never once lost his composure. His evening suit showed no signs of ruffling. Only the paleness of his face showed that anything had happened to excite him.

The policeman and prisoner then walked through the crowd to Fifth Avenue, up the avenue to 30th Street. As they turned the corner at the Holland House, a number of cabmen who knew Thaw tipped their hats to him.

The prisoner reached the station without the usual crowd of curious people following.

Thaw did not seem to be intoxicated, but walked in a sort of daze. He made few comments on the way to the Tenderloin Station, Sgt. McCarthy asked him what his name was, and he answered:

"John Smith, Lafayette Square, Philadelphia."

"What's your business?" he was asked.

"I am a student."

No charge was made on the books against this "John Smith." The detectives were sent out to investigate fully before a charge was made. Sgt. McCarthy asked him: "Why did you do this?"

"I can't say," he replied.

Thaw Sent for Two Friends

Young Thaw walked dazedly to the back room. He then sent for Frederick W. Lowenfellow and Frederick Delafield. When the detectives put on the case had brought in the witnesses and they had been examined in Capt. Hodgins's room, Thaw was charged with homicide and was locked in a cell.

Coroner Dooley reached the Tenderloin Station at 1:30 this morning and asked to see the prisoner. Thaw had sent the doorman out to buy him some cigars. He was smoking and seemed calm when the coroner entered.

"Have you any statement to make to me?" the coroner asked.

"I don't care to make any statement now," Thaw replied. "I would appreciate it if you would tell Burr McIntosh or ex-Judge Hornblower or Joseph H. Choate of what has happened."

"Mr. McIntosh is upstairs," he was told. "Do you want to see him?"

"No," he replied, "just tell him to call up Mr. Hornblower or Mr. Choate."

Mr. Choate is at Stockbridge, Mass. Mr. McIntosh took the message and left the station.

Coroner Dooley said that he found Thaw in good mental condition. He added that he believed the murder was done through jealousy.

When Thaw was searched in the station $125 in paper money, $2.36 in coin, two silk handkerchiefs, two gold pencils, a gold watch, and a little mirror case were found.

Mrs. White at St. James, L.I.

Mrs. Lizzie Hanlon, housekeeper for Mr. White at his residence on East 21st Street, had not heard of the shooting when a reporter from *The Times* called shortly before midnight.

The house is one of the most magnificently decorated in the city. Standing amid elaborate Italian decorations with carved marble and graceful fountains, Mrs. Hanlon gave what information she could. She said: "Mr. White has been alone in the house for some time. Mrs. White has been away in the West for about three weeks or a month, but is now at her country residence at St. James, L.I.

"Lawrence White, Mr. White's son, came down from Harvard the other day. Both he and his father came in and dressed for dinner tonight, but they did not go out together, Mr. White leaving alone a few minutes before his son. I do not know where either of them went."

"Has Mr. Thaw been to the house to see Mr. White recently?" Mrs. Hanlon was asked.

"Mr. Thaw? I never heard of him. As far as I know Mr. White did not have any visitors here today."

Young White, with a friend, Leroy King, dined with his father last night at the Café Martin. Mr. White, his son says, was in the best of spirits. After the dinner the party entered an electric automobile and went up to the New Amsterdam roof garden. There the two boys asked the elder White to stay and see the performance.

Harry Kendall Thaw (in light-colored suit, left) leaving court after his second trial in July 1915, where he was found not guilty.

He said: "No, I thank you," adding that he was going elsewhere.

That was the last they saw of him.

Meant to Go to Philadelphia

Lawrence White says his father was thinking of going to Philadelphia last evening on a matter of business, and only changed his plans in order to dine with the boys.

"If he had only gone!" exclaimed the son in his grief.

Lawrence White said he had never seen Harry Thaw in his life and had never heard his father speak of him, and that he knew of absolutely nothing that could lead to such a tragedy. He was then informed that his father was dead and that the body was still at the Garden. He departed for that place at once.

After the body was taken to the undertaker's a hasty examination was made. Three wounds were found. The fatal bullet entered the left eye. The other two bullets grazed the shoulders, leaving a flesh wound on each. The top of the head showed a mark, this having been caused by striking the edge of the table as the body fell to the floor.

Detectives Look for Mrs. Thaw

Mr. and Mrs. Thaw have been stopping at the [Hotel] Lorraine, Fifth Avenue and 45th Street. Detectives were sent there to get her as a witness, but she had not returned at 3 o'clock this morning. At that hour, Policeman Debes, who arrested Thaw, gave this account of what happened:

"I was on post at 26th Street and Madison Avenue last night, and asked the manager of the Garden if there would be any shooting in the show. I did this because the use of firearms at Hammerstein's last week made me hurry and scurry for awhile, thinking the shooting was done on the street. He told me there was not.

"I heard three pistol shots and started for the Garden. I met the electrician of the place, who was on the run. He said that a man and a woman had been shot in the audience. I hurried upstairs and the first I saw was a woman who had fainted. Then I found Thaw with the fireman. I asked him if he had shot the man whose body I could see by the table.

"'Yes,' Thaw replied.

"Then he added that the man had ruined his life—or wife—I could not distinctly make out.

"'Is he dead?' he asked. I told him he was.

"'Well, I made a good job of it and I'm glad,' he added. Then a woman, who Manager Lawrence told me was Mrs. Thaw, ran up and kissed him.

"'I didn't think you would do it in this way,' she said. He whispered to her, patted her on the shoulder, and said that it would all come out all right."

A dispatch from Pittsburg last night said that Thaw and his wife were to have sailed for Europe tomorrow.

—June 26, 1906

NOTE: *Thaw, Nesbit's husband, was angered because his wife had been White's mistress. The court proceedings, dubbed "the trial of the century" by reporters at the time, ended with Thaw's acquittal by reason of insanity and his commitment to an asylum. Thaw would later escape to Canada and be extradited back to New York, where he was released in 1915 after being found sane. He was arrested again in 1917 for the kidnapping and assault of a 19-year-old boy, again committed to an asylum, and again released in 1924.*

TRIAL UNDER WAY IN YOUTH'S KILLING

By JOHN N. POPHAM

This Deep South town witnessed today a courtroom session in which the touchy race relations subject received extraordinary treatment.

The occasion was the opening of the trial of two white men, Roy Bryant, 24, and his half-brother, J. W. Milam, 36, on charges of kidnapping and murdering Emmett Louis Till, a 14-year-old Chicago Negro alleged to have "wolf whistled" at Bryant's 21-year-old wife, Carolyn.

At the end of the trial today, ten white men had been chosen for the jury that will hear evidence in the case. The trial will resume at 9 a.m. tomorrow when two more jurors and an alternate will be selected.

The highlight of the six-and-one-half-hour trial session, however, concerned the activities that took place inside and outside the courtroom before the eyes of several hundred white persons who strongly support a strict pattern of racial segregation.

Negro newspaper photographers moved freely about the building with their cameras in operation. Approximately 100 Negro spectators moved about the same area while chatting with white visitors. The prospective jurors were asked directly if they would abjure race prejudice in weighing testimony.

Hostility Controlled

For the most part there was an atmosphere of controlled hostility. But in some instances relaxed laughter and good-natured banter carried the day.

The courtroom, seating 250 persons, was jammed with press representatives, a special panel of 120 veniremen chosen for this particular case, a regular panel of 48 veniremen and spectators.

Sheriff H. C. Strider of Tallahatchie County, of which Sumner is the county seat, announced in the courtroom that all persons entering, other than lawyers and court officials, would be searched for weapons by two deputy sheriffs.

At first the deputies patted the pockets of each person. But in a little while they were obviously only half-hearted in their efforts and often joshed with old friends while overlooking the search for arms. There was no searching of the crowd when court reconvened after the luncheon recess.

Mamie Till Mobley, the grief-stricken mother of Emmett Till, at her son's funeral, September 6, 1955.

About 50 to 60 representatives of newspapers, radio and television, many from metropolitan centers throughout the country, were on hand. There were 10 representatives of the Negro press.

Sheriff Strider reserved 22 seats at press tables in the courtroom, behind the railing, for white newspaper representatives, and one table with four seats for Negro reporters, located beyond the rail at the far end of the courtroom.

Circuit Judge Curtis M. Swango, presiding at the trial, gave a 20-minute period for photographers to take pictures at the opening of the session.

The selection of the jurors moved swiftly. Judge Swango, 47 years old and regarded as one of Mississippi's most able jurists, held a firm rein over the procedure. He was dressed in a blue suit, white shirt and dark tie. During the stifling heat of the afternoon session he removed his jacket.

The courtroom was informal in the local rural tradition. Virtually everyone was in shirt sleeves, smoking was permitted at all times, bailiffs carried pitchers of ice water to counsel and press tables and occasionally passed a cup of water over the rail to some friend in the crowd.

Robert B. Smith, special counsel assigned by Gov. Hugh White and Attorney General J. P. Coleman, to prosecute the case, conducted most of the examination for the state. Mr. Smith, 41, is boyish looking with a thick shock of black hair. He is a former FBI agent and a Marine Corps veteran of World War II.

Mr. Smith's questioning of prospective jurors indicated an intensive screening of the veniremen. He seemed to be familiar with everyone's personal habits and family background, even to the nicknames they had for friends who might be interested in the outcome of the trial.

The defendants have five attorneys, with J. J. Breland and C. Sidney Carlton handling the interrogation of the prospective jurors. Both are regarded as outstanding trial lawyers.

During the entire trial session, the wives of Mr. Milam and Mr. Bryant and their children, each couple having two small boys, sat with the defendants.

The children played around the knees of their fathers and occasionally ran up and down the corridors.

—September 19, 1955

NOTE: *An all-white jury acquitted Bryant and Milam after deliberating for just over an hour. Later, in a 1956 interview with* Look *magazine, the men confessed, and tried to justify, their role in the killing. Till's casket is now on display at the National Museum of African American History and Culture in Washington, D.C.*

MANSON, 3 WOMEN GUILTY; PROSECUTION TO ASK DEATH

By EARL CALDWELL

C harles M. Manson and three young women who were members of his hippie family were found guilty today of the Tate-LaBianca murders.

The jury delivered its verdict just before noon, ending more than 42 hours of deliberation spread over nine days.

The defendants showed no emotion as the clerk of the court read the verdicts. But as they were led from the heavily guarded courtroom, Manson again said that he had been denied the opportunity to present a defense and told Superior Court Judge Charles H. Older, "You won't outlive this, old man."

Manson and two of the women—Susan Atkins, 22, and Patricia Krenwinkel, 23— each were convicted on seven counts of murder in the first degree. The fourth defendant, Leslie Van Houten, 21, was convicted on two counts of first-degree murder. All four were also found guilty of conspiracy to commit murder.

All four were also found guilty of conspiracy to commit murder.

In California, conviction of first-degree murder carries an automatic penalty of life imprisonment or death in the gas chamber.

The prosecutor, Vincent Bugliosi, who commented that he was "very pleased" with today's verdict, said that he would ask the jury to impose the death penalty.

Paul Fitzgerald, chief counsel for the defense, expressed some bitterness over the verdict.

"We lost the case when we lost our request for a change of venue," he said. Irving Kanarek, Manson's lawyer, scoffed at both the verdict and the trial in general, "It was just entertainment for the public," he said.

Once the verdicts were announced, Mr. Kanarek asked that the decision be nullified but was ruled out of order by Judge Older. Mr. Kanarek said that he had evidence that the jury had been under pressure to arrive at what he called a group decision.

Judge Older interrupted an in-chambers conference at 10:15 a.m. to notify attorneys that the jury had reached a verdict. Immediately, unusual security precautions went into effect. By the time the jury was brought in, 90 minutes later, there were 13 uniformed bailiffs in the courtroom and more than a dozen others in the spectators' section.

As the verdict was being read, deputies stood behind each of the defendants. The three girls, who had been whispering to each other, stopped to listen as the clerk of the court began to read. Manson, sitting across the table from the girls, often stroked his beard and gazed at the ceiling. He did not speak until he was being led away.

Today's courtroom scene was almost an anticlimax for the trial that was both the longest in the state's history and one of the most bizarre. But the bizarre did not begin with the trial. It began months before, with the murders themselves.

Charles Manson mug shot of April 22, 1968, following an arrest on suspicion of grand theft auto, a year and a half before the Tate-LaBianca murders.

Where Killings Took Place

Five of the murders took place at the Benedict Canyon home of the actress Sharon Tate. The two other victims, Mr. and Mrs. Leno LaBianca, were killed at their home in the Los Feliz district of Los Angeles.

At the Tate residence, the bodies were discovered by a maid on the morning of Aug. 9, 1969. The bodies of the LaBiancas were found the next evening.

Miss Tate, the wife of filmmaker Roman Polanski, was stabbed 16 times. The other victims at the Tate residence were: Abigail Folger, 26, a coffee heiress who was stabbed 28 times; Thomas John Sebring, 35, a Hollywood hair stylist, who was stabbed 7 times and shot once; Voytek Frykowski, 37, a friend of Mr. Polanski's who was stabbed 51 times, shot twice and struck 13 times on the head; and Steven Parent, 18, a student who was shot 4 times and stabbed once.

At the LaBianca residence, Mr. LaBianca, 44, a wealthy supermarket owner, was stabbed 26 times. His 38-year-old wife was stabbed 41 times. According to a coroner's report, at least 13 of her wounds were inflicted after death. Manson and Miss Van Houten were arrested in October, two months after the murders took place, in a police raid on the [Manson] family's commune at Barker's Ranch in Death Valley.

At that time Manson was not charged with murder. He was not even a suspect. The police charged him only with possession of stolen property and arson, and his bail was set at $12,500.

The Hinman Killing

It was in November, after the police had arrested Miss Atkins, that Manson and his family were connected with the crimes.

The police arrested Miss Atkins in connection with the killing of Gary Hinman, a musician who lived in Topanga Canyon and was a friend of Manson's.

Robert C. Beausoleil, 23, who was also once a member of the Manson family, has already been convicted of killing Mr. Hinman. According to witnesses in that case, Manson also ordered that killing. It was reported that Beausoleil linked Miss Atkins with the Hinman murder when Manson failed to get him out of jail after he had been arrested.

Later, Miss Atkins implicated Manson and the family in the Tate-LaBianca killings.

Miss Atkins, after her arrest, told her cellmates at Sybil Brand Institute, the women's house of detention here, that the Manson family had been involved in the killings. The other inmates passed the information on to the police.

Miss Atkins then related her story to the police and later to the grand jury that indicted her, Manson, Miss Krenwinkel, Miss Van Houten and Linda Kasabian.

But on March 5, three months after she had appeared before the grand jury, Miss Atkins and her attorney, Richard Caballero, met with Manson in jail. Afterward, Miss Atkins changed her position. She withdrew her confession, which by this time had been published in book form and in *The Los Angeles Times*. She said that she had fabricated the story of the Manson family's involvement in the murders.

In her confession, Miss Atkins did not admit to stabbing anyone, but said she had been at the murder scene and held Sharon Tate's head in her lap as she was dying.

But the state did not lose its case. Mrs. Kasabian, who had been indicted and charged with murder and criminal conspiracy, agreed to testify against Manson and the other defendants. And in turn, she was granted immunity by the prosecution.

Manson and his three codefendants went to trial July 24, 1970, almost a year after the crimes had been committed. The trial attracted wide attention from the start. It began with the four defendants showing hostility to the court but laughing and joking with one another.

And it was a trial that saw the defense forced to scuttle its plans four months after the proceeding began and rest its case without calling a single witness because three of the defendants, the girls, insisted on giving what Manson's lawyer said would amount to de facto confessions. At the time, it was said that the girls wanted to confess to "save" Manson.

As the trial progressed, the unusual came to be expected. Once Manson angrily lunged across the defense table at Judge Older with a sharpened pencil in his hand.

Bizarre Is Infectious

At another point in the trial, Mr. Bugliosi, the prosecutor, became so enraged with Miss Atkins that he took a swing at her in front of the startled jurors and called her a "little bitch."

The bizarre was infectious, and during the trial it touched all the parties, including the lawyers. Three of them, all defense attorneys, spent at least one night in jail during the trial after having been found in contempt of court. Mr. Bugliosi, the prosecutor, escaped jail when he was found in contempt only after he had agreed to pay a $50 fine.

During the trial, one of the lawyers disappeared and was never found. Ronald Hughes, who was representing Miss Van Houten, apparently was lost when he went to the mountains during a Thanksgiving recess. There were heavy rains at the time, and the authorities said that the area was treacherous during such storms.

When Mr. Hughes disappeared, the court declared a three-week recess and appointed another lawyer, Maxwell Keith, to represent Miss Van Houten.

The trial consumed 121 court days. There were 21,304 pages of transcript containing six million words.

In presenting its case, the state called 84 witnesses. Many were once members of Manson's family and testified that they once believed that he was Jesus Christ. They also told of his almost obsessive belief that the country was on the verge of a black-white race war that he called helter-skelter.

Several of these witnesses said that Manson had been preparing to move his family to the desert to avoid the war, which he believed would end with the blacks killing all the whites.

However, they said that Manson also believed that the blacks would then find themselves incapable of running society and would turn to him and he would assume leadership.

Witnesses said that Manson planned the murders, hoping that blacks would be blamed, and that they would trigger the race war.

The high point of the trial came with the testimony of Mrs. Kasabian, the state's star witness. She said that she had accompanied the killers—all members of the Manson family—to the Tate home on the night the murders there were committed.

"Do What Tex Says"

She said that Miss Atkins, Miss Krenwinkel, Miss Van Houten and Tex Watson entered the Tate house. She said that she served as lookout.

Mrs. Kasabian said that she had gone to the Tate residence not knowing where she was going or for what purpose. But she said that Manson had told her to go and to "do what Tex says."

At the Tate home, a remote mansion high in the hills above Hollywood, she said that Mr. Parent was the first victim and was shot by Watson.

According to other testimony, Mr. Parent had just visited a friend living in the guesthouse at the rear of the Tate residence and was in his car and about to leave when he was apprehended by Watson and the others.

Mrs. Kasabian testified that she heard Mr. Parent beg for his life and saw Watson, who is currently in a mental institution, shoot him four times. She said that when the four entered the house she remained outside, standing watch. When she heard screams, she said, she ran to the house.

Susan Atkins, Patricia Krenwinkle, and Leslie Van Houten heading to the courtroom at the Tate-LaBianca murder trial, August 6, 1970.

The Next Night

She said that she saw Frykowski stumble out with Watson in pursuit. She said that Watson then stabbed and beat him. And then, she said, out of the corner of her eye she saw Miss Krenwinkel, with knife in hand, chasing after Miss Folger.

She said that when they returned to the Spahn movie ranch, where the family was then living, Manson was upset because they had created such a mess and panic. Mrs. Kasabian said in her testimony that the next night Manson accompanied her, Miss Atkins, Miss Krenwinkel, Miss Van Houten, Watson and another family member, Steve Grogan, to the LaBianca home.

She said that he went into the house, returned a short time later and said that the victims were tied up. She said he then told the others to go in but not to let the victims know they were going to be killed.

She said that she, Manson and Grogan drove off in the car, leaving the others at the LaBianca home to do the killing. She said that Manson instructed them to hitchhike rides back to the ranch after they had finished.

Mrs. Kasabian said that while the murders were being committed, she and Manson took a walk on the beach, eating peanuts. Mrs. Kasabian who was on the witness stand for 18 days, said that later that night Manson ordered her to kill an actor she knew. She testified that she replied, "Charley, I'm not you. I can't kill anybody."

Manson was born in Cincinnati to an unwed mother and spent 13 of his first 25 years in reformatories and prisons. He married in 1955, fathered a son and was divorced while serving time in a federal prison for transporting stolen cars.

He was released from the prison, in San Pedro, Calif., in 1967. He moved to San Francisco, and it was there, in the Haight-Ashbury District, that he became involved with the hippies and where he began his family. In 1968, he moved his group to Los Angeles. They finally settled on the old movie ranch, which is in the Santa Susanna Mountains, 30 miles northwest of Los Angeles.

Although the defense rested its case without calling any witnesses, Manson did testify during the trial. However, his testimony was taken in the absence of the jurors, and he refused to repeat it when they were in the courtroom.

While he was on the stand, he was not asked any questions. Instead he was permitted to make a long, rambling statement in which he discussed his philosophy and his background. At the start of that statement he said that he had not killed anyone and had not ordered anyone killed.

—January 26, 1971

NOTE: *Manson was denied parole in 2012 for the twelfth time and is not eligible again until 2027, when he will be 92. Of the other Manson family members who were convicted of the Tate-LaBianca murders, Patricia Krenwinkel, Leslie Van Houten and Charles "Tex" Watson are still serving life sentences. Steve "Clem" Grogan was paroled in 1985. Susan Atkins died in prison in 2009.*

JOHN LENNON OF BEATLES IS KILLED; SUSPECT HELD IN SHOOTING AT DAKOTA

By LES LEDBETTER

John Lennon, one of the four Beatles, was shot and killed last night while entering the apartment building where he lived, the Dakota, on Manhattan's Upper West Side. A suspect was seized at the scene.

The 40-year-old Mr. Lennon was shot in the back twice after getting out of a limousine and walking into an entranceway of the Dakota at 1 West 72nd Street, Sgt. Robert Barnes of the 20th Precinct said.

"Obviously the man was waiting for him," Sgt. Barnes said of the assailant. The suspect was identified as Mark David Chapman, 25, of Hawaii, who had been living in New York for about a week, according to James L. Sullivan, chief of detectives of the 20th Precinct.

Wife Reported Unhurt

Jeff Smith, a neighbor, said that he heard five shots fired shortly before 11 p.m. Other witnesses said they heard four when the shooting occurred at 10:45 p.m.

With the singer when he was shot was his wife, Yoko Ono, who was not hurt by the bullets that struck her husband as they entered an archway that led into the courtyard of the Dakota complex.

Witnesses said Mr. Lennon was wearing a white T-shirt and dungaree jacket when he was shot. They said Miss Ono screamed, "Help me! Help me!"

They said the suspect paced back and forth in the entranceway to the Dakota after shooting the musician, arguing with the doorman and holding the gun in his hand.

There were bullet holes in the structure and blood on the bricks of the building. Immediately after Mr. Lennon was shot, hundreds of people began to gather at West 72nd Street and Central Park West. A number of them were crying. By 1 a.m., the crowd had grown to 500.

Mr. Lennon was taken into the office after being shot. Shortly after, he was taken to Roosevelt Hospital, where he was pronounced dead, according to a hospital spokesman. Police Officer Anthony Palma, who drove Miss Ono to the hospital, described her as "very hysterical" and said she sobbed: "Tell me it isn't true."

Jack Douglas, Mr. Lennon's producer, said he and the Lennons had been at a studio called the Record Plant in midtown earlier in the evening and that Mr. Lennon had left at

10:30 p.m. Mr. Lennon said he was going to get something to eat and then going home, according to Mr. Douglas.

Obtained Autograph Earlier

Lt. John Schick of the 20th Precinct said the gunman let the Lennons pass him and enter the building's passageway before shooting the singer. Lt. Schick said the man called out "Mr. Lennon" and then pulled a gun from under a coat and started firing.

The police said the suspect stepped from an alcove and emptied several shots into Mr. Lennon. Mr. Lennon then struggled up six stairs and inside the alcove to a guard area where he collapsed.

Employees at the Dakota said someone resembling the alleged assailant had obtained an autograph from Mr. Lennon.

Chief Sullivan said the suspect had been seen in the neighborhood of the Dakota for several days.

A bystander, Sean Strub, said he was walking south near 72nd Street when he heard four shots. He said he came around the corner to Central Park West and saw Mr. Lennon being put into the back of a police car.

"A Smirk on His Face"

Mr. Strub said the suspect was put into another police car.

"He had a smirk on his face" when the police took him away, Mr. Strub said.

The suspect, Mark David Chapman, was described by the police as a stocky man wearing a white shirt and brown pants, wire-rimmed glasses and a coat. Sgt. Barnes said a .38-caliber revolver, believed to be the murder weapon, had been recovered.

Continued to Write Songs

Mr. Lennon, who was widely thought to be the most intellectual and outspoken of the Beatles, wrote many of the songs that launched them in the early 1960s and changed the course of rock music.

In an interview this year—his first major interview in five years—Mr. Lennon said he had wanted to leave the Beatles as early as 1966 but did not make the move until four years later because he "just didn't have the guts."

Mr. Lennon made his last Beatles album, *Abbey Road*, in 1969.

After the Beatles broke up in 1970, Mr. Lennon continued writing songs and recording. But in 1975 he dropped out of the music business for five years, saying he wanted to be with his son, Sean.

He was born Oct. 9, 1940, in England's northern industrial seaport of Liverpool, the son of a porter father who deserted the family when John was three.

Mr. Lennon attended secondary school in Liverpool and then went on to Liverpool College of Art, where he married a classmate, Cynthia Powell.

They were later divorced. In 1969, Mr. Lennon married Miss Ono, a Japanese-American artist. He later said, "We went to Paris on our honeymoon, then interrupted our honeymoon to get married on the Rock of Gibraltar."

Emblem of the '60s

The Beatles' music was as much a staple of the revolutionary 1960s as the Vietnam War, whose protesters sang their songs in addition to letting their hair grow long in imitation of the musicians.

"I Want to Hold Your Hand," "Love Me Do" and "She Loves You" stayed on the top of the hit parades for months and heralded Beatlemania, the frenzy whipped up among their teenage fans around the world.

After the breakup of the group, Mr. Lennon and Miss Ono lived in seclusion in New York for several years, but the couple were on the front page again in a messy deportation hearing.

The U.S. government contended that Mr. Lennon, a British subject, was ineligible for permanent residence because of a 1968 drug conviction in Britain. Mr. Lennon eventually was allowed to stay in the United States.

—*December 9, 1980*

NOTE: *Chapman, an obsessed fan, pleaded guilty in the murder, rejecting his lawyers' advice to present an insanity defense. He had bought the .38-caliber handgun for $169 in Hawaii. He is serving a 20-year-to-life sentence.*

MRS. HARRIS FOUND GUILTY OF MURDER AND SHE IS QUICKLY REMOVED TO JAIL

By JAMES FERON

Jean S. Harris was convicted tonight of murder in the second degree in the multiple shooting of her companion and lover for 14 years, Dr. Herman Tarnower.

The 57-year-old former school headmistress, seated at the defense table, took the verdict calmly. Two lawyers at the defense table burst into tears, but Mrs. Harris showed no emotion, watching as each juror was polled. "I can't sit in jail," she said to one of her attorneys. She then walked forcefully from the courtroom, shrugging off a police matron.

Free on bail since soon after the March 10 shooting, Mrs. Harris was remanded to custody by Judge Leggett before she was escorted out of the Westchester County Courthouse. The penalties for second-degree murder range from 15 years to life in prison. She was also found guilty of two counts of criminal possession of a weapon. Mrs. Harris was taken immediately to the women's unit of the Westchester County Jail at Valhalla.

She had testified in the 64-day trial that the 69-year-old physician, a noted cardiologist and author of *The Complete Scarsdale Medical Diet*, died in a struggle over the gun she intended for her suicide, but the jury decided otherwise after 47 hours and 56 minutes of deliberations.

Murder Found "Intentional"

They found her guilty of the most serious of three possible homicide charges against her, agreeing finally that she had "intentionally" murdered the doctor. The prosecutor, George Bolen, contended that Mrs. Harris had shot Dr. Tarnower in a jealous rage over her rival for his affections, Lynne Tryforos, his 38-year-old administrative assistant.

Mrs. Tryforos said tonight that she had no comment except to say that "my reaction is the same as the family's." She was referring to Dr. Tarnower's sister, Pearl Schwartz, who said: "We feel justice was done. I'm emotionally drained. This was a marvelous man, and a terrible loss."

Mrs. Harris left the courthouse at 6:35 p.m. She sat in the back of a sheriff's car, appearing stunned and staring straight ahead. Photographers' flashbulbs glinted on her headband. In the courthouse lobby, Mr. Bolen said that "the jury followed the judge's instructions not to let sympathy or empathy interfere with their role." Joel Aurnou,

Jean Harris with one of her attorneys, Bonnie Steingart, leaving the Westchester County Courthouse in White Plains, February 9, 1981.

Mrs. Harris's lawyer, said he had made no application for bail "because none is possible in a Class A felony."

Will she be able to stand up under all this, he was asked? "I wish I knew," he said.

"Never Spent a Day in Jail"

Asked about a possible sentence for Mrs. Harris, Judge Leggett said it would be based "on the probation report and all the other evidence I get." Mrs. Harris, who has never been convicted of a crime, has told friends she would "never spend a day in jail."

Three times the jury returned to ask the judge to define "intent," and he did so by explaining that it involved the "conscious objective" of Mrs. Harris to cause Dr. Tarnower's death. If they did not find that she had done so beyond a reasonable doubt, they could move on to the lesser charges. The jury finally decided that the frail defendant, who had been headmistress of the Madeira School for girls in McLean, Va., intended to kill Dr. Tarnower. Judge Leggett had explained that "premeditation" was not to be considered, and that "intent" could occur anytime before the shooting, even "as the shots which caused the death were fired."

The verdict brought to an end one of the most sensational murder trials in local history, one that attracted national attention because of the prominence of the people involved and their complex and intriguing relationships.

But the most compelling aspect was Mrs. Harris herself, an articulate and fiercely independent woman whose declarations of affection for the doctor she was accused of murdering, and her scorn for Mrs. Tryforos, her rival, added melodrama to the trial. It also touched many aspects of contemporary life, inspiring articles on a host of related subjects in newspapers, magazines and in forthcoming books. Writers expanded on Mrs. Harris's dependence on prescribed drugs, her struggle for what she felt was a woman's right to be independent and her feeling of losing ground to a younger woman.

The defendant's letters and notes, some ironical and others almost obscene, prompted laughter and tears in a courtroom that was often packed to capacity. Mrs. Harris's eight days of testimony as a witness in her own defense represented a classic courtroom drama.

"Intensely Private Person"

An "intensely private person," she was to become instantly recognizable after the events of the night of last March 10, 1980. They became part of the public record at 10:56 p.m., with a frenzied telephone call to the White Plains Police Department. The call came from Suzanne Van der Vreken, the doctor's house manager, who lived on his six-acre estate with her husband, Henri, the estate manager.

Racing to the house on Purchase Street, Police Officer Brian McKenna saw a car with Virginia license plates operated by a woman "making a U-turn," he later testified. Had she been fleeing, as the prosecution suggested, or was she heading for a public phone to call for help? The doctor's phone, she said later, was inoperable.

Apparently that was because Mrs. Van der Vreken had left the kitchen extension off the hook after the doctor had buzzed for help. According to Mrs. Harris's account, she was deeply depressed over her role as the top administrator of the exclusive girls' school. The school's board of directors, relying on a report critical of Mrs. Harris as headmistress, was seeking her ouster.

Troubles at School

Even the students had become critical of Mrs. Harris. Only a few days earlier she had suspended several after drug paraphernalia was found in their room, and the decision was bitterly criticized in a meeting in Mrs. Harris's house. On March 10 she had received what she perceived to be a critical letter from a student who had been burned in an initiation prank.

Mrs. Harris also had run out of an amphetamine that Dr. Tarnower had been prescribing, and she had called him asking for more. But the prosecution noted that Mrs. Harris was upset about a more personal matter, her fading relationship with Dr. Tarnower.

The 69-year-old doctor had seen Mrs. Harris less and less after she moved to Virginia in 1975, and now Mrs. Tryforos was sharing his bedroom, serving as his dinner hostess and accompanying him on vacations.

"An Empty Chair"

A despondent Mrs. Harris, describing herself as "a person sitting in an empty chair," composed a will, wrote final notes to family members and colleagues, hugged her dogs and then drove to the doctor's home for "a few quiet minutes with Hy, for me to feel safe again" before what she said would be her suicide "at the side of the pond where there were daffodils in the spring."

Mrs. Harris said the doctor knew she was coming, but the house was dark and he was asleep when she arrived at about 10:30 p.m. The front door was locked, so she used the garage entrance. She was carrying daisies, a gift from a Madeira colleague, in one hand and her pocketbook, containing the loaded .32-caliber revolver, in the other.

She said Dr. Tarnower woke up and appeared to be annoyed. He rolled over, she said, and feigned sleep. She looked for a shawl that was to be given to her daughter-in-law, Kathleen Harris. But she also found Mrs. Tryforos's negligee, jewelry and clothing intended for a vacation the younger woman was about to take with the doctor.

Mrs. Harris said she became angry and began to throw things. Dr. Tarnower struck her, "for the first time ever," she said. The second time came a moment later, after she broke a makeup mirror in the bathroom. They were fighting, "two persons who never argued over anything except the use of a subjunctive," she testified.

"Look What You Did"

Mrs. Harris said she had asked the doctor to hit her again, "strong enough to kill," but he walked away to his bed. She picked up her pocketbook, deciding to leave, but "felt the weight of the revolver." Testifying about what she said was her intent to commit suicide, she maintained she had said to herself, "Never mind, I'll do it myself."

Mrs. Harris took out the revolver and pulled the trigger, but she said Dr. Tarnower "pushed my hand down." "Then the gun exploded," she testified. "Hy jumped back. He held up his hand. It was bleeding. 'Jesus Christ, look what you did,' he said. I wasn't aiming the gun at Hy, and he was the one who was shot."

She said the doctor went into his bathroom to inspect his wound, a shot through the palm at the juncture of the thumb and index finger. The prosecution said it was the shot that also entered the doctor's chest, and Dr. Louis Roh, the Westchester County deputy medical examiner, had referred to the shot through the palm as "consistent with a defensive wound."

Mr. Aurnou enlisted the aid of Herbert Leon MacDonell, an expert in bloodstain patterns, fingerprint identification and firearms, to say the bullet that caused the hand wound then went through a glass door.

Put Gun to Head

Mrs. Harris "couldn't believe what had happened," she told a packed courtroom. "I wanted to get dying over with, as pleasant talk was not to be that night." She began to search for the gun, which she said had fallen under a bed. She said she put it to her head again, but the doctor lunged across his bed to grab her wrist. The gun fell again. He picked it up, put it in his lap and buzzed for the Van der Vrekens. Mrs. Harris said she then reached for the gun and he dropped the telephone, which he was now holding, to stop her for a third time.

"There was an instant," she said, "when I felt the muzzle of the gun in my stomach and I had it in my hand." She said she pulled the trigger "and it exploded against me. My first thought was that it didn't hurt at all; I should have done it a long time ago."

Disabling Wound

It was the doctor who had been hit, however, possibly in the upper right arm, she said later, describing a disabling wound that severed a major bone. The doctor also suffered a wound in the right shoulder, with the bullet fracturing three ribs and causing the fatal internal injuries.

Mrs. Harris said she ran to the far side of the bed, still bent on suicide, and fired the gun at her head again, only to hear a click. She looked at the weapon, squeezed the trigger, and a bullet—the last of five in the six-chambered weapon—slammed into a cupboard. Aiming the gun at her head again she fired and fired, but heard only clicks.

Mr. MacDonell supported her account by saying he had found evidence that four of the cartridges had been "double fired," with the firing pin coming down a second time on four of the five empty cartridges.

Mrs. Harris, expecting the "servants," as she called them, to arrive momentarily, ran for her coat, where she had five extra bullets, to reload the gun. She said she did not know how to empty the weapon, however, on either of the occasions that she test fired it from the porch of her home—she got the empty shells out of the chamber with an icepick both times—or that night in the doctor's house. So she banged the gun against the edge of the bathtub, only to see the entire cylinder fall away.

Mrs. Harris said she sought to use the phone to get help, but "there was no outside line." She said she then raced downstairs, heard Mrs. Van der Vreken speaking in the dining room, and shouted, "I'm going for help!" before leaving in her car. She returned in a few minutes, accompanied by Officer McKenna, to answer questions, watch as the doctor was removed and learn an hour later at Harrison Police Headquarters that he had died.

—February 25, 1981

NOTE: *Harris was granted clemency and released in 1993, after serving 12 years in a prison where she won praise for her work in counseling other inmates. Despite police testimony that she admitted to the crime, she insisted until her death in 2012 that the shooting had been her own suicide attempt gone awry.*

NOT GUILTY: THE OVERVIEW; JURY CLEARS SIMPSON IN DOUBLE MURDER; SPELLBOUND NATION DIVIDES ON VERDICT

By DAVID MARGOLICK

O renthal James Simpson, a man who overcame the spindly legs left by a childhood case of rickets to run to fame and fortune, surmounted a very different sort of obstacle today, when a jury of 10 women and two men cleared him of charges that he murdered his former wife and one of her friends.

The verdict, coming 16 months after Nicole Brown Simpson and Ronald L. Goldman were slashed to death in the front yard of Mrs. Simpson's condominium and after nine months of what often seemed like interminable testimony, sidebars and legal bickering, was reached in the end with breathtaking speed. When it was read, much of the nation stopped work to listen to it.

And with the Simpson verdict, as with the Simpson case, the nation once more divided—largely along racial lines. So, too, did defense lawyers, with the onetime chief of Mr. Simpson's legal team, Robert L. Shapiro, criticizing his successor.

"Not only did we play the race card, we dealt it from the bottom of the deck," Mr. Shapiro told Barbara Walters tonight in an interview on an ABC News special.

In a scene that lent a certain symmetry to the entire Simpson saga, Mr. Simpson immediately returned to the freeways of Los Angeles in a white van, and as fans waved from the streets he headed back to his home. While a dozen helicopters flew overhead, and fans festooned the fence with roses and balloons, he was met by A. C. Cowlings, who had been in the driver's seat of the white Ford Bronco on June 17, 1994, five days after the killings.

Mr. Simpson pursed his lips, gulped a few times and wore a forced grin as Deirdre Robertson, the law clerk to Judge Lance A. Ito, read the verdict. Mrs. Robertson tripped over "Orenthal," but not over what came next: "not guilty." When she uttered those words, Mr. Simpson's body instantly uncoiled. He breathed a sigh of relief, and a faint smile appeared.

As Mrs. Robertson's recitation continued—"in violation of Penal Code Section 187A, a felony, upon Nicole Brown Simpson, a human being," Mr. Simpson waved at the panelists and mouthed the words "thank you." The reading then unfolded again, with the name "Ronald L. Goldman" substituted for Mrs. Simpson. Mr. Simpson embraced his chief lawyer, Johnnie L. Cochran Jr., and silently rethanked the jury again.

"Ladies and gentlemen of the jury, is this your verdict, so say you one, so say you all?" Mrs. Robertson then asked. "Yes," the panel members—nine black, two whites and a Hispanic man—replied matter-of-factly. Critics of the jurors' decision maintained that they had been manipulated by a cynical defense team that talked more about the racism of the Los Angeles police than about the guilt or innocence of their client. Mr. Simpson's lawyers countered that prosecutors simply had not proven their case.

As he left court, one juror, a former Black Panther whom prosecutors had inexplicably left on the panel, gave Mr. Simpson a clenched fist salute. Before the verdict was read, the same juror, Lionel Cryer, a 44-year-old black man, had smiled and winked at him. At that point, one defense lawyer, Carl Douglas, whispered to his client, "We won; we won," though Mr. Douglas later said it was because the juror thought most hostile to the defense—Anise Aschenbach, a 60-year-old white woman—had also smiled in their direction.

Within an hour, Mr. Simpson, who faced life in prison for the double killings, traded his blue jailhouse jumpsuit and his courtroom woolens for jeans, checked out of the cell where he has lived for the last 474 days and began what promises to be an awkward new life—a life of glamour and golf games, but a life, too, of bodyguards and ostracism by those passionately convinced of his guilt.

> ## "I think we did the right thing—in fact, I know we did."

"I think we did the right thing—in fact, I know we did," said one juror, Brenda Moran, 44, a black computer technician. As to how jurors could render judgment so quickly, she added simply: "We were there for nine months. We didn't need another nine months to decide."

The victims' families quickly went into seclusion, though Fred Goldman, the father of one of those who died, called the outcome his second biggest nightmare, exceeded only by the murder of his only son.

Mr. Simpson said nothing to reporters. But in a statement read by his elder son, Jason, he expressed relief that an "incredible nightmare" was over. He said his first obligation was to his two youngest children, "who will be raised the way that Nicole and I had always planned." Those children are now in the custody of two people who are convinced that he murdered their daughter. Another task, Mr. Simpson said, was to bring to justice whoever killed their mother and Mr. Goldman.

"They are out there somewhere," he stated. "Whatever it takes to identify them and bring them in I'll provide somehow. I can only hope that some day, despite every prejudicial thing that has been said about me, people will understand and believe that I would not, could not and did not kill anyone."

When the verdict was announced, a strange mix of gasps and sobs arose from the gallery. "Oh, my God!" Mr. Simpson's eldest daughter, Arnelle, exclaimed. Jason Simpson began to weep. Mr. Simpson's elderly mother, Eunice, smiled gently in her wheelchair. At a news conference afterward, she explained her apparent serenity. "I knew that my son was innocent," she said. "The prayer of the righteous prevaileth much." Her daughter, Shirley Baker, was more demonstrative. "I just feel like standing on top of this table and dancing a jig," she said.

Across the aisle, Nicole Brown Simpson's parents, Louis and Juditha Brown, received the verdict stoically, though two of her sisters began crying outside court. But the family of Ron Goldman broke out into paroxysms of grief and anger. His sister, Kimberly, sobbed convulsively. Under their breaths, the Goldmans uttered obscenities at Mr. Simpson.

The jury's decision, made after only three hours of deliberations, was one "rush to judgment" to which Mr. Cochran did not object. Defense lawyers attributed their victory not to racial considerations but to their ability to destroy the chronology of the prosecution's case. No reasonable person, Mr. Cochran said, could have believed that Mr. Simpson killed two people, returned home, changed clothes, cleaned up and hid his weapon in the time that prosecutors had allotted.

"We said that if we could shatter the prosecution's timeline so that O. J. Simpson couldn't have committed this crime, that there would be a reasonable doubt," Mr. Cochran said at a news conference in the courtroom. "That's even before we ever got to the socks, the glove and Fuhrman or anything." By building much of its case around Mark Fuhrman, he added, it was the prosecution, not the defense, that had injected race into the case.

Mr. Cochran began at that news conference on a religious note. "I want to thank God," he said. "He always directs our paths and He's worthy to be praised. We think this verdict bespeaks justice."

At another news conference, District Attorney Gil Garcetti, stunned by a humiliating repudiation of a case based on what he often called a "mountain of evidence," said he was "profoundly disappointed." "This was not, in our opinion, a close case," said Mr. Garcetti, whose political future has clearly been clouded by today's verdict.

At the same news conference, a somber Deputy District Attorney Marcia Clark saluted colleagues for striving to make sure "that the lives of Ron and Nicole were not thrown away." Her fellow prosecutor, Christopher A. Darden, who as a high school football player had aspired to wear Mr. Simpson's number, said: "We came here in search

O. J. Simpson shows the jury a new pair of extra-large gloves similar to the ones found at the crime scene, during his double-murder trial in Los Angeles, June 21, 1995.

of justice. You have to be the judges, I expect, as to whether or not any of us found it today. But I'm not bitter, and I'm not angry."

He then began to thank his colleagues. But as he did so, he broke down, and all he could do was shake his head and briefly wave his hand as if to say, "No more."

For the prosecutors, a new ordeal is about to begin: an orgy of post-mortems and second-guessing. Commentators and political opponents now will debate just what it was that turned the tide: the decision to try the case in downtown Los Angeles, where juries are more predominantly black; relying so heavily on a police officer they knew to be a racist; asking Mr. Simpson to put on the murderer's gloves, or the defendant's overwhelming popularity and wealth.

"What this verdict tells you is how fame and money can buy the best defense, can take a case of overwhelming incriminating physical evidence and transform it into a case riddled with reasonable doubt," said Peter Arenella, a law professor at the University of California at Los Angeles.

Mr. Arenella acknowledged that prosecutors had suffered a number of self-inflicted wounds. But even had they tried a perfect case, he said, they might not have prevailed given the haste with which, prosecutors argued, Mr. Simpson committed his foul deeds and the longstanding antagonism of many blacks, including presumably some jurors, toward the police.

"A predominantly African-American jury was more susceptible to claims of police incompetence and corruption and more willing to impose a higher burden of proof than normally required for proof beyond a reasonable doubt," he said. "This was not a good day for the American criminal justice system."

Mrs. Simpson, 35, had spent virtually her entire adult life dating, living with, being married to, or trying to reconcile with or escape from Mr. Simpson. Prosecutors charged that Mr. Simpson killed her in a jealous rage, and killed Mr. Goldman when he happened upon the scene. Supporting their scenario was a history of domestic violence that had left Mrs. Simpson black and blue and fearful for her life, and a raft of blood, hair and fiber tests linking Mr. Simpson to the crime.

Mr. Simpson's response from the start—indeed, just after the low-speed Bronco chase—was that he was "absolutely 100 percent not guilty."

Many blacks reacted jubilantly today to the exoneration of someone whose heroic status seemed enhanced by what they saw as the bigotry of the police and prosecutors. Many whites, by contrast, were aghast.

"Nicole was right," said Faye Resnick, one of Mrs. Simpson's friends who wrote a book about their relationship. "She said he was going to kill her and get away with it."

When Mr. Goldman's father spoke today, his former indignation had clearly yielded to resignation. "Last June 13, 1994, was the worst nightmare of my life," he began. "This is the second."

—*October 4, 1995*

NOTE: *In 1997, Simpson was held liable in a civil trial for the two deaths. He was subsequently convicted in 2008 of armed robbery and kidnapping in connection with a gunpoint seizure of sports memorabilia at a Las Vegas hotel. He was sentenced to 9 to 33 years in state prison in Nevada. Mr. Simpson's defense in the robbery case had been that he was only trying to recover items that had been stolen from him.*

COLORADO MURDER MYSTERY LINGERS AS POLICE PRESS ON

By JAMES BROOKE

Two weeks after John Bennett Ramsey emerged from the basement of his Tudor home here in Boulder, carrying the battered body of his six-year-old daughter, the question of who killed the child beauty queen has become a murder mystery debated across the nation.

Fueling the fascination is a mix of wealth, sex and child beauty. In her brief life, JonBenét Ramsey sang, danced and pirouetted her way to the top of the nation's child beauty pageants. In death, her doll-like image has become a national icon.

Opening a window on the little-known world of child pageants, the nation's television screens inexorably replay tapes of America's Little Royal Miss—a precocious kindergartner, dressed in sequins and rhinestones, her baby teeth highlighted by fuchsia lipstick, and her large innocent eyes framed by blonde curls, lightened and styled.

After two weeks of detective work, the Boulder police have reconstructed this sequence of events: On Christmas night, hours after JonBenét received a new bicycle, someone sexually assaulted her, fractured her skull, silenced her screams by placing duct tape over her mouth and strangled her with a nylon cord.

The next morning, just before dawn, Patricia Ramsey, her mother, called the police, hysterically screaming that she had found a ransom note on stairs leading to the kitchen. Eight hours later, at the suggestion of a police detective, Mr. Ramsey and a friend searched the 6,000-square-foot home. Opening the door to a windowless basement room that only two days earlier hid Christmas presents, Mr. Ramsey found JonBenét's lifeless body.

Denver newspapers have reported that the three-page note, hand-printed and riddled with misspellings, was apparently written on paper torn from a legal pad that the police found in the house. On Wednesday, they reported that the police had also recovered from the house a portion of a practice ransom letter, written on a sheet from the same pad.

On the night of the killing, only four people were sleeping in the 15-room house: JonBenét, her parents and her nine-year-old brother, Burke.

Since Dec. 26, 30 police officers, or one quarter of this city's police force, have worked the case, Boulder's only murder of 1996. Although detectives have focused heavily on the Ramsey family, the Boulder police publicly say they have no suspects.

"The killing of JonBenét did not appear to be linked to any similar event," Tom Koby, the police chief, said this evening. "We do not believe we have a serial situation to deal with."

In this affluent city of 95,000 people, nestled at Rocky Mountain foothills 25 miles northwest of Denver, a list of possible suspects could be surprisingly long.

On Christmas night, local newspapers have reported, the parents went to bed without turning on the home's burglar alarm system. About 15 people had keys to the residence, including a housekeeper and her husband.

Two days before the killing, about 50 adults and children came to the house for a Christmas party, complete with a visiting Santa Claus and catered food. Since the Ramseys moved here from Georgia in 1991, dozens of workers had been through the $500,000 house, performing $700,000 worth of work.

On a quiet street in a neighborhood of mature trees and brick homes, the Ramseys' house is three blocks from the main campus of the University of Colorado, with 25,000 students, including John Andrew Ramsey, Mr. Ramsey's son by a previous marriage. During the Christmas holidays, John, a sophomore, was staying with his mother in Georgia.

"Patsy will never return to that hellhole," Nedra Paugh, Mrs. Ramsey's mother, told a Denver television reporter, referring to the family home here. "Our friends are mad as hell. America is mad as hell about what happened."

While this winter mystery hangs heavily over an empty Ramsey home, it seems light years from the happy days of last summer, when the family vacationed at a second home at Charlevoix, Mich.

"We're having a great summer—wish you were here," JonBenét's voice was heard last week on an answering machine at the shuttered home on Lake Michigan.

When work permitted last summer, Mr. Ramsey, a former navy pilot, flew his private plane to Michigan to join his family. Named Entrepreneur of the Year in 1995 by the Boulder Chamber of Commerce, Mr. Ramsey is the president of Access Graphics, a Lockheed Martin computer equipment subsidiary.

On vacation, Mr. Ramsey, 53, sailed his boat in a local yacht race while JonBenét, his namesake, won a local beauty contest, Little Miss Charlevoix.

Beauty pageants were a life-absorbing passion for Mrs. Ramsey after she tried out for Miss Teen-Age West Virginia over two decades ago. In 1977, she was Miss West Virginia.

In Boulder, Mrs. Ramsey, a 40-year-old homemaker, was active in the social world, taking part in benefits for Opera Colorado and opening her house for a historic homes tour. But her true love was the beauty pageant circuit, as she decorated her home here with trophies and returned to West Virginia to judge the state contest.

In 1993, she was found to have ovarian cancer. With chemotherapy, the cancer went into remission, but Mrs. Ramsey temporarily lost her hair. About that time, she started dressing up her preschooler as a teenager, and coaching her through the Southern belle routines that captivate child contest judges.

In 1995, JonBenét reigned as Little Miss Colorado, parading through Denver on her own float in the city's annual Christmastime Parade of Lights. Last summer she won the title of America's Little Royal Miss.

A natural performer, she sang last Christmas Eve in the children's choir of her church. At her elementary school's Christmas pageant, she sang "Jingle Bell Rock" while dressed as a Christmas present. Whether sashaying in carnival feathers or dancing in a matching white cowboy hat and boots, JonBenét was such an unbeatable sensation that other mothers sometimes pulled their daughters out of contests where she was to compete.

Beauty pageant trappings accompanied JonBenét to the end of her life. After an open coffin funeral in Georgia last week, she was buried dressed in her favorite contest costume, wearing a rhinestone tiara and holding a teddy bear. On the day her body was found, her parents cooperated with the police, giving hours of interviews. Later, newspapers reported, the police removed carpeting from the room where they believe the killing took place.

But in recent days the Ramseys have declined police requests for formal, videotaped interviews. Last week, the parents hired separate legal counsel, two locally prominent criminal defense lawyers. They also hired Patrick S. Korten, a Washington media consultant who once was the top spokesman for the U.S. Department of Justice, to handle the press attention. "There is a difference between talking with the parents and interviewing the parents," Chief Koby said at the forum. However, he added, "They have given us hair samples, blood samples, handwriting samples—they have participated in this investigation."

In their sole news appearance, on CNN, the Ramseys said last week that they had hired a private investigator and announced that they were offering a $50,000 reward for the capture of their daughter's killer.

Mr. Ramsey dismissed as "nauseating beyond belief" the television reporter's suggestion that he might be a suspect. His wife, visibly upset, warned viewers in Boulder, "There is a killer on the loose."

To this, Leslie Durgin, the mayor, countered, "There was no visible sign of forced entry. The body was found in a place where people are saying someone had to know the house. So there isn't a crazed killer on the loose wandering the streets of Boulder."

—January 10, 1997

NOTE: *No one has been charged in the killing of JonBenét, though suspicion has swept across a wide range of people, including her parents. One detective resigned from the case because he believed her parents had been wrongly targeted.*

KITTY, 40 YEARS LATER

By JIM RASENBERGER

K̲ew Gardens does not look much like the setting of an urban horror story. Nestled along the tracks of the Long Island Rail Road, 16 minutes by train from Pennsylvania Station, the Queens neighborhood is quiet and well kept, its streets shaded by tall oaks and bordered by handsome red-brick and wood-frame houses. At first glance, the surroundings appear as remote from big-city clamor as a far-flung Westchester suburb.

Forty years ago, on March 13, 1964, the picturesque tranquility of Kew Gardens was shattered by the murder of 28-year-old Catherine Genovese, known as Kitty. The murder was grisly, but it wasn't the particulars of the killing that became the focus of the case. It was the response of her neighbors. As Ms. Genovese screamed—"Please help me! Please help me!"—38 witnesses did nothing to intervene, according to reports; nobody even bothered to call the police. One witness later explained himself with a phrase that has passed into infamy: "I didn't want to get involved."

Seldom has a crime in New York City galvanized public outrage so intensely. Newspapers spread the story across the nation and as far away as Istanbul and Moscow. Clergymen and politicians decried the events, while psychologists scrambled to comprehend them.

At a time when the world seemed to be unraveling—Kennedy had been assassinated four months earlier, Harlem was on the verge of race riots, crime rates were suddenly taking off—the case quickly expanded into an all-consuming metaphor for the ills of contemporary urban life. A psychiatrist speculated that television had rendered the witnesses inactive by making them almost delusional. Other observers cited a general moral collapse of modern society.

"When you have this general sense that things are going wrong, you look for events that are going to confirm that," said Neal Gabler, author of *Life: The Movie: How Entertainment Conquered Reality.*

"A society in which people are indifferent to one another; a society in which no one cares; a society in which we are all atomized. Here you had a story that confirmed all of those anxieties and fears."

But for all that has been said and written about Ms. Genovese's murder, important questions persist. Some Kew Gardens residents maintain, even now, that there were fewer than 38 witnesses and that many of them could not have seen much of the killing—in other words, that there was less cold-heartedness in Kew Gardens than has been commonly portrayed. Psychologists continue to grapple with the social implications of the neighbors' response. And then there is the woman who occupies the tragic center of this landmark case: some of the details of Ms. Genovese's life have tended to get lost beneath the appalling circumstances of her death.

A Peaceful Life

Kitty Genovese, the petite eldest child of an Italian-American family, grew up in Park Slope, Brooklyn. When her family moved to New Canaan, Conn., she stayed in the city and, in the spring of 1963, settled in Kew Gardens. With a roommate, Mary Ann Zielonko, she took an apartment in a two-story Tudor-style building on Austin Street, near the village, as residents referred to the central cluster of shops. Across the street rose one of the few high-rises in the neighborhood, an elegant 10-story apartment house called the Mowbray.

Tony Corrado, an 84-year-old upholsterer who has owned a small shop on Austin Street since the 1950s, recalls the day Ms. Genovese moved in. She knocked on his door and asked him to give her help carrying a sofa up the stairs. "That was my introduction to Kitty," Mr. Corrado said. "I remember saying, boy, gonna be a lot of wild parties up there. I thought they were airline stewardesses, which we had a lot coming in."

In fact, Ms. Genovese worked as manager at a tavern in Hollis, Queens, called Ev's 11th Hour, and she and Ms. Zielonko lived a quiet, peaceful life over Mr. Corrado's shop. Crime rates were low in the spring of 1963, and many residents slept with their doors unlocked. "I used to say, gee, nothing ever happens in Kew Gardens," Mr. Corrado recalled. "And all of a sudden, this nightmare."

The nightmare struck a year after Ms. Genovese moved in. Shortly after 3 a.m. on that night in March, she was driving home from work. As she stopped her Fiat at a red light, she caught the eye of Winston Moseley, a business machine operator from Ozone Park. He had been cruising the streets in his white Corvair, searching for a woman to mutilate.

Mr. Moseley tailed Ms. Genovese to Kew Gardens, to the paved lot of the railroad station. When she got out of her car, he followed on foot. Ms. Genovese began to run up Austin Street, but he quickly caught up and stabbed her in the back. As she screamed, he stabbed her again, then twice more. A window opened in the Mowbray and a man's voice called out: "Leave that girl alone!"

Mr. Moseley later told the police he was not that concerned about the voice—"I had a feeling this man would close his window and go back to sleep," he said—but he ran off upon hearing it. He moved his car to a more discreet location, changed his hat, then returned. He found Ms. Genovese collapsed in a foyer in the back of her building and finished what he'd begun on Austin Street, stabbing and slashing her repeatedly, then leaving her to die.

The Community as Villain

Kitty Genovese's murder did not initially attract much attention from the press—*The New York Times* gave it four paragraphs—but 10 days later, A. M. Rosenthal, then metropolitan editor of *The Times*, happened to meet Police Commissioner Michael J. Murphy for lunch. Mr. Moseley had just been arrested and had confessed to the murders of both Ms. Genovese and another young woman. When the subject turned to Mr. Moseley's double confession, Mr. Murphy mentioned the 38 witnesses. "Brother," he said, "that Queens story is one for the books."

As Mr. Rosenthal later recounted in his own book about the Genovese case, *Thirty-Eight Witnesses*, he knew he'd just been handed a scoop, and he assigned it to a reporter, Martin Gansberg, that afternoon. A few days later, Mr. Gansberg filed his story and it appeared on the front page.

"For more than half an hour, 38 respectable, law-abiding citizens in Queens watched a killer stalk and stab a woman in three separate attacks in Kew Gardens," the article began. "Twice the sound of their voices and the sudden glow of their bedroom lights interrupted him and frightened him off. Each time he returned, sought her out and stabbed her again."

Beginning with its indelible first sentence, the article suggested that 38 eyewitnesses had seen all, or at least a substantial part, of the killing; that they had "watched" it for half an hour, almost as if gaping at a performance. *The Times* was first to describe this horrifying spectacle, but it would soon have plenty of company. Writing in *Life* magazine, Loudon Wainwright put it like this: "For the most part, the witnesses, crouching in darkened windows like watchers of a late show, looked on until the play had passed from their view."

A pall fell over Kew Gardens. "People had an impression of Kew Gardens that was unbelievable," said Charles Skoller, a Queens assistant district attorney at the time who would help prosecute the killer at his insanity trial. "The entire community was villainous." Slowly, though, life returned to its tranquil ways. Residents began to shake off their stigma and insist that the portrayal of their neighborhood had been unfair, based on exaggerated accounts by police and journalists.

In the years since Ms. Genovese's death, this charge has been repeated a handful of times in newspaper articles, including a *Daily News* column by John Melia in 1984 and, more briefly, a 1995 account in *The Times*. No one, though, undertook the task of defending Kew Gardens as assiduously as Joseph De May Jr.

A More Complex View

It was never the intention of Mr. De May, a 54-year-old maritime lawyer, to spend hundreds of hours analyzing a decades-old murder. Indeed, he had little interest in Kitty Genovese's death until two years ago. That is when he decided, as a hobby, to create a nostalgic Web site devoted to Kew Gardens, where he'd lived for almost 30 years. If he was going to delve into his neighborhood's past, he reasoned, he'd have to consider its most notorious episode.

In the end, Mr. De May's conclusion about the murder is that, while the behavior of the witnesses was hardly beyond reproach, the common conception of exactly what occurred that night is not in fact what occurred. What did occur, he argues, is far more complex and less damning to the residents of Kew Gardens.

"Yeah, there was a murder," Mr. De May said. "Yeah, people heard something. You can question how a few people behaved. But this wasn't 38 people watching a woman be slaughtered for 35 minutes and saying, 'Oh, I don't want to be involved.'"

Mr. De May began his research with the seminal *Times* article of March 27, 1964. "I remember reading through it, then putting it down and thinking, 'Well, this doesn't hang together at all,'" he said. "And then I read it again carefully. I knew the area. I knew the crime scene because I go by there every day."

Mr. De May soon found himself poring through legal documents related to the case, scouring books and articles, and interviewing neighbors. He even ran the route of Ms. Genovese's flight up Austin Street, timing it with a watch. He became convinced that his first impression was correct. "Here's something that everyone thinks happened," he said, "that isn't so."

His argument boils down to two claims: that the majority of the 38 so-called witnesses did not see any part of the killing; and that what most of them did see, or hear, was fleeting and vague.

To begin, he points out that there were two attacks on Kitty Genovese, not three, as *The Times* initially indicated. The newspaper later acknowledged the discrepancy—it was caused by confused police accounts. Since the extra attack was supposed to have occurred in full view of surrounding windows, it added to an impression of callous disregard by neighbors.

Of the two attacks that did occur, the first was on Austin Street, across from the Mowbray. Contrary to what some accounts imply, Mr. De May, citing courtroom testimony, contends that this first attack must have lasted only minutes before Mr. Moseley jogged off to his car. By the time most witnesses heard the screams and made it to their windows, Mr. De May argues, they saw just a young woman walking or stumbling alone down Austin Street toward the side of her building, then vanishing around the corner.

As significant as the brevity of the first attack, Mr. De May believes, was the location of the second, more sustained attack. This occurred in a narrow foyer at the back of Ms. Genovese's building, indoors and facing away from the Mowbray toward the railroad tracks. This is where Kitty had gone to seek safety, and where Mr. Moseley discovered her. Only one witness, a man who lived at the top of the stairs, could have seen what occurred in that foyer, Mr. De May said.

Charles Skoller, the former assistant district attorney, supports part of Mr. De May's conclusion. "I don't think 38 people witnessed it," said Mr. Skoller. "I don't know where that came from, the 38. I didn't count 38. We only found half a dozen that saw what was going on, that we could use."

But Mr. Skoller is less willing than Mr. De May to forgive the neighbors. Even if not all saw the crime, Mr. Skoller is convinced they heard it. "I believe that many people heard the screams," he said. "It could have been more than 38. And anyone that heard the screams had to know there was a vicious crime taking place."

Many witnesses claimed they thought it was a lovers' quarrel or a drunken argument. Mr. De May points out that many of the witnesses were elderly, and nearly all awoke from deep slumbers, their brains befogged, their windows shut to the cold. Furthermore, he raises the possibility that several witnesses did call the police after the first attack, but that their calls were ignored and never recorded.

A. M. Rosenthal, who went on to become executive editor of *The Times*, stands by the article he assigned to Mr. Gansberg 40 years ago, right down to the word "watched" in its opening sentence. This questioning of details, he said, is to be expected. "In a story that gets a lot of attention, there's always somebody who's saying, 'Well, that's not really what it's supposed to be.'" There may have been minor inaccuracies, he allows, but none that alter the story's essential meaning. "There may have been 38, there may have been 39," Mr. Rosenthal said, "but the whole picture, as I saw it, was very affecting."

Theory, Guilt and Loss

Nowhere was the case more affecting than among America's psychologists. "It was monumental," said Harold Takooshian, a professor of urban psychology at Fordham University. Before the murder, he added, "nobody really had any idea why people did not help, and conversely why people did help. The psychologists were really stunned by their lack of information on this."

The first major studies prompted by the murder, conducted in the 1960s by the psychologists Bibb Latane and John Darley, arrived at a counterintuitive conclusion: the greater the number of bystanders who view an emergency, the smaller the chance that any will intervene. People tend to feel a "diffusion of responsibility" in groups, the two concluded. Kitty Genovese would have been better off, in other words, had one witness seen or heard her attack, rather than the reputed 38.

It is psychology that probably offers the best explanation of the issues the case raised. A raft of behavioral studies performed over the last 40 years suggests that Ms. Genovese's neighbors reacted as they reportedly did not because they were apathetic or cold-hearted, but because they were confused, uncertain and afraid. "Where others might have seen them as villains," Professor Takooshian said, "psychologists see these people as normal."

Normal or not, many of the 38 were consumed by guilt after the crime. Others simply got fed up with the negative attention, and many of them moved away from Kew Gardens. "It was just too much for them, I guess," said Mr. Corrado, sitting in his shop, looking out over the spot where Ms. Genovese was first attacked.

Ms. Genovese's death hit hardest, of course, among those who loved her. This includes Mary Ann Zielonko, the young woman who moved with her to Kew Gardens—and who had the grim task of identifying her remains. One of the many little-known facts about Ms. Genovese was her close relationship with Ms. Zielonko, an omission that perhaps was understandable in 1964. "She was actually my partner," said Ms. Zielonko. "Everybody tried to hush that up."

Ms. Zielonko still becomes emotional remembering the horror of Ms. Genovese's death, but brightens as she recalls what she cherished. "It sounds trite," she said, "but it was her smile. She had a great smile."

William Genovese, one of Kitty's four younger siblings, offers other memories of his sister. He remembers how she would sweep into New Canaan to visit the family, fresh from the city and bubbling with new ambitions and ideas. He remembers how the two of them would stay up late into the night talking about subjects as esoteric as solipsism and Einstein's theory of relativity. "She and I had a special affinity," Mr. Genovese said.

Two years after his sister's murder, Mr. Genovese volunteered for the marines, a decision he attributes to his disgust with public apathy. "I became obsessed with saving people," he said. "When I got to Vietnam, I would have flashbacks of my sister all the time. I'd find myself in situations where I'd think, 'This is a test.' That's the way I viewed it."

—*February 8, 2004*

FREED BY DNA, NOW CHARGED IN NEW CRIME

By MONICA DAVEY

As three men sat nervously on a stage, preparing to recount their nightmarish journeys through a justice system that had sent them away for crimes they had not committed, the moderator had a plea for the crowd in an auditorium here.

Let us not talk about Steven Avery, another man now sitting in a county jail charged with killing a young woman. Not tonight. Not again.

"This event is not about that," the moderator, Lawrence C. Marshall, a law professor who has spent years trying to free wrongfully convicted prisoners, urged. "Tonight we are here to talk about the much bigger issue."

For days, however, the case of Steven Avery, who was once Wisconsin's living symbol of how a system could unfairly send someone away, has left all who championed his cause facing the uncomfortable consequences of their success. Around the country, lawyers in the informal network of some 30 organizations that have sprung up in the past dozen years to exonerate the falsely convicted said they were closely watching Mr. Avery's case to see what its broader fallout might be.

Two years ago, Mr. Avery emerged from prison after lawyers from one of those organizations, the Wisconsin Innocence Project at the University of Wisconsin Law School, proved that Mr. Avery had spent 18 years in prison for a sexual assault he did not commit.

In Mr. Avery's home county, Manitowoc, where he was convicted in 1985, his release prompted apologies, even from the sexual assault victim, and a welcoming home for Mr. Avery.

Elsewhere, the case became Wisconsin's most noted exoneration, leading to an "Avery task force," which drew up a package of law enforcement changes known as the Avery Bill, adopted by state lawmakers just weeks ago.

Mr. Avery, meanwhile, became a spokesman for how a system could harm an innocent man, being asked to appear on panels about wrongful conviction, to testify before the state legislature and to be toured around the capitol by at least one lawmaker who described him as a hero.

But last week, back in rural Manitowoc County, back at his family's auto salvage yard, back at the trailer he had moved home to, Mr. Avery, 43, was accused once more. This time, he was charged in the death of Teresa Halbach, a 25-year-old photographer who vanished on Oct. 31 after being assigned to take pictures for an auto magazine at Avery's Auto Salvage.

After her family searched for Ms. Halbach for days, investigators said they found bones and teeth in the salvage yard, along with her car. In the car, they found blood from Mr. Avery and Ms. Halbach, they said. They also found her car key in the bedroom of his trailer, they said, and, using the very technology that led to Mr. Avery's release two years earlier, they said they identified Mr. Avery's DNA on the key.

"This case has blown us away," Stephen M. Glynn, a Milwaukee lawyer who has represented Mr. Avery in a $36 million civil lawsuit against the former prosecutor and former sheriff in the original sexual assault case, said of the new charges against Mr. Avery. "I haven't taken that hard a punch in a long, long time."

Around the nation, DNA testing has led to the exonerations of 163 people since 1989, including Mr. Avery, said Maddy deLone, executive director of the Innocence Project in New York, where Barry C. Scheck and Peter J. Neufeld were pioneers in the movement. Only one of those exonerated is known to have been convicted of a serious crime since being freed, Ms. deLone said.

At the Wisconsin Innocence Project, leaders said the new accusations against Mr. Avery should not now be linked to his earlier wrongful arrest and release. Keith Findley, co-founder of the Wisconsin group, which describes Mr. Avery's case in its brochure, said the group's intent was not just to release the innocent but to find truth, and properly punish those truly responsible for crimes.

> *Some said Mr. Avery's criminal record revealed telling signs of violence.*

Still, for advocates accustomed to being praised as fighting on behalf of the falsely accused, the backlash here has been unavoidable. On talk radio and on Internet Web logs, critics have said that without the Wisconsin Innocence Project's efforts, one young woman might still be alive. Some said Mr. Avery's criminal record revealed telling signs of violence—with convictions, for example, for burglary and cruelty to animals—long before his 1985 sexual assault conviction.

At the trial, the strongest evidence against Mr. Avery came from the victim. She identified Mr. Avery as the man who had attacked her as she jogged on a beach. She had seen his face just 8 to 10 inches from her own, she said, and had noted his height, his stubby fingers, his hair. Years after the jury found Mr. Avery guilty, his lawyers pressed to have new DNA testing done on pubic hair found on the victim after the attack. The tests revealed not only that the hair did not belong to Mr. Avery, but found that it matched another man, who had lived in the area and who had since been sent to prison for a sexual assault. The case was held up as a perfect example of how eyewitness testimony, even the best intentioned, could simply be wrong.

Even before the sexual assault conviction, Fred Hazlewood, the judge, now retired, who presided over Mr. Avery's case, said Mr. Avery's criminal record showed that he "had a real potential" for violence. "But he served his time," Judge Hazlewood said, "and you can't convict someone for what he might do."

Family members said last week that they were certain Mr. Avery was not guilty of the new charges of first-degree intentional homicide and mutilating a corpse. The authorities were wrong before, Mr. Avery's father, Al, said, and they are wrong again. The evidence, Al Avery said, was planted.

When Steven Avery finally got out of prison, his father said, he had lost his wife and family and found himself living in a tiny ice shanty once meant for winter fishing. Just surviving after so many years in prison was hard enough, Al Avery said.

Steven Avery is escorted out of the Manitowoc County Courthouse in Manitowoc, Wisconsin, after his initial appearance there, Tuesday, November 15, 2005.

"Now it's starting all over again," Mr. Avery's father said. Mr. Avery's mother, Dolores, said she could see the way people were looking at her, again, in the grocery store and on the streets here near Lake Michigan. "He's innocent," Ms. Avery said. "I know it in my heart." Soon, she said, she plans to call the Wisconsin Innocence Project, the lawyers who helped her son once before.

"There are 36 million reasons why they should be doing this to him," Mr. Avery's brother, Chuck, said, referring to the award his brother was seeking in his lawsuit.

The future of that suit now appears in question. Depositions have been postponed. Mr. Glynn said that he still believed that his client had a strong case, but he acknowledged that the case had grown complicated.

The arrest has changed other plans, too. Lawmakers who had pushed to have the state pay Mr. Avery more than $420,000 for his wrongful arrest have grown quiet. And the bill of changes—to the way the police draw up eyewitness identification procedures, conduct interrogations and hold onto DNA evidence—is no longer called the Avery Bill.

"The legislation is very important and very sound for our justice system as a whole," said Representative Mark Gundrum, a Republican who helped organize what was then called the "Avery task force."

"But this does detract a little bit," Mr. Gundrum said. "Obviously, we're not talking about Steven Avery anymore."

—November 23, 2005

NOTE: *Avery and his nephew, Brendan Dassey, were convicted in 2007 of killing Halbach. But a 2015 documentary,* Making a Murderer, *which the filmmakers said was triggered by this article, raised questions about the investigation and prosecution of the case. Lawyers appealed Dassey's conviction on grounds that his confession, at 16, had been coerced. It was overturned by a federal judge in August 2016 but as of this writing he remains incarcerated while the prosecution appeals. Avery continues to fight his conviction in court.*

GRISLY MURDER CASE INTRIGUES ITALIAN UNIVERSITY CITY

By IAN FISHER

"Who is Amanda?" the newspaper *Voice of Perugia* asked Monday. "From brilliant student to cold man-eater."

Two weeks ago, no one here apart from her friends knew who Amanda Knox was. Now in jail, she has emerged as the central character in a killing that has baffled and intrigued this scenic university city, which every year attracts thousands of students from around the world, particularly from the United States and Europe.

On Nov. 2, one of Ms. Knox's three roommates, Meredith Kercher, 21, of London, was found under a blood-soaked duvet cover on her bed with her throat slashed. The police have reported sexual assault, possibly rape, and have arrested Ms. Knox and two others.

The three suspects seem not to fit the bill. There is Ms. Knox, who does not conform to any standard profile for a murderer: 20 years old, well off and pretty, a linguistics major from Seattle who, judging

Amanda Knox arriving at a court hearing in Perugia, September 16, 2008.

from self-posted Internet images, could be accused of little more than occasional rowdiness.

But the police say they do not believe she acted alone.

The third and fatal wound to Ms. Kercher's throat, according to police reports, was inflicted by a man. Also arrested were Ms. Knox's Italian boyfriend, Raffaele Sollecito, 24, and Diya Lumumba, 44, from Congo, the owner of a bar called Le Chic, where Ms. Knox worked as a waitress. He was a fixture in Perugia known as Patrick, the father of a young child and a musician who had put out a reggae record. Ms. Knox's and Ms. Kercher's other two roommates, Italian lawyers who were away during the murder, are not suspects.

Then there is the lack of a clear motive. No one seemed to be hurting for money. Ms. Knox and Mr. Sollecito met at a classical music concert just two weeks ago, and none of the other principals seemed to know one another for a long time. According to a judge's report, the authorities speculate about some combination of drugs and sex, that one or more of the arrested demanded sex from Ms. Kercher and killed her, perhaps accidentally.

All the accused profess their innocence. While Ms. Knox's story has changed repeatedly, all say they were not even at the house the night Ms. Kercher was killed.

The arrest of Mr. Lumumba, an immigrant, seemed to sum up Italy's complicated relationship with the influx of people of different ethnicities who have settled in the country in recent years. There seemed both a popular rush to suspect him and to defend him.

The Internet has provided embarrassing material. Mr. Sollecito said on a social networking site that he was "honest, peaceful, sweet but sometimes absolutely crazy" and posed with a photo holding what looks like a cleaver. Ms. Knox calls herself Foxyknoxy on several sites, and is shown behind a Gatling gun and in a short video with friends in which she appears to be inebriated.

Attention has focused on Ms. Knox. Italian press reports frequently describe what are termed her "icy" blue eyes and her attention to men and standoffishness with women. Newspapers in Italy and Britain have speculated that light bruises found on Ms. Kercher's body could have been from the fingers of a woman holding her down.

Ms. Knox's mother, who traveled to Perugia, strongly defended her. "Amanda is innocent of this and is devastated by the death of her friend," the mother, a teacher, Edda Mellas, was quoted in British newspapers as saying on Sunday.

It has not helped Ms. Knox that she has changed her story several times, according to the judge's report. First she told the police that on the night Ms. Kercher died, Nov. 1, she was with Mr. Sollecito at his house.

But under interrogation, she placed herself in her own house's kitchen, where she claimed she heard Ms. Kercher scream. She said she was there with Mr. Lumumba, whom she described as infatuated with Ms. Kercher, covered her ears, left the house and remembered little else. Last weekend, she again said she was not at the house that night.

Under Italian law, the suspects can be held in jail for a year as the investigation proceeds. But the case gets no clearer. From traces found in the apartment, the police have not ruled out a fourth, unknown assailant.

—November 13, 2007

NOTE: *Knox—whose youth and beauty made her potential involvement in such a heinous crime a worldwide sensation—and Sollecito were convicted of murdering Kercher in 2009. Their convictions were later overturned in 2011. They were reconvicted in 2014, only to have Italy's highest court overturn those convictions finally in 2015. Lumumba had been cleared of any role in the crime years earlier, in 2008, when alibi witnesses said he could not have been at the scene.*

A TRIAL ENDS, BUT FOR SOUTH AFRICANS, THE DEBATE MAY BE JUST BEGINNING

By SARAH LYALL AND ALAN COWELL

The murder trial of the Paralympic star Oscar Pistorius lurched to a close on Friday when he was convicted of culpable homicide in the shooting death last year of his girlfriend, Reeva Steenkamp. But in a case that reflected South Africa's complicated obsession with race, crime and celebrity, many South Africans found understanding the verdict to be as difficult as trying to fathom what was in Mr. Pistorius's mind the night he pulled the trigger.

It is unclear whether Mr. Pistorius, who was acquitted of the two more serious murder charges against him, will do time in jail. The sentence for culpable homicide, a crime roughly commensurate with involuntary manslaughter, is left to the discretion of the judge and can range from no jail time to 15 years in prison.

Completing her two-day reading of the verdict on Friday, Judge Thokozile Matilda Masipa scheduled the sentencing hearing for Oct. 13 and—over the angry objections of the prosecutor, Gerrie Nel—granted bail to Mr. Pistorius until then.

Some South Africans felt that Mr. Pistorius got off too lightly. "Will Oscar Walk?" said the headline in *The Star* newspaper. On the News24 website, a commenter named Peter Tracey called the verdict "a very sad indictment of our justice system."

Friday's proceedings were the culmination of a grueling roller coaster of a trial that began in March, a little more than a year after Mr. Pistorius grabbed a handgun in the middle of the night on Valentine's Day, pumped four shots through the locked door of his bathroom and killed Ms. Steenkamp, 29.

The world may never know what he was thinking that night. But while many saw his account as implausible, the defense he gave—that he believed an intruder had broken into his house and was lurking in the bathroom, and that it did not occur to him that Ms. Steenkamp could have been in there—spoke to many South Africans' deep fear of crime and home invasions.

Mr. Pistorius's story was vehemently disputed by Mr. Nel, the prosecutor, who portrayed him as volatile, spoiled, jealous and obsessed with guns. He contended that Mr. Pistorius had killed Ms. Steenkamp, a law graduate and reality television star, in a fit of rage as the two argued late into the night.

Mr. Pistorius was for years a national hero for the way he rose above his disability, competing against both disabled and able-bodied athletes in international competitions. Born without fibula bones, both his legs were amputated below the knee when he was a baby and he later became known, admiringly, as the Blade Runner, for the scythe-like curved prostheses he used while competing, including in the 2012 London Olympics.

Handsome, charming, gifted as an athlete, Mr. Pistorius became an emblem of South Africa's pride and craving for international acclaim. He carried the flag for his country in the closing ceremony of the London Games.

But the killing of Ms. Steenkamp stripped the sheen off what had been a story of success and celebrity, exposing an uglier side to Mr. Pistorius—a side in which he had a mercurial temper, was a jealous and sometimes angry boyfriend, was irresponsible with guns and used his celebrity to get what he wanted. The case raised many questions— about fame, disability, crime, violence against women, class and race—in a country uneasy about where it stands on many of those matters.

Many of these collided in the courtroom. The trial of Mr. Pistorius—white, rich, privileged—was presided over by a judge who is a 66-year-old black woman who grew up poor in Soweto, began studying law in the throes of apartheid, had been arrested during a protest, and did not earn a law degree until she was in her 40s. The courtroom, too, reflected a reality of race in South Africa: virtually all the principals—the lawyers, the accused, the families—were white, while virtually all the court functionaries, security guards and cleaners were black.

The world may never know what he was thinking that night.

While the verdict enraged some South Africans, who said it sent a terrible message about domestic violence and also gave people the right to kill and then claim they had not meant to do it, it also reflected what seems to be a preoccupation of Judge Masipa: indignation about possible overreach by the prosecution. She raised questions about the defense, calling Mr. Pistorius an unimpressive and evasive witness whose histrionics in court—he sobbed uncontrollably and retched at times—did him no favors. But time and again, she criticized the prosecution for failing to prove its case on the more serious murder charges to the standards required in law, beyond a reasonable doubt.

In a further blow to the prosecution, Judge Masipa on Friday acquitted Mr. Pistorius of two of the three firearms charges against him, saying the state had failed to provide enough evidence. She declared him guilty on one charge, of illegally firing a gun that had been passed to him under a table in a crowded restaurant during a previous episode.

As far as the murder charges, because the prosecution had failed to bring "strong circumstantial evidence," the judge said, Mr. Pistorius's account "could reasonably be true." It was impossible to prove, she said, that Mr. Pistorius "did not entertain a genuine belief that there was an intruder in the house."

As he was pronounced not guilty of murder on Thursday, Mr. Pistorius kept perfectly still. When the judge found him guilty of culpable homicide, he barely reacted at all.

Sometime after court adjourned on Friday, Mr. Pistorius made his way through the scrum of reporters and onlookers, free—at least until his sentencing hearing. And then the uncle with whom he has been living during the trial, Arnold Pistorius, read a statement out loud.

"We as a family remain deeply affected by this devastating tragedy," he said. "There are no victors in this."

—September 13, 2014

NOTE: *Pistorius was sentenced in July 2016 to six years in prison for the death of his girlfriend.*

STRAIGHT FROM TV TO JAIL:
DURST IS CHARGED IN KILLING

By CHARLES V. BAGLI AND VIVIAN YEE

S ince his first wife vanished more than three decades ago, Robert A. Durst, the eccentric and estranged son of one of New York's most prominent real estate dynasties, has lived under the suspicious gaze of law enforcement officials in three states.

They have followed his path from New York City to Los Angeles, where one of his closest friends was found dead in her home in 2000. They have tracked him to Galveston, Tex., where he fled after investigators reopened the case of his wife's disappearance, and where he posed as a mute woman and shot and dismembered a neighbor in 2001.

Mr. Durst was acquitted in the Texas killing, and was never arrested in the disappearance of his wife or the death of his friend. But on Saturday, he found himself in custody once again, arrested on a charge of murder as he walked into a New Orleans hotel he had checked into under a false name.

On Sunday night, in the final moments of the final episode of a six-part HBO documentary about him, *The Jinx: The Life and Deaths of Robert Durst,* Mr. Durst seemed to veer toward a confession that could lift the shroud of mystery that surrounds the deaths of three people over three decades.

"What the hell did I do?" Mr. Durst whispers to himself in an unguarded moment caught on a microphone he wore during filming. "Killed them all, of course."

Robert Durst is driven to Orleans Parish Criminal Court, March 17, 2005.

In the years since his wife, Kathleen Durst, disappeared in 1982 after spending the weekend at the couple's country home in Westchester County, Mr. Durst has bounced in and out of jail for other crimes, cut ties with his family, remarried, and sued his brother for a $65 million share of the family fortune. Through it all, he has maintained his innocence in the disappearance of his wife, while also denying any role in the 2000 death of the Los Angeles friend, Susan Berman.

His arrest on Saturday in a Marriott on Canal Street in New Orleans was in connection with Ms. Berman's death, though the Westchester authorities said they were still investigating him in his wife's case. Mr. Durst was walking toward an elevator, mumbling to himself, when FBI agents intercepted him, a law enforcement official briefed on the investigation said. He had checked in under the name Everett Ward, not the first time he had used an alias.

Mr. Durst is believed to have left Houston on March 10, headed for New Orleans. Investigators involved in the case said they feared that the renewed attention brought by *The Jinx* would lead him to try to flee the country. Mr. Durst will plead not guilty, said one of his lawyers, Dick DeGuerin, who helped win Mr. Durst's acquittal in Galveston in 2003 and who said he expected to head Mr. Durst's defense team in Los Angeles.

"The rumors that have been flying for years will now get tested in court," Mr. DeGuerin said.

It was Mr. Durst himself who may have set the latest twist in his bizarre saga

> *By then, a new investigation was already encircling him.*

in motion. Los Angeles prosecutors reopened their investigation into Ms. Berman's execution-style murder only after Mr. Durst agreed to a series of interviews with the producers of *The Jinx*, Andrew Jarecki and Marc Smerling.

The amount of press coverage Mr. Durst has generated is topped only by the volume of work he has made for his lawyers and police investigators in Westchester, Los Angeles, Galveston and beyond. Yet he had rebuffed overtures from journalists until he saw *All Good Things*, a lightly fictionalized film the producers had previously made of his life in 2010, and approached them to tell his story.

"I will be able to tell it my way," he said in the second episode of *The Jinx*.

In a more recent interview, he brushed off the possibility that the documentary would whet prosecutors' appetites, saying: "It's so long ago. Some D.A. would have to commence a budget-busting investigation."

By then, a new investigation was already encircling him.

"These two producers did what law enforcement in three states could not do in 30 years," said Jeanine F. Pirro, the former Westchester County district attorney, whose office investigated Kathleen Durst's disappearance for six years.

The filmmakers spent nearly 10 years researching Mr. Durst's story: his upbringing as the eldest son of a family that controls 11 major skyscrapers in New York; his marriage to Ms. Durst, a medical student, and its unraveling; his estrangement from his family after his father chose his younger brother, Douglas Durst, to run the business in 1994.

"We are relieved and also grateful to everyone who assisted in the arrest of Robert Durst," Douglas Durst said in a statement on Sunday. "We hope he will finally be held accountable for all he has done."

When prosecutors began pursuing new leads in his wife's disappearance in 2000, Mr. Durst fled to Galveston, posing as a mute woman to rent a $300-a-month room in the Gulf Coast city. The next year, he was on the run again, with a warrant out for his arrest in the murder of Morris Black, a former merchant seaman who had lived across the hall in Galveston. After a nationwide manhunt, he was found in Bethlehem, Pa., where he had shoplifted a sandwich from a supermarket.

Mr. Durst convinced a Texas jury that Mr. Black had died accidentally when the two men were grappling over a gun that discharged as they fell to the floor. He testified that he had carved up Mr. Black's body until he was "swimming in blood."

But he was still under suspicion in the death of Ms. Berman, a friend from graduate school with whom he had become so close that he walked her down the aisle at her wedding. She served as his spokeswoman after his wife's disappearance, and investigators have long suspected that she knew his secrets.

The police had always known Mr. Durst was in California when Ms. Berman was killed, but could not place him in Los Angeles. They suspected he was the author of a short anonymous note sent to the Beverly Hills police on the same day Ms. Berman was found shot in the head, saying there was a "cadaver" in her home. But a handwriting analysis was inconclusive.

The makers of *The Jinx* obtained a letter written by Mr. Durst to Ms. Berman in which the lettering of the address on the envelope appears identical to that of the "cadaver" note, down to the misspelling of Beverly Hills as "Beverley."

Mr. Jarecki, who was also the show's director, and Mr. Smerling struggled with whether to bring the letter to law enforcement authorities. If they did so too soon, their lawyers told them, they could be considered law enforcement agents in the event of a prosecution, possibly jeopardizing the material's admissibility in court, Mr. Jarecki said.

They also wanted to preserve a journalistic privilege not to disclose sources or testify in court. Still, Mr. Smerling said in an interview, "We had a moral obligation and an obligation to the families of the dead to see that justice was done." They began speaking to Los Angeles investigators in early 2013.

Near the documentary's end, the filmmakers were packing up their equipment when Mr. Durst asked to use the bathroom. He did not remove his wireless microphone as he closed the door, however, and began to whisper to himself.

More than two years passed after the interview before the filmmakers found the audio.

It is unclear whether the recording of his comments could be used in court, some legal experts said, since they were made in a bathroom when he was alone and had an expectation of privacy.

"That's pretty damning stuff," said Daniel J. Castleman, the former chief of investigations in the Manhattan district attorney's office. "The question is: Is it admissible in court?"

—March 16, 2015

NOTE: *Durst was convicted in 2016 on federal weapons possession charges in connection with a gun he had with him at the time of his arrest. He was sentenced to seven years in prison and is now awaiting a murder trial in California in connection with the death of Berman.*

CHAPTER 7

PRISON

"Prison should be a place for predators and not dying old men. Some people should die in prison, but everyone should get a hearing."

—Burl Cain, former warden of the
Louisiana State Penitentiary in Angola

FROM ITS EARLIEST DAYS, *The Times* has recognized that incarceration is one of the most serious decisions a society can make. Life inside is, by design, no bargain. As the last stop for our justice system, prisons are built atop the faith that when the cell door clanks, its detainee is guilty. Still, mistakes happen. Conditions erode. Riots occur. And sometimes the people who find freedom are not the unjustly accused, but the real crooks who, with filched chisels and pillow dummies, take matters into their own hands.

OPPOSITE: A cell at Sing Sing prison, Ossining, New York, c. 1910.

SHOWERING AND YOKING

W̲e made a few remarks the other day upon the tortures employed in our state penitentiaries, but were unable to lay hands on the report of the legislative committee respecting the general management of those places. Upon turning to that document we find ample evidence of the inhumanities in habitual practice. The visitors say, overcautiously we think, in view of the testimony they elicited:

"Occasional cases of cruelty still occur, and must so long as such dangerous engines of torture as the shower-bath and yoke are left in the hands of imprudent keepers. Many of the subordinate keepers were free in their opinions that the shower-bath is a much more cruel punishment than the cat [-o'-nine-tails]."

They argue, to be sure, that the effect upon the officer is less brutalizing; but the effect upon the officer has, of course, nothing to do with the question. According to the testimony of Judge Edmonds, formerly inspector of the Sing Sing Prison, it seems that the statements of keepers and sub-keepers are not reliable. The prisoners must be referred to.

"We found that it was absolutely necessary that we should obtain their statements, because to the world at large, all within the walls was darkness and secrecy, and from that source no testimony could be obtained, and from the officers we could not easily procure the knowledge of their own misconduct. How easy it is for the officers to conceal their own conduct was exemplified to me when I was an inspector at Sing Sing. I was astonished and worried by frequent complaints of the prisoners that they did not get enough to eat, and I gave peremptory orders that they should have enough. I directed the assistant keepers to send their men to the kitchen whenever they complained.

"One of them, who saw that one of his best workmen could not do a day's labor from weakness, sent him to the kitchen in vain. He went himself and could get no food for his man. He then complained to the principal keeper. That officer, when he found out who it was complained, beat him over the head with an iron rule until it broke in his hand, then beat him with the hardwood handle of a stone hammer, and when that flew out of his hands, from his own violence, attacked him with a stone axe, and would have struck him with it in his passion, if he had not been prevented. The poor convict was then tied up and whipped with some 50 lashes of the cat, and ended the incident by some two weeks confinement in the hospital, and all for having complained of being hungry."

We turn, therefore, to what is credible authority upon the subject—the evidence of prison physicians. The keepers, when interrogated as to the existence of ill consequences, after the use of the bath or yoke, in several instances denied that there were any. The medical officers report differently. Dr. Fosgate, of Auburn, thus refers to the bath: "To the mechanic who calculates the influence of mere matter upon matter, the power of this column of water must possess considerable importance. But to the physiologist, who can alone judge with any degree of correctness of the influence of a stream, generally at 32° Fahrenheit, falling upon the head, and thence covering the whole body, the suffering induced, and danger incurred, must appear momentous in the extreme."

He further quotes the highest professional authorities for the prejudicial influences of the cold application; and illustrates them by numerous cases that occurred under his own observation. To make the infliction still more severe, ice is sometimes placed in the water.

Dr. Fosgate subsequently remarks: "It would scarcely be credited, should I state that a system of torture to obtain confessions, or information not otherwise to be had, is in full force in this information. Yet such is the fact, and the shower bath is the ready instrument of its execution. This machine is a modification of the water punishments of the Spanish Inquisition,

To make the infliction still more severe, ice is sometimes placed in the water.

and will as certainly extort truth or falsehood from the sufferer, either to gratify the wishes or confirm the suspicions of a keeper of the Auburn prison, as its original did in the hands of the inquisitorial fathers.

"Upon the rehearsal of circumstances so revolting to every feeling of humanity, one is constrained to inquire whether the infliction of so much misery is necessary to maintain the discipline of this prison. The question is affirmatively answered in the fact, that the 'Auburn system of prison discipline' is a system of absolute physical force, in which enters no idea of moral government at all."

And in the course of his examination before the committee he declines to say whether or not death has resulted from punishment; but states that convicts were converted into madmen by them.

Dr. William N. Belcher, of the Sing Sing Prison, gives it as his opinion, that the shower-bath "cannot be generally used with impunity, and that in many cases its use should be prohibited, although punishment should be inflicted in some way. I believe it to be more dangerous than any mode now in use."

These professional dicta are supported by the testimony of all the more intelligent officers of the prisons. Thus Charles W. Pomeroy, agent of the Auburn Prison: "The abuse of the shower-bath, in improper hands, is more injurious than an abuse of the cat.

The bath is more likely to injure the health of a convict than the cat. Have no doubt but that the minds of convicts have been impaired, and in some eases ruined by the bath."

And Chauncey J. Smith, an agent at Sing Sing: "I consider the shower-bath a very cruel punishment. I have seen several showered in the winter when the water froze on the floor as it fell. There would be chunks of ice in the barrel at the time."

Of this character is all the testimony. Nothing was ever more distinctly manifested by legal inquiry than that the shower-bath is a barbarous engine of torment; that it is destructive to the physical and mental health of the convict; and contributes to make those discharged from our prisons, imbecile inmates of lunatic asylums.

To judge the grade of offenses to which it is applied, we may consult the punishment record of the Clinton Prison, the only one where such a roll is preserved. We find the following among the crimes so punished: "Not going to bed when ordered," "leaving the ranks when coming from the mines," "talking and laughing," "insolent language," "profane language," "noise in cell," "attempting to stab," "stealing mittens of another convict," "whistling," "smoking."

These punishments were always inflicted by the offended subjailer authority from a superior, and how judiciously may be judged from the fact, that an attempt to murder is nowhere more severely chastised, than smoking, whistling, laughing or talking. Indeed, few of the offenses deserve any notice whatever; and, nevertheless they subjected the convict to merciless torture, and the prospect of physical weakness and intellectual inanity for life.

Dr. Fosgate says the yoke is not only inefficient, but "derogatory to the discipline of the prison, as well as injurious to the health of the convicts. While wearing the yoke the culprit is the butt through the sly jokes and unfeeling taunts of his fellow convicts, and on this account it is often injuriously and unnecessarily worn to show them of what *stuff* he is made. Their strained and inflamed muscles, and swelled and inflamed skin of neck, breast and arms, often require medical treatment and rest from labor."

Other evidence shows that it is impossible for the victim to stand beneath the intolerable weight and that if strength gave way, he was punished with a cane, tied up with a rope, or turned into a dungeon. The time lost in the workshop, both by the use of the bath and the yoke, was usually three or four days, after each infliction—days spent by the convict in the hospital.

We earnestly hope the recommendations of the committee will be listened to, and these infernal weapons removed from the hands of brutal, irresponsible, case-hardened underlings in our state prisons. We cannot better conclude these extracts than by quoting from the report of Mr. Robinson, warden of the Massachusetts State prison: "I have long looked upon a man as a man, whether he be the occupant of a palace or a prison—and, in whatever situation he may be, entitled to human sympathy, kindness and respect. He is my brother, wherever he may be, whatever of wrong or of crime he may have been tempted to commit.

"We are all liable to fall into temptation: if it were not so we should not have all been taught to beseech our Father in Heaven to 'lead us not into temptation.' I felt my own frailties and imperfections, and resolved to do by others as I should wish to be done by, if I were in their situation. It seemed to me, therefore, in entering upon the duties of this office, I should prefer rather to err on the side of kindness, clemency and humanity, than on that of severity of punishments.

"I know that the laws, rules, regulations and discipline of the prison must be enforced. But I wished, if possible, to enforce them without recourse to corporal punishment or physical suffering. And I have succeeded, thus far, as well as I could have expected. The government of the prison has been administered without corporal punishment. The shower-bath has not been used. And yet I think I can safely say, that the convicts are as orderly, as industrious and obedient as heretofore, and more contented, docile and happy. A feeling of mutual respect, kindness and friendship seems to be growing up between us. I am sure I experience these affections towards the convicts, and every day gives evidence that the same affections are being excited in their breasts towards me."

—*March 1, 1852*

NOTE: *New York State made slow progress toward eliminating measures of prison discipline like the shower-bath and the yoke—a 30- to 40-pound iron bar strapped to the back of the neck and outstretched arms—in the decades to come, though instruments such as the paddle were often brought in as substitute punishments.*

9 HOSTAGES AND 28 PRISONERS DIE AS 1,000 STORM PRISON IN ATTICA—"LIKE A WAR ZONE"

By FRED FERRETTI

The rebellion at the Attica Correctional Facility ended this morning in a bloody clash and mass deaths that four days of taut negotiations had sought to avert.

Thirty-seven men—9 hostages and 28 prisoners—were killed as 1,000 state troopers, sheriff's deputies and prison guards stormed the prison under a low-flying pall of tear gas dropped by helicopters. They retook from inmates the cellblocks they had captured last Thursday. In this worst of recent American prison revolts, several of the hostages—prison guards and civilian workers—died when convicts slashed their throats with knives. Others were stabbed and beaten with clubs and lengths of pipe.

Most of the prisoners killed in the assault fell under the hail of rifle and shotgun fire laid down by the invading troopers.

Doctor Fears More Deaths

A volunteer doctor who worked among the wounded after the assault said the prison's interior was "like a war zone." Standing in front of the prison in a blood-stained white coat, he said that many more of the wounded "are likely to die."

Late today a deputy director of correction, Walter Dunbar, said that two of the hostages had been killed "before today" and that one had been stabbed and emasculated.

Of the remaining 7, 5 were killed instantly by the inmates and 2 died in the prison hospital.

Mr. Dunbar said that in addition to the 28 dead inmates, 8 other convicts of the total of 2,237 were missing. Two of the dead prisoners, he said, were killed "by their own colleagues and lay in a large pool of blood in a fourth-tier cell block."

Oswald Orders Attack

He said he considered the state's recapture of the prison an "efficient, affirmative police action."

The action was ordered with "extreme reluctance" by State Correction Commissioner Russell G. Oswald after consultation with Governor Rockefeller. It followed an ultimatum to the more than 1,000 rebellious prisoners that they release the hostages they held and return to their cells.

Most of the 28 hostages rescued by the invaders and scores of prisoners were treated for wounds and the effect of tear gas dropped into the prison before the assault.

The recapture of the maximum security prison was hampered by trenches dug by the convicts, filled with burning gasoline ignited in cellblock corridors; by electrically wired prison bars separating detention areas; by homemade bombs and booby traps hidden in underground tunnels; by barricades and salvos of Molotov cocktails and bursts from captured tear-gas guns.

The attack began before 10 o'clock and ended 4 hours later as troopers fought hand to hand with stubborn knots of prisoners in the second tier of cellblock D, the portion of the prison that the prisoners had controlled since the riots on Thursday.

It came three hours after Mr. Oswald's ultimatum had been delivered.

The ultimatum was answered, Mr. Oswald said, when the prisoners "callously herded eight hostages within our view with weapons at their throats."

"The armed rebellion of the type we have faced threatens the destruction of our free society," Mr. Oswald declared. "Further delay and negotiations would have jeopardized more lives."

Members of a citizens' observers committee, which had been called to Attica by the state at the request of the inmates, were locked in an administration building office inside the prison walls during the assault.

Kunstler Is Bitter

William M. Kunstler, civil rights lawyer and one of a group of 10 persons who negotiated with the prisoners and acted as agents for Commissioner Oswald, was most bitter.

"A bloody mistake," he said, "this will go down in history as a bloody mistake. They sold the lives far too cheaply. I guess they always do."

The prison uprising began last Thursday when the convicts seized 32 guards and then, through a makeshift megaphone in the yard of cellblock D, issued a list of demands.

The prisoners set fires, broke windows and shredded fire hoses. Twice on that first day, Commissioner Oswald met with the inmates and attempted to negotiate the demands. The demands included "complete amnesty" and freedom from "physical, mental and legal reprisals," "speedy and safe transportation out of confinement to a non-imperialistic country" and "true" religious freedom.

The uprising was viewed as the result of tension that had been building up in Attica for some time. In addition to the customary complaints about services, there were the added

State Correction Commissioner Russell G. Oswald meets with inmates in Attica,
September 10, 1971.

ingredients of a predominantly black body of prisoners being controlled by an armed
white force and the increasing political and radical awareness of the black prisoners.

The assault on the prison followed four days of negotiations in which the convicts
won agreement to 28 demands for social, administrative and legal reforms but held out for
complete amnesty from criminal prosecution and the ouster of the prison superintendent,
Vincent R. Mancusi.

The latter two issues were turned down by Mr. Oswald as nonnegotiable, and the
amnesty demand was rejected Sunday by Governor Rockefeller as being beyond his constitutional authority.

This rejection came a day after the death of a guard, William Quinn, who was
reported injured by the prisoners in the revolt. He was one of 12 guards who had been
hospitalized from injuries during the early rioting.

The action today began at 9:46 a.m., with two national guard CH-34 helicopters
dropping canisters of tear gas into cellblock D, in the northeast corner of the 55-acre
prison compound.

The 500-man contingent of state troopers had received orders to assemble outside the prison walls by 6 a.m. Two hundred more troopers were transported into Attica, and 50 national guard vans with about 600 troops arrived here before dawn. A dense rain began falling as day broke.

Sheriff's deputies from this Wyoming County and 14 other counties arrived in their own automobiles, carrying deer rifles, pistols, surplus army carbines and shotguns. All received riot helmets, rain slickers and gas masks and were sent through the prison's main gate to a vast lawn that lies between the gate and the compound proper. There they were formed into makeshift companies under the direction of Capt. Henry Williams, chief of the local office of the State Bureau of Criminal Investigation.

Tear-gas canisters were loaded into the two helicopters. Troopers armed with high-powered rifles equipped with sniper scopes were sent up to the guard towers atop the prison walls. Squads of troopers, deputies and guards, armed with tear-gas guns, were driven to points around the prison's perimeter.

Deadline Is Set

By 8 o'clock the assault force was in position. Even then members of the committee of observers began to filter into the prison. State Senator Robert Garcia, Democrat of the Bronx; Tom Wicker, columnist for *The New York Times,* and Louis Steel of the National Lawyers Guild were permitted in.

By the time Mr. Kunstler arrived, the assault force was at the ready, and he was barred from the gate. Fifteen more observers had spent the night inside Attica Prison.

At 8:30, an aide to Mr. Oswald, Gerald Houlihan, stepped outside and announced that the Commissioner had sent a memo to a leader of the rebellious inmates, Richard Clark. Clark told him, Mr. Houlihan said, that the memorandum would be referred to the "people's central committee" in the yard of cellblock D.

The memo recounted the concessions made to the convicts and called on them to release the hostages and end the rebellion.

The deadline for answering was set for 8:46 a.m. At that time the prisoners asked for more time to consider. Mr. Oswald gave them until 9 o'clock.

Clark walked back down a corridor that separated the commissioner from the barricaded prisoners. Several minutes later the eight hostages with knives at their throats were paraded before Commissioner Oswald. But even as this final strain of negotiating took place, the last preparations for the assault were made.

At 8:37 a.m. grappling hooks had been brought in. The two national guard helicopters and two state police choppers equipped with public-address sound systems warmed up. At 8:55 a van loaded with riot helmets was backed up to the main gate, and at 9 the state police helicopters took off.

Eight Hostages Threatened

Troopers and deputies atop the prison walls and on the roofs of buildings that surrounded four cellblocks began relaying information by walkie-talkie back to the command post set up in the superintendent's office.

As the observer helicopter circled above the yard of D block, the eight hostages who had been shown to Mr. Oswald were dropped into a pit filled with gasoline. Then they were removed and dragged to a trench full of gasoline, where their feet were thrown in and their bodies were bent backwards so that their throats were exposed. Prisoners stood over them with knives.

At 9:42 Captain Williams's voice came over the short-wave radio: "All forces in position."

At 9:43 he ordered all power in the prison cut off. Only lights powered by portable generators remained on.

At 9:44 he ordered high-powered water hoses connected. At the same time an order was sent out for all available county ambulances to come to the truck gate of the prison.

At 9:45 Captain Williams ordered: "Zero in on targets. Do not take action until the drop." A voice answered: "The drop has been made. Jackpot One has made the drop." This indicated that CS gas was flooding the yard of cellblocks.

At 9:46 Captain Williams shouted: "Move in! The drop has been made."

Gas seeping over the 30-foot-high walls caused those standing outside to weep. Also standing by, silently huddled in the rain, were the relatives of the hostages. Some sobbed openly in parked cars.

The observer helicopter circled the yard. Coming from its sound system continually was this message: "Place your hands on top of your heads and move to the outside of B and D blocks. Do not harm the hostages. Surrender peacefully. Sit or lie down. You will not be harmed. Repeat, you will not be harmed."

But by this time the hostages were dead.

At 9:57 a call came: "I need a stretcher. For God's sake a stretcher!"

At 10:16 the helicopters were ordered down: "Ground your birds. Stand by for evacuations."

Commissioner Oswald came out of the front gate at 10:25. The pops of tear-gas guns and the cracks of rifle shots could be heard over the wall.

"Everything Humanly Possible"

"For the past four days," he said, "I have been doing everything humanly possible to bring this tragic situation to a peaceful conclusion."

He repeated the chronology of negotiations and the concessions he had made and said: "In spite of all these efforts, the inmates have steadfastly refused to release the hostages."

"They continued to make weapons," Mr. Oswald said, "spread gasoline, make booby traps and electrical traps. I extended the deadline. They asked for more time. This was only a delaying tactic."

He then described the prisoners with knives at the throats of hostages.

"We hope to protect the lives of the hostages if possible," the commissioner said. "I pray to God that this works out to the best interests of all of us."

"We Got 30 Out"

Even as he spoke, Captain Williams's voice continued to bark over the radio: "There's 30 out. We got 30 out."

At 10:35 the order was given: "Get as many pictures of these homicides as possible. Take them to the morgue in the maintenance building."

But some of the hostages were alive. A raincoated guard at the main entrance began shouting names to the relatives huddled in the rain.

"They're out!" he yelled. He shouted nine names.

"Steve Wright," the guard yelled. "Miller! Walker's out!"

Standing behind the relatives was another observer, Clarence Jones, publisher of *The Amsterdam News*. "Time was all we asked for," he said quietly. "Time."

At 10:45 Captain Williams asked: "Is D block secured?" Another voice interrupted: "There is a possible explosive device in C block. Get me a demolition detail."

And from Captain Williams: "No shooting unless it's absolutely necessary."

Outside of the gate Mr. Kunstler looked at a guard. "You murdering bastards!" he said. "They're shooting them. They're murdering them."

At 10:55 Captain Williams urged: "Use extreme caution. No gunfire unless absolutely necessary. Utilize gas. We're coming in both ways through D block."

At 11:10 a voice on the radio said: "Thirty came out alive. Eight are dead."

For a long while there was no communication as the troopers gradually gained the upper hand.

Then explosive "gas devices" were found in the prison chapel and in the metal machine shop. At 12:30 p.m. Mr. Houlihan came out to announce the first death toll. "There are 37 dead," he said. "Nine of them hostages."

He said it had been hoped by Commissioner Oswald that the gas dropped by the helicopters "would immobilize them quickly—the plan worked well."

Asked to weigh the success of the plan against the lives lost, Mr. Houlihan said: "No one ever had to make a tougher decision than this." He said Commissioner Oswald had consulted with Governor Rockefeller before ordering the assault.

As for the demands that had been agreed to by Mr. Oswald on Sunday, Mr. Houlihan said: "You must understand that an agreement was never reached, because they refused to talk with us."

Governor Rockefeller's decision not to come to Attica was harshly criticized by two members of the observer committee.

Representative Herman Badillo, New York City Democrat, came out of the prison late today looking haggard. "We wanted time," he said. "More time."

Asked if he had wanted Governor Rockefeller to join in negotiations, he said: "No. We wanted the governor to come to talk with us and get the benefit of our experience before he made a final and irrevocable decision. As far as I'm concerned, there's always time to die."

—September 14, 1971

NOTE: *All told, 39 people were shot dead, including 10 prison employees. The violence, fed in large part by prison conditions, led to a long list of recommended reforms, some of which still have not been implemented decades later.*

NO WAY OUT: DASHED HOPES—SERVING LIFE, WITH NO CHANCE OF REDEMPTION

By ADAM LIPTAK

Minutes after the U.S. Supreme Court threw out the juvenile death penalty in March, word reached death row here in Livingston, Tex., setting off a pandemonium of banging, yelling and whoops of joy among many of the 28 men whose lives were spared by the decision.

But the news devastated Randy Arroyo, who had faced execution for helping kidnap and kill an air force officer while stealing his car for parts.

Mr. Arroyo realized he had just become a lifer, the last thing he wanted. Lifers, he said, exist in a world without hope. "I wish I still had that death sentence," he said. "I believe my chances have gone down the drain. No one will ever look at my case."

Mr. Arroyo has a point. People on death row are provided with free lawyers to pursue their cases in federal court long after their convictions have been affirmed; lifers are not. The pro bono lawyers who

> *More than one in four lifers will never even see a parole board.*

work to exonerate or spare the lives of death row inmates are not interested in the cases of people merely serving life terms. Appeals courts scrutinize death penalty cases much more closely than others.

Mr. Arroyo will become eligible for parole in 2037, when he is 57. But he doubts he will ever get out. "This is hopeless," he said.

Scores of lifers, in interviews at 10 prisons in six states, echoed Mr. Arroyo's despondency. They have, they said, nothing to look forward to and no way to redeem themselves.

More than one in four lifers will never even see a parole board. The boards that the remaining lifers encounter have often been refashioned to include representatives of crime victims and elected officials not receptive to pleas for lenience.

And the nation's governors, concerned about the possibility of repeated offenses by paroled criminals and the public outcry that often follows, have all but stopped commuting life sentences.

In at least 22 states, lifers have virtually no way out. Fourteen states reported that they released fewer than 10 in 2001, and the other 8 states said fewer than 2 dozen each.

The number of lifers continues to swell in prisons across the nation, even as the number of new life sentences has dropped in recent years, along with the crime rate. According to a *New York Times* survey, the number of lifers has almost doubled in the last decade, to 132,000. Prosecutors and representatives of crime victims applaud the trend. The prisoners, they say, are paying the minimum fit punishment for terrible crimes.

But even supporters of the death penalty wonder about this state of affairs.

"Life without parole is a very strange sentence when you think about it," said Robert Blecker, a professor at New York Law School. "The punishment seems either too much or too little. If a sadistic or extraordinarily cold, callous killer deserves to die, then why not kill him? But if we are going to keep the killer alive when we could otherwise execute him, why strip him of all hope?"

Burl Cain, the warden of the Louisiana State Penitentiary in, which houses thousands of lifers, said older prisoners who have served many years should be able to make their cases to a parole or pardon board. Because all life sentences in Louisiana are without the possibility of parole, only a governor's pardon can bring a release.

The prospect of a meaningful hearing would, Mr. Cain said, provide lifers with a taste of hope.

"Prison should be a place for predators and not dying old men," he said. "Some people should die in prison, but everyone should get a hearing."

Television and Boredom

In interviews, lifers said they tried to resign themselves to spending their days entirely behind bars. But the prison training programs that once kept them busy have largely been dismantled, replaced by television and boredom.

The lot of the lifer may be said to be cruel or pampered, depending on one's perspective. "It's a bleak imprisonment," said W. Scott Thornsley, a former corrections official in Pennsylvania. "When you take away someone's hope, you take away a lot."

It was not always that way, said Steven Benjamin, a 56-year-old Michigan lifer.

"The whole perception of incarceration changed in the 1970s," said Mr. Benjamin, who is serving a sentence of life without parole for participating in a robbery in 1973 in which an accomplice killed a man. "They're dismantling all meaningful programs. We just write people off without a second thought."

As the years pass and the lifers grow old, they sometimes tend to dying prisoners and then die themselves. Some are buried in cemeteries on prison grounds by other lifers, who will then go on to repeat the cycle.

Some defendants view the prospect of life in prison as so bleak and the possibility of exoneration for lifers as so remote that they are willing to roll the dice with death.

In Alabama, six men convicted of capital crimes have asked their juries for death rather than life sentences, said Bryan Stevenson, director of the Equal Justice Initiative of Alabama.

The idea seems to have its roots in the experience of Walter McMillian, who was convicted of capital murder by an Alabama jury in 1988. The jury recommended that he be sentenced to life without parole, but Judge Robert E. Lee Key Jr. overrode that recommendation and sentenced Mr. McMillian to death by electrocution.

Because of that death sentence, lawyers opposed to capital punishment took up Mr. McMillian's case. Through their efforts, Mr. McMillian was exonerated five years later after prosecutors conceded that they had relied on perjured testimony. "Had there not been that decision to override," said Mr. Stevenson, one of Mr. McMillian's lawyers, "he would be in prison today."

Judges and other legal experts say the decision to opt for death could be a wise one for defendants who are innocent or were convicted under flawed procedures. "Capital cases get an automatic royal treatment, whereas noncapital cases are fairly routine," said Alex Kozinski, a federal appeals court judge in California.

David R. Dow, one of Mr. Arroyo's lawyers and the director of the Texas Innocence Network, said groups like his did not have the resources to represent lifers.

"If we got Arroyo's case as a non-death-penalty case," Mr. Dow said, "we would have terminated it in the very early stages of investigation."

Gov. Rick Perry of Texas signed a bill in June adding life without parole as an option for juries to consider in capital cases. Opponents of the death penalty have embraced this alternative, pointing to studies that show that support for the death penalty dropped drastically when life without parole, or LWOP, was an alternative.

"Life without parole has been absolutely crucial to whatever progress has been made against the death penalty," said James Liebman, a law professor at Columbia. "The drop in death sentences"—from 320 in 1996 to 125 last year—"would not have happened without LWOP."

But some questioned the strategy.

"I have a problem with death penalty abolitionists," said Paul Wright, the editor of *Prison Legal News* and a former lifer, released in Washington State in 2003 after serving 17 years for killing a man in a robbery attempt. "They're positing life without parole as an option, but it's a death sentence by incarceration. You're trading a slow form of death for a faster one."

Mr. Arroyo shares that view.

"I'd roll the dice with death and stay on death row," he said. "Really, death has never been my fear. What do people believe? That being alive in prison is a good life? This is slavery."

Murder Follows a Kidnapping

Mr. Arroyo was convicted in 1998 for his role in the killing of Jose Cobo, 39, an air force captain and the chief of maintenance training at the Inter-American Air Forces Academy in Lackland, Tex. Mr. Arroyo, then 17, and an accomplice, Vincent Gutierrez, 18, wanted to steal Captain Cobo's Mazda RX-7 for parts.

Captain Cobo tried to escape but became tangled in his seat belt. Mr. Gutierrez shot him twice in the back and shoved the dying man onto the shoulder of Interstate 410 during rush hour on a rainy Tuesday morning.

Although Mr. Arroyo did not pull the trigger, he was convicted of felony murder, or participation in a serious crime that led to a killing. He contends that he had no reason to think Mr. Gutierrez would kill Captain Cobo. "I don't mind taking responsibility for my actions, for my part in this crime," he said. "But don't act like I'm a murderer or violent or that this was premeditated."

That argument misunderstands the felony murder law, legal experts said. Mr. Arroyo's decision to participate in the carjacking is, they say, more than enough to support his murder conviction.

Captain Cobo left behind a 17-year-old daughter, Reena.

"I miss him so much it hurts when I think about it," she said of her father in a victim impact statement presented at trial. "I want to see the murderers punished not necessarily by death. I feel sorry that they wasted theirs and my father's life."

Mr. Arroyo said he was not eager to leave death row, and not just because of dwindling interest in his case.

"All I know is death row," he said. "This is my life."

Most lifers at Angola die of natural causes. The prison operates a hospice to tend to the dying prisoners, and it has opened a second cemetery, Point Lookout Two, to accommodate the dead.

On a warm afternoon earlier this year, men in wheelchairs moved slowly around the main open area of the prison hospice. Others lounged in bed.

The private rooms, for terminal patients, are as pleasant as most hospital rooms, though the doors are sturdier. The inmates have televisions, video games, coffeepots and DVD players.

Robert Downs, a 69-year old career bank robber serving a 198-year term as a habitual felon, died in one of those rooms the day before. In his final days, other inmates tended to him, in four-hour shifts, around the clock. "Our responsibility," said Randolph Matthieu, a hospice volunteer, "is so that he doesn't die there by himself."

Mr. Matthieu, 53, is serving a life sentence for killing a man he met at the C'est La Guerre Lounge in Lafayette, La., in 1983.

At Point Lookout Two the next day, there were six mounds of fresh dirt and one deep hole, ready to receive Mr. Downs. Under the piles of dirt were other inmates who had recently died. They were awaiting simple white crosses like the 120 or so nearby. The crosses bear two pieces of information. One is the dead man's name, of course. Instead of the end points of his life, though, his six-digit prison number is stamped below.

The sun was hot, and the gravediggers paused for a rest after their toil.

"I'm hoping I don't come this way," said Charles Vassel, 66, who is serving a life sentence for killing a clerk while robbing a liquor store in Monroe, La., in 1972. "I want to be buried around my family."

The families of prisoners who die at Angola have 30 hours to claim their bodies, and about half do. The rest are buried at Point Lookout Two.

Timothy Bray, 45, also in for life, added, "It's pretty much the only way you leave."

Wary of a Transformed World

Not all older lifers are eager to leave prison. Many have grown used to the free food and medical care. They worry about living in a world that has been radically transformed by technology in the decades that they have been locked up.

Wardens like Mr. Cain say that lifers are docile, mature and helpful.

"Many of the lifers are not habitual felons," he added. "They committed a murder that was a crime of passion. That inmate is not necessarily hard to manage."

What is needed, he said, is hope, and that is in short supply. "I tell them, you never know when you might win the lottery," Mr. Cain said. "You never know when you might get a pardon."

—October 5, 2005

TALE OF 3 INMATES WHO VANISHED FROM ALCATRAZ MAINTAINS INTRIGUE 50 YEARS LATER

By ROBERT D. McFADDEN

Fifty years ago, on the night of June 11, 1962, the three convicts were locked down as usual. Guards walking the tier outside their cells saw them at 9:30 and checked on them periodically all night, looking in at the sleeping faces, hearing nothing strange. But by morning, the inmates had vanished.

Guards found pillows under the bedclothes and lifelike papier-mâché heads with real hair and closed, painted eyes. Federal agents, state and local police officers, coast guard boats and military helicopters joined the largest manhunt since the Lindbergh baby kidnapping in 1932, scouring the prison complex on Alcatraz Island, the expanse of San Francisco Bay and the surrounding landscape of Northern California.

A crude raft made of rubber raincoats was found on a nearby island. But the fugitives were never seen again. Federal officials said they almost certainly drowned in the maelstrom of riptides, undertows and turbulent, frigid waters of the 10-mile-wide bay, their bodies probably swept out to sea under the Golden Gate Bridge.

> *A crude raft made of rubber raincoats was found on a nearby island.*

But for aficionados of unsolved mysteries, the fantasy that Frank Lee Morris and the brothers Clarence and John Anglin had successfully escaped from the nation's most forbidding maximum security prison and are still alive has been a tantalizing possibility for a half-century.

It seemed wildly improbable. "The Rock" where Al Capone, Machine Gun Kelly and other infamous criminals were held was thought to be escape-proof. In its 29 years as a federal prison, from 1934 to 1963, no one is known to have made it out alive. Forty-one inmates tried. Of those, 26 were recaptured, 7 were shot dead, 3 drowned and 2 besides Mr. Morris and the Anglin brothers were never found.

Had they survived, the three men, all bank robbers serving long terms, would be in their 80s. Their breakout has been a subject of fascination to many Americans, analyzed in countless articles, four television documentaries, a 1963 book by J. Campbell Bruce, *Escape from Alcatraz*, and a 1979 movie of the same name starring Clint Eastwood as Mr. Morris.

Aerial view of Alcatraz Island, off the coast of San Francisco, by Carol M. Highsmith, c. 1993.

The film and television productions, including a 1993 episode of *America's Most Wanted* and a 2011 National Geographic documentary, *Vanished from Alcatraz*, correctly portrayed Mr. Morris as the escape's mastermind and a criminal of superior intelligence.

Federal officials said he had an I.Q. of 133, surpassing 98 percent of the population. Born in 1926, in Washington, he was orphaned at 11, sent to foster homes, convicted of theft at 13 and landed in reform school. He graduated to robbery and narcotics, and while serving 10 years for bank robbery escaped from the Louisiana State Penitentiary. Then, captured in a burglary, he was sent to Alcatraz in 1960 for 14 years.

The Anglins were born in Donalsonville, Ga., John in 1930, and Clarence a year later, two of 14 children of impoverished farmers. The brothers became inept burglars and were imprisoned in Alabama, Florida and Georgia, where they tried to escape repeatedly. Seized after a 1958 Alabama bank holdup, they were sent to the federal penitentiary in Leavenworth, Kan., and later to Alcatraz.

Housed on a tier near one another, Mr. Morris and the Anglins began planning the escape in late 1961. One and perhaps two other inmates were involved. The plan took months to prepare and required daring, ingenuity, careful timing and trust.

Behind their row of cells was a rarely used utility corridor for heating ducts and plumbing pipes. With spoons from a mess hall and a drill improvised from a vacuum cleaner, they dug through thick concrete walls, enlarging small, grille-covered air vents to squeeze through into the utility corridor. The work was concealed with cardboard and paint, and the noise by Mr. Morris's evening accordion playing.

Some worked while others kept a lookout. With absences timed for the guard patrols, they created a secret workshop atop their cellblock. There, they created an inflatable raft of rubber raincoats held together with thread and contact cement, plywood paddles, plastic bags turned into floating devices and dummy heads of plaster and toilet paper, made realistic with paint from prison art kits and hair clippings from the barbershop.

They stole a small accordion-like concertina from another inmate to serve as a bellows to inflate the raft. Finally, they climbed through the utility corridor and up a shaft of pipes and ducts to the roof, where they cut away most of the rivets holding a large ventilating fan and grille in place. Dabs of soap substituted for rivet heads—a little artistic touch, should anyone notice.

On the night of the escape, only one thing went wrong: Allen West, a fourth inmate who had planned to join them, had trouble opening the vent at the back of his cell and was left behind. He later gave investigators many details of the escape.

The others put their dummies to bed, retrieved the raft and other materials from atop the cellblock and climbed the ducts to the roof, where the fan-grille escape hatch had been prepared. In clear view of a gun tower, they stole across the roof, hauling their materials with them, then descended a 50-foot wall by sliding down a kitchen vent pipe to the ground. The wall was illuminated by a searchlight, but no one saw them.

They climbed two 12-foot, barbed-wire perimeter fences and went to the northeast shoreline—a blind spot out of range of the searchlights and gun towers—where they inflated their raft with the concertina. It was after 10 o'clock, investigators later estimated, when they shoved off. A dense fog cloaked the bay that night, and they disappeared into it.

The next day, searchers found remnants of the raincoat raft and paddles on Angel Island, two miles north of Alcatraz and a mile from the Tiburon headlands of Marin County, north of San Francisco. They also found a plastic bag containing personal effects of the Anglins, including a money-order receipt and names, addresses and photos of friends and relatives. Emphasizing their belief that the escapees had drowned, officials said there had been no nearby robberies or car thefts on the night of the escape.

Alcatraz, an aging, 12-acre prison whose crumbling concrete and deteriorated plumbing had grown increasingly expensive to maintain, was closed in 1963 and later became a tourist attraction.

Mr. Morris and the Anglin brothers were officially declared dead in 1979, when the FBI closed the case. But it was reopened by the U.S. Marshal's Service in 1993 after a former Alcatraz inmate, Thomas Kent, told Fox's *America's Most Wanted* that he had helped plan the breakout but had backed out because he could not swim.

Mr. Kent said Clarence Anglin's girlfriend had agreed to meet them on shore and drive them to Mexico. Officials were skeptical because Mr. Kent had been paid $2,000 for the interview. Nevertheless, Dave Branham, a marshal's service spokesman, said, "We think there is a possibility they are alive."

The Eastwood film implied that the escape had been successful. A 2003 *MythBusters* program on the Discovery Channel tested the feasibility of an escape on a raincoat raft and judged it possible. And the 2011 National Geographic program disclosed that footprints leading away from the raft had been found on Angel Island, and that contrary to official denials, a car had been stolen nearby on the night of the escape.

—*June 10, 2012*

HOW EL CHAPO WAS FINALLY CAPTURED, AGAIN

By AZAM AHMED

Stripped to his undershirt and covered in filth, the world's most notorious drug lord dragged himself out of the sewers and into the middle of traffic.

Disoriented from his long trudge underground, with gun-toting marines on his heels, he found himself standing across the street from a Walmart. Joaquín Guzmán Loera, the kingpin known across the globe as El Chapo, would have to improvise. His cavalry was not coming.

He and his top lieutenant commandeered a white Volkswagen from a passing motorist, but only a few blocks later, the car became engulfed in smoke. Desperate for another vehicle, the two men spotted a red Ford Focus at a traffic light, driven by a woman with her daughter and five-year-old grandson.

"Get out of the car now," said the lieutenant, his weapon trained on the woman as he lifted the door handle. She complied, prying the child from the back seat and leaving her belongings in the car. Politely, the lieutenant handed over her purse before speeding off.

The Mexican marines had been on Mr. Guzmán's trail for more than six months, ever since he humiliated the nation by escaping its most secure prison through a tunnel that led into the shower floor of his cell.

The chase had led them into the remote wilds of the Golden Triangle, on the border of Durango and Sinaloa states, an area where Mr. Guzmán is revered. He evaded multiple raids by the Mexican authorities, including a close brush after he sat for an interview with the American actor Sean Penn.

But it had come at a cost. The authorities had swept through 18 of his homes and properties in his native lands. Days on end in the inhospitable mountains, where even a billionaire like Mr. Guzmán was forced to rough it, left him yearning for a bit of comfort.

In early January, he arrived in the coastal city of Los Mochis, in Sinaloa, at a home where the authorities had trailed one of the chief tunnel diggers from his escape. Construction crews had been hard at work on the house for weeks. The final bit of evidence was a food order, Mexican officials said.

Just two blocks away, a big order of tacos was picked up after midnight on Jan. 8 by a man driving a white van, like the one believed to be driven by Mr. Guzmán's associates.

Joaquín "El Chapo" Guzmán is escorted into a helicopter by authorities in Mexico City on January 8, 2016, following his recapture in Sinaloa State.

Hours later, at 4:30 a.m., the marines stormed the compound, meeting a knot of doors and fierce resistance from gunmen. Like many of Mr. Guzmán's homes, this one was equipped with elaborate escape hatches: a decoy beneath the refrigerator and another behind a closet mirror, which he used to flee as the battle raged.

Hours later, on a highway heading out of town, the authorities finally got Mr. Guzmán, arguably the most powerful drug dealer in the history of the trade, for the third time since 1993.

A Potent Symbol

Mr. Guzmán's capture—described using information from interviews with witnesses and government officials, police reports, military video and Mexican news reports—brings to a close, for now, one of the most exhaustive manhunts the Mexican government has conducted, an endeavor that drew in more than 2,500 people across the nation.

That all that effort was committed to the pursuit of a single man—whose arrest, despite his wealth and influence, will do little to alter the dynamics of the drug trade or the war against it—reflects just how potent a symbol Mr. Guzmán has become in Mexico and beyond.

As the head of the Sinaloa cartel, Mr. Guzmán is the embodiment of an identity the country has fought to shed for decades. To some, the uneducated farm boy turned cartel magnate is a modern Robin Hood figure, revered for his fight against the government and generosity to the poor. For others, he is a heartless criminal who floods America's streets with narcotics and leaves Mexico's streets strewn with bodies.

Either way, Mr. Guzmán represents a deep crisis for Mexico's leaders as they struggle to define the country's image. His daring escape from prison last July, in view of the video camera in his cell, cast a lurid spotlight on the incompetence and corruption that has long dogged the Mexican state, driving many to view the government on a par with criminals.

Now, the recapture of Mr. Guzmán, who has escaped prison twice, is about Mexico repairing its security relationship with America, its image globally; and perhaps most important, its leaders' relationship with their own people.

El Chapo's image, by contrast, seemed only to grow after his escapes. Perhaps more than the infamy he gained as a cartel chief—responsible for shipping tons of drugs to more than 50 countries, with a wider reach than even Pablo Escobar in his heyday— Mr. Guzmán has earned a reputation as the world's preeminent escape artist.

Mr. Guzmán has earned a reputation as the world's preeminent escape artist.

After breaking out of prison in 2001, Mr. Guzmán dodged the Mexican and American authorities for over a decade. At a network of homes he owned, his team of engineers and diggers had constructed tunnels enabling him to slip away, time and again.

In February 2014, the authorities arrived at a house in Culiacán only to find a signature Chapo trick—a tunnel entrance beneath a bathtub—through which the kingpin had just fled.

He was, after all, a creator of the border tunnel, underground passages equipped with lighting, ventilation and mechanical carts to smuggle drugs into the United States without having to bother with evading customs agents. Mr. Guzmán's organization is estimated to have burrowed more than 90 such passages between Mexico and the United States.

But those tunnels could hardly compare to the one crafted for his escape last summer from the most secure wing of the country's most secure prison. During the 17 months Mr. Guzmán was locked up, he met often with associates, not only to plan his legal defense, but also to plot his escape. His men purchased land within sight of the prison, constructing an outer wall and an unfinished building on the site. From there, a mile away, the digging began.

They eventually reached the exact spot beneath Mr. Guzmán's cell, tunneling up beneath the shower floor, into a space behind a waist-high wall that gave prisoners some privacy from the 24-hour surveillance camera. At 8:52 p.m. on July 11, 2015, Mr. Guzmán walked into his shower, bent over and disappeared into legend for the second time.

Two Cessna jets later whisked him back to the mountains of his childhood, where the pursuit would begin, again.

Lure of Silver Screen

Even before Mr. Guzmán vanished from custody, though, he was making plans for a vanity project that ultimately helped the authorities pinpoint his whereabouts. By most accounts, Mr. Guzmán was not short on ego. His lawyers had filed papers to copyright his name for a big venture he was working on: a movie about his life. He reached out to several famous Mexican actresses, including Yolanda Andrade, hoping to lure them into his web of influence.

To that end, Kate del Castillo, another Mexican actress known for her portrayal of a drug boss in the series *La Reina del Sur*, or *The Queen of the South*, had caught his attention. She had been sympathetic to him on social media and Mr. Guzmán instructed an associate to contact her.

Before Mr. Guzmán's escape, Ms. del Castillo met with a lawyer in Mexico City to discuss communications with Mr. Guzmán about a potential film. The meetings and communication continued while he was ensconced in the mountains of the Sierra Madre.

The Mexican authorities were monitoring the phones of Mr. Guzmán and his accomplices, reading the unexpectedly tender exchanges between him and the actress. Mr. Guzmán promised to protect Ms. del Castillo as he would his own eyes, an affectionate phrase Mexican parents often say of their children.

Even when Ms. del Castillo suggested bringing along Mr. Penn for an interview, the drug lord did not flinch; perhaps in part, because he seemed to have no idea who Mr. Penn is.

The authorities tracked down Mr. Guzmán and planned an operation to grab him in early October. But the mission was delayed; they said they could not risk taking action while Mr. Penn and Ms. del Castillo were in the vicinity.

On Oct. 2, the parties met for the first time, in the remote reaches of the Golden Triangle, near the city of Cosalá in Sinaloa. Mr. Guzmán left afterward for Durango, where he had a ranch.

The circle had already been drawing tighter around Mr. Guzmán, with the authorities pressing into the villages and homes of his associates. But his meeting with the actors gave them the break they needed: actionable intelligence of his specific location.

Six days later, a detachment of marines swept in to capture Mr. Guzmán on his ranch. During the raid, Mr. Guzmán darted into a gully as he fled.

A Black Hawk helicopter circling the scene spotted him as he darted away, accompanied by his two female cooks and holding one of their children in his arms. A Mexican marine Special Forces sniper trained his rifle on the fugitive drug lord, but was told to stand down. Mr. Guzmán, upon seeing the Black Hawk, leaned back with the child in his arms, Mexican officials said, obscuring himself as a target. The likelihood of hitting one of the women or the child while firing on Mr. Guzmán was too high, they said.

In the following weeks, operations continued in areas under Mr. Guzmán's control. The brutal weather of an approaching winter also concerned the cartel leader—Culiacán, the capital of Sinaloa, where life could be more comfortable, was under constant surveillance. He needed to go somewhere outside his traditional zone of influence.

Los Mochis fit the bill. In 2013, power in the city had begun to shift. The splintering Beltrán-Leyva cartel, long the dominant force, was pushed out, leaving control to Mr. Guzmán's Sinaloa cartel.

The government, aware that Mr. Guzmán was planning a trip to an urban center, followed one of his associates to a house in Los Mochis, on a busy road with shops nearby.

Construction soon started. Neighbors dropped by to take a look. A worker even promised one of them any extra concrete left after the renovation was completed.

"You're welcome to whatever we don't use," he told the neighbor. "We're just doing some repairs."

A Bloody Gun Battle

Toward the beginning of January, there was unusual activity at the house, with the residents inside breaking from their routines of the previous month, the authorities said. They intercepted phone conversations discussing the imminent arrival of someone known by the aliases of "Grandma" and "Aunt."

At dawn on Jan. 7, a car pulled up to the house. The authorities' certainty that Mr. Guzmán had arrived increased. That night, after the taco order, they were nearly sure of it.

Before sunrise the next morning, 17 Special Forces marines from the Mexican navy stormed the house, supported by 50 soldiers charged with surveillance and keeping an eye on the drain system in and around the home. Upon breaking through the metal door, they entered what appeared to be a foyer, surrounded by a maze of doors. Shortly after, gunfire erupted.

"We've got one injured," a marine yelled, referring to one of his own soldiers, according to video of the raid taken by a soldier's helmet camera.

Gunfire continued in the narrow corridors. A commander ordered one of the marines to toss a grenade in front of one of the many doors blocking their advance. Two marines advanced down another hallway, toward a staircase used by the surviving gunmen to escape to the roof.

By 6:30 a.m., the house was secure. Five of Mr. Guzmán's men were killed in the raid, while four others were arrested. Two women discovered inside, cooks for Mr. Guzmán and his men, were also placed under arrest. Just the one marine was wounded.

A sweep of the house revealed two tunnels: one beneath the refrigerator, a false tunnel meant to confuse the advancing troops. The other was in a bedroom closet. A switch by the light bulb activated a trap door behind the mirror, leading to the route Mr. Guzmán used to flee.

On the road, Mr. Guzmán and his associate headed out of town along Highway 15. But the federal police were on alert, and they spotted the two men and arrested them.

Holding two of the deadliest men in Mexico made the police nervous. While they waited for the marines, they took the pair out of sight, afraid that cartel forces might try to stage a rescue. And with good reason: The police had been tipped that 40 assassins were on their way to free their leader.

They selected the Hotel Doux, an hourly-rate place off the highway. They booked rooms and took pictures of Mr. Guzmán in a filthy vest. The drug lord urged the men to free him. He promised them jobs as business leaders. When they refused, he tried threats.

"You are all going to die," he warned them.

After the marines arrived, Mr. Guzmán was taken to Mexico City in a helicopter, the capture finally over. After being paraded before a field of news cameras at the Mexico City airport, Mr. Guzmán was ushered onto another helicopter, headed for the same prison he had escaped from six months earlier.

To keep him locked up this time, the authorities said they would rotate his cells, never allowing him to stay anywhere long enough to burrow his way out again. But to many, the longer the drug lord remains in prison in Mexico, the greater the risk of flight. His imprisonment could drag on for a year, given the numerous—and creative—injunctions filed by his team of lawyers to fight his extradition to the United States, where he faces federal indictments on charges that include narcotics trafficking and murder.

One of them, filed in August while Mr. Guzmán was still at large, stated that it would be impossible for Mr. Guzmán to receive a fair trial in the United States, given the hostile environment there toward Mexicans. They cited, as evidence, the language of a top Republican presidential candidate: Donald J. Trump.

—January 17, 2016

NOTE: *As of this writing, Guzman is in prison in Mexico, awaiting likely extradition to the United States.*

PRISON RATE WAS RISING YEARS BEFORE 1994 LAW

By ERIK ECKHOLM

"**G**angs and drugs have taken over our streets," President Bill Clinton said in 1994 as he signed a far-reaching anti-crime bill to bipartisan acclaim.

Defending the law at the time, a frightened era of crack-cocaine wars and record murder rates, Hillary Clinton, as first lady, warned about an emerging generation of "super-predators"—a notion she later repudiated.

Confronted last week by protesters from the Black Lives Matter movement, Mr. Clinton defended his tough crime stance, even though he, like Mrs. Clinton, has joined in recent calls for sweeping reforms in criminal sentencing.

For some critics, the 1994 crime bill has come to epitomize the late 20th-century policies that sent incarceration to record levels and ravaged poor communities, taking a particularly devastating toll on African-Americans that political leaders are only now working to reverse.

History and statistics tell a more complex story, according to criminologists.

The Violent Crime Control and Law Enforcement Act of 1994 was a composite measure, with elements reflecting opposing impulses. It offered incentives to states to build more prisons if they toughened sentences, and added some mandatory minimum sentences to those that existed. But it also promoted the expansion of community policing and drug courts as alternatives to jail. It established a federal "three strikes" law and expanded the federal death penalty, but outlawed assault rifles.

Some critics portray the law as a critical turning point as the country rushed to put more low-level offenders in prison, ravaging low-income communities.

But in fact, the data shows, the startling rise in imprisonment was already well underway by 1994, with roots in a federal government war on drugs that was embraced by Democratic and Republican leaders alike.

"The trend of increased incarceration had already started two decades before 1994," said Jeremy Travis, the president of the John Jay College of Justice in New York. Mr. Travis led federal research on crime during the Clinton administration and was an editor of a 2014 report by the National Academy of Sciences, "The Growth of Incarceration in the United States."

"To lay mass incarceration and the damages to black communities on the doorstep of the 1994 crime act is historically inaccurate," Mr. Travis said, although elements of the law added to the problem in a modest way.

What the historical record does show is that many federal and state changes in criminal justice policy led to a fourfold rise in the incarceration rate from the early 1970s until it declined modestly in the last few years.

The rise in incarceration was driven by state laws like the 1973 Rockefeller drug laws in New York. It was stoked by a major 1986 federal drug act, which expanded mandatory sentences and set the now-notorious 100-to-1 ratio in the quantities of powdered versus crack cocaine that could trigger severe penalties.

Still, the incentives offered to the states in the 1994 law—nearly $10 billion for prison construction on the condition that states adopt "truth in sentencing" policies—may have added to the prison populations of the 28 states that took advantage of the provision. Incarceration's disproportionate effect on African-Americans continues: In 2014, the Justice Department reported, 6 percent of all black men age 30 to 39 were in prison; the rate was 2 percent for Hispanic men and 1 percent for white men.

The steady rise in incarceration into the 21st century calls for further explanation because it persisted through a steep decline in violent crime.

No one could have known in 1994, but the violent crime rate had already peaked. It plummeted over the next quarter-century, even as more people were sent to prison.

The crime bill passed with enthusiastic and bipartisan support, including a yes vote from Senator Bernie Sanders of Vermont, the current rival to Mrs. Clinton for the Democratic presidential nomination. Mr. Sanders has said that he opposed certain parts of the legislation but voted for the bill because it included an assault weapons ban and language dealing with violence against women.

Mr. Clinton, too, has decried some of the more worrisome parts of the law. In an address before the national convention of the N.A.A.C.P. last July, he acknowledged that the law had gone too far in toughening sentencing standards and had contributed to mass incarceration. "I signed a bill that made the problem worse," he said. "And I want to admit it."

But when confronted by Black Lives Matter protesters last Thursday during a campaign event for his wife in Philadelphia, Mr. Clinton defended his 1994 crime bill.

"I don't know how you would characterize the gang leaders who got 13-year-old kids hopped up on crack and sent them out onto the street to murder other African-American children," Mr. Clinton said to a protester. "Maybe you thought they were good citizens."

"You are defending the people who kill the lives you say matter," he said.

Mr. Clinton later said that he regretted the confrontation.

Criminologists have debated how much of the fall in crime can be ascribed to the rise in incarceration. Most, including the National Academy of Sciences panel that Mr. Travis helped lead, have concluded that extra incarceration played only a modest role compared with wider social changes.

One contributing factor to the persistence of high incarceration is suggested by John Pfaff, a professor of criminal law at Fordham University. Beyond the spread of mandatory sentences and other policies, he said, district attorneys became much more likely to bring felony charges and seek long sentences, perhaps reflecting a changing public mood.

Particularly before the mid-1990s, he said, sentencing laws in the states—which account for 87 percent of the country's prisoners—had become more severe. On top of that, he said, local prosecutors became much more aggressive.

Across the country, the probability that an arrest would result in felony charges roughly doubled between 1994 and 2008, a trend that Mr. Pfaff said seemed unrelated to anything in the 1994 federal law.

Douglas A. Berman, a professor of criminal law at Ohio State's Moritz College of Law, agreed with other experts that the direct effects of the 1994 law on incarceration rates had often been exaggerated. He also said that Mr. Clinton's embrace in the early 1990s of anti-crime rhetoric may have been a political necessity, considering the drubbing that Michael Dukakis received in the 1988 presidential campaign for being considered soft on crime. And Mr. Clinton is right to say that black Americans were disproportionately victimized by runaway crime, and wanted help.

But the Clintons share blame with many others from that era, Mr. Berman said, for overemphasizing "tough" responses at the expense of more thoughtful solutions that did not involve the endless expansion of prisons.

—April 11, 2016

CHAPTER 8

SERIAL KILLERS

"I was born with the devil in me. I could not help the fact that I was a murderer, no more than the poet can help the inspiration to sing."

—H. H. Holmes in confession, 1896

FEAR ENVELOPED NEW YORK CITY in the summer of 1977. One tabloid front page summed up the feeling many were experiencing: "NO ONE IS SAFE FROM SON OF SAM." The sequential, stalking behavior of a serial killer on the loose creates an anxiety that invades entire neighborhoods, even cities. *The Times*'s headline on August 1, 1977, may have been more muted, more factual: ".44 Killer Wounds 12th and 13th Victims." But no one was confused about what it meant.

OPPOSITE: A photograph of H. H. Holmes's "Murder Castle" in Chicago, c. 1914.

DISMAY IN WHITECHAPEL:
TWO MORE MURDERED WOMEN FOUND

The Whitechapel fiend has again set that district and all London in a state of terror. He murdered not one woman but two last night, and seems bent on beating all previous records in his unheard-of crimes. His last night's victims were both murdered within an hour, and the second was disemboweled like her predecessors, a portion of her abdomen being missing as in the last case. He contented himself with cutting the throat of the other, doubtless because of interruption. Both women were streetwalkers of the lowest class, as before.

These crimes are all of the most daring character. The first woman was killed in the open roadway within a few feet of the main street, and though many people were within a few feet, no cry was heard. This was at midnight; before 1 o'clock the second victim was found, and she was so warm that the murder must have taken place but a few minutes before. This was in Mitre-square, which is but a few blocks distant from the

> *These crimes are all of the most daring character.*

Bank of England, in the very heart of the business quarter. The square is deserted at night, but is patrolled every half hour by the police.

These make six murders to the fiend's credit, all within a half-mile radius. People are terrified and are loud in their complaints of the police, who have done absolutely nothing. They confess themselves without a clue, and they devote their entire energies to preventing the press from getting at the facts. They deny to reporters a sight of the scene or bodies, and give them no information whatever. The assassin is evidently mocking the police in his barbarous work. He waited until the two preceding inquests were quite finished, and then murdered two more women. He has promised to murder 20 in all, and has every prospect of uninterrupted success.

—October 1, 1888

Associated Press Dispatches

LONDON, Sept. 30—This morning the whole city was again startled by the news that two more murders had been added to the list of mysterious crimes that have recently been committed in Whitechapel. It was known that another woman had been murdered, and a report was also current that there was still another victim. This report proved true. The two victims, as in the former cases, were dissolute women of the poorest class. That the motive of the murderer was not robbery is shown by the fact that no attempt was made to despoil the bodies.

The first murder occurred in a narrow court off Berners-street at an early hour in the morning beneath the windows of a foreigners' Socialist club. A concert was in progress and many members of the club were present, but no sound was heard from the victim. The same process had been followed in the other cases. The woman had been seized by the throat and her cries choked, and the murderer, with one sweeping cut, had severed her throat from ear to ear. A clubman on entering the court stumbled over the body, which was lying only two yards from the street. A stream of warm blood was flowing from the body into the gutter. The murderer had evidently been disturbed before he had time to mutilate his victim.

The second murder was committed three to four hours later, in Mitre-square, five minutes' walk from the scene of the first crime. The body of the unfortunate woman had been disemboweled, the throat cut, and the nose severed. The heart and lungs had been thrown aside, and the entrails were twisted into the gaping wound around the neck. The work of dissection was evidently done with the utmost haste. The doctors, after a hasty examination of the body, said they thought it must have taken about five minutes to complete the work of the murderer, who then had plenty of time to escape.

Mitre-square, the scene of the second murder, is a thoroughfare. Many people pass through the square early on Sunday morning on their way to prepare for market in the notorious Petticoat-lane. The publicity of the place adds to the daringness of the crime.

The police, who have been severely criticized in connection with the Whitechapel murders, are paralyzed by these latest

DISMAY IN WHITECHAPEL

TWO MORE MURDERED WOMEN FOUND.

ONE NIGHT'S WORK OF THE MYSTERI-
OUS ASSASSIN WHO HAS BAFFLED
THE LONDON POLICE THUS FAR.

BY COMMERCIAL CABLE FROM OUR OWN COR-
RESPONDENT.

Copyright, 1888, by the New-York Times.

LONDON, Sept. 30.—The Whitechapel fiend has again set that district and all London in a state of terror. He murdered not one woman but two last night, and seems bent on beating all previous records in his unheard-of crimes. His last night's victims were both murdered within an hour, and the second was disemboweled like her predecessors, a portion of her abdomen being missing as in the last case. He contented himself with cutting the throat of the other, doubtless because of interruption. Both women were street walkers of the lowest class, as before.

Detail of a *New York Times* front-page headline of October 1, 1888.

279

crimes. As soon as the news was received at police headquarters a messenger was dispatched for Sir Charles Warren, chief commissioner of police, who was called out of bed and at once visited the scene of the murders. The inhabitants of Whitechapel are dismayed. The vigilance committees formed after the first crimes had relaxed their efforts to capture the murderer. The Berners-street victim was Elizabeth Stride, a native of Stockholm, who resided in a common lodging house. The name of the other victim is not known. Dr. Blackwell, who was called to view the remains of the Berners-street victim, gave it as his opinion that the same man, evidently a maniac, had committed both murders. The Berners-street victim had evidently been dragged back by a handkerchief worn around the throat.

NOTE: *The Whitechapel district murderer, who came to be known as Jack the Ripper, was never caught. Although other unsolved murders in the district in 1888 were attributed by some to the Ripper, researchers suggest that five deaths, including that of Ms. Stride, are most persuasively linked.*

HOLMES COOL TO THE END

Murderer Herman Mudgett, alias H. H. Holmes, was hanged this morning in the county prison in Philadelphia for the killing of Benjamin F. Pietzel. The drop fell at 10:12 o'clock, and 20 minutes later he was pronounced dead.

Holmes was calm to the end, even to the extent of giving a word of advice to Assistant Superintendent Richardson as the latter was arranging the final details. He died as he had lived—unconcerned and thoughtless of the future. Even with the recollection still vividly before him of the recent confession, in which he admitted the killing of a score of persons in all parts of the country, he denied everything, and almost his last words were a denial of any crimes except the deaths of two women at his hands by malpractice.

In the murder of the several members of the Pietzel family, he denied all complicity, particularly of the father, for whose death he stated he was suffering the penalty. Then, with the prayer of the spiritual attendants still sounding in his ears, the trap was sprung, and the execution that terminated one of the worst criminal stories known to criminology was ended.

While the exact time of the execution was unannounced, it was supposed that the hour would be about 10 o'clock. Two hours before that time, however, those who were to attend began arriving, but admission to the prison was denied everyone except those officials in direct touch with the institution. The gates were then opened, and the fourscore having tickets pressed into the inner court. Sheriff Clements had preceded the crowd, and was awaiting the arrival of those comprising his jury, that they might be sworn.

Portrait of Herman Mudgett, aka H. H. Holmes, mid 1800s.

The jury comprised six physicians and a like number from other walks in life, all prominent in their respective stations. In response to the calling of their names they ranged about the desk behind which stood Sheriff Clements, and then solemnly swore "to witness the execution of Herman W. Mudgett, alias H. H. Holmes, and certify the time and manner of such execution according to law."

Many prominent men were in attendance, notable among whom were Dr. MacDonald of Washington, the famous criminologist; Det. Frank Geyer, who conducted the case, and Lawyer Rotan, who conducted the defense of Holmes during the trial.

Mr. Rotan was early at the prison, but had been preceded by the Rev. Father Dailey and the Rev. Father MacPake, who administered the last rites to the condemned man. They arrived shortly after 6 o'clock, and remained with him last evening until 10:30.

The deathwatch was then kept by Keeper George Weaver, who remained until 7 o'clock this morning. Weaver said this morning that Holmes had retired about midnight and slept soundly until called at 6 o'clock. So sound were his slumbers that twice was he called before awakening when the arrival of the reverends was announced. They were come to administer the sacrament of communion. For nearly two hours they remained in the cell, and then were succeeded by Lawyer Rotan, the legal adviser of Holmes.

While they were talking, breakfast was served, and Holmes seemed to heartily enjoy the meal. It was substantial, but plain, consisting of eggs, toast and coffee. "He enjoyed it more than I could," remarked Mr. Rotan. "He is the most cool and possessed of all in any way connected with the case."

Shortly before 9 o'clock, Holmes prepared to dress himself. Contrary to the general custom, he refused to don a new suit, but arrayed himself in trousers, vest, and cutaway coat. Collar and necktie were, of course, not worn, but their place was taken by a white handkerchief knotted about the neck.

Ten o'clock had just sounded when a call came from the cell corridor for Sheriff Clements. He had been gone but a moment when the doors leading through the long corridors in which was placed the gallows were opened, and two by two, led by the sheriff's jury, the party passed down. The gallows was halfway down the corridor, and to either side was a high partition that, once through the doors, shut off any view of the approach of the condemned as he came to the scaffold. The greatest stillness prevailed among the group watching for the first glimpse of the condemned.

Preceded by Sheriff Clements and Superintendent Perkins, Holmes soon stepped onto the trap. On the right was Father Dailey, to the left, Father MacPake, and bringing up the rear were Lawyer Rotan and Assistant Superintendent Richardson. The little party stood for a moment and then Holmes stepped forward and spoke.

He spoke slowly and with measured attention to every word; a trifle low at first, but louder as he proceeded, until every word was distinctly audible. "Gentlemen," he said, "I have a very few words to say. In fact, I would make no statement at this time except that by not speaking I would appear to acquiesce in life in my execution. I only want to say that the extent of my wrongdoings in taking human life consisted in the deaths of two women, they having died at my hands as the result of criminal operations, I wish to also state, however, so that there will be no misunderstanding hereafter, I am not guilty of taking the life of any of the Pietzel family, the three children or father, Benjamin F. Pietzel, of whose death I am now convicted and for which I am today to be hanged. That is all."

As he ceased speaking, he stepped back, and, kneeling between Fathers Dailey and MacPake, joined with them in silent prayer. Again standing, he shook the hands of those about him, and then signified his readiness for the end.

Coolest of the entire party, he even went to the extreme of suggesting to the Assistant Superintendent Richardson, that the latter not hurry himself. "Take your time: don't bungle it," he remarked, as the official exhibited some little haste, the evident outcome of nervousness. Those were almost his last words. The cap was adjusted. A low-toned query: "Are you ready?" and an equally low-toned response, "Yes, good-bye," and the trap was sprung.

The neck was not broken, and there were a few convulsive twitches of the limbs that continued for about ten minutes. "But he suffered none after the drop," said Dr. Scott, the prison physician. The trap was sprung at precisely 10:12, and 15 minutes later Holmes was pronounced dead.

The body was placed in a vault in Holy Cross Cemetery. The last act at the vault was performed at Holmes's express command. The lid of the coffin was taken off and the body was lifted out and laid on the ground. The bottom of the coffin was filled with cement, and the body was replaced in the coffin and covered with the cement. It was Holmes's idea that this cement would harden around his body and prevent any attempt at grave robbery. The coffin was left in the receiving vault under the guard of two watchmen. Tomorrow afternoon the body will be interred in a grave in the cemetery.

Holmes made no will and left no confession. The two women referred to by Holmes in his confession from the scaffold were Julia Connor of Chicago, who, with her daughter, was believed to have been murdered by him, and Emily Cigrand of Anderson, Ind.

Holmes the Murder Demon

Harry Howard Holmes was only 36 years old, but into those few years he had succeeded in crowding a series of crimes that many older scoundrels had achieved only in a much longer life. The man who has just received the heaviest penalty of the law was convicted of one murder. Three more were in evidence against him. He had apparently planned to kill three more persons, and he accused himself of having taken the lives of 27 human beings.

After giving this list, the charges against him of bigamy, train robbery, horse stealing and general swindling sink into insignificance.

H. H. Holmes is the name by which this slayer will be enrolled in the list of the world's great criminals. Herman Webster Mudgett was his real name, and he was born in Gilmanton, N.H., May 16, 1860. By what stages of wickedness he rose to the crime of murder is not known, or when he committed his first great crime. He says it was in 1886. At that time he was the proprietor of the "Castle," in Chicago, which subsequent research by the police has shown to be a veritable man trap, with furnaces, concealed rooms, cells and many other devices for putting victims speedily and secretly out of the way. Whatever he did there, he first appeared prominently in September 1894, to assist in the identification of a man who was found dead in a room on Callowhill Street in Philadelphia.

This man was Benjamin F. Pietzel, for whose murder Holmes has been hanged. Pietzel, under the name of B. F. Perry, had hired the house, ostensibly as a dealer in patents. On Sept. 4 his body was found there, the face burned, and indications of an explosion. A coroner's jury decided that death was due to congestion of the lungs, caused by inhalation of flames, chloroform or some poisonous drug. Whether it was suicide or murder was a mystery.

The next development was a notice to the Fidelity Mutual Life Association of Philadelphia that Perry was really Benjamin F. Pietzel, and that his widow held a policy for $10,000 insurance on his life. The notice came from Jephtha D. Howe, a lawyer of St. Louis. In the investigation, H. H. Holmes appeared to assist in the identification of the body, as well as the dead man's daughter, Alice. The insurance company was satisfied, and the money was turned over. Alice was the only one of a family of a widow and five children to appear on the scene. Apparently the incident was ended.

But the insurance company had a detective, Inspector W. E. Gary, who was suspicious of wrongdoing somewhere. The next month, when he was in St. Louis, he was given the confession of M. C. Hedgepeth, a convicted train robber who laid bare the whole scheme. Holmes had visited him in jail, and had asked the name of a lawyer to assist in a fraud upon an insurance company. This was to insure Pietzel for $10,000, substitute a corpse and collect the money. Hedgepeth said he recommended J. D. Howe, and for this was to receive $500 out of the money, but he had never been paid. The company began an investigation, evidences of fraud multiplied. Holmes was eventually arrested in Boston, but, strangely, on a telegram from Fort Worth, Texas, accusing him of horse stealing. Mrs. Pietzel was also arrested.

Then Holmes made confession No. 1. He admitted a conspiracy to defraud the insurance company and said Pietzel was alive, with three of his children, in South

America, and his supposed body was a cadaver bought in New York. Holmes, Pietzel, Howe, the lawyer, and Mrs. Pietzel were indicted for conspiracy to defraud.

In the meantime, many suspicious facts became known. No trace could be found of Pietzel or his children. Holmes made a second confession, that it was Pietzel's body that had been found, and that Pietzel had probably committed suicide; that he (Holmes) had discovered this, and then arranged the body and left it in the house where it was found. This made necessary a second indictment, under which he was convicted, and sentence was deferred.

Here comes in the most dramatic part of the story—the tracing of the three children, whom Mrs. Pietzel had entrusted to Holmes at the time of the identification of her husband. She was anxious to see them. Holmes was told he was suspected of murdering the father and the son, Howard, and the daughters, Alice and Nellie. He was told he could clear himself partially by telling where the children were. He said he had given them to a Miss Williams, who had taken them to London.

This was not believed. There were ugly rumors about the disappearance of two sisters, Nettie and Minnie Williams, last seen in the care of Holmes, and a piece of real estate in Fort Worth, Texas, was found to have been conveyed by them to Pietzel under the name Benton T. Lyman. Holmes said that Minnie, in a moment of passion, had killed Nettie, and he had shielded her by sinking the body in the lake at Chicago.

So strong became the suspicions of a hideous crime that Det. Frank P. Geyer of the Philadelphia force was put on the track of the missing children. While the police were gathering evidence to prove Holmes guilty of the father's murder, Geyer revealed a more horrible chapter. He followed the footsteps of Holmes and the three children, and found where he killed the boy Howard and burned his body at Irvington, near Indianapolis; dug up the corpses of the two little girls in a cellar, in Toronto, and found their toys even, in the houses where the crimes were committed. The detective found that Holmes had been leading three parties around the country from place to place. One was composed of the broken-hearted wife, with her oldest daughter, Dessie, 16 years of age, and her one-year-old baby daughter, the woman continually deceived with promises of soon meeting husband and children. Another was made up of the boy and his two sisters. In the third was Holmes and his third wife, Georgiana Yohe. Neither party, Holmes excepted, knew of the others. It is believed that Holmes was planning to kill the mother and two remaining children had not his arrest at Boston interfered.

The finding of the children's bodies and the proofs connecting Holmes with the death of Pietzel had by this time roused a feeling of horror toward Holmes that overran the whole country. On Sept. 12, 1895, he was indicted for the murder of Pietzel. His trial began Oct. 28, and on Nov. 2 he was found guilty. On Nov. 28 he was sentenced to death.

As to the motive for these crimes, one theory is that Holmes feared that Pietzel, who had been his partner for years, might betray him when on a drunken carouse. By killing him he could get rid of an embarrassing witness and make some money at the same time. Holmes's behavior since his sentence has been marked by great hardihood. His third and last confession is a document, which, if true, marks him as one of the most depraved monsters of any age. In it he excuses himself for his crimes by calling himself a "degenerate." He gives a list of 27 murders, mostly committed in his "Castle" in Chicago—men and women whom he lured there, forced to give up their property,

An artist's rendering of H. H. Holmes's "Murder Castle" hotel in Chicago, April 1896.

and then killed, and whose bodies he sold for use in dissecting rooms. He tells of all these with an attention to detail which is sickening. Holmes, as a bigamist, appears to have been married under his real name first near his native town, to Clara A. Lovering, on July 4, 1878. From her he obtained a divorce in February 1987, in Illinois. Two weeks before this, he had married Myrta Z. Belknap, with whom he lived at Wilmette, Ill., under the name of Holmes. Next, without even the formality of legal separation, he was married, as Henry Mansfield Howard, at Denver, Col., to Miss Georgiana Yohe. This last was the woman who was with him in all his later wanderings.

One of the last scenes in this horrible drama took place April 17—Holmes's reception into the Catholic Church. For five or six weeks the Rev. P. F. Dailey, in whose parish the Moyamensing Prison is situated, had been laboring with him. He became convinced that Holmes's change of heart was sincere. On the day mentioned, assisted by a band of Franciscan monks, and aided by all the ritual that could be carried out in a cell in Murderers' Row, Holmes was given the rite of baptism.

On April 29, Holmes sent a communication to Gov. Hastings asking for a respite. He asserted his innocence of many of the charges against him, and said that he wanted to get himself into a spiritual condition to meet his God. His attorney intimated that Holmes would divulge the names of men who aided him in his crimes. The governor, however, refused the application.

After the first of the month, Holmes lost his cheerfulness and became morose, seeming to realize his position. He made a will, in which, it is said, he made provision for each of his wives, and also for Mrs. Pietzel.

Holmes's Many Confessions

If the "murder confessions" which Murderer Holmes wrote can only partially be believed, he was without a peer as a bloodthirsty demon. His recent ingenious "confession," wherein he claimed to have killed 27 persons, was disproved, partly, at least, by the appearance of several of the so-called victims; but Holmes's object in making the "confession" was realized—the obtaining of a sum, said to be $7,500, to have been settled upon the criminal's 18-year-old son.

Holmes was captured in Boston, Mass., in the latter part of 1894 by Owen Hanscom, the deputy superintendent of police, upon the strength of a telegram from Fort Worth, Texas, where he was wanted for horse stealing and other charges. At that time, officials of the Fidelity Mutual Life Association of Philadelphia were hot on Holmes's trail for defrauding the concern out of $10,000 in connection with Pietzel's death, the latter having been insured for this amount, and, as the accused believed horse stealing to be a high crime in Texas, he voluntarily confessed to Deputy Superintendent Hanscom to the insurance fraud. He did not dream that he was then suspected of the murder of Pietzel. He came to Philadelphia and expressed a willingness to be tried here on the conspiracy charge in preference to that of horse stealing at Fort Worth.

Before leaving Boston, Holmes made this "confession" to Mr. Hanscom: "When I concluded it was time to carry out our scheme to defraud the insurance company I secured a 'stiff' in New York and shipped it in a trunk to Philadelphia. I turned the check for the trunk over to Pietzel on the Sunday nearest the first of September. I instructed him how to prepare the body, and in three hours we were on our way to New York. Ten days after the payment of the money I saw Pietzel in Cincinnati. I took the three children to that city, where the father saw them.

"Pietzel agreed to go south, and he took one child. Howard. I took the two girls to Chicago because I had business there. We all met again in Detroit. Pietzel took the children and went to South America. During all this time Mrs. Pietzel knew her husband was alive, but she did not know that he had the children. To keep Mrs. Pietzel away from her husband, I had to tell her he was here and there, traveling from one city to another."

This was the first of a number of alleged admissions that Holmes subsequently made. The insurance officials had good grounds for believing Holmes had murdered Pietzel and the three children. So when the prisoner arrived in Philadelphia he was urged to make another confession. He did so, but it varied from the one he made in Boston. It graphically narrated how the body was substituted for Pietzel in the Callowhill Street house, and its identification by Alice Pietzel as that of her father. Holmes also related how the money was received from the insurance company and its division between Mrs. Pietzel, Jephtha D. Howe, the St. Louis lawyer, and himself. In this "confession" Holmes accused Howe of receiving $2,500 for his share in the transaction.

Soon after Holmes was taken to Philadelphia, Det. Geyer visited him in the county prison in relation to the finding of the body at Callowhill Street, Sept. 4, 1894. After an hour's conversation with the wily Holmes the detective emerged from the prison with a "confession," in which the accused said that the body was not that of Pietzel, but was one substituted to defraud the insurance company.

Holmes honored Mr. Geyer a week later with still another "confession." "Mr. Geyer," he said, "that story I told you about a substitute body is not true. It is the body of Benjamin Pietzel, but I did not murder him or his children. On Sunday morning, Sept. 2, I found Pietzel dead in the third story of the Callowhill Street house. I found a note in a bottle telling me that he was tired of life and had finally decided to commit suicide. He requested me to look after the insurance money, and take care of his wife and family. I then fixed up the body in the position it was found. These children you speak of are all right. They are with Minnie Williams in London."

When the bodies of Nellie and Alice Pietzel were unearthed in Toronto, Holmes denied having killed them. When Howard's charred bones were located in a stove in Irvington, Ind., Holmes denied any knowledge of the lad's death. When the murders of Minnie Williams and her sister were discovered, Holmes said Minnie killed Nancy in a jealous frenzy, and he buried the body in Lake Michigan. He denied having put Minnie to death to secure her property. The disappearance of Emily Cygrand was traced to Holmes, hut the criminal said he knew nothing of the girl's fate. The partially consumed bones found in the Chicago "Castle" are known to be those of some of Holmes's victims.

The last time that Holmes was taken to the district attorney's office to "confess," Mr. Graham lost patience with him. "Holmes, you are an infernal, lying murderer," Mr. Graham said. "I will hang you in Philadelphia for the murder of Benjamin Pietzel."

Holmes's nerve was still with him, and he said "I defy you. You have no evidence to prove me guilty."

Mr. Graham looked with disgust and determination at Holmes and said: "You will surely hang in Philadelphia for murdering Benjamin Pietzel."

—May 8, 1896

DESALVO, CONFESSED "BOSTON STRANGLER," FOUND STABBED TO DEATH IN PRISON CELL

By JOHN KIFNER

Albert H. DeSalvo, who became known as the "Boston Strangler," was found stabbed to death at Walpole State Prison this morning. The prison authorities said the 40-year-old inmate's body was discovered in his cell bed in the prison's hospital wing at 7 o'clock. DeSalvo, who worked as an orderly in the hospital, was said to have died of multiple stab wounds.

The Norfolk County district attorney, George Burke, said that a possible suspect had been questioned, but that no arrest had been made.

Although DeSalvo confessed the details of the slayings of 13 women from the Boston area to a psychiatrist and became widely known as the "Boston Strangler" through a book and movie of the same name, he was never tried for those crimes. Later DeSalvo retracted the confession.

> *"The only problem we had with Albert DeSalvo was his trafficking in drugs."*

"The only problem we had with Albert DeSalvo was his trafficking in drugs," said Mr. Burke. "We don't know if this murder is drug-connected. It's possible . . . anyone who deals in drugs has enemies, because it's competitive."

The medical examiner, Nolton Bigelow, said it appeared DeSalvo had been dead for "up to 10 hours."

John Irwin, chief of the Criminal Investigations Division of the State Attorney General's Office, recalled today that there was considerable doubt among law enforcement officers over whether DeSalvo was indeed the strangler.

The slaying of the 13 women—most of them strangled with a stocking—between 1962 and 1964 spread terror through the Greater Boston area, and the Boston Strangler became a part of the folklore of crime.

Tried and Convicted

Some police officials who investigated the case, however, believed that only five of the victims were killed by the same assailant. Mr. Irwin recalled that some police officers were satisfied that DeSalvo committed all the crimes, while others believed he might have committed some.

DeSalvo was tried and convicted in January, 1967, for a separate series of crimes, including burglaries, assaults and sex offenses against four other women.

He was at first ruled mentally unable to stand trial, but F. Lee Bailey, the defense attorney, entered the case and won him a trial.

He had DeSalvo examined by a psychiatrist, Dr. Robert R. Mezer, who shocked the courtroom when he testified: "DeSalvo told me he was the strangler. . . . He told me he strangled 13 women . . . and he went into details of some of them, telling me some of the most intimate acts he committed."

"Gleaned the Details"

Mr. Bailey argued, unsuccessfully, that DeSalvo should be found "not guilty by reason of insanity."

The month after he was sentenced to life in prison, DeSalvo and two other convicts escaped from the Bridgewater State Hospital, where he was undergoing mental tests, but they were soon recaptured.

In 1968, George Harrison, DeSalvo's cellmate and one of the men he had escaped with, said that DeSalvo, rather than being the "Strangler," had been tutored for the role by another convict. He said he had overheard 15 to 20 conversations between DeSalvo and the other man in Bridgewater.

Mr. Irwin recalled in an interview today that many officers had suspected that DeSalvo had "gleaned the details" of the crimes he had committed from other convicts.

A one-time handyman and boxer, DeSalvo was a big, husky man who wore his black hair slicked back in a pompadour and dressed neatly, typically with a freshly laundered white shirt. He had become skilled in making costume jewelry, and many of his products were on display in the prison lobby.

—November 27, 1973

NOTE: *Despite his confession, DeSalvo was never charged with the murders of the 13 women to which he admitted. He was instead tried on other charges, including assault, and sentenced to life in prison, where he was stabbed to death in 1973.*

.44 KILLER WOUNDS
12th AND 13th VICTIMS

By ROBERT D. McFADDEN

With massive police patrols focused elsewhere in the city, the killer who calls himself "Son of Sam" shot and critically wounded a young couple early yesterday as they sat in a car parked on the Brooklyn waterfront a mile south of the glittering lights of the Verrazano-Narrows Bridge.

At midafternoon yesterday, more than 12 hours after the shootings, police department ballistics experts confirmed that the attack had been carried out with the same .44-caliber revolver that had been used to kill five young people and wound six others in seven incidents during the last year.

The killer's strike yesterday had the earmarks of a deadly cat-and-mouse game with the police. It came two days after the anniversary of his first murder, an anniversary marked by increased patrols, wide publicity and spreading public fears. And it came for the first time in Brooklyn, more than 10 miles from his previous attacks, which were clustered in northern Queens and the east Bronx—where the weekend's patrols were concentrated.

Throughout the weekend in many parts of the city, people warned one another about the killer stalking the streets, seemingly able to strike at will. Such warnings had been made to both of the victims in this, the killer's eighth attack.

According to witnesses—the police said at least two persons and possibly more saw the attack—the killer this time emerged from the shadows of a nearby park into the faint light of a full moon and walked up behind the couple's car at Shore Parkway and Bay 14th Street in the Bath Beach section about 2:50 a.m.

The couple, Robert Violante, a 20-year-old clothing-store salesman, of Bensonhurst, and Stacy Moskowitz, 20, a secretary, of Flatbush, were on their first date and had attended a movie before stopping near Dyker Beach Park on a lane known as a local trysting place.

They did not see the gunman approach, but witnesses, including a man who watched it all through the rear-view mirror of his car, said the assailant crouched, aimed with both hands and fired four shots through the open window on the passenger side.

Each victim was shot in the head, Mr. Violante once and Miss Moskowitz twice. Mr. Violante sounded his car horn to attract help and witnesses said he staggered out, screaming: "Help me! Don't let me die!" The assailant, meantime, was said to have walked away calmly, across a street and into the park, vanishing near the spot where he had appeared.

A police contingency plan dubbed Code 44 was put into effect immediately after the shooting was reported. Police patrols saturated the Bath Beach area and halted lone male motorists, but the effort proved futile.

The victims were taken to Coney Island Hospital and then transferred to Kings County Hospital Center where both underwent extensive operations.

Doctors later said that Miss Moskowitz had suffered brain damage from a bullet that passed through her head and lodged in her neck, and they listed her chances of survival at 50 percent. Mr. Violante's survival chances were said to be better, but a bullet that passed through his head destroyed his left eye and damaged his right eye, his doctors said.

One bullet fired in the attack had lodged in the car's steering column, but the fragment was too badly mangled for ballistics experts to say definitely that it had come from the .44-caliber killer's gun. Not until surgeons removed a nearly whole bullet from Miss Moskowitz's neck could the police conclusively state that the "Son of Sam" had struck again.

But even before that bullet was analyzed, Chief of Detectives John F. Keenan and other police officials had said they were nearly certain that the attack had been mounted by the psychopath, who has become the object of one of the biggest manhunts in the city's history.

The pattern of the crime seemed to fit—a gun assault in the early morning hours of a weekend on a young woman with long hair seated in a car with a friend. Specifically, the number of shots fired seemed to fit—"Son of Sam" had, in each of his seven previous assaults, fired four shots from his five-round, .44-caliber Charter Arms Bulldog revolver.

Assailant Fits Description

The description of the assailant also seemed to fit—a man in his 20s, of medium build and dressed in dungarees and a gray shirt with the sleeves rolled up.

In his previous assault, on June 26, the killer shot and wounded another couple sitting in a parked car in Bayside, Queens, after they had left a nearby discotheque. Despite the efforts of a special task force of 70 detectives who have worked on the case full time since April, the police have conceded mounting frustrations and a dearth of leads.

Expectations that the killer would strike again ran high on Friday, the anniversary of the July 29, 1976, killing of 18-year-old Donna Lauria, his first victim, as she sat with a girlfriend in a car in the Bronx.

In one of two taunting notes written in recent months—one to the police and one to Jimmy Breslin, the columnist—the killer asked: "What will you have for July 29? You must not forget Donna Lauria. . . . She was a very very sweet girl, but Sam's a thirsty lad and he won't let me stop killing until he gets his fill of blood." Amid mounting tensions in the city, many women pinned up their long hair or passed up offers of weekend dates in town, and the police mobilized hundreds of officers in plainclothes for street patrols, and decoy operations focused heavily in areas where the killer had struck before.

The date that was to end in tragedy began, according to the police, with a movie in Brooklyn.

Mr. Violante's father, Pasquale, said that he had warned his son before the date about the danger of the killer on the loose. "I told him to stay out of Queens," he said in an interview at Kings County Medical Center. "'O.K., dad,' he quoted his son as having said. "'I'll hang around in Brooklyn.'"

The police said it was uncertain what time the couple had parked at Shore Parkway and Bay 14th Street in Mr. Violante's brown 1968 Buick. They stopped under a streetlight, and there were other parked cars with couples in the area, a quiet spot with little traffic right off the busy Belt Parkway. A chain-link fence separated the parked couple from a view of Gravesend Bay and the necklace of bridge lights arcing across the Narrows of New York Harbor from Fort Hamilton in Brooklyn to Staten Island.

Miss Moskowitz was shot twice, doctors said later. One bullet grazed the top of her scalp and apparently did not inflict a serious wound. The second crashed into the back of her skull, passed through a portion of her brain and lodged in the back of her neck.

Mr. Violante was struck once by a bullet that entered just behind his left eye, passed above the bridge of the nose and exited above the right eye. The bullet shattered his left eye and inflicted some damage to the right eye.

At Kings County Medical Center, Dr. Jeffrey Freedman, a surgeon who operated on Mr. Violante, declined to offer a prognosis for the right eye, but described Mr. Violante's condition as "very stable." After an eight-hour operation, during which the bullet in Miss Moskowitz's neck was removed along with bone fragments from the brain, her condition was listed as critical.

"Paranoid, Neurotic, Schizoid"

After the assailant's escape, which was described by witnesses as an almost casual retreat, the police yesterday appeared to be no closer to the identity of the gunman, whom they have called a "paranoid, neurotic, schizoid," and who seems to hate women.

At police headquarters in New York on August 6, 1977, detectives view a composite sketch of the .44 caliber killer, part of a videotape describing the killer and his methods. The tape was played in all 73 precinct houses.

Chief Keenan noted at a news conference that "the witnesses have been very poor, physical evidence is scant and we have no motive."

A number of bullet fragments, apparently from the slugs that struck the victims with full force, were found in Mr. Violante's car. One bullet, believed to be the one that had grazed Miss Moskowitz's scalp, was found lodged and mangled in the steering column and was of little use to ballistics experts the police said.

List of Killer's Victims

Following is a list of the victims of the killer who calls himself "Son of Sam."

1. Donna Lauria, 18, of the Westchester Heights section of the Bronx, was shot and killed about 1 a.m. on July 29, 1976, while sitting in a parked car outside her home. Jody Valenti, 19, of Hutchinson River Parkway, was wounded in the left thigh as she sat in the car with Miss Lauria.

2. Carl Denaro, 20, was wounded in the head Oct. 23 as he sat in a parked car with Rosemary Keenan on 160th Street in Flushing, Queens. The injury required doctors to place a steel plate in his skull. Miss Keenan was uninjured.

3. Joanne Lomino, 18, of Bellerose, Queens, was shot in the back of the head at 12:40 a.m. on Nov. 27, 1976, while sitting on the porch of her home with a friend. She is now paralyzed from the waist down. Donna DiMasi, 17, of Floral Park, Queens, was shot through the neck Nov. 27, 1976 while sitting on the porch with Miss Lomino.

4. Christine Freund, 26, of Ridgewood, Queens, was shot to death at 12:30 a.m. last Jan. 30, as she sat in a parked car near the Long Island Rail Road station in Forest Hills, Queens. With her, and unhurt, was John Diel, 30.

5. Virginia Voskerichian, 19, of Forest Hills, Queens, was shot to death at about 7:30 p.m. last March 8 as she walked on Dartmouth Street on her way home from college. She was slain a half block from where Miss Freund was killed five weeks earlier.

6. Valentina Suriani, 18, of Baychester, the Bronx, and Alexander Esau, of West 46th Street, were shot to death at 3 a.m. last April 17 as they sat in a parked car on Hutchinson River Parkway, near Miss Suriani's home.

7. Judy Placido, 17, of the Pelham Bay section of the Bronx, was shot in the right temple, right shoulder and back of the neck as she sat in a parked car with Salvatore Lupo at 3:20 a.m. on June 26, 1977, in Bayside, Queens. Mr. Lupo, of Maspeth, Queens, was wounded in the right forearm.

8. Robert Violante, 20, of the Bensonhurst section of Brooklyn, was shot in the head at 2:50 a.m. yesterday as he sat in a parked car with Stacy Moskowitz in a lovers' lane area near Dyker Beach Park in the Bath Beach section of Brooklyn. Mr. Violante was critically wounded. Miss Moskowitz, 20, of the Flatbush section of Brooklyn, was shot once in the head and also was critically wounded.

—*August 1, 1977*

THE SUSPECT IS QUOTED ON KILLINGS: "IT WAS A COMMAND ... I HAD A SIGN"

By HOWARD BLUM

"**F**or more than a year I had been hoping for just one thing—a chance to talk to the 'Son of Sam,' a chance to ask him why," said Det. Gerald Shevlin. He was part of the special homicide task force that had conducted the search for the .44-caliber killer, the largest manhunt in New York's history.

Just after 3 o'clock yesterday morning, Det. Shevlin had his chance.

Ten detectives who had been assigned to the task force headed by Inspector Timothy Dowd since its formation after the .44-caliber killer claimed his fourth and fifth murder victims in April, crowded into Room 1312 in police headquarters and for a half hour "fired every question we could think of" at the 24-year-old suspect, David Berkowitz of Yonkers.

> *"He was talkative and calm and answered whatever we asked."*

"From the beginning I had just wanted 10 minutes with him in a motel room so I could find out about the guy I had been hunting for six months," Det. Shevlin said. "Room 1312 became our motel room. We went in there and wrapped up all the loose ends."

"Berkowitz was very cooperative," said Sgt. Joseph Coffey who, with Sgt. Richard Conlon, was directing the questioning. "He was talkative and calm and answered whatever we asked."

"It Was a Command"

But as task-force members formed a semicircle around the suspect seated in the chief of detectives' office, an orderly interrogation was abandoned as detectives sought answers to questions they had been pondering for more than a year.

"Why? Why did you kill them?" a detective asked the suspect.

"It was a command," a detective reported Mr. Berkowitz as responding. "I had a sign and I followed it. Sam told me what to do and I did it."

Sam, the 24-year-old postal worker explained in a passive voice, is Sam Carr, a neighbor in Yonkers, "who really is a man who lived 6,000 years ago."

"I got the messages through his dog," Mr. Berkowitz said. "He told me to kill. Sam is the devil." Mr. Carr is a neighbor whose dog Mr. Berkowitz is accused of having shot.

At this point, some of the detectives expressed doubt that they were questioning the right man.

"But," said a detective, "when we asked him about the letter he left after the murder of Valentina Suriani, he knew things that only Sam could have known."

The suspect was asked how the letter was signed.

"The Monster," he responded.

"What did you call yourself in the note?"

"The Chubby Behemoth."

"Did you say anything about Queens?"

"I wrote that Queens girls are prettier."

Hours later, Inspector Dowd, the commander of the task force, explained the questioning on the letter as detectives gathered around a desk turned into a bar in the chief of detectives' office:

"It's because we always knew tonight would come that I never released the first letter to the press," he said.

David Berkowitz, aka "Son of Sam," being taken into police custody in New York, August 11, 1977.

Earlier, the detectives had Mr. Berkowitz reconstruct each of the .44-caliber killer's eight attacks.

The suspect, according to officers at the interrogation, said he was "out driving every night since last July [1976] looking for a sign to kill."

"The situation would be perfect," the suspect was quoted as having said. "I would find a parking place for my car right away. It was things like that which convinced me it was commanded."

Mr. Berkowitz, who said a "'buddy in Houston" had bought the gun for him, reportedly told the police he had the Charter Arms Bulldog revolver, the .44-caliber weapon the police say was used as the murder weapon, "for about a month" before the first shooting.

As the suspect detailed the attacks, the police learned that many of the theories—and even a few aspects of the investigation that they had accepted as facts—were unsubstantiated. According to detectives, Mr. Berkowitz made the following statements:

- He fired one-handed for the first three attacks, not in the two-hand combat-style position, as the police believed.
- At least twice he fired five times, emptying the .44-caliber revolver. He did not keep one bullet in the chamber, as the police believed.
- He never went inside a discotheque.
- He never wore a wig.
- The attacks were random, his targets always the young girls.
- He insisted he was never jilted by a girlfriend. His only explanation for the attacks was that "they were commanded."

Never Shot through Bag

Speaking in terse sentences, the suspect explained how he always parked about a block and a half away from the scene of each attack "and then ran like hell to my car."

He said he had kept his revolver in a plastic bag, but never shot through it as police had theorized.

Why did he carry his gun in a plastic bag?

"I don't believe in holsters," the police quoted Mr. Berkowitz as stating with a smirk.

The constant hurling of questions at the suspect was interrupted, however, as Mr. Berkowitz explained what he had planned to do on the night when he was captured.

"I was going out to kill in the Bronx," he allegedly explained. "I was going to look in Riverdale."

And then Mr. Berkowitz for the first time posed a question: "Do you know why I had a machine gun with me tonight?"

"I'll tell you," he said: "I wanted to get into a shootout. I wanted to get killed, but I wanted to take some cops with me."

Mr. Berkowitz also told the police how he had visited the sites where he had murdered Donna Lauria, in the Bronx on July 29, 1976, and Christine Freund last Jan. 30 in Forest Hills, Queens, a couple of times after the shootings.

Sought Victim's Grave

He also went, the detectives related, to St. Raymond's Cemetery to visit the grave of Miss Lauria, his first victim.

"But," he said, "the grave was impossible to find."

Why did he want to go to the grave?

"I felt like it," Mr. Berkowitz allegedly responded.

"He also told us that the length of hair, the color—all that had nothing to do with his picking out victims," said, a detective.

In fact, Stacy Moskowitz, the last victim, was not even his target that night, the police reported.

"He had planned to get the girl Tommy Z. was sitting with," the detective continued, referring to the young man who had witnessed the murder of Miss Moskowitz through his rearview mirror. "But when Tommy Z. moved his car into a darker spot, Berkowitz told us he changed his target."

Another detective added that Robert Violante, the young man who was seriously wounded when Miss Moskowitz was shot on July 31 in the Bath Beach section of Brooklyn, had told the police about a man who had been sitting on the swings for nearly an hour in the park near when the couple's car was parked.

"It was while we were questioning Berkowitz that we realized he was the guy on the swings," the detective explained. "Robert Violante had been staring at the guy who was going to shoot him all night, except he didn't know it."

The suspect also answered questions about specific attacks.

Why, he was asked, had he murdered Virginia Voskerichian as she walked home alone from the subway on a Tuesday night? She did not fit into the .44-caliber killer's pattern.

"It was commanded," the suspect allegedly replied.

Asked if he had any remorse," he reportedly said, "No, why should I?"

—August 12, 1977

NOTE: *Berkowitz, a 24-year-old postal clerk who said he heard voices that commanded him to kill, confessed to six murders and pleaded guilty. He is serving six consecutive 25-years-to-life sentences in a New York State prison.*

SUSPECT IN MASS DEATHS IS PUZZLE TO ALL

By DOUGLAS E. KNEELAND

In the clean, well-lighted world of middle-class America, the hardworking, outgoing, community-spirited man next door is not supposed to be the suspect in the worst instance of mass killings in the United States in this century.

But John Wayne Gacy is that.

Tomorrow, Mr. Gacy, a short, round, 36-year-old remodeling contractor, is scheduled to appear in a Cook County, Chicago, courtroom for arraignment in a case that may ultimately involve the deaths of at least 32 young men over several years. A grand jury has indicted him in seven murders, and the prosecutors are seeking further indictments as more of the 29 bodies recovered so far are identified.

But who is John Wayne Gacy?

Affable, Driven Businessman

Is he the affable businessman, driven, often boastful, but as eager to please as puppy? The clown, Pogo, who entertained children at picnics and parties? The outgoing man most neighbors, friends and family members knew here, in Springfield, Ill., and in Waterloo, Iowa?

Or is he the night wanderer portrayed by investigators, a man who cruised the homosexual scene's meanest streets in his black Oldsmobile with police-like spotlights, picking up young male prostitutes or other willing partners? The man who lured youngsters into his contracting business, brutalized them sexually and killed them? The unreformed former convict who served 18 months in an Iowa reformatory after he was convicted in 1968 of having engaged a Waterloo teenager in sodomy?

Or is he both?

A close look at his past does not provide easy answers as to why and how John Gacy became the prime suspect in the bizarre sex murders. Most people who knew him will not discuss him, and those who will seem confused by the charges against him. But a look at Mr. Gacy's life does provide a picture, puzzling, perhaps even troubling, in its contradictions, of the man who sits quietly in the hospital wing of the Cook County jail awaiting tomorrow's proceedings.

John Wayne Gacy was born in Edgewater Hospital here in Chicago on March 17, 1942. His parents were John and Marian Gacy, both factory workers, and he grew up with his sisters, one older and one younger, in a working-class neighborhood on the northwest side. His father died nine years ago and his mother, who is 71, lives with his younger sister in Arkansas. The elder sister lives in Chicago. All three family members have desperately sought anonymity. But his younger sister, an articulate, sandy-haired mother of three, agreed to an interview if her identity was not disclosed.

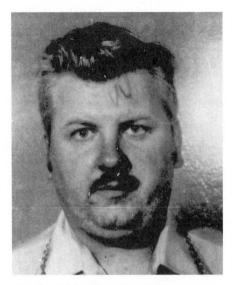

Mug shot of John Wayne Gacy, 1978.

"Just a Normal Person"

"He was a normal person like everyone else," she said, "just a normal person. My mother just can't believe it. All she does is cry. I hope people know we're being torn apart by this."

The only unusual thing that she could recall about her brother's younger years, she said, was that he occasionally had blackouts. The problem, she continued, was diagnosed when he was 16 as a blood clot on the brain thought to have resulted from an earlier playground accident.

John Gacy went to Cooley Vocational High School, where he took business courses, his sister said. After a year, he transferred to Prosser Vocational High School, then dropped out after a few months. Later, he attended Northwestern Business College of Chicago.

Visited Once or Twice Yearly

Mr. Gacy's sister said that he had always been the sort of brother and son who could not do enough for his family, who stayed in close touch by telephone and who visited once or twice a year.

The family knew of his sodomy conviction in Iowa, she said, but considered it "an incident in his life that he paid for."

Turning to happier memories, such as her brother's penchant for playing Pogo in clown costumes he had designed for himself, she said that he had always enjoyed entertaining children.

In 1964, shortly before he turned 22, Mr. Gacy, who had been hired by a local shoe company here, was transferred to Springfield as manager of the concern's retail outlet.

Married Springfield Co-Worker

There he met Marlynn Myers, who also worked at the store. They were married nine months later and moved into the home left behind by his wife's parents, who had purchased a string of fried chicken franchises in Waterloo.

In Springfield, Mr. Gacy plunged furiously into his job and into community life, joining the Jaycees, a service club. "He was a very bright person, energetic and never displayed any abnormal signs," recalled Ed McCreight, who worked with Mr. Gacy in the Springfield Jaycees.

Mr. Gacy's former father-in-law, Fred W. Myers, sold his chicken franchises in Waterloo a year and a half ago and moved back to Springfield. Speaking through the door of his home, open a crack, Mr. Myers said, "I can't understand why they would have let him out of prison in Iowa."

> *"He was a very bright person, energetic and never displayed any abnormal signs."*

In 1966, the Gacys moved to Waterloo, where he helped Mr. Myers manage the fast-food outlets. Mr. Gacy again threw himself into Jaycees' activities. In 1967, he was vice president of the Waterloo Jaycees, chaplain of the chapter and chairman of its prayer breakfast.

"A Real Go-Getter"

"He was a real go-getter," said Charles Hill, manager of a Waterloo motel and a friend of Mr. Gacy. "He did a good job and was an excellent Jaycee."

Others were less receptive to Mr. Gacy's outgoing ways.

"He was a glad-hander type who would go beyond that," said Tom Langlas, a lawyer who knew Mr. Gacy through the Jaycees. "He'd shower too much attention on you as a way of getting more attention himself."

And Peter Burk, a lawyer who opposed Mr. Gacy in 1968 for the local Jaycees presidency, which he subsequently won after Mr. Gacy was charged in the sodomy case, said: "He was not a man tempered by truth. He seemed unaffected when caught in lies."

In May 1968, two teenage boys told a Black Hawk County grand jury that Mr. Gacy had forced them to commit sexual acts with him.

Youth Said Gacy Chained Him

According to the grand jury records, one of the youths said that Mr. Gacy had chained him and had begun choking him, but that when he stopped resisting his assailant loosened the chains and let him leave.

He was indicted, convicted and sentenced, in December 1968, to 10 years at the state reformatory at Anamosa.

While he was in the reformatory, on Sept. 18, 1969, his wife, Marlynn, was granted a divorce on the grounds of cruel and inhuman treatment and was given custody of their children.

Now remarried, she was reticent about discussing her past with Mr. Gacy, but agreed to an interview if her new name was not divulged.

"I just couldn't believe it," she said. "I never had any fear of him. It's hard for me to relate to these killings. I was never afraid of him."

No Signs of Homosexuality

She said that she had "problems believing that he was homosexual" at the time of the Iowa sodomy indictment. She said nothing in their married life had indicated that. She added that he had never been violent and that he had been a good father.

At the reformatory in Anamosa, Mr. Gacy is remembered as a model prisoner who headed the Jaycees chapter, worked in the kitchen and was paroled after 18 months.

"He had no particular problem during his stay," said Warden Calvin Auger. "His adjustment was exceptionally good. He was a good worker, a willing worker with only one minor disciplinary thing on his record, just a hassle with another resident with nobody injured."

In Des Moines, Donald L. Olson, executive secretary of the Iowa State Board of Parole, which released Mr. Gacy from prison on June 18, 1970, said that the contents of Mr. Gacy's file were privileged.

"There are psychiatric reports," he added. "But I can tell you this: If there were any red flags, he wouldn't have been paroled."

When Mr. Gacy left the reformatory, he returned to Chicago, where he worked at a restaurant and lived with his mother. After four months in an apartment on the northwest side, he is reported to have borrowed money from his mother to buy his house in Norwood Park Township.

Later, he started his own business, P.D.M. (for painting, decorating and maintenance) Contractors, which he operated out of his home. He specialized in remodeling work at retail stores and subcontracted work on larger construction projects.

Youths Said They Rebuffed Him

Over the years, he hired a succession of youths to work with him. The bodies of two have been identified from among those discovered at his home. Since his arrest, others who worked for him have said that he made sexual overtures toward them, but that they had rebuffed him and he had laughed the matter off.

Meanwhile, the Chicago police have acknowledged that they staked out Mr. Gacy's home for two weeks in January 1976, when a nine-year-old boy was missing. The police said they questioned a number of young men going in and out of the Gacy home, but none would say anything against him.

No Links Found to Gacy

The police also investigated, in 1975 and in 1976, the separate disappearances of the two youths who had worked for him, but did not turn up anything linking Mr. Gacy to them.

On Dec. 31, 1977, a 19-year-old man charged that Mr. Gacy had kidnapped him at gunpoint and forced him to commit sexual acts, but no criminal charges were filed, according to the police records. The officials said that Mr. Gacy had acknowledged the acts, but had said the man was a willing participant who later tried to blackmail him.

Last March, another young man accused Mr. Gacy of having abducted, chloroformed and raped him. A misdemeanor charge of battery is still pending.

"When these things come up, people say the police should have come up with a pattern," said David M. Mozee, a spokesman for the police, "but we have a good conscience. We questioned Gacy, we followed Gacy, but we found nothing wrong. We knew of the conviction in Iowa, but that doesn't make him a mass killer."

All the while, to his neighbors in Norwood Park Township, he was just the man next door, a trustee of the township's street lighting district, a Democratic precinct captain, a fun-loving person who gave parties for as many as 400 friends and then shared the leftover liquor and food with those who lived nearby.

In June 1972, Mr. Gacy married Carole Hoff, a divorced woman with two daughters.

Then one time, she said, she found several wallets apparently belonging to teenage boys in his car. He exploded in anger.

"He would throw furniture," she said. "He broke a lot of my furniture. I think now, if there were murders, some must have taken place when I was in that house."

The couple was divorced March 2, 1976.

She has said recently on television that he was sexually dysfunctional with women.

Even when he was being followed openly by the Des Plaines police shortly before he was arrested and charged with murder, Mr. Gacy's neighbors could not believe what was happening.

Sam and Jennie DeLaurentis, who lived across the street, recalled that they had asked him why the police cars were following him all the time. They said he told them that the police were "trying to pin a murder rap on me." They said he laughed and they laughed.

That was before the police found evidence at Mr. Gacy's home that Robert Piest, a 15-year-old who disappeared after going to see him on Dec. 11 about a summer job, had been there. The contractor is reported to have told the authorities that he threw the youth's body into the Des Plaines River.

Since they began digging three days before Christmas, Cook County sheriff's investigators have dug up 27 decomposed bodies from under Mr. Gacy's garage and three-bedroom ranch house.

The authorities have said that Mr. Gacy has told them that he killed 32 youths after having sexual relations with them, burying 27 at this home and throwing the bodies of five into the Des Plaines River.

Two bodies have been recovered from the river, making the 29 linked to the case so far the largest number of victims attributed to a murder suspect in the United States in this century.

—January 10, 1979

NOTE: *Gacy was convicted of killing 33 young men, many of whom he buried in his home. He was executed in 1994 by lethal injection.*

BUNDY IS PUT TO DEATH IN FLORIDA AFTER ADMITTING TRAIL OF KILLINGS

By JON NORDHEIMER

Theodore Bundy, among the most notorious killers in recent times, was electrocuted today, and about 200 people gathered outside the entrance of the Florida State Prison cheered when they heard the news.

He went quietly to his death nearly 15 years after he embarked on a trail of murder that investigators believe took the lives of 30 or more young women across the nation.

"Give my love to my family and friends," the former law student told his lawyer and a minister as guards strapped him into the wooden chair in an execution chamber separated from two-dozen official witnesses by a large glass window.

He was pronounced dead at 7:16 a.m. after 2,000 volts of electricity surged through his body for one minute, prison officials said.

Outside the prison gates, the crowd cheered and whooped when a signal came from the floodlit cellblock 400 yards away, where the execution took place, that Mr. Bundy was dead.

A few opponents of capital punishment were lost in the crowd that had come in the predawn chill of northern Florida's piney woods to applaud the death of a man whose "boy-next-door" good looks and intelligence concealed the impulses that led him to hunt down women and murder them.

> *"Some of us have waited 11 years for this moment."*

"Thought He Was So Clever"

"This is a big deal," said Carey Harper, 26, of nearby Gainesville. "Some of us have waited 11 years for this moment."

His companion, Jeannine Gordon, 21, expressed a widely held view that reviled not only Mr. Bundy's murderous acts but also his personal demeanor. "He thought he was so clever, so smart, that he could get away with his crimes," she said. The execution came on the fourth death warrant signed by a Florida governor. Three of them were issued in 1986, only to be stayed while his appeals were heard in the courts.

The final warrant was for the 1978 murder of Kimberly Leach, a 12-year-old Lake City, Fla., girl who was abducted, mutilated and slain, and whose body was dumped in an abandoned animal pen. He was convicted in 1980 of her killing, a year after he had been found guilty of murdering two Florida State University students who were bludgeoned and strangled as they slept in their beds in a sorority house in Tallahassee three weeks before Kimberly Leach was killed.

Spurt of Confessions

The condemned man spent the last few days confessing at least 16 other killings to police detectives who had come here from the states of Washington, Utah, Idaho and Colorado in an attempt to clear up numerous murder investigations before Mr. Bundy was silenced by his date with the executioner. Some of the confessions were made in killings with which the authorities had not connected him, and federal and state officials still link him to a dozen or more similar crimes since his spree began in February 1974, in Seattle.

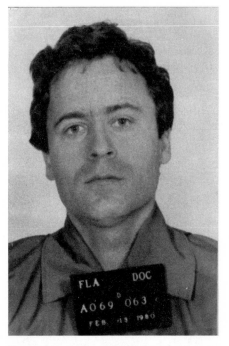

Florida Department of Corrections mug shot of Ted Bundy, February 13, 1980.

Over the years he maintained his innocence, saying he had been drawn into a web of circumstantial evidence woven by "conniving investigators."

Finally running out of appeals that would be heard by the federal courts, his confidence apparently crumbled. Described as "visibly shaken," he supplied the detectives with the names of victims in four western states and the dates he killed them.

By the time he entered the death chamber shortly before 7 o'clock this morning, he appeared tense but composed, apparently resigned to his fate, according to the witnesses.

One of these, Jerry Blair, was the state prosecutor in the Leach murder trial. Mr. Bundy nodded to him in recognition as he was being strapped into the chair. "I think he was trying to say there were no hard feelings," Mr. Blair said later. But Mr. Blair and a host of others who had worked on the Bundy crimes over the years, conceded they were no closer now to the central mystery of what had turned a handsome, articulate, urbane young man into one of the most savage and unpredictable killers in the nation's history.

"Killed for the Sheer Thrill"

"Ted Bundy was a complex man who somewhere along the line went wrong," Mr. Blair said. "He killed for the sheer thrill of the act and the challenge of escaping his pursuers. He probably could have done anything in life he set his mind to do, but something happened to him and we still don't know what it was."

The killer, who stalked victims in the Pacific Northwest in the mid-1970s, terrorized several university communities, selecting coeds for abduction from campuses at night or crowded parks in daytime when their defenses were lowered in familiar settings. Accounts of witnesses and other evidence show that he typically used his good looks and soft-spoken charm to lure them to their death.

He usually throttled them and then sexually abused and mutilated them before disposing of their bodies in remote areas. If the skeletons were found months or years later there was nearly always evidence of fractured skulls and broken jaws and limbs.

"This kind of mutilation reveals a hatred of the female body," said Dr. David Abrahamsen a New York psychiatrist who is an authority on those who kill people in a series and is author of *The Murdering Mind*.

"The victim is not really the target," he said. "The victim is a substitute, and that is why these crimes seem so random and capricious."

Dr. Abrahamsen theorized that when a man commits a violent sexual crime against an unknown woman, the real motive is rooted in acting out "strong and repeated fantasies of revenge and power" subconsciously directed at his mother.

Mr. Bundy previously hinted that alcohol played a role in his mood swings. On Monday he tearfully told James Dobson, a psychologist and religious broadcaster who served on a federal pornography commission, that hard-core pornography became an obsession and drove him to act out his fantasies in murder.

Boy Scout and B-Plus Student

Theodore Robert Bundy was born to a young, single Philadelphia woman who raised him in Tacoma, Wash. But his mother, Louise Bundy, said there was never a shred of evidence in her son's first 28 years, before he became a murder suspect for the first time, to hint at any aberrant behavior.

People familiar with his early years say he was a Boy Scout, a B-plus college student; he loved children, read poetry and was a rising figure in Republican politics in Seattle. The year the murders began there he was the assistant director of the Seattle Crime Prevention Advisory Commission and wrote a pamphlet for women on rape prevention.

"If anyone considers me a monster, that's just something they'll have to confront in themselves," he said in a 1986 interview with *The New York Times*. "For people to want to condemn someone, to dehumanize someone like me is a very popular and effective, understandable way of dealing with a fear and a threat that is incomprehensible."

—January 25, 1989

JEFFREY DAHMER, MULTIPLE KILLER, IS BLUDGEONED TO DEATH IN PRISON

By DON TERRY

Jeffrey L. Dahmer, whose gruesome exploits of murder, necrophilia and dismemberment shocked the world in 1991, was attacked and killed today in a Wisconsin prison, where he was serving 15 consecutive life terms.

Mr. Dahmer was 34, older than any of his victims, who ranged in age from 14 to 33. He died of massive head injuries, suffered sometime between 7:50 and 8:10 a.m., when he was found in a pool of blood in a toilet area next to the prison's gym, said Michael Sullivan, secretary of the Wisconsin Department of Corrections.

A bloodied broomstick was found nearby, and a fellow inmate who is serving a life sentence for murder, Christopher J. Scarver, 25, of Milwaukee, is the prime suspect, the authorities said.

E. Michael McCann, the Milwaukee County district attorney, who sent Mr. Dahmer to prison in 1992, said, "This is the last sad chapter in a very sad life."

"Tragically," Mr. McCann said, "his parents will have to experience the same loss the families of his victims have experienced."

A third inmate, Jesse Anderson, himself a notorious figure in the history of Milwaukee crime and race, was critically injured in the attack.

Mr. Sullivan would not comment on a possible motive for the beatings. Mr. Scarver, who is black, was convicted in 1992 of murdering Steve Lohman, who was shot in the head at the Milwaukee office of the Wisconsin Conservation Corps, where he worked, officials said. Mr. Scarver is not eligible for parole until 2042.

But both Mr. Dahmer, whose victims were mostly black, Hispanic and Asian men and boys, and Mr. Anderson, a white man who killed his wife and blamed it on two black men, had badly shaken Milwaukee's racial peace.

Mr. Dahmer and the two other inmates had been assigned to clean the toilets and the showers near the gym and had arrived there under guard at 7:50 a.m. Then the inmates were apparently left unattended for up to 20 minutes.

"They followed procedures," Mr. Sullivan said of the guards. "There was no irregular gap in supervision."

The three inmates, all convicted murderers, had been on the routine work detail together for three weeks without incident—until today. At 8:10 a.m., a guard returned to find Mr. Dahmer bleeding on the floor. The guard sounded the alarm and then found Mr. Anderson several rooms away in the shower area.

When Mr. Dahmer arrived at the prison, the Columbia Correctional Institute in Portage, about 40 miles north of Madison, his safety was a major concern.

The blond former chocolate-factory worker was the most prolific killer in the state's history, so, the authorities feared, killing him might earn a convict an honored place in the prison world, especially for someone with a long sentence and with little to lose.

Mr. Dahmer's first year in prison had been spent in protective isolation, away from the general inmate population. But in the last year, Mr. Dahmer and the prison authorities had deemed it safe for him to be integrated into the general population of 622 inmates.

Last July, however, an inmate tried to slash Mr. Dahmer's throat with a plastic homemade knife during a chapel service. Mr. Dahmer was not injured and it was determined that the attack was an isolated incident.

"He never told me he was afraid," said Stephen Eisenberg, a lawyer representing Mr. Dahmer in several civil suits filed by the families of his victims. Mr. Dahmer confessed to 17 killings, 16 in Wisconsin and one, his first, he said, in his hometown of Bath Township, Ohio, a suburb of Akron. He pleaded guilty and was convicted of 15 killings in Wisconsin. Prosecutors said there was not enough evidence to charge Mr. Dahmer with the 16th slaying.

> *"There was no irregular gap in supervision."*

Mr. Dahmer also pleaded guilty to the Ohio slaying of a young hitchhiker, Steven Hicks, in his parent's home in 1978.

Mr. Dahmer met most of his victims at bus stops, bars, malls and adult bookstores in Chicago and Milwaukee. He then lured them to his apartment in a hard-pressed section of Milwaukee with promises of beer or money in exchange for posing for nude photographs. Then he would drug their drinks, strangle and stab them while they were unconscious. He ate part of the arm of at least one man and stored the remains, including the hearts, of several others in his refrigerator.

Mr. Dahmer told investigators he killed to ward off loneliness. "I didn't want them to leave," he said.

Mr. Dahmer was almost caught in May 1991 when a 14-year-old Laotian boy, Konerak Sinthasomphone, stumbled into the street bleeding when Mr. Dahmer left the apartment for a six-pack of beer. Two Milwaukee police officers ignored the pleas of a woman who said the boy was in trouble, and allowed Mr. Dahmer to take him back into his apartment, apparently believing Mr. Dahmer's story that he and the boy were lovers after a spat.

Mr. Dahmer later told investigators that shortly after he got the boy back into his apartment, he killed him. After the Dahmer case broke, the two officers who found the boy bleeding were dismissed, but they won reinstatement last April after a lengthy court battle. One has since left the department.

Mr. Dahmer was finally arrested after another intended victim broke free and ran into the street with a handcuff dangling from his wrist.

While Mr. Dahmer is now dead, the legal battle over his estate remains alive. Several families of his victims sued him and were awarded millions of dollars. Ever since, they have been trying to gain control of the contents of his Milwaukee apartment, where he killed most of his victims.

The families want to auction off some 312 items, including a 55-gallon vat he used to decompose the bodies, the refrigerator where he stored hearts, a saw, a hammer and his toothbrush. Tom Jacobson, the lawyer for the families, said the auction could bring more than $100,000.

Rita Isbell, the sister of one of Mr. Dahmer's last victims, Errol Lindsey, 19, said she always knew that this day would come sooner or later. For the past two years, she said, she has been getting telephone calls from men identifying themselves as prison inmates, offering condolences and promises that Mr. Dahmer would be "taken care of." The last call came about six months ago.

"You don't know me," Ms. Isbell quoted the caller as saying. "I'm up here with Jeffrey Dahmer. Don't worry. We'll take care of it.'"

—November 29, 1994

RETRACING A TRAIL: THE SNIPER SUSPECTS; SERIAL KILLING'S SQUAREST PEGS: NOT SOLO, WHITE, PSYCHOSEXUAL OR PICKY

By N. R. KLEINFIELD AND ERICA GOODE

The middle-aged man and the teenager were footloose traveling companions on a fathomless mission of horror. For three weeks, investigators say, they killed—callously, wantonly, ceaselessly, driven by a logic known only to themselves—and thus qualified themselves for inclusion in the macabre fraternity of the serial killer.

When the police captured a slumbering John Allen Muhammad, a 41-year-old army veteran and expert marksman, and John Lee [Lee Boyd] Malvo, a 17-year-old Jamaican citizen, at a highway rest stop early Thursday morning, the authorities declared an end to the sniper shootings that left 10 people dead and millions panic-stricken in the Washington, D.C., suburbs.

If the men are convicted, they will add a highly peculiar chapter to the already saturated history of the multiple killer. If anything is clear in that roll call of malevolence, it is that all serial killers are their own story, with their own idiosyncrasies and twisting plot lines, their own tumble of complexities. The only true common denominator among them is skill at bringing about death.

But as criminologists and academicians try to find the proper context for the sniper suspects, they have been struck by how unconventional the pair appear to be. In many ways, based on the still sketchy information known about them, they seem to defy the broad connections that have been drawn among their criminal predecessors.

"This is certainly out of the realm of what I've seen in the past," said Peter Smerick, a former agent and criminal profiler with the FBI now in private practice with the Academy Group, a forensic science–consulting firm. "Of all the thousands of cases I've analyzed, I haven't seen one exactly like this one."

The Team Killer

The fact that there are two of them sets them apart. Serial killers are usually loners, who strike without accomplices or companions, propelled by their personal demons and objectives.

It is unclear whether both Mr. Muhammad and Mr. Malvo actually killed, but investigators say they traveled together in the three weeks of the shootings.

Several experts estimate that no more than 10 to 28 percent of serial killers are teams, although some of the pairs qualify as among the most infamous of all criminals. The Hillside Strangler, for instance, was actually two cousins, Angelo Buono Jr. and Kenneth Bianchi, who were convicted of kidnapping, raping, torturing and murdering young women in Los Angeles in the late 1970s.

In team killings, according to students of serial killers, one member usually dominates.

"Typically, what you have is a dominant offender who is the driving force and the second individual is usually more subservient," said Gregg McCrary, who for 25 years worked in the FBI's behavioral sciences unit. "Rarely are they real peers."

Mr. Muhammad seemed to hold considerable sway over Mr. Malvo. Though apparently unrelated, Mr. Malvo called Mr. Muhammad father and is said to have adhered to a rigid diet of crackers, honey and vitamin supplements he insisted upon. Even among teams, though, the sniper suspects were unusual because of the 24-year disparity in their ages.

The Race Factor

He would be white. That was the consensus of many experts who furnished educated guesses on the sniper's identity before the arrests. Serial killing, they said, was a white man's game.

Both suspects are black.

There have been few studies of the race and ethnicity of serial killers, but the handful that have been done suggest that black serial killers occur in roughly equal—or even slightly greater—proportion to the number of blacks in the population. These studies estimate that between 13 and 22 percent of American serial killers are black.

But the cases so indelibly imprinted on the public consciousness by Hollywood and book publishing are generally white killers like David Berkowitz, the Son of Sam killer.

Most serial killers, black and white, kill within their race. This was true of Wayne Williams, who killed at least five black children in Atlanta in the 1980s, and Henry Louis Wallace, who killed nine young black women in Charlotte, N.C., between 1992 and 1994. The sniper suspects are particularly atypical in that the police believe they killed whites and blacks.

The Nonspecialist

White. Black. Men. Women. Young. Old. The snipers killed them all. To be a target, one person suggested early on, all it took was a pulse.

Almost always, though, serial killers specialize, and by now the categories of choice are familiar: prostitutes, children, young women, gay men, hitchhikers. But investigators have been unable to establish any links between the sniper victims. Some investigators suspect that the snipers may have been killing by location, that they intentionally chose to focus on the suburban areas outlying Washington, D.C., to attract maximum attention.

"It wasn't the process of killing so much," said Dr. Eric Hickey, a criminologist at California State University at Fresno who studied 399 serial killers, in his speculation about the choice of victims. "It was about eliciting a response from the community."

The Speeded-Up Timeline

The timing was strange.

Most serial killers begin slowly, tentatively, almost testing the waters of death. With success, their confidence builds and they begin to speed up the death count. Generally, though, there are pauses between killings that can last days, weeks or years.

"Serial killers generally start slowly," Dr. Fox said. "Their first kill may be something that is not really planned." For example, Dr. Fox said, a killer might pick up a prostitute and then, without premeditation, kill her. "If they don't like what they've done, they won't do it again," he said. "But sometimes they find they enjoy it."

Mr. McCrary agreed that the serial killers he has studied "start out more cautiously, trying it out, waiting to see what happens."

"They wait and pull back and watch," he said. But as time goes on, he said, "they get more confident. They act more quickly and you get an intensification of the frequency of the crime."

The snipers, the authorities say, turned that protocol on its head. They began with a burst of violence, gunning down six people in just over 24 hours, and then followed that explosion with a series of single killings that slowed in frequency as time passed.

The Childhood

Are serial killers made or born?

Criminologists still know little about what makes these killers kill.

Some experts cite a so-called homicidal triad—fire setting, bed-wetting beyond an appropriate age, and animal torturing—that frequently shows up in the backgrounds of murderers. Other experts say physical or sexual abuse in childhood may be a factor.

Many serial killers interviewed by researchers after they were convicted have described parents who were brutal, neglectful or, at the very least, difficult. Dr. Donald Lunde, a professor emeritus of psychiatry at Stanford University and the author of *Murder and Madness*, interviewed Edmund Kemper, who murdered his mother and a string of college women in Santa Cruz, Calif., in the 1970s. He said Mr. Kemper told him that after killing his mother he put her head on a bookshelf in his apartment and "said all the things to her that he could never say before without her interrupting."

Other specialists in violent crime maintain that the role of child abuse is exaggerated. Some killers appear to have had normal childhoods, while most people with histories of abuse do not kill.

"I'm not saying that child abuse or trauma or even adoption isn't important," Dr. Fox said. "But adolescent and adult experiences are just as important. If it were just childhood, why would it be that so many serial killers are in their 30s or older?"

The Motives

Why kill? Why kill again and again?

The motivation of serial killers is one of the murkier areas of inquiry, and even their own interpretations often prove unsatisfying. Ted Bundy said pornography made him kill, but did it?

Various profilers and researchers try to divide motivations into broad classifications. Dr. Fox settles on five: power and control, profit, revenge, terror, and loyalty.

But he and others find that the most common drive is power and control, usually expressed in sexual fixation. The majority of serial killers, experts said, use their crimes to act out elaborate sexual fantasies, sometimes involving rape or torture. The very process of killing—seeing that look of terror in a victim's eyes, hearing a victim beg for mercy—often elicits a sexual thrill. "Traditionally, that's what it's all about, having a victim at your disposal, holding life and death authority over that person, enjoying inflicting pain and suffering," said Robert K. Ressler, a former FBI agent and expert on serial killers.

Jerry Brudos, who preyed on young women in Oregon in the late 1960s, had a foot fetish and a fascination with women's shoes. According to Dr. Hickey, Mr. Brudos would hack up his victims and store their body parts in a freezer.

It is unclear what motivated the snipers, or whether there was only one motivation, though there have been certain indications that Mr. Muhammad harbored anti-American sentiments. And there was a written demand for $10 million, an unusual request for a serial killer.

Experts say the manner in which the crimes were carried out suggests that the snipers were not sexually motivated. They delivered death from a distance and are not known to have touched any of the victims. The suffering of the victims appears to have held little interest for them, since they apparently left the scenes quickly.

Revenge or anger does occasionally disclose itself in serial killings, and some serial murderers embark on their crimes after experiencing life failures—the dissolution of a marriage, a financial crisis, the loss of a job. Such killers, Mr. Ressler said, are usually devoid of hope and have set upon an irreversible course of self-destruction. "These guys are not thinking, 'I'm going to do this for a couple of weeks and then go back to my family,'" he said. "A person doing this is heading for death. They know there is nowhere to go but to hell."

Mr. Muhammad is known to have gone through two divorces and to have suffered financial setbacks. The two men were believed to be close to destitute. Such circumstances alone, of course, do not bring on murder.

The Catch-Me Killer

Most kill in silence.

As a rule, experts said, serial killers do not want to be lured into a cat-and-mouse game with the police. They are often arrogant. But they want to kill, and while they may relish the idea of outsmarting the police, it is a fringe benefit rather than a goal.

So they deliberately avoid communicating with the rest of the world. For every Keith Hunter Jesperson, the Happy Face Killer who wrote letters to newspapers about his killing women in the Northwest, signing them with a smiling face, or Theodore J. Kaczynski, the Unabomber, who sent letters and offered up his bitter anti-technology manifesto, there are scores upon scores of killers who remain mum about their acts.

The snipers felt the need to talk. They left letters at their sniper perches. They called the police. In one conversation, they even offered up the clue about having committed a murder-robbery in Montgomery, Ala., that set off the chain of events that the police say solved the case.

They behaved as serial killers generally do not behave. They could not shut up. In the end, it was their mouths that got two suspects caught.

—*October 28, 2002*

NOTE: *Muhammad was convicted in several of the killings and was executed by lethal injection in Virginia in 2009. His accomplice, Malvo, was sentenced to six consecutive life sentences, which he is serving in a Virginia penitentiary.*

CHAPTER 9

SEX CRIMES

"No verdict can undo the pain and suffering caused by Mr. Sandusky, but we do hope this judgment helps the victims and their families along their path to healing."

—From a statement released by Penn State University
on June 22, 2012, when Jerry Sandusky,
a former Penn State assistant football coach,
was found guilty of sexually abusing boys

A STAR FILM DIRECTOR. A football coach. Priests. The range of people pursued as sex offenders runs the full gamut. But in so many of the cases the predatory behavior is enabled, not by the threat of a gun, but by the power of leverage, of age, of authority. That power, which feeds on trust, surfaced repeatedly in *The Times* coverage of the child sex-abuse trial of former Penn State football coach Jerry Sandusky and similar charges filed against members of the Boston archdiocese.

OPPOSITE: Jerry Sandusky, right, arrives at the Centre County Courthouse in Bellefonte, Pennsylvania, on August 12, 2016, for an appeals hearing on whether his 2012 conviction for sexually abusing 10 young boys was improper.

POLANSKI GUILTY PLEA ACCEPTED IN SEX CASE

By GRACE LICHTENSTEIN

Roman Polanski, the film director, pleaded guilty today in superior court here in Santa Monica, California, to one felony count of "unlawful sexual intercourse" with a 13-year-old girl.

The plea, entered as a result of plea bargaining, could result in Mr. Polanski's being deported or sentenced to a jail term. It was the least serious of six drugs and sex felony counts handed up by a grand jury after he allegedly seduced the girl last March in the Los Angeles home of Jack Nicholson, the actor.

In accepting the plea, the deputy district attorney, Roger Gunson, said the girl's family was afraid that a trial on the original charges would be traumatic for her. He also suggested that the prospect of extensive news media coverage was a major consideration in choosing not to put the girl on the witness stand.

Roman Polanski entering court in Santa Monica, on August 8, 1977.

A lawyer representing the family read a letter before Judge Laurence J. Rittenband, saying his clients wished the plea to be accepted to spare the "emotional well-being" of the victim. He said the family was "not seeking the incarceration" of Mr. Polanski, only an admission of wrongdoing and a rehabilitation program for the director.

Knew Age of the Girl

Standing in a pinstriped gray double-breasted suit, the 43-year-old director of *Rosemary's Baby* and *Chinatown* replied, when asked what crime he had committed, "I had sexual intercourse with a person not my wife, under the age of 18." He said he knew the girl was 13 at the time.

The crime used to carry a penalty of from 1 to 50 years in prison. But a new sentencing law that went into effect July 1 in California changed that to 16 months to 3 years. The judge may decide which to apply and also can suspend any sentence he pronounces. Before being sentenced, Mr. Polanski was ordered to undergo examination by two court-appointed psychiatrists as an "alleged mentally disordered sex offender." Judge Rittenband said that their report would help determine if the defendant needed treatment or should be committed to a state hospital or mental health facility.

The assistant district attorney also said the judge could recommend that Mr. Polanski, a French citizen, not be deported. Under immigration law, aliens convicted of a crime involving "moral turpitude" and sentenced to confinement of more than one year are to be deported.

Mr. Gunson conceded that the acceptance of the guilty plea to the lesser charge departed from normal procedures used by the district attorney's office. But in a statement, the district attorney, John K. Van de Kamp, said it was being done because "it may achieve substantial justice" yet "provide the victim with the opportunity to grow up in a world where she'll not be known as the young girl with whom Roman Polanski had sexual intercourse."

Lawrence Silver, attorney for the family, said that no money was involved in his clients' decision to urge acceptance of the plea.

The trial was to have begun tomorrow, the eighth anniversary of the murder of Mr. Polanski's pregnant wife, Sharon Tate, and others by the Charles M. Manson cult.

Mr. Polanski was originally charged with rape by use of drugs, furnishing drugs to a minor, lewd and lascivious acts on a child under 14, unlawful sexual intercourse, sodomy and perversion. The first two counts carry penalties of three to five years under the new sentencing law.

According to published crime reports and material disclosed at preliminary hearings, the director allegedly first photographed the San Fernando Valley girl with the permission of her stepmother in February, saying it was for a French magazine.

—August 9, 1977

NOTE: *Polanski fled to Europe on the eve of his sentencing in February 1978, after serving 42 days in jail. In 1996, he settled a lawsuit filed by his victim. He was arrested in Switzerland in 2009 and held under house arrest until 2010, when the Swiss government announced it would not extradite him to the United States. In May 2016, the Polish government said it would revive the extradition effort, but later that year a Polish court said it would not order Polanski's extradition. (Polanski has dual French-Polish citizenship).*

CRIMMINS FOUND GUILTY OF MURDER AS THE JURY ACCEPTS HIS CONFESSION

By E. R. SHIPP

C raig S. Crimmins was found guilty yesterday of murdering a violinist at the Metropolitan Opera House in New York City last July 23. The 22-year-old former stagehand remained impassive when the verdict was announced, but his girlfriend, Mary Ann Fennell, wept loudly. After Mr. Crimmins had been led away, she sobbed and kept repeating: "They're wrong, they're wrong. He didn't do it."

The jury in state supreme court in Manhattan determined that Mr. Crimmins had killed Helen Hagnes, who had been performing in an orchestra for the Berlin Ballet, by pushing her down an airshaft in his flight following his attempt to rape her.

Homicide in the commission of, or flight from, another felony is known as "felony murder." The jurors found that Mr. Crimmins was not guilty of intentionally killing Miss Hagnes, as had been charged in the first count of the indictment against him. Both intentional murder and felony murder are punishable by a maximum of 25 years to life in prison. The minimum sentence is 15 years to life.

Mr. Crimmins will be sentenced July 2 by Acting Justice Richard G. Denzer. The jurors deliberated five and a half hours Wednesday and three and a half hours yesterday. As Mr. Crimmins's mother, Dolores Higgins, waited outside the courtroom, she asked a companion if a jury could decide in a short time "all these years in somebody's life?"

At that moment, a court officer summoned Lawrence Hochheiser, one of the defense attorneys, and Mrs. Higgins and an entourage of relatives followed him inside.

At 2:49 p.m., Mr. Crimmins was brought into the courtroom. Seated behind him, trembling, was Miss Fennell. Mr. Hochheiser then walked over to the railing separating the defense table from the audience and asked the family to try to remain calm "no matter what happens."

When the jury foreman, Christine Overton, announced, "Not guilty," to the intentional murder charge, Mrs. Higgins cried out, "Oh, my God!" Seconds later, however, Miss Overton said that Mr. Crimmins was guilty of felony murder. Once the import of the verdict registered, Miss Fennell began weeping. Mrs. Higgins moved to the seat beside her and tried to comfort her.

Mr. Crimmins was originally charged with attempted rape in addition to murder, but Justice Danzer ruled that there was no proof, independent of an alleged confession, that that crime had actually occurred. Under the law, there must be such corroboration. A confession alone is not considered enough.

For felony murder, however, there must only be independent proof that a murder took place, and the body of Miss Hagnes was sufficient evidence in this case. The jury could then consider the confession in determining whether Mr. Crimmins had killed Miss Hagnes while attempting to flee from another crime. The judge instructed the jurors that if they did not believe the confession, they must acquit Mr. Crimmins of the murder charge.

In returning its verdict, the jury apparently rejected the defense contention that Mr. Crimmins was "entirely innocent," but had been tricked into confessing to the crime by shrewd and experienced detectives who "put words in his mouth."

One juror, Vernon Symmonds, 70, said, "It was the palm print and the confession. We explored the confession. That is why we wanted to see the tape played because we wanted to make sure it was his lips that were moving, saying, 'Yes.' We intended to make sure that the confession came from him."

Mr. Symmonds was referring to a videotape made Aug. 30 showing Mr. Crimmins acknowledging answers he had made earlier in a statement.

Called "Highly Suggestible"

From the beginning of the trial on April 27 through his closing statement to the jury on Monday, Mr. Hochheiser had maintained that Mr. Crimmins had severe learning disabilities, a low intelligence level and was "highly suggestible" to a confession containing questions asked by Detective Gennaro Giorgio and answers he said Mr. Crimmins had given him.

The case began with the disappearance of Miss Hagnes sometime between 9:40 p.m. and 10:19 p.m. at a performance of the Berlin Ballet. Miss Hagnes, 31, had performed with various orchestras in this country and in Europe since her graduation in 1974 from the Juilliard School of Music. She had been married for nearly four years to Janis Mintiks, a sculptor.

At the end of the pas de deux from *Don Quixote* at 9:29, the orchestra left the pit for their break. And, "because she didn't feel well," according to another violinist, Elena Barere, "we went to the women's lounge," one floor beneath the stage level. About 9:40 Miss Hagnes left the lounge, ostensibly to try to speak to Valery Panov, the Soviet émigré dancer and choreographer, about giving work to her husband.

When she failed to return for the final number, a search began which continued throughout the night. At 7:45 a.m., Lawrence Lennon, a maintenance mechanic, went to the sixth-floor roof that contains six large fans that make up part of the building's cooling system.

Noticing a pair of women's shoes, he went downstairs to alert Detectives Giorgio and Patrick Heaney, who returned to the roof with him and with several other police officers. There they spread about the roof and "within minutes," Detective Giorgio said, he heard an outcry from an officer. "I looked down through an opening and observed the body of the victim," he said.

Bound Body Discovered

It was 8:20 a.m. The body was found dangling on a steel ledge midway down a six-story ventilation shaft beneath those roof fans. It was supine and nude, with the arms and legs bound with rope and old rags and with a gag stuffed in the mouth.

That afternoon, police officers found a partial palm print on a pipe on the roof. On Aug. 29, Charles J. Heffernan, an assistant district attorney, thought there was enough information to believe that Mr. Crimmins was the killer.

The police theory, according to testimony by Mr. Heffernan at a pretrial hearing, was that Miss Hagnes "had been abducted and killed by somebody intricately familiar with the Metropolitan Opera House." They had observed that her bindings contained a "particular knotting device or style commonly used by craftsmen and especially by stagehands" at the Met.

Mr. Crimmins had begun working at the Met when he dropped out of Manhattan Vocational High School in 1976. By Aug. 29, according to the state's case, the detectives thought he resembled a police artist's sketch of a suspect.

The palm print from the pipe had been identified as his. They knew that he had disappeared from his assigned post at 9:15 and did not return to work until the next day. They knew from other Met employees that he had not been asleep either behind the main stage or in a lounge as he had said. And they had his admission that he had been on an elevator with Miss Hagnes the night she was slain.

At 11 that night, according to Detective Giorgio, Mr. Crimmins said, "I killed the lady." The detective then took down the stagehand's statement. Each page was signed by Mr. Crimmins.

—June 5, 1981

NOTE: *Crimmins was sentenced to 20 years to life. He remains in custody in a New York State prison.*

DARKNESS BENEATH THE GLITTER: LIFE OF SUSPECT IN PARK SLAYING

By SAMUEL G. FREEDMAN

Both the victim and the suspect in the strangling death Tuesday of an 18-year-old woman moved in the same Manhattan circle of privileged young people, a circle centered on the Upper East Side singles bar where the two spent the hours before the murder, the police and others close to the case say.

For Jennifer Dawn Levin and Robert E. Chambers Jr., life was private schools, fancy apartments, foreign vacations and underage drinking at a preppy hangout called Dorrian's Red Hand. But for Mr. Chambers, it was also unemployment, academic futility and signs of cocaine abuse.

The two had known each other for about two months and dated several times, the police said, before they met early Tuesday morning at Dorrian's Red Hand, at 300 East 84th Street. The owner, Jack Dorrian, said he knew both as regulars.

Arrived Separately, Left Together

Mr. Chambers and Miss Levin each had arrived with a separate group of friends, but they left together at 4:30 a.m., exchanging "boy-girl talk" as they walked toward Central Park, the police said. It was there, the police believe, that she was killed.

Less than two hours later, a passer-by found Miss Levin's body—strangled with her bra and apparently sexually abused, according to the authorities—in the park, just behind the Metropolitan Museum of Art. An autopsy yesterday confirmed that she was strangled. Further tests were to be conducted today.

Early this morning, Mr. Chambers was arraigned on a charge of second-degree murder.

> *Mr. Chambers was arraigned on a charge of second-degree murder.*

The police picked up Mr. Chambers at his East 90th Street apartment Tuesday afternoon and brought him to the Central Park Precinct for questioning. Mr. Chambers had scratches on his face that the police said he sustained in a struggle with Miss Levin.

Mr. Chambers's lawyer, Jack Litman, entered a plea of not guilty at the arraignment early this morning in Manhattan Criminal Court before Judge Richard Lowe 3d.

Mr. Litman told the court that Miss Levin had sought out Mr. Chambers in the bar and that they had had a prior relationship. "But that night she was the one who was the aggressor," he said.

He asked that bail for Mr. Chambers be waived, but Judge Lowe ordered Mr. Chambers remanded to jail.

The charge against Mr. Chambers was presented by Stuart D. Schwartz, an assistant district attorney, who told the court that Miss Levin had bite marks on her face and breast and that Mr. Chambers had "lied to the police to protect himself."

Mr. Schwartz said Mr. Chambers had thought out a story and then changed it when he realized it was not working.

"An Accident?"—"Yes"

Judge Lowe asked the defense attorney, "Are you saying this was an accident?" "Yes, your honor," said Mr. Litman. "At the hands of the defendant?" asked the judge. "Yes, your honor, a tragic accident." During the arraignment, Mr. Chambers wept. His parents sat quietly behind him.

Mr. Litman said Mr. Chambers had been about 100 feet from the body of Miss Levin when the police arrived in the park Tuesday morning. But he said Mr. Chambers left because he was in a state of confusion.

The details of both Mr. Chambers's life and Miss Levin's began to emerge yesterday—details that contradicted Mr. Chambers's golden-boy image and revealed a naiveté beneath Miss Levin's worldly exterior.

Mr. Chambers, in the recollection of friends, possessed charisma and mature good looks rare for a 19-year-old. He stood 6 feet 4 inches tall and was a gifted athlete who had played for three years on the soccer team at York Preparatory School on East 85th Street.

"Nothing less than total success," said the caption beneath Mr. Chambers's photograph in his yearbook.

A Way with Women

Mr. Chambers had a particular way with young women. Mr. Dorrian, the bar owner, said: "He didn't have to chase girls. They chased him."

Mr. Chambers, an only child, lived with his mother in an apartment in a town house

Robert Chambers, left, with his lawyer, Jack T. Litman, on October 2, 1986, a day after being released on bail.

on East 90th Street. Robert Chambers Sr., the police said, is a record promoter who has been separated from his wife for a year.

As a teenager, Robert Chambers Jr. was a cadet in the Knickerbocker Greys, a drill team for the children of prominent families; his mother, Phyllis, was at one time the president of the Greys' all-female board.

Both Robert Chambers and his mother were interviewed in an article about the Knickerbocker Greys in the May 1981 issue of *Town and Country* magazine. "Discipline is still the main theme," Mrs. Chambers was quoted as saying. "The Greys teaches what society should be about, the niceties of life."

"Boss Other People Around"

Robert, then 14, added: "The best part is becoming an officer. Then you get to boss other people around. That's a whole lot better than taking orders."

But self-discipline, it appears, was something Mr. Chambers lacked. If anything, he seemed to try to coast on his good looks and charm, not always with success.

"He was bright, charming and not a particularly good student," recalled Ronald P. Stewart, the York headmaster. A friend from York, Larry J. Greer, said: "He could have been captain of the soccer team, but he was lackadaisical. He was an underachiever."

Before attending York, Mr. Chambers had lasted one year at the Choate School in Wallingford, Conn., and less than one semester at the Browning School in Manhattan.

Dropped Out of College

Mr. Chambers entered Boston University in the fall of 1984, but dropped out at the end of one semester, university records show.

Back in New York, Mr. Chambers worked briefly as a restaurant host, but for the most part he was unemployed.

Still, Mr. Chambers had enough money to drink and flirt "five or six nights a week" at Dorrian's Red Hand, Mr. Dorrian said.

The bar owner described Mr. Chambers as "the nicest kid you'd want to meet," someone who would help calm rowdy customers and pick up litter from the floor. But he added that Mr. Chambers had "a drug problem" and had gone to treatment program in Michigan about three months ago.

"We hear rumors that at one time he did have a cocaine problem," said the deputy police commissioner for public information, Alice T. McGillion. "We're pretty sure it's true." Miss Levin, meanwhile, was a young woman who "was always happy," said Eric Barger, the manager of Flutie's Pier 17, the restaurant in the South Street Seaport where she worked as a hostess this summer.

"Never once, from the time I hired her, did I ever see her come to work with anything but a smile," he said.

Boyfriend Gone for the Summer

"She was a lovely, lovely little girl," Mr. Dorrian said. He said Miss Levin's regular boyfriend, whom he recalled only as "Brock," was vacationing in Europe this summer. Miss Levin had dated several different co-workers from Flutie's, according to Mr. Barger.

Miss Levin was living with her father and stepmother on Mercer Street in SoHo and had graduated last spring from the Baldwin School on West 74th Street in Manhattan.

This fall, Miss Levin was going to enter Chamberlayne Junior College in Boston, an expensive, two-year school that does not require Scholastic Aptitude Tests for admission. Miss Levin's father, Steven, said yesterday that his daughter was "always the straight kid of her crowd." Her stepmother, Arlene Levin, added that the young woman might even have been considered "a prude."

Still, Mr. Levin acknowledged that his daughter "liked to go out at night." Mr. Dorrian said she came into his bar several times a week. And amid Miss Levin's belongings at the murder scene, the police found a learner's driving permit giving her age as 22.

It had been her passport into Dorrian's Red Hand.

—August 28, 1986

NOTE: *In 1988, as a jury was deliberating his fate, Chambers pleaded guilty to first-degree manslaughter. He was sentenced to five to 15 years in prison. Levin's parents sued him for $25 million, a claim he opted not to contest. In prison, Chambers racked up more than two dozen disciplinary violations and ended up serving the maximum sentence before his release in 2003. In 2008, he was sent back to prison, sentenced to 19 years for selling cocaine.*

LORENA BOBBITT ACQUITTED IN MUTILATION OF HUSBAND

By DAVID MARGOLICK

In a verdict that highlighted the plight and rights of abused women, a jury today found Lorena L. Bobbitt not guilty of all criminal charges, concluding that she was temporarily insane last June when she cut off her husband's penis with a kitchen knife.

When the jury of seven women and five men announced its decision, acquitting Mrs. Bobbitt of malicious wounding, an offense for which she could have been imprisoned for 20 years, a gasp went up among her supporters in the courtroom.

Mrs. Bobbitt, who was born in Ecuador and raised in Venezuela, apparently did not understand what the jury foreman had said. Turning to one of her lawyers, Lisa Kemler of Alexandria, Va., she asked, "Is that good?" Ms. Kemler replied, "You're free." Mrs. Bobbitt smiled briefly, then resumed her customarily serious, slightly sorrowful expression.

She still faces one more hurdle—a psychiatric examination that could last 45 days.

To Undergo Evaluation

Moments after the verdict, Mrs. Bobbitt left through the rear of the courtroom and was taken for psychiatric evaluation, as state law provides for people acquitted for reasons of insanity. She was taken to Central State Hospital in Petersburg, Va., where a psychiatrist and a psychologist will determine whether she poses any danger to herself or the public.

The doctors are to decide on a course of treatment for Mrs. Bobbitt, which will determine how long she is held. She could be released after 45 days under an order to seek private treatment.

The defense had argued that Mrs. Bobbitt, flooded with nightmarish images of her husband's abuse and suffering from various mental illnesses, snapped psychologically after her husband raped her and yielded to an "irresistible impulse" to strike back.

In testimony, Mrs. Bobbitt said she had not realized what she had done until later, when she fled their home and was in her car. She said she then discovered the knife in one hand and her husband's penis in the other. She threw what she called his "body part" in the underbrush, from which it was retrieved, and, after nine hours of surgery, reattached.

The verdict brought to an end the eight-day trial, during which the Bobbitt marriage became one of the most highly publicized and minutely scrutinized ever. Forty-eight witnesses, including Mrs. Bobbitt and her husband, John W. Bobbitt, graphically depicted a relationship gone sour.

The disintegration culminated early on the morning of June 23, Mrs. Bobbitt said, when, moments after her drunken husband raped her and while she was drinking a glass of water in the kitchen, she spotted a 12-inch knife, picked it up, approached the sleeping man and cut him.

"Seek Her American Dream"

In a statement read in English by Janna Bisutti, owner of the nail salon where Mrs. Bobbitt has worked as a manicurist, Mrs. Bobbitt thanked her supporters and urged other battered women to seek the help of friends and counselors. "She did once and will again seek her American dream when she is able, and if the publicity of her abuse can help one person find freedom, then all of this is not in vain," said the statement, which was later read in Spanish.

The prosecutor in the case, Paul B. Ebert, expressed fears that the verdict could send the wrong message about deterrence and punishment.

"I have a certain amount of sympathy for Mrs. Bobbitt, but that doesn't justify what she did," Mr. Ebert said. "A lot of people go to the penitentiary who in some ways tug at your heart strings, but when you violate the law, you've got to be punished, in my opinion, and this is no exception. I'm happy she went out the back door rather than the front."

Kim Gandy, executive vice president of the National Organization for Women, said today, "We're glad the jury rejected the twisted argument that a battered woman should be locked up in a prison cell."

Marital Abuse Corroborated

In remarks in the courtroom after the verdict, Mr. Ebert said he had no regrets about calling Mr. Bobbitt to testify, even though the prosecution's own experts concluded that he had abused and raped his wife.

"I don't think we could begin to have a successful prosecution without calling the victim in this case," Mr. Ebert said. "John Bobbitt is what he is and he testified, I'm sure, to the best of his ability." He also said he felt he had done nothing wrong by handling the prosecutions of both Mr. and Mrs. Bobbitt. Last November, a jury cleared Mr. Bobbitt of charges of marital sexual abuse in a case that examined evidence from only the five days immediately preceding the mutilation.

A procession of witnesses corroborated Mrs. Bobbitt's account of marital abuse, saying they often saw her with bruises on her body. Two forensic psychologists and a psychiatrist from the hospital in Petersburg concluded she was a battered woman. They also concluded that she was seriously depressed when she cut her husband; two held that she was suffering from post-traumatic stress disorder.

But all rejected the diagnosis of a defense expert that Mrs. Bobbitt had suffered a "brief reactive psychosis," one that left her defenseless when the thought of mutilating her husband came to her. Her actions, they concluded, were too purposeful to meet the definition of "irresistible impulse," which impel random attacks without regard for the consequences.

At the insistence of the defense, Judge Herman A. Whisenant's charge to jurors on irresistible impulse was considerably less stringent, requiring only that they find that Mrs. Bobbitt's mind "was so impaired by disease that she was unable to resist the impulse to commit the crime." The jury wrestled with the language of the charge, once asking Judge Whisenant whether they could use the doctors' broader definition. He told them they could not; moments later, they returned with their verdict.

Memories of Mutilation

The jury rejected the prosecution's assertion that Mrs. Bobbitt acted intentionally and maliciously. It also acquitted her of a lesser charge, unlawful wounding, rejecting the assertion that she acted with intent and "in the heat of passion."

The prosecution maintained that Mrs. Bobbitt's testimony of remembering nothing about the episode—an assertion, they hinted, that fit her insanity defense—was belied by more credible statements that she had made earlier.

"He always have orgasm and he doesn't wait for me to have orgasm," she told a police lieutenant hours after the incident. "He's selfish. I don't think it's fair, so I pulled back the sheets then and I did it."

While Mrs. Bobbitt's memories of the mutilation waned over time, her memory of the prelude grew more expansive as she detailed how her mind clouded over with what she called "pictures" and what psychiatrists call flashbacks, common to people who have suffered severe trauma. But with witness after witness, along with Mrs. Bobbitt herself, attesting to Mr. Bobbitt's psychological, physical and sexual abusiveness, and with Mrs. Bobbitt's having won sympathizers nationwide through broadcasts of the trial, prosecutors appeared fearful of challenging Mrs. Bobbitt's credibility too explicitly.

The verdict ended, at least in the courts, what began as a depressingly ordinary domestic dispute between two mismatched people—one a 26-year-old former marine, bar bouncer, cab driver and construction worker, the other his Ecuadorean-born wife, whom he married in 1989.

The matter would surely have remained that way had Mrs. Bobbitt amputated any of her husband's other appendages. Whether generated by concern for the problem of domestic violence, voyeurism or the way it has broken numerous social and journalistic taboos, however, public appetite for the Bobbitts seems insatiable.

Mr. Bobbitt was not in the courtroom for today's verdict.

Appearing on *Larry King Live*, his parents, Marylyn and Bill Biro, who were with him elsewhere in Manassas at the

Lorena Bobbitt meets reporters outside court in Manassas, Virginia, February 28, 1994, after Circuit Judge Herman Whisenant Jr. ordered her release from a mental hospital.

time of the verdict, said their son was "dumbfounded" by the results and asked, "You mean she got away with it?"

Throughout, the case juxtaposed images of normalcy and perversity. Mr. Bobbitt, Ms. Kemler said in her opening statement, was everything Mrs. Bobbitt wanted: "He was handsome, he seemed nice, he was a U.S. marine, after all."

Mrs. Bobbitt depicted herself as an unworldly and deeply religious Roman Catholic but one who admitted stealing dresses from Nordstrom and manicuring equipment from Ms. Bisutti.

Together, they made an unusual couple, whose bitter, bruising fights were interspersed with trips to Luray Caverns and the Kings Dominion amusement park, who engaged in consensual sex 72 hours before the amputation, even as they planned to divorce.

—January 22 1994

A CRIME REVISITED: THE DECISION;
13 YEARS LATER, OFFICIAL REVERSAL IN JOGGER ATTACK

By ROBERT D. McFADDEN AND SUSAN SAULNY

Thirteen years after a Central Park jogger was beaten and raped on a night of teenage violence that horrified New York, prosecutors pointed to a convicted killer yesterday as the probable lone rapist and asked a court to throw out the convictions of five Harlem men whose graphic but unsupported confessions had sent them to prison.

In a remarkable turn in the infamous case, the office of the Manhattan district attorney, Robert M. Morgenthau, submitted to state supreme court a report on new evidence that not only presaged a reversal of the convictions early next year but also appeared to raise the curtain of mystery that has long shrouded the events in the park on the night of April 19, 1989.

The prosecutor's report reopened a window on an era of rampant crime and racial tensions in New York that had generated a climate of fear and a sense of vulnerability in a citizenry that felt helpless against marauding teenagers in the streets, subways and parks.

Contradicting a longstanding theory that the jogger had been gang-raped, the report said that an 11-month re-examination of the case had found DNA and other persuasive evidence that the woman had been brutally beaten, raped and left for dead by one man, Matias Reyes, a murderer and serial rapist who confessed last January that he alone had attacked the jogger.

The report, a motion by Nancy E. Ryan, Mr. Morgenthau's chief of trials, to join the defense in seeking a dismissal of all charges, said that a fresh look at the confessions of Antron McCray, Kevin Richardson, Yusef Salaam, Raymond Santana and Kharey Wise, and a reconstruction of the events that night suggest that the youths could not have raped the jogger because they were elsewhere in the park, assaulting, robbing and harassing joggers, bikers and others, on a night of what one suspect called "wilding," a term police investigators had never heard before.

The report also said that the convicted youths' confessions—videotaped, written and so powerful that they persuaded two juries who had heard almost no other evidence— were so full of discrepancies and errors regarding the rape, even about where, when and how it took place and who was involved, as to make the statements implausible as evidence of the rape.

In addition, the report said, many details in the confessions were never corroborated. None of the DNA evidence linked the youths with the jogger, and their descriptions of her clothing and injuries, the weapons used and other details were at odds with the facts. The report also noted that these weaknesses were not exploited by defense lawyers in two trials. The report said nothing about investigators' using coercion or trickery to obtain the confessions, as supporters of the convicted men have charged. But it suggested that the youths' statements regarding the rape—each minimizing his own role while implicating others—might have amounted to false claims by the teenagers trying to become witnesses rather than defendants.

The report also undercut the only physical evidence offered by prosecutors in the trials to link the youths directly to the jogger. It said that strands of hair found on Mr. Richardson and on another youth who was charged but never prosecuted in the rape had been shown in recent DNA tests not to have come from the jogger, though prosecutors had exploited them in the trials as matching or "consistent with" hers.

The report contained no sweeping admonitions about a miscarriage of justice, and did not portray the convicted men as innocents who committed no crimes in the park the night of the rampage. But in an avalanche of facts, it focused narrowly on legal grounds and argued that, given the new evidence, the verdicts probably would tip in the defendants' favor if new trials were held.

But in carefully constructing an argument that the five men had been wrongly convicted, the report made no attempt to assign blame for how it happened, and it did not criticize or name any of the detectives and prosecutors who handled the case, one of the most important in Mr. Morgenthau's 29-year tenure.

Besides the dismissal of rape and assault charges in the jogger case, the report recommended that the men's convictions for other assaults, robberies and crimes that night should also be set aside. While there was ample evidence to show they were part of a pack of 30 youths who beat and harassed eight other victims, the report said the youths had been portrayed in court as predators in a vicious sexual assault, and thus jurors' perceptions of them would have been tainted for judgments on the secondary charges.

"We conclude that there is a probability that the new evidence, had it been available to the juries, would have resulted in verdicts more favorable to the defendants, not only on the charges arising from the attack on the female jogger but on the other charges as well," the 58-page report concluded.

There was no reaction from the jogger, now 42, married and a resident of Connecticut. She was unable to provide an account of what happened after the attack. After 12 days in a coma she emerged with no memory of what happened. She testified at the trials, but only on her injuries and experiences before and after the attack. As a rape victim, her identity has been withheld by the news media, but she intends to use it in a book she is writing about the case.

Barring unforeseen developments, the prosecutor's report made it all but certain that Justice Charles J. Tejada, at a hearing set for Feb. 6, would dismiss all the convictions of the five men, both in the jogger case and the attacks on eight other people in the park that night.

The five convicted men, now 28 to 30 years old, who have all completed their prison terms of 7½ to 13½ years for the park offenses, made no comments yesterday. But their lawyers and families praised the district attorney's office and expressed relief that the men's long ordeal would soon end.

"To really breathe and really take a deep breath and not have to go back under—you don't know how good it feels," said Linda McCray, the mother of Antron. "I was never ashamed of my son."

Myron Beldock, another lawyer, praised Mr. Reyes for confessing. "We wouldn't be here but that Matias Reyes found a conscience and came forward," he said.

Whoops of joy from a cluster of relatives greeted Mr. Beldock as he emerged from the district attorney's office in the Criminal Courts Building at 100 Centre Street at 1 p.m., and announced the prosecutor's move.

A police spokesman, Michael P. O'Looney, said that Commissioner Raymond W. Kelly was reviewing the report and had no immediate comment. The department is conducting a parallel investigation of the jogger case, and the two agencies are said to be sharply divided over the convictions. Some prosecutors and detectives continue to believe that the youths had some contact with the jogger, perhaps starting an assault that Mr. Reyes finished. Thomas J. Scotto, president of the Detectives' Endowment Association, the union that represents police detectives in New York, sharply criticized the report and said the detectives who worked on the case "did an outstanding job."

Michael Sheehan, a detective originally on the case, said he was outraged by the report. He scoffed at its description of Mr. Reyes as candid, calling him a manipulative, untrustworthy person.

The investigation found no evidence that Mr. Reyes knew any of the men in the park rampage and was "a loner" who stalked, raped, robbed and murdered on the Upper East Side and in Central Park. One of his victims was raped in the park two days before the jogger, a fact that could have helped the defense had the lawyers known of it, the report said.

Detailing his attack on the jogger, the report said Mr. Reyes first saw her running north on the East Drive near the 102nd Street Transverse. He followed to rape her, and along the transverse picked up a fallen branch, hit her head and dragged her into a secluded wooded ravine. He pulled off her jogging tights and raped her.

Afterward, he said, she broke away and ran, and he recalled "an image of her running naked from the waist down." He had already beaten her, but his violence escalated and he hit her face and head repeatedly "with a rock and other things," fracturing her skull.

He said he had no memory of tying her up, but when found she was bound with her shirt looped around her neck and used to gag her and tie her wrists near the neck, a method he had used before.

DNA tests established . . . that Mr. Reyes was the source of the DNA.

He said he took her Walkman and, as he left the park, stopped to speak with a police detective he knew who was working undercover in a taxi. The detective recalled working in a cab that night, but not the brief encounter. The report said the victim had a cross-shaped wound on her left cheek, and Reyes had worn a ring with a cross that apparently had made the wound, it said.

But the most telling evidence that he raped the jogger was scientific. DNA tests established—"to a factor of 1 in 6,000,000,000"—that Mr. Reyes was the source of the DNA found on the jogger's sock and in her cervix. It was the only DNA found. In addition, DNA tests established that Mr. Reyes was the source of a pubic hair found on the sock.

"In short, the DNA tests showed the Matias Reyes's claim that he raped the jogger was true, and confirmed that no one else's DNA was present in samples taken from the victim or the evidence at the scene," the report said.

Moreover, three strands of hair found on Mr. Richardson were re-examined with more sophisticated DNA tests than were available in 1989. "None of the DNA matched the victim's," the report said.

The report said the youths' confessions had "serious weaknesses," adding: "Perhaps the most persuasive fact about the defendants' confessions is that they exist at all. While all of the defendants began by denying knowledge of the attack, each ultimately made himself an accomplice in a terrible crime."

The statements seem powerful, it said, but "they differed from one another on the specific details of virtually every major aspect of the crime—who initiated the attack, who knocked the victim down, who undressed her, who struck her, who held her, who raped her, what weapons were used in the course of the assault and when in the sequence of events the attack took place."

None accurately described the attack's location; with one exception all put the attack at or near the park reservoir, a half-mile to the south. And at 9:15 p.m. when the jogger was being raped, they apparently were elsewhere, attacking other victims, the report said.

It added: "It is difficult to construct a scenario that would have allowed the defendants the time to interrupt their progression south, detour to the 102nd Street Transverse and commit a gang rape. All of these issues were apparent at the time of trial."

—December 6, 2002

NOTE: *The five men whose convictions were vacated sued the city, alleging their confessions had been coerced and citing a conspiracy among law enforcement officials. The suit ended in 2014 with a settlement of $41 million—roughly $1 million for each year the men had spent in prison. In the settlement, the city denied any wrongdoing.*

BOSTON CHURCH PAPERS RELEASED; A PATTERN OF NEGLIGENCE IS CITED

By PAM BELLUCK

Hundreds of pages of church documents released today show that officials of the Roman Catholic Archdiocese of Boston allowed priests accused of abuse to remain in ministry or failed to persuade them to receive residential psychiatric treatment.

The documents, 2,200 pages concerning eight priests, were released by lawyers for plaintiffs in a lawsuit involving the Rev. Paul R. Shanley, who is accused of molesting several boys. The lawyers, who got the documents from the archdiocese, are trying to strengthen their case by showing that the Boston church officials engaged in a pattern of mishandling abusive priests.

In one case, a priest from Youngstown, Ohio, was placed in a Boston parish just after being treated for pedophilia, despite warnings by the treatment center and the Youngstown bishop that the priest not be allowed to have contact with children. Several young men in Boston parishes later said the priest abused them, and he was convicted of sexual abuse in New Hampshire.

In another case, a priest was transferred in 1984 to a different parish after he admitted sexual activity with a teenage boy. Three years later, the church received more reports of sexual misconduct by the priest. He was finally removed from ministry in 1993.

In two other cases, priests accused of abuse did not receive long-range in-patient treatment despite recommendations by church officials. The records show the priests resisted such treatment.

Some of the documents also suggest that Cardinal Bernard F. Law was more directly informed about complaints against priests than he has previously asserted in his public statements.

The records contain letters from Cardinal Law to accused priests that are more personal and sympathetic than those released in other cases. In them, he compliments or sympathizes with the priests.

In one case, responding to a letter from a priest accused of sexually assaulting young women studying to be nuns, he said, "Our recent conversation and your written reflection are a beautiful testament to the depth of your faith and the courage of your heart." Cardinal Law added, "It is important that all of us be reminded by the pain endured by those who have been accused."

Donna M. Morrissey, a spokeswoman for the archdiocese, said today: "We can't change the past. We can recognize the inadequacy of our policies and change them and recognize the suffering and the pain the victim-survivors have gone through and are continuing to go through.

"For the past 11 months our comprehensive new policy has not allowed any priest with a credible allegation of abuse of a minor to serve in ministry in the Archdiocese of Boston. We wish it would have been our policy for the last 50 years."

The archdiocese sought last month to delay the public release of the documents, and 10,000 other pages concerning 57 other priests, but a judge denied their motion, saying the church was trying keep information from public view.

The release of documents comes at a time when tensions are high over settlement negotiations in the Shanley case and hundreds of other lawsuits over priests accused of abuse.

Financial advisers to the archdiocese have said that the church is considering filing for bankruptcy. Lawyers in the Shanley case, who also represent about 200 other plaintiffs, have accused the archdiocese of threatening bankruptcy to persuade plaintiffs to accept less compensation. The lawyers have said they will quit negotiating unless the church puts off consideration of bankruptcy.

"These documents are going to be very important to us in the trial of this case," said Roderick MacLeish Jr., a plaintiff's lawyer. "Now there's more context and understanding of what was happening."

Advocates for abuse victims said today that the documents were more troubling than the records released earlier this year on a handful of priests accused of abuse because they appeared to show a more consistent pattern of mishandling abusive priests.

"What is striking to me about these documents is that it is very clear from them that Cardinal Law and other top archdiocesan officials knew far more, far earlier about far more priests and their abusive behavior than the officials have ever let on and yet did so very little," said David Clohessy, national director of the Survivors Network of Those Abused by Priests, a group based in Chicago.

In some cases, the documents suggest that archdiocese officials tried to discourage accusers of priests from filing lawsuits seeking compensation. In the case of the Ohio priest, Father Robert M. Burns, a memo from the Rev. John B. McCormack, now the bishop of Manchester, N.H., said he told a meeting with a family complaining of Father Burns's abuse: "I didn't think compensation would be helpful to their son. It is not what he needs."

A spokesman for Bishop McCormack said he could not comment on any of the cases because he had not seen the documents.

Experts on the sexual abuse cases said the Burns case was an example of a pattern of dioceses around the country accepting troubled priests from other dioceses, particularly in the 1970s and early 1980s.

"There was a general practice of these guys helping each other out," said Patrick J. Schiltz, a professor at the University of Saint Thomas School of Law in St. Paul, Minn., who has represented religious institutions in sexual abuse lawsuits. "It was often thought by bishops that what these guys needed was a fresh start."

In the case of Father Burns, it was no secret to the Archdiocese of Boston that he had molested children. In 1982, when Father Burns applied to be a pastor here, he had just finished treatment for

> *"It was often thought by bishops that what these guys needed was a fresh start."*

pedophilia at an institution, the House of Affirmation, which recommended that he not be given a clergy job involving contact with children, the documents show. The priest's bishop in Youngstown, Ohio, James W. Malone, said later in an affidavit that although he supported Father Burns for the job, he urged Boston church officials to keep him away from children.

Boston archdiocese notes about the priest at the time state next to Father Burns's name: "Problem: little children."

Mr. MacLeish said the note had been written by the second highest-ranking archdiocesan official in Boston, Bishop Thomas V. Daily, now the bishop of Brooklyn. The notes also say that Bishop Daily had "reservations" about placing Father Burns in a parish but that after consultation with the archbishop at the time, Cardinal Humberto Medeiros, he was made a part-time associate pastor in a church in the Jamaica Plain neighborhood. Calls seeking comment from Bishop Daily were not returned.

The documents show that Father Burns was recommended for the post by Bishop Alfred Hughes, now the bishop of New Orleans. A spokesman for Bishop Hughes, the Rev. William Maestri, said today: "Sometimes after treatment a new environment and new placement after treatment, a new beginning, is important. Bishop Hughes was thinking he'd be in a very limited ministry, he would not be in a parish assignment." Father Maestri added, "In hindsight, that judgment did not turn out to be a sound judgment."

In 1991, with Father Burns now in his second Boston parish, the archdiocese received a detailed complaint that the priest had repeatedly raped and molested a boy.

Cardinal Law removed Father Burns from ministry, but wrote him an unusually consoling note.

"Life is never just one moment or one event and it would be unrealistic to have too narrow a focus," he wrote. "It would have been better were things to have ended differently, but such was not the case. Nevertheless I still feel that it is important to express my gratitude to you for the care you have given to the people of the Archdiocese of Boston."

The letter continues, "I am certain that during this time you have been a generous instrument of the Lord's love in the lives of most people you served."

In 1999, after publicity about the 1996 conviction of Father Burns for molesting boys in New Hampshire and after more accusations had surfaced in Boston, Cardinal Law wrote to the Vatican, acknowledging that the archdiocese was warned in 1982 "that Father Burns ought not receive an assignment that placed him in a position to minister to minors."

He continued: "Through a misjudgment of the severity of his past behavior and the likelihood of its recurrence, Father Burns received the full faculties of the archdiocese and was twice assigned as part-time parochial vicar to parishes within the city of Boston. Neither of the pastors with whom he was assigned was informed of a need to restrict Father Burns's ministry with children."

While events in the Burns case straddle the tenures of two cardinals, some cases occurred solely during Cardinal Law's tenure, which began in the spring of 1984.

In November of that year, the Rev. Robert H. Morrissette admitted to accusations that he had invited a boy to his room and run his hand along the boy's leg while the boy was wearing a bathing suit, the documents show. The priest received treatment by a therapist and Bishop Robert J. Banks, now head of the diocese of Green Bay, approved his transfer to another parish.

In 1988, a note apparently written by Bishop Banks said about Father Morrissette that "he should come out" of the priesthood. But Father Morrissette was allowed to remain in ministry until 1993, when the case of the Rev. James Porter, who was accused of molesting more than 100 people in the nearby diocese of Fall River, Mass., prompted archdiocesan officials to review the files of Father Morrissette.

Bishop Banks did not return calls seeking comment.

In another case, Bishop Banks fielded a complaint about the Rev. Robert V. Meffan in 1986, an anonymous accusation that in the 1960s he had seduced girls who were studying to be nuns. A memo Mr. MacLeish said was written by Bishop Banks said that Father Meffan's reactions in a meeting suggest "that the allegations might well be true: not upset, but matter-of-fact, no desire to know who or attempt to puzzle it out, no indignation."

The documents provide no indication that the archdiocese did anything in response to the accusations. In 1993, after the archdiocese received similar complaints from women about Father Meffan's luring them into sex, in one case telling a girl to imagine that Christ was touching her, he was pulled from ministry.

Although the archdiocesan review board recommended residential treatment, Father Meffan refused and was allowed to live at home. In 1996, he wrote Cardinal Law that he missed the joys of ministry, but was still devoted to Christ.

Another priest, the Rev. Thomas P. Forry, was the subject of a number of accusations over more than 15 years, including one he admitted—beating up a housekeeper in 1979—as well as accusations in 1984 that he had had an 11-year affair with a woman.

In 1984, the archdiocesan personnel secretary wrote to Cardinal Law that psychiatrists who evaluated Father Forry felt he should be in a psychiatric hospital because "he is in grave need of some long-range assistance." Documents indicate that after Father Forry refused, he had two months of outpatient treatment.

Later the woman's son complained that Father Forry had molested him. A doctor at a treatment center found he had "an underlying personality disorder" but did not believe the abuse accusations were true. In 1999, while Father Forry was serving as a prison chaplain, the Department of Corrections complained of "scandalous" behavior, saying he was screaming and shouting and exhibiting emotional and behavioral problems.

An archdiocese official wrote, "I think Father Tom Forry is a deeply troubled person, that he should be held accountable for his behavior."

After that complaint, Cardinal Law placed Father Forry on the emergency response team, meaning he would fill in at parishes when the regular priests were on vacation.

In October 2001, the archdiocese received a complaint that Father Forry molested a girl and inappropriately touched her brother "some years ago." The girl, now a woman, was uncomfortable because Father Forry had been assigned to fill in at her parish and felt "he should not be allowed to preside in a parish setting to protect other children."

In February 2002, the archdiocese removed Father Forry from active ministry.

—December 4, 2002

NOTE: *Cardinal Law resigned as archbishop of Boston on December 13, 2002. A 2004 report by the United States Conference of Catholic Bishops found that 10,667 people had made allegations of children having been sexual abused by U.S. priests between 1950 and 2002 and that 95 percent of dioceses had received at least one complaint.*

SANDUSKY GUILTY OF
SEXUAL ABUSE OF 10 YOUNG BOYS

By JOE DRAPE

—————

Jerry Sandusky, a former Penn State assistant football coach, was convicted Friday of sexually abusing young boys, completing the downfall of a onetime local hero in a scandal that shook a proud Pennsylvania community, a prominent American university and the world of major college football.

A jury in Centre County Court, in Bellefonte, Penn., convicted Sandusky, 68, of sexually assaulting 10 boys, all of them children from disadvantaged homes whom Sandusky, using his access to the university's vaunted football program, had befriended and then repeatedly violated. The jury, more than half of whom had ties to Penn State, returned a verdict on the second day of deliberation.

Sandusky stood stoically as the jury foreman read off the verdicts on the 48 counts against him. The foreman said guilty 45 times. Many of the charges, which include rape and sodomy, carry significant prison terms, and it seems likely that Sandusky will spend the rest of his life behind bars.

The case against Sandusky, even before his trial, had exacted an enormous toll. Joe Paterno, the university's famed head coach who had been alerted to at least one of Sandusky's attacks on a boy, was fired, went into a kind of exile and was dead of cancer within months. The university's longtime president, Graham B. Spanier, was dismissed as well, and Penn State officials, alumni and students were forced to confront the possibility that the interests of big-time college sports had trumped concern for the welfare of vulnerable children.

Sandusky, who had been Paterno's longtime defensive coordinator, had also founded a charity, The Second Mile, to work with troubled youths. In a trial that lasted two weeks, prosecutors asserted that Sandusky had used the charity as his private hunting ground, scouting for potential victims. He gave them gifts and money, invited them to his home, took them to Penn State football games, showered with them at the university's football building and slept with them in hotel rooms on the road.

Eight men testified during the trial, offering graphic accounts of repeated assaults by Sandusky—on the Penn State campus, in hotel rooms and in the basement of Sandusky's home. It was painful testimony, the men telling their horrifying stories in public for the first time. Some wept. Others said, with anger and relief both, that they wanted to move on at last.

Jerry Sandusky, during a December 2011 interview with Jo Becker of *The New York Times* to answer questions about his indictment on sexual abuse charges.

In one of the case's final startling chapters, coming after the case went to the jury, another man came forward to assert that Sandusky had molested him: it was one of Sandusky's adopted children, Matt, who said he had offered to testify at the trial.

Sandusky's lawyer, Joseph Amendola, said outside the courthouse that he and Sandusky's wife "accepted the verdict," but complained that he had been rushed in preparing a defense. "There are a lot of people sitting in jail who are innocent," he said, prompting booing from the crowd that had gathered.

The verdict against Sandusky will not bring an end to Penn State's problems. Lawsuits loom. At least two formal investigations, including one by a former director of the FBI at the behest of the university's board of trustees, are under way. And two senior university officials—the athletic director and the administrator in charge of the campus police—face criminal charges that they failed to act when informed that Sandusky had assaulted a 10-year-old boy in a university shower in 2001 and then lied about that knowledge before a grand jury.

The university, in a statement issued after the verdict, said: "The legal process has spoken, and we have tremendous respect for the men who came forward to tell their stories publicly. No verdict can undo the pain and suffering caused by Mr. Sandusky, but we do hope this judgment helps the victims and their families along their path to healing."

Sandusky's arrest, on a Saturday last November, registered with seismic force in this corner of Pennsylvania known as Happy Valley. He was regarded as a local pillar, a former Penn State standout who had played for Paterno and then spent 30 years on the sideline with him building the Nittany Lions defense into "Linebacker U" and the football team into a national power.

People expressed shock that a man they knew as a committed coach, a prominent fund-raiser for charity and a father figure to scores of aspiring football players and other children could be capable of such crimes.

But things got worse for Penn State, as charges and revelations were laid out by the state attorney general's office: Sandusky had been investigated by the campus police for possible sexual crimes against children as far back as 1998; in 2001, a graduate assistant in the football program, who was a former Penn State quarterback, had told Paterno and then other university officials that he had seen Sandusky sexually attacking a 10-year-old boy in the football building showers.

No one . . . ever reported the attack to the police.

No one—not Paterno, not the graduate assistant, not the other university officials— ever reported the attack to the police. Sandusky, who had retired two years before but retained an office and privileges on campus, was merely told not to take boys onto campus any longer.

The university erupted with upset. Paterno's reputation was badly tainted. The outsize importance of college sports was debated anew, but this time with a wrenching soul-searching.

Sandusky's own behavior in that first week only deepened the sense of bewilderment. He gave a strange, almost incriminating interview to Bob Costas of NBC. He seemed not to grasp the severity of the accusations. Amendola insisted his client was innocent, and began what would become a prolonged assault on the credibility of Sandusky's accusers.

Soon, though, more accusers came forward. Sandusky's house, where he raised a family and apparently carried out many of his attacks, was vandalized. And Sandusky became a subject of national scorn and curiosity. At one point in his interview with NBC, Sandusky was asked if he was sexually attracted to boys.

"Sexually attracted, you know, I, I enjoy young people," Sandusky answered. "I, I love to be around them. No, I'm not sexually attracted to young boys."

Joseph E. McGettigan III, the lead prosecutor, cited that reply in his closing argument on Thursday as evidence that Sandusky was a guilty man.

"I would think that the automatic response, if someone asks you if you're a criminal, a pedophile, a child molester or anything along those lines would be: 'You're crazy. No. Are you nuts?'" McGettigan said.

In the end, Sandusky chose not to take the stand. Amendola said he made that decision after learning from prosecutors that they would have called his son Matt to testify as a rebuttal witness if Sandusky testified. That, Amendola said, would have devastated Sandusky.

The repair work for Penn State, the university made clear Friday night, is far from complete.

The university said it planned to invite Sandusky's victims to work with its officials to settle legal claims, stating, "The purpose of the program is simple—the university wants to provide a forum where the university can privately, expeditiously and fairly address the victims' concerns and compensate them for claims relating to the university."

—June 23, 2012

NOTE: *Sandusky was sentenced in October 2012 to 30 to 60 years in prison. He is seeking a new trial, claiming his legal representation had been ineffective.*

CHAPTER 10

VICE

"I receive some 700 letters a day, and many of them are about speakeasies. After policemen are sent there to close the place complained about, it sometimes reopens and the people write me again. They cannot understand why. The only justification the police have for closing a place summarily is in case it is harboring criminals or gangsters, when we can invoke the nuisance act."

—New York Police Commissioner Grover Whalen in 1929, as he tried to explain why so many bars continued to operate despite Prohibition

THE LURE OF THE illicit entangles all manner of men and women. Pablo Escobar, the son of a farmer, was drawn to the immense money and power that came with being a cocaine kingpin. Eliot Spitzer, the one-time governor of New York and son of a wealthy real estate developer, became the client of a high-end prostitution ring. Articles in *The Times* have chronicled the full span of vice, from the brutality unleashed during drug wars to the venial sins that forced a promising politician to resign from office.

OPPOSITE: New York City Deputy Police Commissioner John A. Leach, right, watches agents pour liquor into a sewer following a raid during Prohibition, c. 1921.

MARIJUANA SMOKING IS REPORTED SAFE

A Panamanian judge recently sentenced an American seaman, Hamilton Main, to a year of penal confinement for smoking and having in his possession cigarettes made of the leaves of the *Cannabis indica,* known also as marijuana, canjac and by various other names, and often incorrectly referred to as hashish.

About a year ago there was considerable comment on the fact that this weed was being grown in the public parks of New York City by a group said to be Mexicans. Sunday newspaper features are still being printed about the fearful consequences of using this allegedly habit-forming and dreadful weed.

An investigation made by a special committee appointed by Colonel M. L. Walker, governor of the Panama Canal, raises grave doubts as to the effects produced by smoking marijuana.

Literature Was Studied

The investigation took the form of studying available literature on the subject, writing to the authors for sources of information and actual experiment with subjects smoking marijuana, which is the Latin-American name for the hemp and is probably a combination of the names "Mary" and "Jane" in Spanish: Maria y Juana.

Some articles by men of supposed scientific knowledge were based on sources other than actual experiment, and the authors of some apparently learned monographs on the use of marijuana had never seen a subject under the influence of the weed, nor did they know of first-hand knowledge of the dire results alleged to lie due to its use, according to the committee.

"While anybody can gather the plant and prepare it for use, it is sold more or less openly already made up," a recent Sunday feature story in an American newspaper said. "Mixed with tobacco, or made straight into a cigarette, a few puffs are enough to send the smoker into the realm of half-dream, half-reality."

"School children are smoking it, prisoners are growing it secretly in the jail yards, grown-ups soak it in perfume. Scores have already gone crazy from it and hundreds are getting that way as fast as they can."

The weed, really Indian hemp, came up for discussion at the Geneva conferences on narcotics. Chapter XIX of *Opium as an International Problem,* a book by Professor W. W. Willoughby of Johns Hopkins University, carries the title "Indian Hemp (Hashish)," and gives a resume of what was done on the subject at the conference.

Mixed with Other Materials

The question was brought up by M. El Guindy, the Egyptian delegate, who referred to the "*Cannabis indica* or *sativa* as hashish." He explained that hashish was used in the form of a paste made from the resin of the flowers, mixed with sugar and cooked with butter and aromatic substances, the resulting concoction being known in Egypt by the names of "*manzui, maagun* and *garawish.*" It was also cut into small fragments and mixed with tobacco for smoking in cigarettes, or simply smoked in hookahs, he said.

Apparently M. El Guindy made no distinction between the use of the hemp as a part of the paste known as "*manzui ect,*" and as a weed for smoking either pure or mixed with tobacco. Of the effects he said:

"Taken in small doses, hashish at first produces an agreeable inebriation, a sensation of well-being and a desire to smile; the mind is stimulated. A slightly stronger dose brings a feeling of depression and of discomfort. There follows a kind of hilarious and noisy delirium in persons of a cheerful disposition, but the delirium takes a violent form in persons of violent character. The habitual use of hashish brings on chronic hashishism. The addict very frequently becomes neurasthenic and eventually insane."

Canal Tests Made by Smoking

The experiments carried out in the Canal Zone were confined to the smoking of the weed, some of which was cultivated in the plant introduction gardens of the Panama Canal, some collected from wild plants, but all properly identified.

The most thorough study of the subject in the investigations was that of Dr. M. V. Ball of Warren, Pa., the results of which were published in the *Journal of the American Medical Association* under the title "The Effects of Hashish Not Due to *Cannabis Indica.*"

Cannabis indica, according to one commission member, seems to have got into bad company, and it is the association with other drugs that has brought an undeserved reputation to marijuana.

"It seems to me," writes Dr. Ball, "that all the symptoms ascribed to the use of *Cannabis indica* are to be explained by the admixtures which are ordinarily contained in the hemp preparations as they appear in the ganja shops and the hashish joints of the Oriental countries. There is no record to my knowledge of any habitués of *Cannabis indica* among the Anglo-Saxons."

Ganja is one of the forms in which the hemp is used in India, although always with other ingredients, and on this subject the Indian Hemp Commission reported in part:

"The alleged cases of insanity due to ganja smoking were for the most part not clearly proved; those who indulged in crime were not driven to it by excessive use of this drug, but when excesses were noted they were usually connected with other vices, such as alcohol and opium. Not a single medical witness could clearly prove that the habit gave rise to mental aberration."

Seventeen Subjects Took Part

Seventeen subjects smoked marijuana during the course of the investigation made in the Canal Zone. All were under careful medical observation. In two investigations 12 volunteers smoked from 2 to 12 cigarettes of marijuana. Only one experienced incoordination and mental confusion. In the report of the test made of 2 soldiers about 20 years of age, who said that they were habitual smokers of the weed, it is stated:

"Both soldiers said that the smoke from the drug tasted the same as the smoke from the plant which they had been accustomed to smoking, and that they felt fully as much effect or 'kick' from it as they usually did. This they described as a feeling of lightness and of happiness. However, their general conduct and behavior appeared perfectly normal. Each had a very dry throat and mouth and a slight increase in pulse rate, and—face was somewhat flushed. They had perfect coordination and showed no other signs either mental or physical."

Each of these men smoked six marijuana cigarettes in a little more than one hour.

Smoked It from Childhood

Three soldiers were the subjects of a later test, and one of them, a man of 25, from Texas, said he had smoked marijuana since he was a child. He declared he had no craving for marijuana and did not think it habit forming. He felt no ill effects from it the following day and did not think it had ever done him any harm.

Another had been smoking marijuana for just over a year, sometimes smoking it every day and at other times going for quite a while without it. He does not crave it and does not think it is habit forming. He prefers tobacco. The third said that he had been smoking marijuana every three or four days for about a year, from one to three cigarettes at a time, and that he felt the effect from the first cigarette, but preferred tobacco.

He said he could not describe the effect produced, but that "time flies, and it puts you in a sleepy condition." This subject smoked three cigarettes within an hour and no appreciable effects were noticed.

A poster for the film *Reefer Madness*, a melodramatic morality tale about the dangers of marijuana that came out in 1936, a decade after this article appeared in *The New York Times*.

The subject who had used marijuana from childhood showed moderate reaction after smoking four cigarettes, and could not walk a chalk line, his left foot usually being out of line. However, he showed fair coordination in hands and arms.

The third subject smoked four cigarettes and at no time did he show any effect from smoking the drug.

Reports Effects Exaggerated

The committee, in reporting to the governor of the Panama Canal, stated: "The influence of the drug when used for smoking is uncertain and appears to have been greatly exaggerated. The reports seem to have little basis in fact, and there is no medical evidence that it causes insanity. Tests conducted by our local board confirm the evidence that the plant is not a habit-forming drug, and no pleasurable sensations nor acts of violence were observed.

The board concluded that there is no evidence that the marijuana grown locally is a habit-forming drug in the sense of the term as applied to alcohol, opium, cocaine, &c., or that it has any appreciable deleterious effect on the individuals using it."

The board recommended that no steps be taken by the authorities of the Canal Zone to prevent the sale or use of marijuana, and that no special legislation on that subject was needed.

In some states of the United States, marijuana is classed with cocaine, heroin, opium and other dangerous narcotic drugs, and penalties are applied for violation of the regulations governing its use.

—November 14, 1926

SPEAKEASY CENSUS SHOWS BRISK TRADE

By C. G. POORE

W hen Police Commissioner Whalen announced recently his belief that some 32,000 speakeasies were operating in the city, attention was dramatically drawn to the fact that the speakeasy, in the infinite variety of its manifestations, has become one of the outstanding social institutions of New York.

The widespread popularity of the speakeasy is graphically indicated by Mr. Whalen's estimate. In response to the demand of thousands of patrons, speakeasies are operated in all parts of New York despite the penalties of the law that may or may not reach them through a police department occupied with a multitude of other duties and a prohibition service that allots 200 men to cover the entire metropolitan area. How many speak-easies there are altogether in New York at any given time it is impossible to say. But authorities point out that you have only to ask the New Yorkers around you to learn of several places where liquor is served in comfortable surroundings.

The officials charged with abating the speakeasy nuisance find it a physical impossibility to deal effectively with them all. So in several instances they have devised programs for dealing first with those that in their estimation have the most harmful aspects. Thus the police department, finding that there are almost twice as many speakeasies as there are policemen, makes its most determined drives against places known to harbor

Prohibition agents destroying a bar, c. 1928, location unknown.

criminals and sell poisoned liquor. The federal enforcement authorities work primarily at attempts to cut off the wholesale sources of liquor supply, and usually carry out raids and padlocking proceedings against speakeasies in cooperation with the city police force.

And in recent months a development among certain of the speakeasies whose original function was simply the illegal selling of liquor has aroused concern. This is the hostess problem, to which Commissioner Whalen drew attention the other day. It has been engaging the attention of welfare organizations for some time, notably the Committee of Fourteen, devoted to research work and legislation against commercialized vice.

In his office at police headquarters, where the records of the 32,000 speakeasies known to the police are kept, Commissioner Whalen one day last week discussed the question fully.

"Those 32,000 speakeasies are the ones we actually know exist because patrolmen all over the city have reported them," said the Commissioner. "How many more there may be we have no way of knowing. The great difficulty in dealing with the speakeasy is that, as its name and nature imply, it is undercover. The saloon was always out in front, where the police could put their finger on it when the need arose. But the speakeasies, hidden away anywhere from an upper apartment to a sub-basement, makes the problem of obtaining legal evidence far more difficult."

Difficult to Combat

Commissioner Whalen emphasized how simple is the equipment necessary to start a speakeasy as compared to the old saloon, with its larger premises, bar fixtures and a complete stock of liquors.

"That makes them able to grow rapidly," he remarked. "Then there is this fact: As fast as we close them they start up again in another location." He pointed out the difficulties in making closed speakeasies stay closed.

"Even after arrests have been made; the speakeasies continue to operate under other men," he said. "Why, in some cases we have made as many as 30 arrests in one place, and still the speakeasy continues to operate.

"The only effective measure that can be taken is to station a policeman on the premises to see that the speakeasy does not reopen. But there are only 18,000 policemen altogether. And if we attempted to station one on the premises of every known speakeasy, we would still be short the difference between 18,000 and 32,000.

> *As fast as we close them they start up again in another location.*

"Actually, the number of policemen available is much smaller, of course. In the first place, the 18,000 men on the force are divided into three tours of eight-hour duty. Then the 2,000 that are on traffic duty and the 1,700 on the detective forces must be subtracted, as well as the men on vacation and sick leave. So that there is a maximum of perhaps 3,000 men on active patrol duty on each eight-hour tour. These men are doing all the work of preserving law and order that falls to the police department. If we set them all to watching the premises of raided speakeasies, there would be considerable resentment felt on the part of the public at their neglecting all the other duties of the police force in the city of New York.

"Padlocking offers the best method for closing speakeasies. Here we work in cooperation with the federal prohibition forces who have charge of padlock proceedings. The legal processes involved require considerable investigation for the gathering of the evidence that must be submitted. Affidavits must show conclusively that liquor was sold on the premises to a particular person signing the affidavit. The chemical analysis of the liquor must accompany the affidavit. Then the United States court issues an order which must be served to the owner of the speakeasy and it is often exceedingly difficult to locate the actual owner and serve the order on him."

"It became a pretty well-established policy in the days of the saloon that the wisest practice was to keep women out of them. So the danger of the vice question arising in connection with them was kept as distant as possible. But the speakeasy encourages the patronage of both men and women, and the introduction of hostesses has brought the problem forward again.

"The sympathetic cooperation of the public in combating speakeasies would be very helpful, if it were forthcoming," Commissioner Whalen concluded. "But there is no evidence shown in the enforcement process that the public is enthusiastic. Indeed, the work of officers engaged in the work is sometimes hampered by the active antagonism of people in the neighborhood."

The most casual inquiry about the different sorts of speakeasies brings forth a flood of directions and reminiscences from persons who have visited them. They are to be found in all manner of places—from the Roaring Forties, where they flourish most luxuriously, to penthouse apartments just off Park Avenue, cellars in Greenwich Village and rooms in office buildings in the financial district. Recalling that the police have actual records of 32,000 of them, it becomes apparent that no section of the city can be entirely bereft.

The intricate and mysterious rites observed before patrons are allowed to enter seem to be chiefly intended to add romantic excitement to the adventure. Introduction by someone who has been there before it usually required. Then there is the business of registering the new patron's name and perhaps the issuing of a card of admittance to be presented on the next visit. Many persons carry a dozen or more such cards.

Elaborate Precautions

The devious means employed to protect the entrances to speakeasies adds to the general mystification. Bells are to be rung in a special way. A sliding panel behind an iron grill opens to reveal a cautious face examining the arrivals. Behind the ground-floor doors of many old brownstone residences there is often a long room furnished with a salvaged saloon bar and tables and chairs.

Where does all the liquor for the 32,000 speakeasies come from? Arrests and convictions have shown that some of it is smuggled in from Canada by train and truck and perhaps even through the pipeline that was reported to have been connected to a Detroit brewery. Though rum row is said to be gone, foreign ships still bring liquors to our shores. And one genuine bottle of liquor so imported often goes to give the more or less convincing bouquet to the other bottles that are cut from it with the addition of adulterants. But the main source of supply is believed to be domestic—either produced in establishments here in New York or in the metropolitan area—and then brought in by truck.

—April 14, 1929

NOTE: *Prohibition, in effect from 1920, ended with the ratification of the 21st Amendment to the Constitution in 1933.*

KINGPIN OF CRIME SYNDICATE

By ROBERT D. McFADDEN

"**H**e would have been chairman of the board of General Motors if he'd gone into legitimate business," an agent of the FBI once said of Meyer Lansky with grudging admiration. And in a moment of triumph, Mr. Lansky once boasted to an underworld associate: "We're bigger than U.S. Steel."

Maier Suchowljansky, the Russian-born immigrant better known as Meyer Lansky, always called himself a lucky gambler. But, according to law enforcement officials, he was for decades a kingpin of organized crime in the United States, a ruthless onetime "director" of Murder Inc. who bet only on a sure thing.

While he was said to have had experience as a hired gunman in the 1920s, he had not, by most accounts, personally done anything violent for 50 years.

The authorities described him as a genius of finance who applied his Midas touch to bootlegging in the Prohibition era, to gambling in Cuba, the Bahamas and the United States and to loan-sharking, stock manipulation and underworld penetration of legitimate businesses throughout the United States.

From an impoverished childhood on New York's Lower East Side, Mr. Lansky maneuvered his way up through the ranks of organized crime, parlaying Prohibition profits into hundreds of illicit and legitimate ventures.

He was said to have been a key figure in the 1934 creation of a national crime syndicate, which brought fragmented gangland empires into a loosely organized national federation. Later he was said to have devised schemes to infiltrate legitimate business and to have set up sophisticated means to skim receipts and evade taxes.

One biographer said a few years ago that Mr. Lansky had amassed a personal fortune of $300 million, most of it tucked away in Swiss bank accounts, real estate and hidden investments.

Went to Jail Only Once

Mr. Lansky was accused of many crimes, ranging from assault to contempt of court. But, aside from a few minor run-ins with the law as a teenager, he went to jail only once. That was for two months in 1953, on a gambling conviction in Saratoga Springs, N.Y.

His record included a conviction on only one other charge—a contempt citation in 1973 that was overturned on appeal. Repeated prosecutions ended in acquittals or were thwarted by trial delays arranged by his attorneys or prompted by his frequent bouts of assertedly poor health.

Mr. Lansky's interests were apparently unhindered by any of the prosecutions, or by changes of government in the United States or the Bahamas. It took the Castro revolution in Cuba to put him out of business in Havana.

Mr. Lansky became an international cause célèbre in the early 1970s, when he retired to Israel and refused to return to the United States to face two federal indictments. He sought to remain in Israel under that country's Law of the Return, which says every Jew has the right to immigrate to Israel, and a two-and-a-half-year legal battle ensued.

The episode posed a dilemma for the Israeli government. Had it allowed him to stay, it would have been criticized for harboring a reputed criminal. When it asked him to leave, it was criticized for turning away a Jew seeking refuge.

Mr. Lansky was born in 1902, in Grodno, Byelorussia [Belarus], and was brought to the United States with a sister and a brother in 1911. His parents could not remember his birth date, so an immigration officer listed it as July 4.

He was said to have been a key figure in the 1934 creation of a national crime syndicate.

Meyer Lansky was physically small—at maturity he was only 5 feet 4 inches tall and weighed 136 pounds—but his teachers at Public School 34 on the Lower East Side regarded him as clever and remarkably self-possessed. He graduated from eighth grade in 1917 and got a job with a tool and die maker.

To supplement his small income, he organized a floating dice game. It was about this time that he met and became friends with Charles "Lucky Luciano" Luciana and Benjamin "Bugsy" Siegel, who, according to investigators, were to be his partners in later years. In 1921, he switched jobs, became an auto mechanic and soon found himself servicing and camouflaging stolen cars for bootleggers.

By 1928, when he became a naturalized citizen, Mr. Lansky had attracted a gang of his own, forming what was known as the Bugs and Meyer Mob with Bugsy Siegel, and was at the helm of a burgeoning rum-running operation. The gang also hired out gunmen as "enforcers" for other bootleggers.

After the repeal of Prohibition in 1933, Mr. Lansky and Frank Costello opened illegal gambling casinos in upstate New York, New Orleans and Florida.

In 1935, after the slaying of the top New York crime figure, Arthur "Dutch Schultz" Flegenheimer, Mr. Lansky and five others were identified by the authorities as the heirs of all rackets in Manhattan, Brooklyn and Newark.

Later in the 1930s, Mr. Lansky went to Cuba and, after getting Fulgencio Batista, the dictator, to legalize gambling, set up several casinos there.

The Kefauver Investigation

The expansion of organized crime in the United States after World War II was huge, and Mr. Lansky was among its top investors. The authorities said he acquired major interests in the Flamingo Hotel in Las Vegas and in choice Miami Beach real estate.

Mr. Lansky's name became virtually a household word after hearings by the Senate Crime Investigating Committee in 1950 and 1951. The committee, headed by Senator Estes C. Kefauver of Tennessee, conducted the most far-reaching study of organized crime ever undertaken. Mr. Lansky, named as a major boss, was called to testify, but he provided little helpful information.

Twelve years later Joseph M. Valachi, an informer testifying before a Senate sub-committee headed by Senator John L. McClellan of Arkansas also named Mr. Lansky.

In 1953, after his brief jail term for running a gambling operation in Saratoga Springs, Mr. Lansky moved to Florida and concentrated on his investments there, in Nevada and in Cuba. Mr. Lansky also reportedly became involved at that time in gambling operations in the Bahamas.

In 1957, he was said to have been a participant at the Apalachin, N.Y., meeting of gangland's top leadership.

Profit in Other Ventures

Two years later, when the Cuban revolution brought Fidel Castro to power, his troops smashed hundreds of slot machines, roulette tables and other gaming devices in the Havana tourist hotels and ended a multimillion-dollar industry and Mr. Lansky's substantial interests in it.

But the 1960s proved highly profitable for Mr. Lansky's other ventures that, according to law-enforcement officials, included loan-sharking and policy and numbers rackets, as well as legitimate businesses backed by underworld money. Mr. Lansky's intended retirement in Israel in 1970 touched off a legal fight that went to Israel's highest court, which ruled he was not entitled to citizenship because he was a "danger to public safety."

Seven countries—Switzerland, Brazil, Argentina, Paraguay, Bolivia, Peru and Panama—rejected his offer of $1 million for sanctuary, and he was arrested when he landed in Miami on Nov. 7, 1972.

"That's life," a haggard Mr. Lansky said at the time. "At my age, it's too late to worry. What will be will be. A Jew has a slim chance in the world."

He posted $250,000 cash bail and was ultimately cleared of, or was adjudged too ill to stand trial on, all the tax evasion, conspiracy and skimming charges against him. His own doctors and court-appointed physicians found he was suffering from heart trouble, bronchitis, ulcers, bursitis and arthritis.

—January 16, 1983

NOTE: *This story was published with the announcement of Meyer Lansky's death from cancer on January 15, 1983, in Miami Beach, at the age of 81.*

HEAD OF MEDELLÍN COCAINE CARTEL IS KILLED BY TROOPS IN COLOMBIA

By ROBERT D. McFADDEN

Pablo Escobar, who rose from the slums of Colombia to become one of the world's most murderous and successful cocaine traffickers, was killed in a hail of gunfire yesterday in a rooftop shootout with security forces in his hometown of Medellín, officials in Bogota reported.

Caught in a hideout in the heart of the city that served as the base of a drug empire that once reached across the Western Hemisphere and Europe, the 44-year-old fugitive with an $8.7 million price on his head was surrounded by 500 police officers and soldiers and shot to death, officials said.

Authorities said that a barefoot Mr. Escobar and his bodyguard raced to the roof and fired at troopers in camouflage fatigues who had raided their two-story house, and that the two were shot dead as they tried to escape over the rooftops.

Pablo Escobar watching a soccer game in Medellín in 1983.

Witnesses said the raiders fired weapons into the air in jubilation and shouted, "We won!"

The death is not expected to seriously affect cocaine traffic, but President Clinton, in a message to President César Gaviria Trujillo, said: "Hundreds of Colombians—brave police officers and innocent people—lost their lives as a result of Escobar's terrorism. Your work honors the memory of all these victims."

Officials said Mr. Escobar had been traced through telephone calls he had made while planning the kidnapping of prominent Colombians to pressure the government into accepting his conditions for surrender, chiefly protection for his wife and children from rival drug gangs bent on revenge.

The killing of Mr. Escobar, who had amassed a $4 billion fortune and was blamed for the murder of hundreds—from presidential candidates and judges to police officers, journalists and innocent bystanders—ended a 16-month manhunt begun after his escape from prison in July 1992.

It also ended a life of crime that made him an uncrowned king with estates and airplane fleets, a seat in the National Assembly and a reputation as a killer who blew up neighborhoods, shopping centers and even a jetliner. But he was also seen as a Robin Hood who built houses for the poor, paved roads, erected sports stadiums and provided jobs for thousands.

"The Triumph of Law"

Life on the run and the death or surrender of many of his lieutenants had severely eroded the volume of cocaine that Mr. Escobar could ship to the United States and Europe.

But he once supplied what experts said was 80 percent of the cocaine used in the United States, and his death ended, at least symbolically, an era of terror in which the Medellín ring used the income of a multinational corporation to make war against a modern nation.

In Washington, D.C., Lee P. Brown, director of the Office of National Drug Control Policy, said, "Escobar was the most ruthless of the drug kingpins, and his fate should serve as an example to others who traffic in death and misery."

But beyond its symbolism, his death was not expected to affect the flow of cocaine that continues to flood cities and ruin the lives of millions of addicts, their families and others.

In recent months, with Mr. Escobar's organization in ruins, rival gangs in Cali and elsewhere in Colombia, and in Bolivia and Peru, have taken over much of the market. They are expected to become the targets of redirected enforcement resources.

The killing of Mr. Escobar was a major victory for an elite military and police corps known as the Search Block, a 3,000-member force, aided by U.S. and British communications and technology, that was set up at the time of Mr. Escobar's escape to hunt drug traffickers in Colombia.

Vigilantes Join Hunt

After Mr. Escobar's escape last year, the CIA stepped up its anti-drug programs in Colombia, the Pentagon sent surveillance aircraft to help, and the National Security Agency used electronic eavesdropping to intercept Mr. Escobar's telephone conversations, officials in Washington said yesterday.

Mr. Escobar had been hunted not only by government troops but also by vigilante squads known as People Persecuted by Pablo Escobar, or Pepes, which have killed scores of his associates and turned the tables on Mr. Escobar, burning his homes and those of his family and blowing up his fleet of antique cars.

Just three days ago, Mr. Escobar's wife, Victoria Eugenia Henao, his 16-year-old son, Juan Pablo, and his 5-year-old daughter, Manuela, flew to Germany seeking political asylum but were turned away. The family returned to Bogotá and are staying in a hotel under army protection.

A Life of Crime Begins

Pablo Escobar Gaviria, who just turned 44, was born on Dec. 1. 1949, in Rio Negro, 25 miles east of Medellín. His father was a farmer and his mother a teacher. A year later, they moved to a rundown suburb of Medellín, where he finished high school and went to work for a smuggler of stereo equipment.

The teenaged entrepreneur began selling tombstones he had stolen from a cemetery and sanded flat. He was first arrested in 1974 for stealing a car.

Behind a soft-spoken facade, he came to be known to associates and enemies as brilliant, ambitious, a quick learner with a talent for business and an unforgiving memory. By 1976, he was an established drug smuggler with a growing fleet of airplanes. Caught with 39 pounds of cocaine in a pickup truck, he walked out of jail three months later, his arrest mysteriously revoked; both officers who arrested him were later killed.

Liked His Luxuries

With his potbelly and greased-down hair, he never outgrew the appearance of a thug. But he surrounded himself with luxury. In 1980, he bought a Miami Beach mansion; a year later, he paid $8.3 million for an apartment complex in Florida and filled his Medellín condominium with paintings and Chinese porcelain.

A 7,000-acre ranch in Colombia, said to cost $63 million, was his favorite estate. He imported hundreds of exotic animals, including giraffes, camels and a kangaroo. Hiding his drug dealing behind claims of legitimate business wealth and the image of a bene-factor, he had his own radio show and was often accompanied by Roman Catholic priests.

He built housing projects for the poor, soccer stadiums and roller rinks, often naming them after himself. In 1982, he won an alternate representative's seat in Colombia's con-gress. Two years later, he was forced out of office when a justice minister exposed his criminal record. The minister was later slain.

Others believed killed by Mr. Escobar and his henchmen included an attorney general, a newspaper publisher, three presidential candidates, scores of judges and hundreds of others. A terrorist bomb believed to have been set by his gang destroyed a Colombian jetliner in 1989, killing all 107 people aboard.

Mr. Escobar's empire continued to grow. At their peak in the late 1980s, Mr. Escobar and others loosely associated in the cartel produced 60 percent of the cocaine in Colombia, which in turn supplied 80 percent of the U.S. market. *Forbes* magazine listed him among the world's richest people.

A Good Life in Jail

After an intense manhunt, Mr. Escobar negotiated his surrender in June 1991: He was to be in charge of the jail, presiding over his drug enterprises with cell phones, computers and meetings at a boardroom table. In what was more like a bachelor-pad-in-a-fortress, he had a waterbed, a video-cassette player, a stereo system, a bar, a 60-inch color television, a whirlpool bath and a wood-burning fireplace. Handpicked guards served as waiters at parties with prostitutes.

Fearing his enemies might try to bomb the jail, Mr. Escobar demanded and got a bomb shelter. Aviation authorities closed the airspace over the prison and guards doused the lights when a plane loomed at night.

When accounts of this luxury emerged, in July 1992, the government decided to move him to a regular jail. But en route, he escaped. He then began a purge of suspected traitors and a vendetta against rivals. As Mr. Escobar's cartel crumbled, an emboldened government began the hunt that led to yesterday's deaths in Medellín.

—December 3, 1993

SPITZER, LINKED TO A SEX RING AS A CLIENT, GIVES AN APOLOGY

By DANNY HAKIM AND WILLIAM K. RASHBAUM

G ov. Eliot Spitzer continued to weigh whether to resign Tuesday, a day after law enforcement officials said he was a client of a high-end prostitution ring broken up last week by federal authorities.

Mr. Spitzer received counsel from his advisers late Monday at his Fifth Avenue apartment, and had not emerged as of early Tuesday. A top administration official said Tuesday morning that no announcement had been scheduled.

The disclosure of Mr. Spitzer's involvement with the prostitution operation threatened to end his career and upended the state's political world.

His involvement came to light in court papers filed last week, officials said, as federal prosecutors charged four people with operating the service Emperor's Club V.I.P. Mr. Spitzer was caught on a federal wiretap discussing payments and arranging to meet a prostitute in a Washington, D.C., hotel room last month. The affidavit, which did not identify Mr. Spitzer by name, indicated that he had used the prostitution service before.

Mr. Spitzer, 48, who is married with three daughters, appeared briefly with his wife at his Manhattan office on Monday to apologize, but did not specifically address involvement with the ring. He said he needed to repair his relationship with his family and decide what was best for the state, but he declined to take questions.

"I have acted in a way that violates my obligations to my family and violates my, or any, sense of right and wrong," the

In the wake of a prostitution scandal, New York governor Eliot Spitzer announces his resignation at his New York office, March 12, 2008.

governor said. "I apologize first and most importantly to my family. I apologize to the public to whom I promised better."

The governor, a Democrat in his first term, then returned to his apartment on Fifth Avenue. *The New York Times* began investigating Mr. Spitzer's possible involvement with a prostitution ring on Friday, the day after the prosecutors arrested the four people on charges of helping run the Emperor's Club. After inquiries from *The Times* over the weekend and on Monday, the governor canceled his public schedule. An hour after *The Times* published a report on its Web site saying Mr. Spitzer had been linked to the ring, the governor made his statement.

The news was met with disbelief and shock in Albany, a capital accustomed to scandal. Some legislative assistants said they were too stunned to speak.

Mr. Spitzer has not been charged with a crime. But one law enforcement official who has been briefed on the case said that Mr. Spitzer's lawyers would probably meet soon with federal prosecutors to discuss any possible legal exposure. The official said the discussions were likely to focus not on prostitution, but on how it was paid for: Whether the payments from Mr. Spitzer to the service were made in a way to conceal their purpose and source. That could amount to a crime called structuring, which carries a penalty of up to five years in prison.

If Mr. Spitzer were to resign, Lt. Gov. David A. Paterson would serve out the remainder of his term. Mr. Paterson would become the state's first black governor.

The governor learned that he had been implicated in the prostitution inquiry when a federal official contacted his office on Friday, according to the person briefed on the case. On Saturday night, he attended the Gridiron Club annual dinner, a political roast put on by Washington journalists, and appeared ebullient, according to people in attendance.

The governor informed his top aides on Sunday night and Monday morning of his involvement.

Mr. Spitzer's family and his top assistants debated Monday morning at Mr. Spitzer's apartment whether he should step down, a person who spoke to the governor said. Silda Wall Spitzer, who was among them, told her husband that he should not resign in haste. But most of the others saw no way for him to survive.

According to prosecutors, the Emperor's Club provided women to clients in London, Paris, Miami and other cities, and charged them between $1,000 and $5,500 an hour.

> *"I apologize first and most importantly to my family. I apologize to the public to whom I promised better."*

The affidavit details a Feb. 13 encounter between a prostitute named Kristen and a man described as "Client 9," whom law enforcement officials identified as Mr. Spitzer. Mr. Spitzer traveled to Washington that evening, according to a person told of his travel arrangements, and stayed at the Mayflower Hotel.

He testified before Congress about the bond insurance crisis the following morning. The affidavit says that he met with the woman in Room 871 but does not identify the hotel. Room 871 at the Mayflower that evening was registered under the name George Fox.

One law enforcement official said that several people running the prostitution ring knew Mr. Spitzer by the name of George Fox, though a few of the prostitutes came to realize he was the governor of New York.

Mr. Fox is a friend and a donor to Mr. Spitzer. Asked whether he accompanied Mr. Spitzer to Washington on Feb. 13 and 14, Mr. Fox responded: "Why would you think that? I did not."

Told that Room 871 at the Mayflower Hotel had been registered in Mr. Fox's name with Mr. Spitzer's Fifth Avenue address, Mr. Fox said, "That is the first I have heard of it. Until I speak to the governor further, I have no comment."

In a wiretapped conversation after the encounter, the prostitute, Kristen, called her booker to inform her that the session had gone well, and that she did not find the client "difficult," as other prostitutes apparently had, according to the affidavit.

The booker responds that he, in an apparent reference to Client 9, sometimes asks the women "to do things that, like, you might not think were safe."

Mr. Spitzer was elected in a landslide in 2006, capitalizing on his popularity he won as the "Sheriff of Wall Street" during eight years as attorney general. With a reputation for personal probity and independence, he pledged to bring higher ethical standards to the statehouse.

After promising change in Albany from "day 1," Mr. Spitzer was quickly plunged into political turmoil, and much of his legislative agenda was sidelined. He gained a reputation for being intemperate and alienated even some members of his own party.

The revelation about Emperor's Club and the attendant disruption in Albany comes at a particularly bad time: The state faces a $4.4 billion deficit and is weeks away from its deadline to complete a new budget.

"Every year you say you've seen it all, but you haven't," said Matthew Mataraso, a lobbyist who started his career at the capitol in 1962 as a lawyer for a Republican assemblyman. "It's a shame. It's awful. This is why people lose faith in government. But I guess it shows that he's human like everybody else."

Republicans were quick to pounce, with the state party and a top lawmaker calling for him to resign.

"The governor who was going to bring ethics back to New York State, if he was involved in something like this," said James N. Tedisco, the Republican minority leader of the assembly, "he's got to leave. I don't think there's any question about that."

When he was attorney general, Mr. Spitzer's signature issue was pursuing Wall Street misdeeds. But he also oversaw the prosecution of at least two prostitution rings by the state's organized crime task force, which reports to the attorney general. In one such case in 2004, Mr. Spitzer spoke with revulsion and anger after announcing the arrest of 16 people for operating a high-end prostitution ring out of Staten Island.

"This was a sophisticated and lucrative operation with a multitiered management structure," Mr. Spitzer said at the time. "It was, however, nothing more than a prostitution ring."

—March 11, 2008

NOTE: *Spitzer resigned later that month as governor. He was never criminally charged in connection with the case.*

CHAPTER 11
WHITE COLLAR

"Sentence this monster named Madoff to the most severe punishment within your abilities. We are too old to make up what we lost. We have to start over."

—Randy Baird, an investor and victim of
Bernard Madoff's fraud, in a 2009
letter to Judge Denny Chin

THOUGH TYPICALLY OBSCURED BY the complexities of commerce and buried in layers of phony paperwork, few crimes have wider impact than financial frauds. They often erase a lifetime of savings. More broadly, they cripple the investor confidence on which our economic system relies. For decades, *The Times* has been helping readers untangle the myriad schemes that put them at risk, from the wizardry of Charles Ponzi to the flimflams of Bernie Madoff.

OPPOSITE: Bernie Madoff departs court following a hearing in New York, March 9, 2009.

EXCHANGE "WIZARD" IS PAYING CLAIMS

Charles Ponzi, head of the Securities Exchange Company, began today to pay in full all matured claims against him and the investments of all who wanted their money back, following his announcement yesterday that he had suspended operations in international exchange, by which he claims to have made several million dollars within a few months.

Meanwhile, an application was made by one of Ponzi's creditors in the superior court today for a receivership for the Ponzi concern, and a temporary injunction restraining Ponzi from drawing on funds on deposit in several banks here in Boston.

Judge Wait declined to grant the temporary injunction, and the application for a receivership was withdrawn.

Judge Wait's decision to withhold temporary action against the firm followed a statement by Samuel L. Ballen, appearing for Ponzi, that Ponzi and his firm are meeting all obligations, and that Ponzi declares his ability to meet them in full.

Secret selection of an auditor to investigate the affairs of Ponzi, the newest "financial wizard," whose promise to "double your money within 90 days" has set Boston wild: a near riot in the School Street offices of the Securities Company, in which four women were exhausted by hours of frantic endeavors to reach the inner offices to collect their money during one of the periodic attempts of the crowd to force entrance to the rooms; the injury to several men in the crowd who were cut by flying glass from the doors when they attempted to force their way inside; and a constantly growing demand for repayments of credits, marked the day's developments in the $8,500,000 financial sensation.

District Attorney Joseph C. Pelletier announced today that he had appointed an auditor to examine carefully the standing of Ponzi's business venture. Pelletier refused to answer any questions as to why he concealed the name of the auditor, or to speculate or comment in any way upon the case.

Shortly before the announcement, a crowd of persons who had invested money with Ponzi, most of whom were Italians from the North End colony, rushed his offices, forced admittance, and gave the police a merry time before order was restored.

A second disturbance occurred during the luncheon hour when a flying wedge of creditors jammed the doors of Ponzi's office. So many creditors appeared at the School Street offices that Ponzi took over the Bell-in-Hand, famous for years as a barroom in Pie Alley, and transformed the place into a temporary office. There applicants for return of loans were received, their applicants checked, and those approved paid from a hastily constructed cashier's booth.

At least a thousand claims were settled today before the business closed, actual cash on hand in Ponzi's offices had been exhausted, and clerks were giving out bank checks. At the close of business this afternoon, Ponzi gave out a statement to the press that said that, in accordance with an agreement he had made with the district attorney, he had paid "every obligation presented at my office today in the form of notes issued by me during the past 45 days. "The amount paid out by me during the day amounted to several hundred thousands of dollars. I shall continue every day until all of my obligations have been presented."

Ponzi Tells His Methods

U.S. District Attorney Daniel J. Gallagher today issued the following statement as coming from Ponzi, in which Ponzi himself explained the methods he was using to double money with 90 days:

"The method is the conversion of American money, first into depreciated foreign currency, no matter what it is; or the conversion of foreign money, not depreciated, into foreign money that is depreciated. I am making this statement because I do not actually send money abroad, but I use funds I have abroad between one country and another. That is the first part of the transaction.

"The second part is the purchasing of the depreciated currency in international reply coupons.

"The third part is the reduction of these international reply coupons in countries in which the currency is not depreciated, and the conversion, of course, into postage stamps.

"The fourth part is the disposal of the postage stamps, and the fifth is either the conversion of the money that I derive the sale of the stamps into American money, or the credit of such money into some foreign money to have at my disposal to repeat the operation."

Continuing, Mr. Gallagher's statement said:

"Mr. Ponzi said he has in the United States upward of $5,000,000 and between $8,000,000 and $99,000,000 in depositories abroad. He was asked why it was that, having eight or nine millions of dollars in American money, he should maintain an office here to solicit and receive more money, or why he should pay agents a commission for soliciting people to invest. He said he did not use the money, but that he would eventually need the people.

"When asked for what purpose he would need the people he said it was possible that he might want to run for office. On being asked if he was a citizen of the United States, he replied, 'almost.' On being asked if his international reply coupon enterprise was a preliminary to something bigger, he answered, 'Very much so.'

"He said he was going to start a different banking system, that instead of giving the net profits entirely to stockholders the net profits would be divided equally between the stockholders and the depositors, because the stockholders are taking the depositors' money and paying the depositors only 5 percent. He declared he would make Boston the largest importing and exporting center in the United States and that his present enterprise was only preliminary to that end. He said that he needed popularity and if he made $100,000,000 he would keep $1,000,000 and spend the other $9,000,000 in charitable work or something that would do good for the people.

"'Today,' said Mr. Ponzi, 'that official would be tickled to death if he had put in $5,000, and he is not the only one.'

"To all intents the business has been based upon the wide variation in the rates of foreign exchange. Ponzi, according to his explanations, took advantage of the discrepancies in the money rates through the medium of the international postal reply coupon. These coupons have constant value throughout the countries in the international postal agreement. A coupon worth three two-cent stamps here is worth stamps to equal value in Bulgaria, or any of the other countries, but coupons in Bulgaria, where the money rate is low, are at a discount. The same amount of American money will buy more value in coupons in Bulgaria than in the United States.

He was offering interest in investments at the rate of 200 percent annually.

"Ponzi had agents throughout Europe, he maintains. These bought coupons where they were cheap. The coupons were taken to countries where money rates were high and converted into stamps. These stamps were sold to big business houses or other large users, Ponzi said.

"The official U.S. Postal Guide sets forth the details of how international reply coupons were to be used. They were intended merely as a business convenience, but it seems that Ponzi was the first one to conceive how they could be exploited.

"His customers did not invest directly in these coupons. They simply deposited their money with him and took in return a note for one and one-half times the amount, redeemable in 90 days. He was offering interest in investments at the rate of 200 percent annually, and in many cases he was actually giving returns at a far greater rate."

Washington Is Puzzled

WASHINGTON, July 27—Postal authorities are investigating closely the manipulations whereby Charles Ponzi, of Boston, says he has made millions out of dealings in "international reply coupons." The post office officials said today they were going into every angle of the affair.

From all that can be gathered, it appears that the Ponzi story has the authorities here puzzled. One thing is said to be certain, and that is, if the promoter is not engaged in an enterprise entirely within the law, he will be barred from the mails, and perhaps prosecuted.

Officials here say that no great increase in the sale of international reply coupons has been shown, as would be the case if Ponzi's agents abroad had purchased them wholesale.

The statements from Boston that Charles Ponzi, head of the Securities Exchange Company there, had made

Charles Ponzi in Italy, 1935.

more than $8,000,000 by manipulating international postal reply coupons was characterized as "impossible" by postal authorities here yesterday. The coupons are only worth five cents a piece when redeemed, it was pointed out, and the total number sold in 1919 throughout the country amounted only to $1,819.00

—July 27, 1920

NOTE: *Ponzi was convicted of mail fraud in 1920 and served three and half years in federal prison. After his release, he was convicted of larceny in Massachusetts and imprisoned there until 1934, when he was deported to Italy. He moved to Brazil before the outbreak of World War II and died a pauper in Rio de Janeiro in 1949.*

VAN DOREN PLEADS GUILTY; IS FREED

By ALFRED E. CLARK

Charles Van Doren and nine other former contestants on rigged television quiz shows pleaded guilty yesterday in New York to perjury charges and received suspended sentences from Justice Edward F. Breslin, who said the humiliation was evident in their faces. The court could have imposed prison terms up to three years along with fines of $500 on each. The defendants had been among 20 persons accused of second-degree perjury, a misdemeanor, in telling a grand jury they had not been coached on questions and answers prior to appearing on such television shows as *Twenty-One* and *Tic Tac Dough*.

Yesterday morning, they changed earlier not-guilty pleas to guilty.

Besides Mr. Van Doren, 35, who won $129,000 on *Twenty-One*, those entering guilty pleas included Miss Elfrida Von Nardroff, who won the record amount of $220,500 on the show, and Hank Bloomgarden, who won $98,500.

Justice Notes Humiliation

Assistant District Attorney Joseph Stone read the charges against Mr. Van Doren, a former instructor at Columbia University and a member of a distinguished literary family,

Charles Van Doren, shown in profile at center right, at a news conference in New York in October 1959, several weeks before his appearance at a congressional investigation committee in Washington.

who appeared gaunt and nervous. Then, in a loud, clear voice, he replied, "Guilty." "How deep and how acute your humiliation has been is quite evident," said Justice Breslin. "I have seen it on your face and on the faces of other defendants in this case."

The justice continued: "I understand that you were one of the first who wanted to throw himself on the mercy of the court. The punishment began the day the matter was exposed to the press and not the day you went before the grand jury.

"This is your first offense, and you are entitled to a chance."

Defendants Nervous

The courtroom was tense as each defendant appeared before the bench. All the contestants seemed nervous and contrite. Each pleaded guilty in a low voice, some almost in whispers.

The 10 defendants brought to 17 the number of former TV contestants who have pleaded guilty and received suspended sentences. Another received youthful offender treatment. A 19th has never been named because of being outside the court's jurisdiction, and the 20th, Mrs. Ruth Klein, 30, a housewife, had her case put over until next Wednesday because her lawyer was hospitalized.

So far as is known, there has been no indication that any of the contest winners have returned the money received from a fixed program.

> *"This is your first offense, and you are entitled to a chance."*

Mr. Van Doren, who was accompanied by his wife, Geraldine, spoke outside in the corridor. He said he had not been working regularly recently but had received several job offers.

"I'd like to drop out of the limelight altogether and get back to teaching," he said.

Asked if he had learned any moral from his experience, he replied:

"That's for you to say. All I want to do is just go home and try to forget the whole thing."

Late in 1958, Mr. Van Doren denied he had received advance answers to difficult questions on the quiz show. But a year later he appeared before a congressional investigation committee in Washington and admitted he had been coached in his replies. After a second grand jury inquiry, he was charged with perjury along with other contestants.

—January 18, 1962

MILKEN GETS 10 YEARS FOR WALL ST. CRIMES

By KURT EICHENWALD

Michael R. Milken, the once-powerful financier who came to symbolize a decade of excess, was sentenced to 10 years in prison yesterday for violating federal securities laws and committing other crimes.

The sentence, handed down by Federal District Judge Kimba M. Wood in Manhattan, was the longest received by any executive caught up in the Wall Street scandals that began to unfold in 1986. But Judge Wood left open the possibility that Mr. Milken could be eligible for parole at any time during his sentence and that his sentence could be reduced if he cooperated in future investigations. Some legal experts said they did not expect him to be paroled until he served at least a third of the prison term.

After Mr. Milken serves his term, he faces a three-year period of probation. Mr. Milken, who paid $600 million in fines and restitution when he pleaded guilty to the violations, will also be required to perform 1,800 hours of community service during each of three years of probation.

Judge Wood said the former financier had to be sentenced to a long jail term to send a message to the financial community, and because he chose to break the law despite his advantages of position and intelligence.

"When a man of your power in the financial world, at the head of the most important department of one of the most important investment banking houses in this country, repeatedly conspires to violate, and violates, securities and tax laws in order to achieve more power and wealth for himself and his wealthy clients, and commits financial crimes that are particularly hard to detect, a significant prison term is required," she said.

A Lengthy Investigation

The sentencing of Mr. Milken closes the most significant chapter of the longest investigation ever of crime on Wall Street. Over four years, numerous top Wall Street executives confessed to criminal activities and testified for the government. But Mr. Milken did not cooperate with the inquiry and admitted his guilt only last April.

As head of the "junk bond" operations of Drexel Burnham Lambert Inc., which collapsed earlier this year, Mr. Milken financed some of the largest corporate takeovers in the 1980s. He pioneered the use of high-yield, high-risk junk bonds as instruments for corporate warfare, convincing investors that the bonds' high returns more than compensated for the risk that the issuers would default.

The sentence came at the end of an emotional hearing, in which Mr. Milken frequently broke into tears as he listened to one of his lawyers plead for leniency.

Mr. Milken made only one comment during the proceeding, tearfully telling Judge Wood: "What I did violated not just the law but all of my principles and values. I deeply regret it, and will for the rest of my life. I am truly sorry."

Mr. Milken did not flinch when the sentence was handed down, but his lawyers and family seemed momentarily stunned by the sentence.

When the hearing ended, Mr. Milken's wife, Lori, and other family members came to his side. They quickly left the courtroom, and cries of sorrow were heard inside the court after the door closed behind them.

One Lawyer's Reaction

Lawyers and legal experts also expressed surprise. "This is an incredibly long sentence," said Michael Feldberg, a partner at Shea & Gould. "If there is a message to be gained from this experience, it is, at least for this judge, cooperation is enormously important."

In his settlement, Mr. Milken had agreed to respond truthfully to any questions asked him by the government after he is sentenced. Judge Wood said that if that testimony proves to be valuable in future investigations, she would consider reducing the sentence. Judge Wood said yesterday that although she did not accept that Mr. Milken committed insider trading or manipulated a particular security, as the government tried to prove, she believed that the former financier had tried to prevent investigators from uncovering his crimes by suggesting to subordinates that they dispose of important documents.

Some See Vindication

Government officials indicated that the sentence was a vindication of the four-year inquiry into Mr. Milken's practices in the financial markets.

"This sentence should send the message that criminal misconduct in our financial markets will not be tolerated, regardless of one's wealth or power," said Richard C. Breeden, the chairman of the Securities and Exchange Commission.

Mr. Milken agreed to plead guilty in April to six felonies. He admitted to a conspiracy between himself and two clients, Ivan F. Boesky and David Solomon, the manager of an investment fund. Mr. Milken pleaded guilty to hiding stock for Mr. Boesky to allow the speculator to file false information with the government, and at another time to allow him to avoid minimum capital requirements for a stock-trading firm.

28 Years Was Possible

Mr. Milken had faced a maximum of 28 years in prison, but few legal experts were estimating that his sentence would exceed eight years.

Mr. Milken's lawyer, Arthur L. Liman, had asked Judge Wood to sentence his client only to a term of community service.

Mr. Liman repeatedly stressed that his client was not a criminal on a par with Mr. Boesky, the stock speculator whose settlement of insider trading charges in 1986 and subsequent cooperation with the government helped expose the Wall Street scandals.

"Two conflicting pictures have been presented of Michael Milken," Mr. Liman said. "The government, which has not spent time with him, tries to cast him in the Boesky mold, but I would say to Your Honor that that template does not fit."

Mr. Boesky, who pleaded guilty to filing a false statement with the Securities and Exchange Commission, was sentenced in 1987 to three years in prison. He was released on parole this year.

Charitable Work Described

Mr. Liman described Mr. Milken's philanthropic works. He said Mr. Milken had contributed more than $360 million to charity, and Mr. Liman read numerous letters from people who said they had been personally helped by the financier.

During the reading of the first of those letters, from a mother whose child was injured in an accident, Mr. Milken began to sob quietly.

Mr. Liman added that he could not explain why his client had committed his crimes. "I am not a psychiatrist," he said. "I have worked very closely with Michael, and I can't offer an explanation as to how Michael slipped."

In his response, Jess Fardella, an assistant U.S. attorney, said Mr. Milken was a brilliant and decent man, but added that because of that, his crimes should be judged in a harsher light.

The Government's Viewpoint

That perspective, Mr. Fardella said, showed that Mr. Milken had abused his advantages and his position for personal benefit. "That the defendant was blessed with intelligence, energy, education and the support of family and friends makes his choice to engage in persistent violations of the law all the more inexcusable," he said. "Despite his talents and opportunities, Mr. Milken sought to multiply his success through the vehicle of criminal fraud."

Mr. Milken is acknowledged to be the highest-paid financier ever; he took home $550 million in compensation from Drexel in 1987 alone. Yet Mr. Fardella said the financier committed his crimes out of desire for more money.

The prosecutor also argued that Mr. Milken's crimes should not be taken lightly just because there was not an immediately apparent victim.

"Such deceptive and unlawful practices inevitably have a corrosive effect on these markets," Mr. Fardella said. "Left unchecked and unpunished, they threaten the entire process of savings and capital formation."

The Deterrence Factor

Mr. Fardella also asked Judge Wood to consider the importance of sending a message to the financial community that would deter other criminal conduct.

In describing her reasoning, Judge Wood said yesterday that she did not find the government's portrayal of Mr. Milken as "one of the most villainous criminals Wall Street ever produced" to be persuasive. But she also said she did not accept the defense position that Mr. Milken's crimes were aberrations in which he went beyond the law to help a client.

"Your crimes show a pattern of skirting the law," she said, "stepping just over to the wrong side of the law in an apparent effort to get some of the benefits of violating the law without running a substantial risk of being caught."

Immediately before sentencing Mr. Milken, Judge Wood praised him for his generous nature, adding that she hoped he would continue on that path.

"You are unquestionably a man of talent and industry and you have consistently shown a dedication to those less fortunate than you," the judge said. "It is my hope that the rest of your life you will fulfill the promise shown early in your career."

—November 22, 1990

NOTE: *A judge later reduced Milken's sentence to two years. Barred for life from the securities industry, Milken turned his focus to philanthropy. Today his foundations support educational programs and medical research.*

2 ENRON CHIEFS ARE CONVICTED IN FRAUD AND CONSPIRACY TRIAL

By ALEXEI BARRIONUEVO

Kenneth L. Lay and Jeffrey K. Skilling, the chief executives who guided Enron through its spectacular rise and even more stunning fall, were found guilty Thursday of fraud and conspiracy. They are among the most prominent corporate leaders convicted in the parade of scandals that marked the get-rich-quick excesses and management failures of the 1990s.

The Houston jury reached the verdicts after just over five days of deliberations. Mr. Skilling was convicted of 18 counts of fraud and conspiracy and one count of insider trading. He was acquitted on nine counts of insider trading. Mr. Lay was found guilty on six counts of fraud and conspiracy and four counts of bank fraud.

The conspiracy and fraud convictions each carry a sentence of 5 to 10 years in prison. The insider trading charge against Mr. Skilling carries a maximum of 10 years.

"The jury has spoken and they have sent an unmistakable message to boardrooms across the country that you can't lie to shareholders, you can't put yourself in front of your employees' interests, and no matter how rich and powerful you are you have to play by the rules," Sean M. Berkowitz, the director of the Justice Department Enron Task Force, said outside the courthouse.

Both men are expected to appeal. Judge Simeon T. Lake III, the judge in the case, set sentencing for Sept. 11. Until then, the two men are free on bail. If they lose their appeals, Mr. Skilling and Mr. Lay face potential sentences that experts say could keep them in prison for the rest of their lives. "Obviously, I'm disappointed," Mr. Skilling said as he left the courthouse, "but that's the way the system works."

Once jurors and the judge cleared out of the courtroom, Mr. Lay's family members huddled around him. Elizabeth Vittor, Mr. Lay's daughter and a lawyer who had worked on his defense team, sobbed. After he emerged from court, Mr. Lay said, "I firmly believe I'm innocent of the charges against me."

For a company that once seemed so complex that almost no one could understand how it actually made its money, the cases ended up being simpler than most people envisioned. Mr. Lay, 64, and Mr. Skilling, 52, were found guilty of lying—to investors, employees and regulators—in an effort to disguise the crumbling fortunes of their energy empire.

The 12 jurors and three alternates, who talked to reporters at a news conference after the verdict, said they were persuaded—by the volume of evidence the government presented and by Mr. Skilling's and Mr. Lay's own appearances on the stand—that the men had perpetuated a far-reaching fraud by lying to investors and employees about Enron's performance.

The panel rejected the former chief executives' insistence that no fraud occurred at Enron other than that committed by a few underlings who stole millions in secret side deals. For years, Enron's gravity-defying stock price made it a Wall Street darling and an icon of the "New Economy" of the 1990s. But its sudden collapse at the end of 2001 and revelation as little more than a house of cards left Enron the premier public symbol of corporate ignominy. Investors and employees lost billions when Enron shares became worthless.

Former Enron Corp. executive Kenneth L. Lay speaks to the media outside the Bob Casey Federal Courthouse in Houston, Texas, Thursday, May 25, 2006.

Enron's fall had a far greater impact than on just the energy industry by heightening nervousness among average investors about the transparency of American companies. "The Enron case and all the other scandals and cases that trailed after it may have finally punctured that romance with Wall Street that has been true of American culture for a while now," said Steve Fraser, a historian and author of *Every Man a Speculator: A History of Wall Street in American Life.*

At Enron, Mr. Skilling was the visionary from the world of management consulting who spearheaded the company's rapid ascent by fastening on new ways to turn commodities, like natural gas and electricity, into lucrative financial instruments.

Mr. Lay, the company's founder, was Enron's public face. Known for his close ties to President Bush's family, he built Enron into a symbol of civic pride and envy here in its hometown of Houston and throughout the financial world.

The verdicts are a vindication for federal prosecutors, who had produced mixed results from their four-year investigation of wrongdoing at the company. The investigation resulted in 16 guilty pleas by Enron executives, and four convictions of Merrill Lynch bankers in a case involving the bogus sale of Nigerian barges to the Wall Street firm.

Last year, however, the Supreme Court overturned the obstruction-of-justice verdict that sounded the death knell for the accounting firm Arthur Andersen, Enron's outside auditor. And a jury either acquitted or failed to agree on charges in the fraud trial of former managers of Enron's failed broadband division.

In the 56-day trial, defense lawyers repeatedly criticized prosecutors for bringing criminal charges against Mr. Skilling and Mr. Lay, saying the government had set out to punish the company's top officers regardless of what the facts might be. The lawyers said the government was criminalizing normal business practices and accused prosecutors of pressuring critical witnesses to plead guilty to crimes they did not commit.

The defense lawyers also complained about a lack of access to witnesses who they contended could have corroborated their clients' versions of events. Several jurors said they would have liked to hear from more witnesses, in particular Richard A. Causey, the chief accounting officer, whom neither side called. The Enron trial, more than any other, punctuates the era of corporate corruption defined by the failure of WorldCom, the telecommunications giant whose bankruptcy following revelations of $11 billion in accounting fraud exceeded even Enron's in size; the prosecution of Frank P. Quattrone, the technology industry banker; and scandals at Tyco, Adelphia and HealthSouth.

From the beginning, the Enron leaders' trial was not what many people expected after revelations of secret off-the-books schemes that earned a small fortune for Andrew S. Fastow, Enron's former chief financial officer, and his co-conspirators. Some of those transactions were used by Mr. Fastow without approval by anyone to enrich himself at Enron's expense; others were used to manipulate Enron's financial reports with what Mr. Fastow testified was the full knowledge of his bosses. Rather than delve into those intricate structures, prosecutors focused on what they cited as the false statements Mr. Skilling and Mr. Lay made to employees and outside investors.

The "lies and choices" theme transformed the case into a test of credibility between the former chief executives and the more than half a dozen witnesses from inside Enron who testified for the government.

During the trial, the government called 25 witnesses and the defense called 31, including Mr. Skilling and Mr. Lay. Government witnesses, including the former Enron treasurer, Ben F. Glisan Jr., testified that the executives had sanctioned or encouraged manipulative accounting practices and crossed the line from cheerleading into outright misrepresentations of financial performance.

Mr. Fastow's emotional turn on the stand offered some of the most devastating evidence against Mr. Skilling, and to a lesser extent, Mr. Lay. He said he had struck "bear hug" side deals with Mr. Skilling guaranteeing that his off-the-books partnerships, called

LJM, would not lose money in their dealings with Enron. Mr. Fastow also described how Mr. Skilling had bought into using the LJM's to bolster earnings.

But Mr. Fastow's own admitted history of extensive crimes at Enron was dissected by Skilling's lead lawyer, Daniel Petrocelli, and jurors said they did not find Mr. Fastow particularly persuasive. "Fastow was Fastow," said a juror, Donald Martin. "We knew where he was coming from."

The jurors said they were moved, in contrast, by the testimony of Mr. Glisan. "We kept on going back to that testimony to corroborate things," said one juror, Freddy Delgado, a school principal.

The surprise testimony of David W. Delainey, the former chief of a retail unit called Energy Services, also helped pave the way for Mr. Skilling's conviction. Mr. Delainey, who pleaded guilty to fraud, said that Mr. Skilling took part in a decision to shift $200 million in losses from Energy Services to the more profitable wholesale energy division to avoid having to admit to investors that Energy Services was failing.

On the stand, Mr. Skilling offered differing and confusing explanations for the shift, and proved evasive and sometimes forgetful.

His resignation in August 2001, after only six months as chief executive, led to a bout of heavy drinking as a depressed Mr. Skilling watched in horror as the company he helped build edged closer to the brink.

For Mr. Lay, a turning point came when Sherron S. Watkins, the former Enron vice president, took the stand to describe how she confronted him with concerns about Enron's accounting. Ms. Watkins suggested that the subsequent investigation Mr. Lay ordered was intentionally limited in scope to conclude that there were no problems.

Other issues plagued Mr. Lay's defense, notably his own testiness on the stand and the sudden illness of his lead lawyer, Michael W. Ramsey, a well-regarded criminal defense lawyer who was forced to miss more than a month of the trial because of coronary disease that required two operations. Mr. Lay decided to carry on without Mr. Ramsey rather than seek to delay the trial and fight another day.

—May 26, 2006

NOTE: *Lay died of a heart attack six weeks after the verdict. A federal judge vacated Lay's conviction on the grounds that he could no longer appeal, thereby thwarting the government's plan to seize more than $43.5 million from Lay's estate. Skilling was sentenced to 24 years, but the sentence was trimmed by 10 years in 2013.*

MADOFF GOES TO JAIL AFTER GUILTY PLEAS

By DIANA B. HENRIQUES AND JACK HEALY

When Bernard L. Madoff entered a federal courtroom in Manhattan on Thursday to admit that he had run a vast Ponzi scheme that robbed thousands of investors of their life savings, he was as elegantly dressed as ever. But, preparing for jail, he wore no wedding ring—only the shadowy imprint remained of one he has worn for nearly 50 years.

He admitted his guilt for the first time in public, and apologized to his victims, dozens of whom were squeezed into the courtroom behind him, before being handcuffed and led away to jail to await sentencing.

"I knew what I was doing was wrong, indeed criminal," he said. "When I began the Ponzi scheme, I believed it would end shortly and I would be able to extricate myself and my clients."

But finding an exit "proved difficult, and ultimately impossible," he continued. "As the years went by I realized this day, and my arrest, would inevitably come."

Mr. Madoff acknowledged that he had "deeply hurt many, many people," adding, "I cannot adequately express how sorry I am for what I have done."

His testimony was shaped not only by expressions of regret, but also by his determination to shield his wife and family.

As a result, those who thought his guilty plea would shed more light on Wall Street's biggest and longest fraud left the courtroom unsatisfied and uncertain—about where their money had gone and who may have helped Mr. Madoff steal it. The hearing made clear that Mr. Madoff is refusing to help the government build a case against anyone else.

> *"I knew what I was doing was wrong, indeed criminal."*

Repeatedly, Mr. Madoff insisted that the stock-trading business run by his brother and two sons was legitimate and untainted by his crime. That contradicted the criminal charges against him and statements made in court by Marc O. Litt, the federal prosecutor handling the case, who asserted that at times Mr. Madoff's firm "would have been unable to operate without the money from this scheme."

Mr. Madoff also claimed his fraud began in the early 1990s, not in the 1980s, as the government contends—an assertion that seemed aimed at limiting how far back into the family business history the government can reach for restitution.

No family members have been accused of any wrongdoing and they all—Mr. Madoff's wife, Ruth, his brother Peter and his sons, Mark and Andrew—have denied any knowledge of the fraud. Mrs. Madoff is seeking to retain almost $65 million that she says are her own assets.

And when one of Mr. Madoff's victims urged a public trial to shed more light on the crime, Mr. Litt promised that the government was vigorously investigating what had happened to the money and who else had been involved—questions that could have been answered by Mr. Madoff if he were willing.

"Did we get answers? Not at all," said George Nierenberg, an award-winning film-maker, whose family lost nearly everything to Mr. Madoff.

Mr. Nierenberg was one of a handful of victims that Judge Denny Chin of Federal District Court allowed to speak at the hearing. As he went to the podium, he suddenly turned to the defendant and prodded him to "turn around and look at the victims."

For a moment, a startled Mr. Madoff did look at Mr. Nierenberg, before Judge Chin warned Mr. Nierenberg to address the court, not the defendant. "What I saw was a hollow, empty man," the filmmaker said later.

The inconsistencies between Mr. Madoff's version and the government's charges are evidence that no plea agreement could be reached, said Joel M. Cohen, a former federal prosecutor in Brooklyn.

"Clearly, he's light-years away from being cooperative," Mr. Cohen said after reviewing a transcript of the hearing. "Essentially, Madoff is saying, 'I'll plead guilty—but I'm not going to plead guilty to exactly what you say I did.'"

But Thursday's hearing probably is not the final forum for exploring Mr. Madoff's crime. Typically, before sentencing, the court conducts what is called a Fatico hearing in which the government and the defense lawyers try to resolve factual disputes remaining in the case.

"While we do not agree with all the assertions made by Mr. Madoff today, these admissions certainly establish his guilt," said Lev L. Dassin, the acting U.S. attorney in Manhattan, in a statement after the hearing. "We are continuing to investigate the fraud and will bring additional charges against anyone, including Mr. Madoff, as warranted."

The 11 counts of fraud, money laundering, perjury and theft to which Mr. Madoff, 70, pleaded guilty carry maximum terms totaling 150 years.

After Mr. Madoff's plea was accepted, his lawyer, Ira Lee Sorkin, tried to persuade Judge Chin to allow Mr. Madoff to remain free on bail, confined to his apartment on the Upper East Side, until he was sentenced.

Judge Chin refused.

"He has incentive to flee, he has the means to flee, and thus he presents the risk of flight," Judge Chin said. "Bail is revoked."

Some of Mr. Madoff's victims began to applaud that ruling before Judge Chin cautioned them to remain silent. As Mr. Madoff's hands were cuffed behind his back, some victims nodded with satisfaction.

And as he was led out of the paneled courtroom into an antiseptic tiled hallway, Adriane Biondo, of Los Angeles, wept with anger. Her family's devastating losses have left elderly relatives "sick with fear," she said. "It's emotional—120 cumulative years of hard work is gone."

Raw emotion had been an undercurrent throughout the day, from the moment Mr. Madoff arrived at the courthouse, and was ushered into a 24th-floor courtroom that was already packed with lawyers and victims.

Mr. Madoff stood, was sworn in and reminded that he was under oath. Noting that he had waived indictment, Judge Chin asked, "How do you now plead, guilty or not guilty?"

"Guilty," Mr. Madoff responded.

Then the judge said, "Mr. Madoff, tell me what you did."

Mr. Madoff began: "Your honor, for many years up until my arrest on Dec. 11, 2008, I operated a Ponzi scheme through the investment advisory side of my business, Bernard L. Madoff Securities LLC."

Mr. Madoff's fraud became a global scheme that ensnared hedge funds, charities and celebrities. He enticed thousands of investors, including figures like Senator Frank Lautenberg of New Jersey, the Hall of Fame pitcher Sandy Koufax and a charity run by Elie Wiesel, the Nobel Peace Prize laureate.

The fraud's collapse erased as much as $65 billion that his customers thought they had. It remains unclear how much victims will recover. A court-appointed trustee liquidating Mr. Madoff's business has so far been able to identify only about $1 billion in assets to satisfy claims.

—March 13, 2009

NOTE: *Madoff was sentenced in 2009 to 150 years in federal prison. Though others on Madoff's staff or in his employ were convicted of having played some role in the fraud, neither his wife nor his sons were ever the subject of a criminal investigation related to the case.*

ACKNOWLEDGMENTS

The New York Times Book of Crime reflects the expertise of a whole range of the newspaper's talents, stretching back to its founding days when many of them toiled anonymously without bylines. I tip my hat to them and to the tradition of excellence they created and that we hope to build on today.

Though I'm listed as the editor, my partner in all of the work was Susan Campbell Beachy, my tireless researcher. Her good judgement is reflected in the quality of the articles she recommended for inclusion, and her way with words is evident in the many annotations she crafted.

Our work was overseen expertly by Alex Ward, the editor who shapes the books created by *The New York Times*, and Barbara Berger, the executive editor at Sterling Publishing who took a special interest in our project and pushed it to be even more ambitious than we first conceived.

Richard Price was wonderfully generous in agreeing to provide a foreword that brims not only with his voice, but also with his deep understanding of crime and criminals and the people who chase them.

Evan Sklar and Darcy Eveleigh were photo editors whose devotion to capturing the right images is apparent in the book's many compelling pictures. Jeff Roth, *The Times*'s photo archivist, was also essential in that effort, as was Phyllis Collazo, who arranged the photo clearances.

At a point where the sheer magnitude of crimes that cried out to be included in the book seemed overwhelming, Constance Rosenblum, an editor of rare talent, stepped forward with a sharp pencil and a sharper eye to trim and, in many cases, improve articles so that the richest variety of material could appear in these pages.

The experience I brought to shepherding this work was largely honed during my years at police headquarters where I learned much from the fine reporters who worked alongside me, including William K. Rashbaum, Al Baker, C. J. Chivers, Michael Cooper, Kareem Fahim, Jodi Rudoren, Lydia Polgreen, Kit Roane, Elissa Gootman, Michael Wilson, Richard Lezin Jones and Shaila Dewan.

Finally, there are many who never seek bylines but whose work fosters a project like this, making it more beautiful, more accessible to readers and better known to the public at large. I am most grateful for the work in this regard done by many people at Sterling Publishing, including Senior Art Director (interior) Chris Thompson, Cover Designer David Ter-Avanesyan, Senior Art Director (cover) Elizabeth Lindy, Editorial Director Marilyn Kretzer, Publicist Ardi Alspach and Production Manager Terence Campo; and, at Tandem Books, Ashley Prine and Katherine Furman.

CONTRIBUTORS

Azam Ahmed is *The New York Times* bureau chief for Mexico, Central America and the Caribbean, where he took over in the summer of 2015. In his six years with the newspaper, he has previously served as a bureau chief in Afghanistan and as a reporter on the Business desk.

Lizette Alvarez has been the Miami bureau chief for *The Times* since January 2011. Her previous assignments for the newspaper include work as a Metro reporter, a foreign correspondent based in London and a reporter in the Washington bureau, covering Congress.

Charles V. Bagli is a Metro reporter for *The Times* who covers the intersection of politics and real estate. He is the author of *Other People's Money: Inside the Housing Crisis and the Demise of the Greatest Real Estate Deal Ever Made.*

Alexei Barrionuevo worked at *The Times* for eight years, serving as a reporter on the Business desk and later as a foreign correspondent based in Brazil. He currently works as an executive with Sitrick and Company, a public-relations firm.

James Barron is a reporter and columnist on the Metropolitan staff of *The Times*. He is the author of *Piano: The Making of a Steinway Concert Grand* as well as *The One-Cent Magenta: Inside the Quest to Own the Most Valuable Stamp in the World*, and he was editor of *The New York Times Book of New York.*

Pam Belluck, a *New York Times* staff writer for two decades, has served as a National bureau chief and a health and science writer. She shared the 2015 Pulitzer Prize for International Reporting and is the author of *Island Practice: Cobblestone Rash,* *Underground Tom, and Other Adventures of a Nantucket Doctor,* a true story that has been optioned for television.

Dan Bilefsky is a London-based correspondent for *The New York Times*. He has previously reported from Paris, Prague, Brussels, Istanbul and New York, and has been at the paper 11 years.

Howard Blum worked at *The New York Times* for nearly a decade, mostly reporting on investigations, and is now an author, most recently of *The Last Goodnight: A World War II Story of Espionage, Adventure, and Betrayal.* He is also a contributing editor at *Vanity Fair.*

James Brooke worked for *The New York Times* for 24 years, serving as a foreign correspondent reporting from the Soviet Union, Russia, Pakistan, Afghanistan and India, among other places. He is currently the founding CEO and editor in chief of *The Ukraine Business Journal.*

Fox Butterfield was a national and foreign correspondent for *The Times* who also wrote for the Metropolitan desk over a career that stretched for several decades. He is the author of *China: Alive in the Bitter Sea*, which won the 1982 National Book Award, and was a member of *The Times* reporting team that won the Pulitzer Prize for its publication of *The Pentagon Papers.*

Earl Caldwell, a pioneering reporter and columnist, was the only reporter present when Martin Luther King Jr. was assassinated. His coverage while at *The Times* of the Black Panther Party led to a Supreme Court decision that clarified reporters' rights. He now teaches at the Scripps Howard School of Journalism and Communications at Hampton University.

Alan Cowell was a *Times* foreign correspondent for 34 years, serving in Africa, the Middle East and Europe. A winner of the George Polk Award, he is also the author of several works of fiction and nonfiction, including *The Terminal Spy*, an account of the life and death of a former KGB officer who was poisoned.

Monica Davey, who joined *The Times* in 2003, is a national correspondent and editor currently working in the Midwest bureau, based in Chicago. She was part of a team from *The St. Petersburg Times* that was a finalist for the 1998 Pulitzer Prize in investigative reporting.

Shaila Dewan is a national correspondent for *The Times* who has reported on a variety of issues in her 16 years with the newspaper. Her recent reporting has explored the devastating effects of low-level arrests and convictions and the cycle of criminal justice debt that results from high fines and fees.

Joe Drape has been writing about the intersection of sports, culture and money since coming to *The Times* in 1998. He has also pursued these lines of reporting as a book author, most recently in *American Pharoah: The Untold Story of the Triple Crown Winner's Legendary Rise* and *Our Boys: A Perfect Season on the Plains with the Smith Center Redmen*.

Peter Duffy wrote for the Metropolitan section of *The Times* for more than a decade. He is the author of several books, including *The Bielski Brothers: The True Story of Three Men Who Defied the Nazis, Built a Village in the Forest, and Saved 1,200 Jews*.

Erik Eckholm left *The Times* in 2016 after serving in multiple roles over 31 years with the newspaper, including national legal correspondent, foreign correspondent, Beijing bureau chief, deputy foreign editor, science editor and editor of the Week in Review. A former Nieman Fellow, he is the author of several books, including *Down to Earth: Environment and Human Needs*.

Kurt Eichenwald worked for 20 years at *The Times* as an investigative reporter, columnist and senior writer. He has won the George Polk Award twice and, in 2000, was a finalist with Gina Kolata for the Pulitzer Prize for Investigative Reporting. He is the author of several books, including *The Informant*, which was made into a major motion picture starring Matt Damon in 2009.

John Eligon is a national correspondent for *The Times* based in Kansas City. Over his 11 years with the newspaper he has covered a range of topics, including sports, politics, legal affairs and the issue of race. He has filed reports from the funeral of Nelson Mandela; the Olympic venues in Turin, Italy; the Minnesota environs of the late musician Prince, and the protests in Ferguson, Missouri, where he was a lead reporter on the police shooting of Michael Brown.

William E. Farrell, who died in 1985, spent 23 years as a reporter, editor, columnist and foreign correspondent for *The Times*. A writer with a vivid eye, Farrell's evocative details enriched his reports from both the streets of New York and the turmoil of the Middle East, where he was bureau chief in Jerusalem.

Richard Fausset, who joined *The Times* in 2014, is the Atlanta bureau chief. He was previously a foreign correspondent for *The Los Angeles Times* working in Mexico and Central America.

James Feron, who died in 2004, worked for *The Times* for 40 years, and during his long career he was a foreign correspondent based in London, Jerusalem and Warsaw. He also reported from the United Nations and for 18 years was the Westchester bureau chief.

Fred Ferretti worked as a food writer, television critic and reporter for *The Times* over a career that spanned several decades. He is also the author of several books and was a columnist for *Gourmet* magazine.

Ian Fisher is the weekend editor for *The Times*, one of a number of senior management roles he has held in the newsroom in his 26 years at the newspaper. Those roles have included work as the assistant managing editor for content operations, associate managing editor for news and deputy foreign editor. As a reporter, he largely worked as a foreign correspondent and bureau chief with postings in Rome, Baghdad, Eastern Europe and East Africa.

Samuel G. Freedman was a staff reporter for *The Times* from 1981 through 1987 and currently writes the On Religion column for the newspaper. He is the author of seven books, including *The Inheritance: How Three Families and America Moved from Roosevelt to Reagan and Beyond*, which was a finalist for the 1996 Pulitzer Prize in nonfiction.

Dan Frosch worked as a reporter in the Rocky Mountain bureau of *The Times* for seven years. He is currently a national correspondent for *The Wall Street Journal*, covering Texas and the Southwest.

Carlotta Gall is a senior foreign correspondent for *The Times* who has been based in North Africa since 2013. A former Nieman Fellow, she is the author of *The Wrong Enemy: America in Afghanistan, 2001–2014*. She was also a member of the team that won the 2009 Pulitzer Prize for International Reporting.

Erica Goode has spent 18 years at *The Times* in a variety of editing and reporting posts and most recently has been writing about criminal justice, mental health and environmental science issues. She came to the newspaper to cover human behavior and was the newspaper's first environment editor.

Abby Goodnough has worked at *The Times* for more than 20 years, covering politics, education, Florida, New England and, most recently, health care. In 2004, she authored a book, *Ms. Moffett's First Year: Becoming a Teacher in America*, based on a series of articles she had written.

Jack Gould, who died in 1993, was a television and radio critic and reporter for *The Times* from 1944 to 1972, a period in which his opinion had an influence on the burgeoning television market during its formative years.

Danny Hakim, an investigative reporter based in London, has also been a bureau chief in Albany and Detroit during his 16-year career at *The Times*. He was one of the lead reporters on a *Times* team that won the 2009 Pulitzer Prize for Breaking News Reporting for their coverage of former New York governor Eliot Spitzer's involvement with prostitutes.

Jack Healy has reported on stories from New York, Afghanistan, Iraq and a snow-buried yurt in North Dakota. He is currently a national correspondent for *The Times*, which he joined in 2008.

Diana B. Henriques has written for *The Times* since 1989, specializing in investigative reporting on white-collar crime, market regulation and corporate governance. The winner of the 2005 George Polk Award, she has been recognized three times as a Pulitzer Prize finalist, either individually or as a member of a team. HBO has made her book, *The Wizard of Lies: Bernie Madoff and the Death of Trust*, into a film, scheduled for release in May 2017.

Gladwin Hill, who died in 1992, worked for 44 years with *The Times*, including a time when he served as a pioneering environmental reporter—one of the first in the nation to devote his focus to topics like pollution and conservation.

Jason Horowitz joined *The Times* in 2013 as a political profiles and features writer in the paper's Washington bureau. Before that, he worked as a staff reporter for *The Washington Post* and *The New York Observer*. He has written for *The New York Times Magazine*, *GQ* and *Vogue*.

Kirk Johnson, the chief of the Seattle bureau, has worked at *The Times* for 35 years. A former environmental writer for the Metro desk, he has been involved in some of the paper's major projects, including "How Race Is Lived in America" in 2000, which won the Pulitzer Prize. He is the author of *To the Edge: A Man, Death Valley, and the Mystery of Endurance*.

John Kifner, who joined *The Times* after graduating from Williams College in 1963, served in many capacities, including senior foreign correspondent, until his retirement in 2008. Kifner reported extensively from the Middle East during his career and was often assigned to war zones. In 1979, he received the George Polk Award for his reporting excellence.

Peter Kihss, who died in 1984, was a leading reporter for *The Times*'s Metropolitan staff during much of the 1960s and 1970s. He also covered South America, the civil rights movement and assorted other topics during a reporting career that spanned 49 years, with 30 of them spent at *The Times*.

N. R. "Sonny" Kleinfield is a reporter on the Metro staff of *The Times*, where he has worked for 39 years. He is the author of eight nonfiction books and was a finalist for the 2016 Pulitzer Prize for Feature Writing.

Douglas E. Kneeland, who died in 2007, was a reporter for *The Times* who covered some of the major stories of the 1960s and 1970s and later became a high-level editor at *The Chicago Tribune*.

Les Ledbetter, who died in 1985, joined *The Times* in 1969 as a news assistant in the Washington bureau and spent 14 years at the newspaper, serving as a reporter on *The Times*'s Metro staff, the editor of a New Jersey section of the daily newspaper and a national correspondent in the San Francisco bureau.

Mark Lewis wrote for the International desk of *The Times* and was one of the lead reporters on the coverage of the killings by Anders Breivik in Norway.

Grace Lichtenstein, the author of several books, including *A Long Way, Baby: Behind the Scenes in Women's Pro Tennis*, was a reporter and national correspondent at *The Times* for more than a decade, serving for a period as head of the Rocky Mountains bureau, based in Denver. In New York, her beats included transportation and consumer affairs.

Adam Liptak joined The New York Times Company in 1992 as a lawyer, moved to the paper's news staff in 2002 and started covering the Supreme Court in 2008. He was a finalist for the 2009 Pulitzer Prize for Explanatory Reporting.

Sarah Lyall has worked for *The Times* for 28 years, much of it spent as a foreign correspondent based in London. Now a writer at large based in New York, she is the author of *The Anglo Files: A Field Guide to the British*.

Leslie Maitland was a reporter and national correspondent for *The Times* who specialized in legal affairs and investigative reporting. She covered the Justice Department for the Washington bureau during part of her 14 years with *The Times* and is the author of *Crossing the Borders of Time: A True Story of War, Exile, and Love Reclaimed*, a family memoir.

David Margolick was a legal affairs correspondent for *The Times* for 15 years. He has been a contributing editor at *Vanity Fair* and held similar posts at *Newsweek* and *Portfolio*. He is also the author of several books, including *Dreadful: The Short Life and Gay Times of John Horne Burns*.

Salman Masood is based in Islamabad, Pakistan, and has covered the country for *The Times* since 2003. He mostly writes about politics and terrorism.

Robert D. McFadden has been a reporter at *The Times* since 1961 and has often served as the newspaper's primary rewriteman to shepherd major stories into print, among them important articles about crime. A skilled wordsmith, McFadden was awarded the Pulitzer Prize for Spot News Reporting in 1996 and has authored two books with *Times* colleagues, including *Outrage: The Story Behind the Tawana Brawley Hoax.*

Jesse McKinley is the Albany bureau chief for *The Times*; he has previously covered culture, written features and served as national correspondent based in San Francisco. McKinley has been on staff since 2000, has written a half-dozen plays and is working on a novel.

Adam Nagourney has been chief of the Los Angeles bureau of *The Times* since 2010. Before that he served as the paper's chief national political reporter. He co-authored a book on gay history, *Out for Good: The Struggle to Build a Gay Rights Movement in America*, with Dudley Clendinen, and is currently writing a book on the contemporary history of *The New York Times.*

Jon Nordheimer served in a variety of capacities during a long career at *The Times*, including deputy national news editor; chief of the Miami, Atlanta and Los Angeles bureaus; London correspondent, and deputy editor of *The New York Times Magazine.*

Richard Pérez-Peña has been a reporter at *The Times* since 1992, covering breaking national news, higher education, media, health care, government and politics, transportation and the legal system. He was part of a team that was a finalist for a 2007 Pulitzer Prize for Explanatory Reporting, and is a former five-time champion on *Jeopardy!*

Emanuel Perlmutter, who died in 1986, worked for *The Times* as a reporter for more than 40 years after joining the newspaper in 1929. He was an expert on organized crime and for years taught a class in police and crime reporting at Long Island University.

C. G. Poore, who later went by the byline Charles Poore, was a book reviewer for *The Times* for nearly 40 years after writing for a number of departments earlier in his career. He served as assistant editor of the Book Review and wrote reviews in the daily paper twice a week. He was the author of a biography of Goya and the editor of *The Hemingway Reader*, published in 1953.

John N. Popham, who died in 1999, was the first northern newspaper correspondent to cover the American South regularly. He worked for *The Times* for 25 years and later edited *The Chattanooga Times* for 20 years.

Selwyn Raab worked at *The Times* from 1974 to 2000, largely covering criminal justice as a reporter. He is an expert on organized crime and is the author of several books, including *Justice in the Back Room* and *Mob Lawyer.*

Jim Rasenberger wrote multiple articles for *The Times* over a period of several years, primarily for the Metropolitan desk. He is the author of several books, including *The Brilliant Disaster: JFK, Castro, and America's Doomed Invasion of Cuba's Bay of Pigs.*

William K. Rashbaum has covered corruption, terrorism and crime—organized and otherwise—in New York for more than three decades, much of that period at *The Times*. He was a lead reporter on a *Times* team that won the 2009 Pulitzer Prize for Breaking News for their coverage of former New York governor Eliot Spitzer's involvement with prostitutes.

Frances Robles, who joined *The Times* in 2013, is a Miami-based correspondent for the paper's National and International desks. As a Metro reporter, her work exposed the corrupt tactics of a homicide detective, led to 10 murder convictions being overturned and earned a George Polk Award. She spent 19 years at *The Miami Herald*, where she shared in two team Pulitzer Prizes.

Jack Roth, who died in 1987, was a reporter for *The Times* after serving as its City College correspondent during his years as an undergraduate. He worked for the newspaper for 32 years, working primarily on the staff that covered the news of New York City.

Susan Saulny is a former national correspondent for *The Times* who spent 13 years at the paper in a variety of roles after beginning in 2000 as a Metro reporter. Her work included coverage of Hurricane Katrina, the aftermath of the attacks on the World Trade Center and the 2008 and 2012 presidential campaigns.

E. R. Shipp was a reporter and editor for *The Times* for 13 years. She won the 1996 Pulitzer Prize for Commentary as a columnist for *The New York Daily News*. She is now a journalist in residence at Morgan State University's School of Global Journalism and Communication and a columnist for *The Baltimore Sun*.

Alessandra Stanley worked at *The Times* from 1990 to 2016 as a reporter, foreign correspondent and chief television critic. She was in Moscow during the post-Communism era and was Rome bureau chief when Silvio Berlusconi was prime minister of Italy and John Paul II was pope.

Don Terry spent more than 12 years at *The Times*, most of it as a national correspondent based in Los Angeles and Chicago, where he served as bureau chief. He is currently the press secretary for the Rainbow PUSH Coalition and the Reverend Jesse Jackson.

Robert Trumbull, who spent 38 years at *The Times*, died in 1992. He was present when Pakistan was born in 1947, and his report on the assassination of Gandhi is part of a long career chronicling the affairs of Asia—including a 1946 interview with Ho Chi Minh soon after he became president of the Democratic Republic of Vietnam.

Wallace Turner, who died in 2010, shared in a Pulitzer Prize for exposing corruption in Portland, Oregon, as a reporter there for *The Oregonian* before joining *The New York Times* in 1962. He reported for the paper for 26 years and served as its bureau chief in San Francisco and Seattle.

Austin C. Wehrwein, who died in 2008, spent nine years at *The Times* and served as its Chicago bureau chief. He went on to become an editorial writer with *The Minneapolis Star*. In 1953, he won the Pulitzer Prize for International Reporting for articles he wrote for *The Milwaukee Journal*.

Tom Wicker, who died in 2011, spent 31 years at *The Times*, as a reporter, Washington bureau chief and columnist. He would become one of America's more famous journalists but was relatively unknown when he covered the assassination of President Kennedy from Dallas.

Vivian Yee, a *Times* reporter since 2012, covers politics, with a focus on New York State government. In 2015, she covered the escape of two convicted murderers from an upstate New York prison.

INDEX

Note: Page numbers in *italics* include photo captions.

Abernathy, Ralph W., 28, 31
Adonis, Joe, 153
Ahmed, Azam, article by, 266–272
Airline, Lufthansa heist and murders, 65–69
Airplane hijacking mystery (D. B. Cooper), 76–77
Alcatraz, escapes from, 262–265
Alcohol. *See* Prohibition
Amurao, Corazon, 115
Anastasia, Albert, 75, 156, 158, 176
Anglin, Clarence and John, 262–265
Arroyo, Randy, 257, 259, 260
Art, theft from Boston museum, *45*, 70–72
Asaro, Vincent, 69
Assassinations, 1–43
    about: overview of articles, 1
    Bhutto, Benazir, 40–43
    Ferdinand, Archduke Francis, 6–7
    Gandhi, Mohandas K., 8–11
    Kennedy, John F., *1*, 12–20
    Kennedy, Robert F., 32–35
    King, Martin Luther, Jr., 27–31
    Lincoln, Abraham, 2–5
    Malcolm X, 21–26
    Sadat, Anwar el-, 36–39
    Seward, Secretary of State, 2, 4–5
Atkins, Susan, 201, 203–204, 205–*206*, 207
Attica prison revolt and deaths, 250–256
Aurora (CO) theater shootings, 124–127
Avery, Steven, 231–234

Bailey, F. Lee, 97, 98, 100, 290
Bank heists. *See* Heists
Barrionuevo, Alexei, article by, 382–385
Barron, James, article by, 131–133
Basciano, Vincent, 182, 183, 184
Belluck, Pam, article by, 339–343
Berkowitz, David ("Son of Sam"), 291–295, 296–299
Berman, Susan, 241, 242, 243
Bevins, Reginald, 56–57
Bhutto, Benazir, 40–43
Biggs, Ronnie, 59
Bilefsky, Dan, article by, 78–81
Black, Morris, 242
Blair, Jerry, 307–308
Blum, Howard, article by, 296–299
Bobbitt, Lorena and John, 330–333
Bonanno family, 166, 169, 170, 174. *See also* Massino, Joseph C.
Bonanno, Joseph, 159, 162
Booth, John Wilkes, 5
Boston Archdiocese, sex crimes within, 319, 339–343
Boston museum, art heist, *45*, 70–72
"Boston Strangler," 289–290
Boulder (CO), JonBenét Ramsey murder, 222–224
Breivik, Anders Behring, 128–130
Bronfman, Samuel 2d, kidnapping of, 92–95
Brooke, James, articles by, 117–120, 222–224
Browning, James L., 97–98
Bryant, Roy, 198, 200
Bugliosi, Vincent, 201, 204
Bulger, James "Whitey," 185–189
Bundy, Ted, 306–309
Burke, James, 67, 68, 69

Butterfield, Fox, article by, 70–72
Byrne, Dominic, 92–93, 95

Cain, Burl, 245, 258
Caldwell, Earl, articles by, 27–31, 201–207
Capone, Al, *145*, 147, *148*, 149, 152, 161, 262
Capuzzi, Nick, 159, 160
Carbone, Steve, 65, 66, 69
Castellano, Paul, 175, 178, 179, 180, 183
Catania, Joseph, 158
Catholic priests, sex crimes by, 339–343
Central Park rape, decision overturned, 334–336
Chambers, Robert, 325–329
Chapman, Mark David, 208, 209, 210
Charleston (SC) church shootings, *109*, 134–139
Chicago, nurse slayings, 114–116
Chicago, Valentine's Day Massacre, 146–152
Cho, Seung-Hui, Virginia Tech massacre by, 121–123
Clark, Alfred E., article by, 376–377
Clark, Dr. Kemp, 15–16, 18
Clark, James, 146
Clark, Roger Frederick, 60, 63–64
Clark, Russell, 51, 52, 53
Clinton, Bill, 102, 119, 273, 274, 275, 362
Clinton, Hillary, 273, 274, 275
Cochran, Johnnie L., 217, 219
Collins, John, 78, 80, 81
Colombo family, 169, 170, 180, 183. *See also* Persico, Carmine
Connally, Gov. John and Mrs., 12, 13, *14*, 15, 16, 17, 19
Connecticut (Newtown) school shootings, 131–133
Cooper, D. B., 76–77

Coppolla, Leonardo, 164, 167
Corallo, Anthony, 67, 169–170
Cosa Nostra. *See also specific mobster names*
Costello, Frank, 153, *154*, 155, 359
Crimmins, Craig S., 322–324
Crittenden, Thomas, 49
Cronin, Cory, 70, 71
Croswell, Edgar, 156, 157–158

Dahmer, Jeffrey, 310–312
The Dark Knight Rises, theater killings and, 124–127
Darrow, Clarence, 84, *86*, 88
Dassey, Brendan, 234
Davey, Monica, article by, 231–234
DeFreeze, Donald, 98, 99, 100
Del Castillo, Kate, 269
Dellacroce, Aniello, 174, 177, 178–179, 180
DeLong Star ruby, 60, 64
De May, Joseph, Jr., 227–229
Denaro, Carl, 295
DeSalvo, Albert H. ("Boston Strangler"), 289–290
DeSimone, Thomas, 68, 69
Dillinger, John, escapades of, 50–54
DiMasi, Donna, 295
DNA, cases overturned with, 232–233, 234, 334, 335, 337
Drape, Joe, article by, 344–347
Drug kingpins. *See* Escobar, Pablo; Guzmán Loera, Joaquín (El Chapo)
Duffy, Peter, article by, 73–75
Dugard, Jaycee, 105–107
Durst, Kathleen, 240–241, 242
Durst, Robert A., 240–243
Dynamiter, school slayings by, 110–113

Eckholm, Erik, article by, 273–275

Eichenwald, Kurt, article by, 378–381

El Chapo, 266–272

Eligon, John, article by, 134–139

Ellington, Gov. Buford, 27, 30

Emanuel African Methodist Episcopal Church shootings, 109, 134–139

Enron fraud and conspiracy, 382–385

Erickson, Frank, 153

Esau, Alexander, 295

Escobar, Pablo, 362–365

Fardella, Jess, 380–381

Farrell, William E., article by, 36–39

Fausset, Richard, article by, 134–139

Ferdinand, Archduke Francis, 6–7

Feron, James, articles by, 55–59, 211–216

Ferretti, Fred, article by, 250–256

Ferrigno, Steve, 159, 160, 161

Folger, Abigail, 203, 206

Foote, L. (train engineer), 46–47, 48

Ford, Robert, 49

Ford's Theatre, 2–3

Fox (express messenger), 47, 48–49

Franks, Robert, kidnapping of, 84–88

Freedman, Samuel G., 325–329

Freund, Christine, murder of, 295, 298

Frosch, Dan, article by, 124–127

Frykowski, Voytek, 203, 206

Gabrinovics, 6, 7

Gacy, John Wayne, 300–305

Galante, Carmine, murder of, 164–167

Gall, Carlotta, article by, 40–43

Gambino, Carlo, 159, 165, 169

Gambino family, 169, 170, 174, 183. See also Castellano, Paul; Gotti, John

Gandhi, Mohandas K., 8–11

Garrido, Phillip and Nancy, 105–107

Gasko, Charlie. See Bulger, James "Whitey"

Gay nightclub massacre (Orlando, FL), 140–143

Gems, theft recovery, 60–64

Genovese, Catherine "Kitty," murder of, 225–230

Genovese family, 169–170, 180

Genovese, Vito, 156, 159, 162, 166

Genovese, William, 230

Gentleman bandit (Willie Sutton), 73–75

Godse, Nathuram, 8, 11

Goldman, Ronald L., 217, 218, 219, 221

Goode, Erica, article by, 313–317

Goodnough, Abby, article by, 185–189

Gotti, John, 145, 170, 173–174, 175–181

Gould, Jack, article by, 153–154

Gravano, Salvatore, 175, 176, 179, 181

Greig, Catherine, Whitey Bulger and, 185–189

Gusenberg, Frank, 146, 149, 151

Gusenberg, Peter, 146, 150

Guzmán Loera, Joaquín (El Chapo), 266–272

Hagan, Thomas, 21, 22, 25, 26

Hagnes, Helen, murder of, 322–324

Hakim, Danny, article by, 366–369

Halbach, Teresa, murder of, 231–234

Hamilton, John, 51, 52, 54

Harris, Eric, Littleton (CO) killings and, 117–120

Harris, Jean S., 211–216

Hauptmann, Bruno, 91

Healy, Jack, article by, 386–389

Hearst, Patricia "Patty," 96–102

Hearst, Randolph A. and Catherine, 96

Heists, 45–81
   about: overview of articles, 45
   bank, by gentleman Willie Sutton, 73–75

Boston art museum (Isabella Stewart Gardner Museum), 45, 70–72

Dillinger (John) escapades, 50–54

Hearst, Patty and, 96–102

hijacking mystery (D. B. Cooper), 76–77

London bank, by graying thieves, 78–81

Lufthansa heist and murders, 65–69

Star of India/other gems recovered, 60–64

train robbery (Jesse James gang), 46–49

train robbery (London area, multimillions), 55–59

Henriques, Diana B., article by, 386–389

Hijacking mystery (D. B. Cooper), 76–77

Hill, Gladwin, article by, 32–35

Hinman, Gary, 203

Hogan, Frank S., 60, 61, 62–63

Holmes, H. H. (Herman Mudgett), 281–288

Holmes, James, Colorado theater murders by, 124–127

Horowitz, Jason, article by, 134–139

Hurd, Cynthia Graham, 138–139

Indelicato, Anthony, 167

Isabella Stewart Gardner Museum heist, 45, 70–72

Islambouli, Khalid, 39

Islamic State terrorism, Orlando shootings and, 140–143

Italian politician, kidnapping/murder of Moro, 103–104

Italy, murder in, Amanda Knox and, 235–236

Ito, Lance A., 217

Jackson, Susie, 138

Jack the Ripper, 278–280

James, Jesse, train robbery, 46–49

Johnson, Kirk, article by, 124–127

Johnson, Lyndon B., 1, 12, 13–15, 16, 17, 18, 32

Johnson, Sylvia, 135, 138, 139

Jones, Daniel, 78, 80, 81

Kanarek, Irving, 201

Kasabian, Linda, 204, 205–207

Kaufman, Peter, 93–94

Kefauver, Estes W., 153, 155, 360

Kehoe, Andrew, 110–113

Kennedy, Jacqueline, 13, 14, 16–17, 18–20, 34

Kennedy, John F., 1, 12–20

Kennedy, Robert F., 1, 32–35

Kew Gardens, Kitty Genovese murder and, 225–230

Kidnappings, 83–107
   about: overview of articles, 83
   of baby Lindbergh, 83, 89–91
   of bank robber Patty Hearst, 96–102
   of 18-year-captive Jaycee Dugard, 105–107
   of fourteen-year-old Robert Franks, 84–88
   of heir Samuel Bronfman 2d, 92–95
   of Italian politician Aldo Moro, 103–104

Kifner, John, article by, 289–290

Kihss, Peter, articles by, 21–26, 92–95

King, Martin Luther, Jr., 27–31

Klebold, Dylan, Littleton (CO) killings and, 117–120

Kleinfield, N. R., article by, 313–317

Klutas, Jack, 52

Kneeland, Douglas E., article by, 300–305

Knox, Amanda, 235–236

Krenwinkel, Patricia, 201, 204, 205, 206, 207

Krugman, Martin, 67, 69

Kuhn, Allan Dale, 60, 61, 63–64

Kunstler, William M., 251, 253, 255

LaBiancas, Tate-LaBianca murders and, 201–207

Lance, Ethel, 138

Lansky, Meyer, 358–361

Lanza, Adam, Sandy Hook school shootings and, 131–133

LaPrade, J. Wallace, 93, 94, 95

Lauria, Donna, murder of, 292–293, 294, 298, 299

Law, Cardinal Bernard F., 339, 340, 341–342, 343

Lay, Kenneth L., 382–385

Ledbetter, Les, article by, 208–210

Lennon, John, murder of, 208–210

Leopold, Nathan F., 84–88

Levin, Jennifer, murder of, 325–329

Lewis, Mark, article by, 128–130

LiCastri, Paolo, 65, 66, 69

Lichtenstein, Grace, 320–321

Life sentences, realities of, 257–261

Liman, Arthur L., 380

Lincoln, Abraham, 2–5

Lindbergh kidnapping, 83, 89–91

Liptak, Adam, article by, 257–261

Little, Dick, 48

Littleton (CO) school shootings, 117–120

Locascio, Frank, 181

Loeb, Richard A., 84–88

Lomino, Joanne, 295

London bank heist, 78–81

London, Jack the Ripper and, 278–280

London train heist, 55–59

Lucchese family, 67, 169, 170

Lucchese, Thomas, 159

Luciano, Charles "Lucky," 162, 359

Lufthansa heist and murders, 65–69

Lupo, Salvatore, 295

Lyall, Sarah, articles by, 128–130, 237–239

Lynch, Mel Patrick, 92–93, 94–95

Madoff, Bernie, 371, 386–388

Mafia. See Mob crimes

Magliocco, Joseph, 159

Maitland, Leslie, article by, 65–69

Makley, Charles, 51, 52–53

Malcolm X, 21–26

Maline, Richard, 61–62

Malvo, John Lee, 313–317

Mangano, Philip and Vincent, 162

Mankiewicz, Frank, 32, 33–34

Manri, Joseph, 65, 69

Manson, Charles,
    Arrest on suspicion of grand theft auto, 202
    Tate-LaBianca murders and, 201–207, 321

Maranzano, Salvatore, 161–162

Margolick, David, articles by, 217–221, 330–333

Marijuana, safety of, 350–353

Masood, Salman, article by, 40–43

Masseria, Giuseppe "Joe the Boss," 161–162

Massino, Joseph C., 182–184

Mass murder, 109–143
    about: overview of articles, 109
    of Chicago nurses, 114–116
    of Colorado (Aurora) theater-goers, 124–127
    of Colorado (Littleton) high-schoolers, 117–120
    of Connecticut (Newtown) school children, 131–133
    of Florida (Orlando) nightclub attendees, 140–143
    of Michigan (Bath) school children (by dynamiter), 110–113
    of Norwegian citizens, 128–130
    of South Carolina (Charleston) church members, 109, 134–139
    of Virginia Tech students, 121–123

Mateen, Omar, Orlando (FL) nightclub shootings and, 140–143

May, John, 146, 148

McBratney, James, 177

McClellan, John L., 162, 163, 360

McCray, Antron, rape conviction vacated, 334–336

McFadden, Robert D., articles by, 164–167, 168–174, 262–265, 291–295, 334–338, 358–361, 362–365

McKinley, Jesse, article by, 105–107

McMahon, Robert, 65, 69

Mehsud, Baitullah, 43

Michigan (Bath), dynamiter killing school children, 110–113

Milam, J. W., 198, 200

Milken, Michael, 378–381

Mineo, Alfred, 159, 160, 161

Mob crimes, 145–189. See also specific mobster names
    1980s mob (divided, under siege), 168–174
    about: overview of articles, 145
    boss telling all about, 182–184
    drugs and, 172, 178–179
    Galante/others murdered at restaurant, 164–167
    Gotti and. See Gotti, John
    Irish mob legend and, 185–189
    organization of mob and, 170–171
    Prohibition, Meyer Lansky and, 358–361
    roundup of 65 hoodlums, 156–158
    TV hearings on, 153–154
    Valachi naming bosses and hits, 159–163
    Valentine's Day Massacre, 146–152

Mobley, Mamie Till, 199

Morello, Peter "The Clutching Hand," 161

Moro, Aldo, 103–104

Morris, Frank Lee, 262–265

Moseley, Winston, 226–227, 228, 229

Moskowitz, Stacy, murder of, 291–292, 293, 294, 299

Mubarak, Hosni, 36, 37

Mudgett, Herman (aka H. H. Holmes), 281–288

Muhammad, Elijah, 22, 23

Muhammad, John Allen, 313–317

Murder, 191–243. See also Assassinations; Mass murder; Mob crimes; Serial killers
    about: overview of articles, 191
    community ignoring, of Kitty Genovese, 225–230
    confession on TV microphone, Robert Durst and, 240–243
    Franks kidnapping and, 84–88
    Gentleman bandit Sutton and, 75
    in Italy, Amanda Knox and, 235–236
    life sentence realities and, 257–261
    Lufthansa heist and murders, 65–69
    by Manson cult (Tate-LaBianca murders), 201–207
    Moro kidnapping and, 103–104
    of Negro Emmett L. Till, 198–200
    previously wrongly-accused felon (Steven Avery) and, 231–234
    trial of O. J. Simpson, 217–221
    trial of Oscar Pistorius, 237–239
    of violinist Helen Hagnes, 322–324

Murphy, Jack "Murph the Surf," 60, 62, 63–64

Nadjari, Maurice, 61, 62–63

Nagourney, Adam, article by, 185–189

Nehru, Pandit, 8, 10, 11

Nesbit Thaw, Evelyn, 191, 192, 193, 197

Newtown (CT) school shootings, 131–133

Nierenberg, George, 387

Nightclub massacre (Orlando, FL), 140–143

Nordheimer, Jon, article by, 306–309

Norway, mass murder in, 128–130

Nurse slayings, in Chicago, 114–116

Oates, Chief Dan, 125–126
Obama, Barack, 109, 131, 135, 141–142
Ono, Yoko, 208, 210
Organized crime. See Mob crimes
Oswald, Lee Harvey, 12, 20
Oswald, Russell G., 250–251, 252, 253, 254–255, 256

Paintings, priceless works stolen, 45, 70–72
Parent, Steven, 203, 205
Paterno, Joe, 344, 346
Penn, Sean, 266, 269
Penn State, Jerry Sandusky and, 344–347
Perkins, Terrence, 78, 79, 80–81
Perlmutter, Emanuel, article by, 159–163
Perry, Dr. Malcom, 15
Persico, Carmine, 169–170, 171, 173, 183
Pierpont, Harry, 51, 52–53
Pietzel, Benjamin, murder of, 281–288
Pinckney, Clementa C., 134–136, 139
Pistorius, Oscar, 237–239
Pizzolo, Randolph, 182, 184
Placido, Judy, 295
Polanski, Roman, 203, 320–321
Ponzi, Charles, original Ponzi schemer, 372–375
Ponzi scheme, of Madoff, 371, 386–388
Poore, C. G., article by, 354–357
Popham, John N., 198–200
Priests, sex crimes by, 339–343
Princip, Gavrilo, 7
Prison
    about: overview of articles, 245
    Alcatraz escapes, 262–265
    Attica revolt and deaths, 250–256
    El Chapo's captures and escapes, 266–272
    life sentence realities, 257–261

rising incarceration rate and 1994 anti-crime bill, 273–275
    shower-bath and yoking discipline/torture in, 246–249
Profaci, Joseph, 162
Prohibition
    crime syndicate, Meyer Lansky and, 358–361
    liquor poured down sewer, 349
    speakeasies and, 354–357

Quiz show scandal, 376–377

Raab, Selwyn, article by, 175–181
Ramsey, John Bennett, 222, 223, 224
Ramsey, JonBenét, murder of, 222–224
Ramsey, Patsy, 222, 223
Rao, Vincent, 163
Rasenberger, Jim, article by, 225–230
Rashbaum, William K., articles by, 182–184, 366–369
Ray, James Earl, 31
Reina, Gaetana, 161
Reiner, Tom, 9
Reyes, Matias, 334, 336–337
Richardson, Kevin, rape conviction vacated, 334–336
Robberies. See Heists
Robles, Frances, article by, 134–139
Roof, Dylann, Charleston (SC) church shootings and, 109, 134, 135–139
Roth, Jack, article by, 60–64
Ruby (gemstone), DeLong Star, 60, 64
Ruby, Jack, 20
Ruggiero, Angelo, 177–179
Russell, William F., 148

Sadat, Anwar el-, 36–39
Salaam, Yusef, rape conviction vacated, 334–336
Salerno, Anthony, 169–170, 171
Sanders, Felicia, 138
Sanders, Tywanza, 138

Sandusky, Jerry, 319, 344–347
Sandy Hook Elementary school shootings, 131–133
Santana, Raymond, rape conviction vacated, 334–336
Santuccio, Girolamo, 159–160
Saulny, Susan, articles by, 76–77, 334–338
School shootings. See Mass murder
Schuster, Arnold, 73–74, 75
Schwimmer, Reinhardt, 146, 150
Seagram liquor heir, kidnapping of, 92–95
Sebring, Thomas John, 203
Sepe, Angelo J., 67–68
Serial killers
    about: overview of articles, 277
    "Boston Strangler" Albert H. DeSalvo, 289–290
    Bundy, Ted, 306–309
    Dahmer, Jeffrey, 310–312
    Gacy, John Wayne, 300–305
    Holmes, H. H. (Herman Mudgett), 281–288
    Jack the Ripper, 278–280
    sniper team of Muhammad and Malvo, 313–317
    "Son of Sam" David Berkowitz, 291–295, 296–299
Seung-Hui Cho, Virginia Tech massacre by, 121–123
Seward, Secretary of State, 2, 4–5
Sex crimes, 319–347
    about: overview of articles, 319
    acquittal of Lorena Bobbitt, 330–333
    jogger case decision vacated/changed, 334–336
    murders and, 322–324, 325–329. See also Bundy, Ted; Gacy, John Wayne
    of Catholic priests, 339–343
    of Robert Chambers, 325–329
    of Craig Crimmins, 322–324
    of Roman Polanski, 320–321
    of Jerry Sandusky, 344–347

Shillitani, Salvatore, 159, 160
Shipp, E. R., 322–324
Shower-bath and yoking, in prisons, 246–249
Simmons, Daniel Lee, Sr., 139
Simpson, Nicole Brown, 217, 218–219, 221
Simpson, Orenthal James "O.J.," 217–221
Sing Sing Prison, 245, 246, 247, 248
Sirhan, Adel, 34
Sirhan, Munir "Joe," 34, 35
Sirhan, Sirhan Bishara, 33, 35
Skilling, Jeffrey K., 382–385
SLA (Symbionese Liberation Army), Patty Hearst and, 97, 100–102
Sniper killers, Muhammad and Malvo, 313–317
Snyder, John, 146, 150
Sollecito, Raffaele, 235–236
"Son of Sam," 291–295, 296–299
South Carolina (Charleston) church shootings, 109, 134–139
Speakeasies during Prohibition, 354–357
Speck, Richard Franklin, 114–116
Spitzer, Eliot, 366–369
Stanley, Alessandra, article by, 103–104
Star of India, theft of, 60–64
Steading, John, 46, 48
Steenkamp, Reeva, murder of, 237–239
Stride, Elizabeth, murder of, 280
Suriani, Valentina, murder of, 295, 297
Sutton, Willie, 73–75

Tarnower, Herman, murder of, 211–216
Tate-LaBianca murders, 201–207
Tate, Sharon, 203, 204
Television
    confession, of Robert Durst, 240–243
    hearings on mob crimes, 153–154
    rigged quiz shows, 376–377

Terranova, Ciro, 163
Terry, Don, article by, 310–312
Thaw, Evelyn Nesbit, *191*, 192, 193, 197
Thaw, Harry Kendall, *191*, 192–197
Theater (Colorado), killings at, 124–127
Till, Emmett L, murder of, 198–200
Train robberies. *See* Heists
Trumbull, Robert, article by, 8–11
Turano, Giuseppe, 164, 166–167
Turner, Wallace, article by, 96–102

Valachi, Joseph M., 159–163, 360
Valenti, Jody, 294

Valentine's Day Massacre, 146–152
Van Doren, Charles, 376–377
Van Houten, Leslie, 201, 203, 204–205, *206*, 207
Vario, Paul, 67
Vice, 349–369
  about: overview of articles, 349
  cocaine cartel head Escobar killed, 362–365
  crime syndicate, Meyer Lansky and, 358–361
  marijuana safety, 350–353
  sex ring and Eliot Spitzer, 366–369
  speakeasies during Prohibition, 354–357
Violante, Robert, 291–294, 295

Violent Crime Control and Law Enforcement Act of 1994, 273–275
Virginia Tech massacre, 121–123
Voskerichian, Virginia, murder of, 295, 299

Wall Street crimes. *See* White collar crime
Wehrwein, Austin C., article by, 114–116
Weinshank, Albert, 146, 150
Werner, Louis, 66, 67, 69
Whitby, David, 57–58
Whitechapel killings, Jack the Ripper and, 278–280
White collar crime, 371–388
  Enron fraud and conspiracy (Lay and Skilling), 382–385
  Michael Milken, 378–381

Bernie Madoff, *371*, 386–388
Ponzi scheme originator Charles Ponzi, 372–375
rigged TV quiz shows and Charles Van Doren, 376–377
White, Stanford, murder of, 192–197
Wicker, Tom, article by, 12–20
Wise, Kharey, rape conviction vacated, 337

Yoking and shower-bath, in prisons, 246–249
Yorty, Samuel W., 33, 34
Young, Andrew, 29, 31

Zielonko, Mary Ann, 226, 230

PICTURE CREDITS

Associated Press: 14; Dayton Daily News: 50; 62; © Stephen B. Morton: 108; © Paul Cannon: 115; 118; © RJ Sangosti/The Denver Post: 124; © Chuck Burton: 134; 147; 148; © Daniel Sheehan: 180; Chicago-Sun Times: 199; 206; © Morry Gash: 233; © Antonio Calanni: 235; Chicago Tribune: 281; 301; © Gene J. Puskar: 318; 320; © J. Scott Applewhite: 333; 362; 375

European Press Photo Agency: © Oliver Matthys: 41

Getty Images: © Makaram Gad Alkareem/Agence France-Presse: 37; Daily Express/Hulton Archive: 56; Bettman: 86; 101; BIPS: 89; © Mark Boster: 106; Hulton Archive: 202; © Vince Bucci/Agence France Press: 220; © Alfredo Estrella/Agence France Press: 267

Federal Bureau of Investigation: 76, 144

Federal Bureau of Prisons: 187

Florida Department of Corrections: 307

Courtesy Internet Archive: 353

Library of Congress: 3; 5; Taylor Copying Co.: 48; New York World-Telegram & Sun Collection: 82; Gertrude Käsebier: 190; Bain News Service, via Library of Congress: 196; 244; Carol M. Highsmith Archive: 263; 276; 286; New York World-Telegram and the Sun Collection: 348

National Archives and Records Administration (NARA), College Park, MD: vxi, 354

The New York Times: 7; Jack Manning: 21; Don Hogan Charles: 31; Keith Myers: 44; 74; 112; 154; 165; Joyce Dopkeen: 212; Edmund D. Fountain: 240; William E. Sauro: 252; 279; Fred R. Conrad: 294; Sara Krulwich: 327; Rob Harris: 345; Hiroko Masuike: 366; Damon Winter: 370; Robert Walker: 376; Michael Stravato: 383